HATERS, BAITERS AND WOULD-BE DICTATORS

For fifty-five years, from 1919 until 1975, The Britons published Jew-hating literature. For the forty years until his death in 1948, the founder and president of The Britons, Henry Hamilton Beamish, devoted his life to touring the world as an obsessive preacher of this hatred. Using material he has collected over the past thirty years, Nick Toczek tells their story. This is the first complete history of the organisation, which was the most prolific and influential advocate of extreme prejudice against all things Jewish – not least as the publisher of that notorious forgery *The Protocols of the Elders of Zion*. Likewise, this is the first biography of Beamish.

Putting both The Britons and Beamish into context, this book also examines and explains their precursors, their contemporaries and their legacy. Here, then, are detailed accounts of several anti-Jewish organisations and individuals. These include the late Victorian anti-Semitism of Arnold White and the British Brothers League; the curious life of Rotha Lintorn-Orman, who was the unlikely founder of British Fascisti, Britain's first fascist party; Anglo-American supporters of Hitler; the lives and roles of extreme haters such as Arnold Leese and Colin Jordan; and the whole history of *The Protocols*, including the key role played by American motor magnate Henry Ford. This shocking history of hatred takes us from South Africa to Nazi Germany, from America to Rhodesia.

Nick Toczek is a writer, performer and political researcher.

Oh, mind of man, what can you not be made to believe?

>Johann Adam Weishaupt (6 February 1748–18 November 1830)
>(German law professor, philosopher and founder of The Illuminati)

HATERS, BAITERS AND WOULD-BE DICTATORS

Anti-Semitism and the UK Far Right

Nick Toczek

Routledge
Taylor & Francis Group
LONDON AND NEW YORK

First published 2016
by Routledge
2 Park Square, Milton Park, Abingdon, Oxon OX14 4RN

and by Routledge
711 Third Avenue, New York, NY 10017

Routledge is an imprint of the Taylor & Francis Group, an informa business

© 2016 Nick Toczek

The right of Nick Toczek to be identified as author of this work has been asserted by him in accordance with sections 77 and 78 of the Copyright, Designs and Patents Act 1988.

All rights reserved. No part of this book may be reprinted or reproduced or utilised in any form or by any electronic, mechanical, or other means, now known or hereafter invented, including photocopying and recording, or in any information storage or retrieval system, without permission in writing from the publishers.

Trademark notice: Product or corporate names may be trademarks or registered trademarks, and are used only for identification and explanation without intent to infringe.

British Library Cataloguing in Publication Data
A catalogue record for this book is available from the British Library

Library of Congress Cataloging in Publication Data
A catalog record for this book has been requested

ISBN: 978-1-138-85348-5 (hbk)
ISBN: 978-1-138-85350-8 (pbk)
ISBN: 978-1-315-72274-0 (ebk)

Typeset in Bembo
by Book Now Ltd, London

Printed and bound in Great Britain by
TJ International Ltd, Padstow, Cornwall

DEDICATION

To my father, John Toczek (né Hans), who died in 2012 at the age of ninety-one.

It was his experiences during and after the Second World War that first awakened my interest in the politics of prejudice. He and his twin brother, then in their teens, were among the very few members of my extended paternal family to escape the Holocaust. As a pair of Germans arriving in wartime Britain, they were arrested under Defence Regulation 18b as enemy aliens and jailed on the Isle of Man alongside British fascists. The war years persuaded my father there could be no God. After the war, as a naturalised British Jew with a strong German accent who had chosen to reject his faith and to marry outside it, he learned to deal with a broad spectrum of prejudices. A couple of years before he died, the BBC contacted him to say that they had found his father's grave in France, close to the camp in which he and many other Jews had died. This was the first my father knew of the camp and of the existence of a grave. So, more than fifty years after that death, Dad featured in a documentary which ended with him placing flowers on the grave of my grandfather Otto.

CONTENTS

Acknowledgements ix
Introduction xi

1 The life of Henry Hamilton Beamish   1
2 Arnold White and the British Brothers League   74
3 The Britons: the first three decades, 1919–1949   83
4 The Britons Publishing Company throughout the 1950s   103
5 The Britons Publishing Company: the 1960s and 1970s   124
6 Arnold Leese and The Britons   143
7 Colin Jordan and The Britons   159
8 *The Protocols*: origins, circulation and influence   168
9 Henry Ford and *The Protocols*   182
   Postscript: the legacy of Henry Hamilton Beamish
   and The Britons   190

Illustrations   134–142
Appendix 1 Precursors of The Britons: 1900–1919   192
Appendix 2 Peer groups of The Britons: 1920–1939   202
Appendix 3 Some independent right-wing British journals   232
Appendix 4 Key figures in The Britons   244
Appendix 5 Draft constitution of The Britons   259
Appendix 6 Publications by The Britons   268
Appendix 7 Addresses of The Britons   273
Some selected further reading   274
Conclusion   276
Afterword   278
Index   280

ACKNOWLEDGEMENTS

I owe special thanks to my friend, the author and researcher Martin Durham, for repeatedly urging me to get back to undertaking far-right research after AK Press published my slim book *The Bigger Tory Vote* back in 1991. Over the years, I have given Martin and other researchers access to the vast right-wing archive I have collected. However, until now I have not made the time to use these resources myself. It was with Martin's admonishments in mind that, twenty-two years later, during 2013, I eventually sat down and began this book.

For the most part, I have not had to leave my house for research purposes. My own collection supplied the core source material, checked and embellished through internet research. I do, however, owe a debt of gratitude to the Churchill Archive Centre at the University of Cambridge, where I was able to look through some of the Beamish family papers.

I would also like to acknowledge the generous help given by two key suppliers of rare far-right literature – Blog Rare Books here in the UK (www.blograrebooks.co.uk) and the Patriot Bookshop in the USA (on AbeBook.com).

My thanks go to Craig Fowlie at Routledge for being keen to consider this book for publication from the moment I first phoned him to offer it, and for being such a knowledgeable, informative and constructive editor; and to his assistant, Emma Chappell, for her hard work on my behalf, especially in replying helpfully, quickly and cheerfully to all my procedural queries.

Finally, I owe thanks to my wife, Gaynor, not just for patiently tolerating my often obsessive work on this book, but also for constantly reminding me that there's more to life than writing!

INTRODUCTION

I started this book almost two years ago with the intention of writing a history of The Britons, the small specifically anti-Jewish organisation founded in 1919 by a little-known man called Henry Hamilton Beamish. However, as the book came together, I began to realise the importance of extending it to include coverage of The Britons' precursors and of the numerous contemporary bigoted organisations with which they and their members cooperated, interacted, feuded and campaigned. The result is a book that has expanded to cover twentieth-century British anti-Jewish activism as a whole. In the course of doing so, it also deals with broader British xenophobia, American and European Jew-hatred, and anti-Jewish activity as far afield as Russia and the British colonies.

It's a popular misconception that twentieth-century Jew-hatred in Britain was spearheaded almost exclusively by Oswald Mosley and his followers via his pre-war British Union of Fascists and his post-war Union Movement, but there is a much bigger picture. While the Mosleyites played an important and high-profile role, this has been covered extensively by other authors and researchers. I have therefore focused on the rest of the story.

Before starting into this book, readers may find it useful first to skim through appendices 1 to 4. In doing so, they will familiarise themselves with many of the organisations, journals and individuals referred to in the text.

Throughout, I have avoided footnotes in an effort to make the book an uninterrupted linear narrative (the note cues that appear in the text refer to the list of main sources of information which is given at the end of each chapter). It's also inevitable that occasional reference to the first four appendices serves as a useful means of clarifying what would otherwise be a confusing text milling with characters and organisations.

In order to avoid further clogging up the whole text with a mass of people, organisations, incidents and other details, I have opted for a series of chronological accounts, beginning with the life of Henry Hamilton Beamish. Much of this is new. Most accounts elsewhere devote little more than a few paragraphs to his life.

My second chapter tackles Britain's seminal anti-Jewish organisation the British Brothers League, of which little has previously been written. In the course of this chapter I also introduce the key political writers whose work deeply influenced the anti-Jewish thinking of Beamish and his compatriots in The Britons.

The next three chapters are devoted to a chronological history of The Britons, based primarily on information gleaned from their four key journals – *Jewry Über Alles*, the *Hidden Hand*, the *British Guardian* and *Free Britain* – of which I have near complete collections. Again, much of this material is previously unpublished.

Chapters 6 and 7 deal respectively with the lives of two notorious racist campaigners – Arnold Leese and Colin Jordan – both of whom had great influence over the course taken by The Britons after the Second World War. A third activist, A. K. Chesterton, deserves a similar chapter but, as I shall be devoting an entire future book to his activities, I have simply incorporated his role into my account of The Britons.

In Chapter 8 I discuss the role, origin and influence of The Britons' primary publication, *The Protocols of the Learned Elders of Zion*, while Chapter 9 looks at how *The Protocols* fared in America, with particular reference to the role played by Henry Ford, founder of the Ford Motor Company.

Finally, my appendices provide an array of useful addenda and summaries.

Nick Toczek
May 2015

1

THE LIFE OF HENRY HAMILTON BEAMISH

For bigotry to thrive, rather than merely persist, it requires the steady sustenance of justification. To achieve this, it needs to build itself a culture, one within which prejudice has the appearance of rationality and reason. And, for those who would have it evolve into hatred, that culture must be all-embracing. It has to have its own literature, history, art, faith and philosophy. Within such an environment, even the most outlandish of views can gain the appearance of authority, authenticity and, indeed, normality. Since the 1920s, for those in the English-speaking world who have a propensity to dislike Jews, there's just one person and one organisation which have together established this milieu more successfully than any other. They are Henry Hamilton Beamish and The Britons.

Remarkably little has been published about either of them. As an avid collector of material from and about far-right activity in Britain, I was curious. I began to pursue every fragment I could find. I started to collate these pieces, to build time lines, to plug the gaps, to fill in the details. I wanted to understand this strange and elusive man, the nature of his obsessive zeal and the story of his organisation. Before you can counter prejudice, you need to understand it.

At the root of twentieth-century Jew-hatred there is a single book, *The Protocols of the Learned Elders of Zion*. Beamish, who had founded The Britons, based his life's work on the content of this book. It was one of the first books that The Britons published, and for more than fifty years it would consistently remain their best-selling title. Working on this material I was gathering, I knew there was a story to be told here.

The truth is never easy. Beamish and The Britons could both be secretive. And, when they weren't, they could and did embellish their achievements. Also, where there's no complete story, falsities thrive, so some widely accepted details are simply wrong. Thus, for example, we are often told that Beamish was born in Ireland.

Henry Hamilton Beamish was born in London on 2 June 1873, his birth registered in the civil parish of St George, Hanover Square. He was the fifth of nine surviving children born to Blanche and Henry Beamish. His was a family with a long history of political influence. For generations, most of his male antecedents had been military or naval officers. Many went on to become notable figures in the spheres of legal, clerical or political service. Those in his paternal line had, for centuries, also been wealthy Irish landowners, although this inheritance had dissipated well before his birth, or even that of his parents. Who were they?

Henry's mother, Blanche Georgina Hughes (1840–1904), was the granddaughter of Loftus William Otway (1775–1854), who was born in the family home, Castle Otway in Tipperary, Ireland. Like his forebears, he had an extensive and influential military career, as did his brother, Robert Waller Otway, who became both an admiral and a baronet.

Henry's father, also named Henry Hamilton Beamish (1829–1901), was a rear-admiral and naval aide-de-camp to Queen Victoria. His was an illustrious career which almost didn't happen. In 1871 he had been the commander of HMS *Agincourt*, 'the noisiest and worst disciplined ship in the squadron', when it ran aground on the Pearl Rock off Gibraltar and very nearly sank. He was relieved of his command, court-martialled and severely reprimanded. With the help of an inherited arrogance, he refused to let this setback hinder his progress. He had come through tragedy too. In 1864, three years before his marriage to Blanche, he had married Louisa Mary Ann Harrison. The following year she and their daughter, Louisa Esther, died in childbirth.

The Beamish men were expected to achieve greatness in serving their country. It was a long familial tradition. Go back, for example, a further six generations and you find Sir Richard Cox (1650–1733), himself born into an ancestral history of high public office. He was an Irish lawyer and judge who served as lord chancellor of Ireland (1703–7) and then lord chief justice of the queen's bench for Ireland (1711–14).

The year after Henry was born, Blanche gave birth to Tufton Percy Hamilton Beamish (1874–1951) who followed their father in becoming a rear-admiral before entering politics. He was MP for Lewes in Sussex from 1924 to 1932 and again from 1936 to 1945, when his place was taken by his son Tufton Beamish (1917–1989), MP for Lewes from 1945 until 1974.

The couple's surviving children – six boys and three girls – were all born in the twelve years between 1868 and 1880. In order of birth they were Robert Otway (1868–1949), Maude Louisa (1869–1951), Evelyn Frances Jane (1871–1913), Sackville Edward Cecil (1872–1947), our Henry (1873–1948), Tufton Percy (1874–1951), the short-lived Gustavus William Loftus (1875–1877), John Spread (1877–1915) and, finally, Margaret Esther (1880–1957).[1]

The 1881 census tells us that, at the age of seven, Henry was the youngest pupil boarding at Romanoff House Boys' School in Tunbridge Wells, Kent. And ten years later we find him, via the 1891 census, as a seventeen-year-old agricultural student boarding at the Colonial College in Hollesley, Suffolk. This was an establishment which specialised in taking the sons of well-to-do families, especially boys who had proved academically unfit for university.

Henry would later claim that, in his youth, it was his father who first informed him of the 'Jewish question', enlightening him about the 'intrigues of international Jewry'.[2] That may well be true. Anti-Jewish sentiment was widespread at this time. And there is one specific piece of evidence that casual familial anti-Jewish attitudes existed between Henry's siblings. On 17 November 1941, Sackville wrote a letter to Tufton, who devoted much of his spare time during the 1930s and 1940s in obsessively researching Beamish family history. His letter read:

My dear Tuf,

I have taken a copy of the enclosed & many thanks for it. I was glad to see you on Thursday, & as I told you then, to the best of my recollection from the old Adam & Eve bible, a big tome, practically all the younger members of Rev.d H.H.B's family were born at Hamilton Terrace, London with the exception, I think, of Katie Palmer.* I also think I remember our father stating that he was born at Youghal.** This would be easily possible, as the Rev.d Spread (rector) father in law of Rev.d H.H.B. was probably living there.*** I have discovered a resemblance between the Southern Irish and the Jews. They both clamour for independence, and both take damned good care they don't get it.

Yrs ever
Sack.[3]

Notes: *Catherine Emily Beamish (1852–1930), their aunt, who married Joseph Blades Palmer in 1887.
**Youghal is an Irish seaside resort town in County Cork.
***Rev. Edward Spread (1752–1814), their great-grandfather, lived in Ireland and was father-in-law of their grandfather, Rev. Henry Hamilton Beamish (1796–1872).

Intensely aware of his family history, our Henry Hamilton Beamish reached adulthood certain that he was destined for military and political greatness. It lent him a self-righteous determination in all he attempted, together with a generous and ill-concealed combination of vanity and arrogance.

During 1891, while still only seventeen, exhibiting a wanderlust that would last him a lifetime, Henry went to Canada, where he took up wheat farming. During 1892 he is reported to have taken part in an expedition to the North Pole.[4] In 1895 he went to Ceylon, where he worked for several years on tea plantations, and from 1898 to 1899 held the post of assistant manager on the Hope Estate in Upper Hewaheta.[5] During the Second Boer War (1899–1902) he served as second lieutenant with the South African contingent of the Ceylon Planters Rifle Corps. They left Ceylon for South Africa on 22 April 1900 aboard the P&O SS *Syria* and returned to Ceylon on 15 July 1902 after just over two years' service.[6]

During 1901, Beamish appears to have been given leave to attend his father's funeral. The admiral, who had been ill for some time and was bedridden, had died at his home – Mount House, Braxted, Kent – on 18 July 1901. Beamish then stayed on in England, presumably to help sort out his father's estate, which was settled that October (he left £3,465 11s. 8p.).[7] Beamish then sailed from Liverpool on 14 November 1901 aboard the SS *Staffordshire*, bound for Colombo in Ceylon.[8] It's not clear if he rejoined his regiment, but within a year he had left Ceylon for good and was back in South Africa.

Beamish was now in his mid-thirties and living in Bloemfontein. Here, in 1903, he and a friend were running the Empire Tea Rooms.[9] In 1904 he started the *Farmer's Advocate*, one of the country's first agricultural newspapers. This appears to have been his first venture into publishing. The paper's full title was the *South African Farmer's Advocate and Home Magazine*, it being a pair of co-published but separately edited his-and-her journals which ran from 1904 until 1933.[10] (NB: Beamish appears to have based his publication on a well-established Canadian journal, also called *Farmer's Advocate and Home Magazine*, which had been founded around 1865 and was owned and edited by William Weld.) He remained the owner of the *Farmer's Advocate* for fifteen years. Thus, for example, when he returned briefly England in 1910, we find him described as a newspaper proprietor travelling as a second-class passenger aboard the SS *Briton*, which sailed from Natal and arrived in Southampton on 28 May.[11]

Beamish seems to have been full of ideas for new enterprises. Also in 1904, he wrote as follows to the Secretary of the Industrial Commission in Bloemfontein:

Dear Sir,
I have the honour to say that I am still prepared to put down and work a modern Tobacco Manufacturing Plant in the Parys or Vredefort District, provided that the Government are willing to give me assistance in the way of a bonus or bounty on the produce of the factory.
I have made enquiries about the tobacco growing industry in the Vredefort district, and I find that the tobacco is put on the market in a very crude state.
With proper treatment and packaging a substantial trade might develop, and I believe with a good factory in the district there is every prospect of great improvement both in quantity and quality of the local crops.
I am awaiting replies to my enquiries in the United States about the engagement of an expert in manufacturing and packaging, and should certainly engage such a man should my proposal be accepted by the government.
I have the honour to be,
Sir,
Your obedient servant,
H. H. Beamish[12]

During 1905 he was also on the six-strong executive council of an Orange River Colony consortium promoting the establishment of a Bloemfontein Consumptive Sanatorium on a piece of land in the Eagle's Nest district of Bloemfontein.[13]

It was in South Africa, during and after the Boer War, that Beamish first began to encounter the kind of extreme anti-Jewish sentiment that he would later so vehemently preach.[14] There was a belief, widely held within the post-Victorian southern African ex-pat community, that Jewish business interests – particularly of those involved in gold, diamonds and broader finance – had invested in that war, promoting it and profiting from it. One author in particular wrote extensively on this theme, thereby doing much to legitimise such prejudices. He was J. A. Hobson, a journalist who, in the autumn of 1899, had a series of articles published in the *Manchester Guardian*. These then formed the basis of his influential book *The War in South Africa: Its Causes and Effects*, published in February 1900. In a chapter entitled 'For Whom Are We Fighting?', Hobson wrote:

> A few of the financial pioneers in South Africa have been Englishmen, like Messrs. [Cecil] Rhodes and [Charles] Rudd; but recent developments of Transvaal gold-mining have thrown the economic resources of the country more and more into the hands of a small group of international financiers, chiefly German in origin and Jewish in race. Before I went there, the names Beit, Eckstein, Barnato, &c., were of course unknown to me; the very ship in which I crossed bore many scores of Jewish women and children. But until I came to examine closely the structure of industry and society upon the Rand I had no conception of their number or their power. I thus discovered that not Hamburg, not Vienna, not Frankfort, but Johannesburg is the New Jerusalem. It is not too much to say that this little ring of international financiers already controls the most valuable economic resources of the Transvaal. The first and incomparably the most important industry, the gold-mines of the Rand, are almost entirely in their hands.[15]

To reinforce the currency of such ideas among the non-Jewish white populations of southern Africa in the early years of the twentieth century, we have the work of another popular author, Arnold White, whose best-selling title *Efficiency and Empire* was published in 1901 and tackled this same subject. It included a chapter entitled 'Our Moral Inefficiency', which he blamed variously on 'German Jews' and 'foreign Jews'. The main thrust of the book concerned the Boer War and the malign effect of Jewish influence – their 'character flaws', their devotion to materialism and their desire for 'unearned' wealth. All this, White believed, was counter-British. The British nation, he asserted, had become 'infected' by 'bad smart society' which was dominated by Jews, his solution being to create a new 'true aristocracy' characterised by patriotism, independence and hostility to 'financial schemers'.[16]

These ideas expounded by Hobson and White are so strongly and directly echoed in those later expressed by Beamish that it's fair to conclude that he gleaned much from their work, either by reading their books himself or from discussions with others who had read them. Beamish was never an original thinker. However, in developing his rabid speeches on the subject more than twenty years later, he would self-importantly claim identical themes to be his personal observations. By extension, he would claim that Jews had therefore secretly worked actually to bring about the war – that they had caused it. That being the case, he began attempting to prove that they had done the same in the past and would do so again. Of course, he wasn't alone in embracing such prejudices. There was a strong climate of antipathy towards Jews in South Africa, throughout the British Empire and, indeed, in Britain itself. Beamish would have no problem finding like-minded allies.

This conspiracy theory, that the Jews were behind all the ills of the Western world and its empire territories, had long lingered in the wings. Coming conflicts, notably the Great War (1914–18) and the 1917 Russian Revolution, would see Beamish and co. strive to place that prejudice centre-stage.

Pinning down what predisposes a person to bigotry is difficult. When we look at how this possessed Beamish, several factors surface. Given his antecedents, he was under-achieving. The greatness that was expected of him by his family was proving elusive. Deprived of what he thought he deserved, he naturally looked for a scapegoat. At the same time, the world was in turmoil and was looking for a scapegoat too. For many white settlers in southern Africa, this was a difficult time. Anglo-German divisions in particular put black–white racial issues on the back-burner. Much more important was the cause of unrest between white Christians of European descent. As the Boer Wars demonstrated, these divisions were real, deep and very damaging. It was such a simple solution to blame the Jews. In that sense, what Hobson and White and their ilk wrote simply reflected pre-existing prejudices. However, the authority with which they wrote and the popularity of their books certainly served to reinforce and disperse anti-Jewish sentiment. One direct result was the Jew-hatred that would permanently characterise The Britons, the expressly anti-Jewish organisation which Beamish would found in 1919.

Beamish, meanwhile, became more involved in southern African issues. In 1907 he represented the Orange River Colony settlers at a London conference with the British government on the subject of land settlement. This was an ongoing issue, one which stemmed from the fact that many of the British settlers in the Orange River Colony had bought their land at the end of the Second Boer War, at which time land prices had been inflated. The settlers were now campaigning for the imperial government in London to readjust these evaluations because the current repayments meant that most of them faced losing both their land and much of their original investment. Thus, in the late summer of 1908, Beamish, who was still living in Bloemfontein, revisited London with H. A. Cole of the Heilbron district of the Orange River Colony. The two men, serving as representatives of the settlers, met with Lord Crewe (secretary of state for the colonies, 1908–10) to try to renegotiate terms. Although little came of these discussions, an offer surfaced two months later, in late November, under which the British Southern Africa Company, eager to recruit experienced settlers in Rhodesia, would sponsor resettlement by offering virtually free transport from South Africa to Rhodesia to those willing to make the move and generous grants towards the purchase of new land.[17] As we shall see, Beamish himself appears to have taken advantage of these terms when, in 1920, he moved to Rhodesia to make it his permanent home. Meanwhile, he remained in Bloemfontein and later claimed to have worked closely in or around 1912 with the prominent South African barrister Percival Frere Smith on labour issues.

Beamish was also involved in further business enterprises. From a history of the town of Parys comes the following for 1912:

> About this time Mr H. H. Beamish who had been connected previously with Parys as the promoter of a jam and sweet factory, which was carried on for several years until the government subsidy for these undertakings was withdrawn, proposed to the Council a plan to build rondawels and bungalows on Woody Island, which is just opposite the town. To advertise them to let for holiday-makers, also to have boats to hire, and to carry on a bioscope in the Town Hall. The Council agreed to all these ideas, and Mr. Beamish duly carried out his plans. The scheme was carried on for several years, the Council receiving a monthly rental for the rights they granted.
>
> The island plan idea was not as successful as was expected, mainly because of difficulty in access, particularly when the river was in flood. Years later the cinema and the whole scheme was bought from Mr. Beamish and formed the beginning of the present recreation department of the town.[18]

We learn some more about Beamish from the pro-Apartheid politician and journalist Arthur G. Barlow, who, in South Africa, spent a great deal of time in his company. In his entertaining South African memoir *Almost in Confidence*, Barlow paints a picture of Beamish that's both surprising and revealing. Having described him as 'one of the strangest personalities with whom I have come into contact', he continues:

> Beamish, who stuttered, was the son of a British admiral who had been an A.D.C. to Queen Victoria, and was a happy-go-lucky, humorous fellow. He had lived in Canada, where he had been a farm labourer. In South Africa, he was a British officer in the Boer War, then a waiter in a café, a shopkeeper, owner of the *Farmer's Advocate*, a building contractor who specialised in constructing Dutch churches, a policeman, an owner of buildings to let to church congregations, a coconut grower in the Seychelles (where he was considered to be 'somewhat of a nuisance') ... On the Jewish question he was cracked – quite 'barmy'.[19]

From the outbreak of the Great War in 1914, Beamish was instrumental in the formation, organisation and promotion of several political bodies which – though nominally simply pro-British – echoed similar patriotic organisations in Britain in being intensely anti-German. Such sentiments were already rife within the British ex-pat community in southern Africa, stoked by regular reports of atrocities alleged to have been committed by German troops and their allies.

During 1914, Beamish had founded and become the chairman of the British Citizen Movement (BCM),[20] an anti-German organisation which campaigned for patriots to buy British products (or, failing that, allied products) in order to support the war effort in Europe. He also became a prime mover within a second organisation, the Johannesburg-based Consumers' Alliance (CA, the full name of which was the British Patriotic Traders' and Consumers' Alliance of South Africa), which campaigned for the exclusion of Germans from the business community.

By 1915, the CA committee had begun drawing up lists of businesses funded by German or Austrian money, employing German or Austrian subjects, or owned by or otherwise associated with enemy subjects. And some of these findings began appearing in the press. Businesses not deemed to be enemy-linked were encouraged to join the CA. On payment of the 1 guinea subscription, each new member received a certificate of membership to display in their premises. In March of that year a pressure-group, the Petitioner's Committee (PC), was formed as an offshoot of the CA, founded and led by Beamish and three others – Catesby Holland, A. E. O'Flaherty and Fred W. Denbigh. Beamish, their spokesperson, was described by the authorities as the most vocal and troublesome of the four. The purpose of the PC was 'to procure the holding of a public meeting to protest against the attitude of the Government in the matter of the internment of enemy subjects, and against the carrying on of business by persons of enemy origin'.

Anti-German sentiment reached fever-pitch following the sinking of the British ocean liner RMS *Lusitania*, which was torpedoed by a German U-boat on 7 May 1915 with the loss of almost 1,200 lives of the almost 2,000 people on board. In sinking a non-military ship, the Germans had certainly broken international law; however, so had the British, because the ship – as the Germans claimed at the time and as was finally admitted by the British Foreign Office in 1982 – was secretly carrying a cargo of war munitions.

News of the sinking appeared in the South African press on Saturday 8 May. On the following Wednesday, a half-holiday, posters for that day's issue of the *Rand Daily Mail* featured the headline 'German shops sacked', referring to incidents in Liverpool and Birkenhead in England prompted by the sinking. This, it seemed, triggered events in Johannesburg (and other South African cities). Rioting began. In the centre of Johannesburg alone, 168 properties were wrecked or damaged, fifty of them totally destroyed by fire. The police did little to stop it all. While large crowds gathered to witness these events, relatively few individuals were directly or actively involved. Furthermore, properties displaying a CA membership certificate went undamaged. The inference was that this rioting was not only organised but planned, with suspicion inevitably falling on the CA and those connected with it.

A year later, during May 1916, the Select Committee on Incendiarism met to investigate the riots. Beamish was one of the twenty-one witnesses called to testify. On Tuesday 9 May he appeared before the committee on behalf of both the Petitioners' Committee and the British Citizens Movement (of which he was chairman):

Chairman: You reside in Johannesburg?
Beamish: Yes.
C: What is your occupation?
B: I am a journalist.

C:	We should like to have some information from you as to the anti-German riots that took place in Johannesburg in May of last year and more particularly with respect to the Consumers' Alliance and the Petitioners' Committee, of which we understand you are a member. When was the Consumers' Alliance first formed?
B:	Shortly after the war broke out, as far as I remember. I had nothing to do with it then.
C:	Do you know who formed it?
B:	Yes, Mr. Frank Brown; and a man named Parnham was the honorary secretary.
C:	What were its objects?
B:	To promote trade between Great Britain and her Allies. I was not a member when it started but became a member afterwards. I remained a member until after the riots. Here is a circular addressed to the Patriotic Traders' and Consumers' Alliance of South Africa. [Document handed in.]
C:	I take it that these circulars were sent round to the business men and traders of Johannesburg?
B:	Yes.
C:	Did you get many replies?
B:	Yes, a fair number. I had nothing to do with it at that time. I became a Vice-President of it afterwards.
C:	This circular is issued by the Patriotic Traders' and Consumers' Alliance which was a body known as the Consumers' Alliance?
B:	Yes.
C:	Mr. Frank Brown was the President?
B:	Yes, and Mr. Ward Jackson of the *Rand Daily Mail*, Mr. T. R. Purchus, and Senator Tucker.
C:	You resigned from this body after the riots?
B:	Yes, in May.
C:	Can you tell us when the Petitioners' Committee was formed?
B:	It was before the riots, about ten days I should think. I was connected with them. The principal member was myself, because I took the most prominent part in organising it, and there were three or four others.
C:	What were the objects of that committee?
B:	The object was to have a public meeting in order to draw the attention of the Government to the fact that all those Germans who had been interned had been let out, or the bulk of them had, and that they were really trading within the British Empire rather more strongly than they were before. Business with them was a great deal better than usual in many cases.
C:	Did you obtain a list in Johannesburg of people who were trading and were not British subjects? Of Germans?
B:	No. I have never lived in Johannesburg. I am not a Johannesburg man.
C:	Where did you live?

B: In Bloemfontein mostly. At that time if you had offered me a hundred pounds I could not have given you the names of three German firms. That did not interest me, that part of it. It was the Government allowing these people to get out and so irritating the people.

C: You did not at that stage trouble very much about the men who were trading in Johannesburg, Germans or Austrians? It was all over South Africa, not in Johannesburg alone.

B: That was well known. They were trading and they are still trading. In many cases there is no difference now from that time.

C: Did I understand you to say that the immediate object of the formation of that Committee was the holding of a public meeting in Johannesburg?

B: Yes.

C: What was done in connection with that meeting?

B: The government would not allow the meeting.

C: How was that?

B: They said it would embarrass the Government.

C: Who are they?

B: General Smuts. The mayor refused to hold it. He wanted me and others to look at a confidential wire he had received, but I refused to look at it as it was confidential.

C: What steps did the Government take to prevent the holding of that meeting?

B: They wired the mayor that it would embarrass the government to hold the meeting.

C: They suggested that it should not be held?

B: The mayor told the Government that there was a big agitation. The country was under Martial Law and I presume the mayor wired to General Smuts and he was told that it would embarrass the Government if the meeting was held.

C: Was there any refusal on the part of the Government to permit the meeting to be held?

B: Well, under Martial Law I take it to be quite enough for them to say that it would embarrass the Government. At any rate it was made a refusal because the meeting was not held.

C: What did you do after that?

B: An extraordinary coincidence took place, for which I have been blamed. The Lusitania was sunk. I had not arranged for that, but I have been blamed for it all the same.

C: Blamed for having arranged what?

B: The sinking of The Lusitania.

C: Who blamed you for such a thing?

B: A few intriguers in the country. There was a very specific story spread about, as they will do in this country without the least foundation. I wonder that it has not been stated that I arranged for the rebellion, the armed protest.

C: Was this meeting held eventually?

B: Yes. The Mayor showed me a telegram which he said he had received from General Smuts, but I would not look at it because he said it was confidential. That was the same telegram that was afterwards published from Senator Ware. In the middle of this agitation the sinking of The Lusitania took place.

C: Did you see the same wire published in the press afterwards?

B: I presume it was the same wire, but I cannot tell you, as I refused to look at it when the Mayor offered to show it to me. The situation was of course completely altered by the sinking of The Lusitania. There had previously been just an ordinary desire on the part of the public to hold a meeting. That had been refused. They sent in one petition signed by 1,600 names some weeks before that, but I had nothing to do with that. The Mayor then refused to hold a meeting and it was felt that all these enemy alien people were being allowed out and that they were behaving in an extraordinary way. Then a second petition was got up, in the middle of this agitation the sinking of The Lusitania took place, and then it was not a question of whether you would like to hold a public meeting or not. The public were very incensed that they would have held their meeting if they had had to smash the doors open. Unfortunately the Mayor, still having this confidential telegram from General Smuts, still refused to hold the meeting. He could not have had any knowledge of human nature, could not see that, as happened in France, there was a revolution coming along. Still he hung out, and he hung out, until I pointed out in his office that the people were beginning to smash up things. He had only to look out of the window to see that. He would not consent to hold the meeting until he looked out of the window and saw that the people meant mischief. Then he gave in.

Beamish seemed to think that it was the banning of his meeting rather than the sinking that triggered the riots. As we'll see, throughout his life, evasive repetition coupled with an exaggerated perception of his own role in key events would prove typical of Beamish whenever he was questioned or called to account. When asked if the PC was an offshoot of the CA he replied:

> It was when it started. There were certain people getting up the petition. They had no machinery of their own such as typewriters and stationery, so they came to me and I said I would help them. I was a member of the Consumers' Alliance and a Vice- President before the riots. The Petitioners' Committee was merely concerned in getting up that meeting, and it was to be dissolved immediately after the meeting. The Petitioners' Committee took upon itself the organisation of the meeting. There was nothing to be ashamed of in getting up the meeting. The Consumers' Alliance is still in existence, and the British Citizens' Movement. The latter is quite a different body from the Consumers' Association.

The meeting demanded by the PA was eventually held on 15 May in Johannesburg Town Hall, just after the two days of rioting. It was chaired by Beamish. Questioned about the meeting during his testimony, he said that an earlier meeting would have prevented the rioting:

C: Might not the fact of a large number of people coming together and perhaps getting excited and hearing strong speeches have done more to inflame public feeling?

B: It all depends on how you organise your public meeting. If you have an inflammatory man speaking, naturally he will inflame the people, but there was nothing of that kind. I started the agitation for the meeting, which I conducted myself, and not only was it all orderly, but they went home extremely quietly.[21]

This post-riot PA meeting, described by Beamish as 'the best and most enthusiastic ever held in Johannesburg', passed four resolutions which Beamish circulated to the press throughout the British Empire. They were:

1   That this meeting of citizens, Boer and British men and women of South Africa, themselves beset by treacherous enemies working in secret against the people who have afforded them a free life and prosperity on British soil, send to the headquarters of Empire this message – 'We share your horror at the cowardly outrages of Germany, of which the destruction of the Lusitania is as yet the most hideous and towering crime; we sorrow with those made to mourn innocent victims; we vow to serve to the glorious end the righteous arms of Britain and her Allies.' – Sent from Johannesburg Town Hall by the Mayor of Johannesburg, in the presence of assembled citizens.

2   That this meeting records its abhorrence of German barbarity, especially its revolting cold-blooded murdering of non-combatants, women, and children, and its brutality towards British prisoners of war, and binds itself to take all steps necessary to ensure that all Germans shall be interned or deported, and resolves that it shall be neither lawful nor possible for any German or his agent within our borders to transact business, in person or by deputy, or to occupy any position of authority or control over British subjects.

3   That whereas German trade and finance and fictitious naturalisation have been used as a mask for espionage and hostile preparation, we demand that the Government shall now order – (a) That all property and financial interests held by or on behalf of Germans be sequestered to the State, and be administered in such a way that no profit shall now or later be derived by such enemy or their assignees. (b) That all persons acting on behalf of German interests shall be required to hand over to the State such agencies, together with all securities, and documents belonging thereto, and that the same be administered for the benefit of genuine British subjects.

4   That copies of these resolutions be forwarded to the Prime Minister, and also to the Governor-General, for transmission to the Imperial Government. Together with an assurance of our resolve to aid to the uttermost his Majesty's resistance and the overthrow of an enemy self-outlawed from the humane world.[22]

As we shall see, within four years, in setting up The Britons and in publishing his book *The Jews' Who's Who*, Beamish would transfer this very language and these attitudes from Germans to Jews.

Following the riots, Beamish resigned from the CA, ostensibly in disgust after discovering that they had been selling their guinea membership and issuing membership certificates to non-British business owners. Here he is during his May 1916 testimony to the Select Committee:

C: We have evidence that one firm took as many as nine of these certificates for their branches.
B: One took forty-four, and he was not a British subject. He got as many as he wanted. They were being issued like cards to anybody, whether British subjects or not. That upset the whole thing and that is why I left it.
C: Then the whole business was a farce?
B: A perfect one. There is a Mr. Schlesinger, who is not even an ally, and he took out forty-four of the certificates for his places ... This man Schlesinger is a hyphenated Yankee Jew with a German name, so I do not know what nationality you make him out to be.

Throughout, his testimony Beamish repeatedly contradicted himself. Thus the man who 'could not have given the names of three German firms' later responded as follows:

C: You say you informed the Government of some people whom you took to be German spies?
B: Yes.
C: Was it particularly your business to look out for spies?
B: I think so, certainly, I think it is everybody's business to look after burglars and spies and people like that. I am very much interested in that, and I am of the opinion that one of the firms I mentioned were German spies and I informed the Government of that. The property of the firm was not touched during the riots. I had informed the Government about lots of other people in Johannesburg. I am always even now informing the Government, every day.
C: Then you are acting as a kind of C.I.D.?
B: I do not know whether I am a C.I.D. It is a question of my own country. I am a Nationalist, meaning an Irish Nationalist.
C: You mean a South African Nationalist?
B: I mean the same thing. They are both excellent bodies. I consider it my business to find out the enemies of my country and of the Empire.

Why Beamish should try to pass himself off as Irish is anyone's guess. That the Select Committee was unimpressed by him soon became clear, as expressed by one of their number, Reverend Vorster:

Vorster: I rather got this impression that you were a sort of responsible person, but your utterances this morning are very irresponsible. I may say that you make random utterances.

Beamish: All right. Put it that way. That is your personal view, Vorster. I have here a letter that you put in from the Commissioner of Police in which the following occurs: 'Will your committee kindly supply me with the names of enemy subjects which are known to them and which are at large, and it will render me great assistance in carrying out the duties I have to perform.'

The Select Committee had reason to suspect (a) that, before the riots, the CA had indeed prepared lists of non-British businesses and had probably been instrumental in provoking the rioting, and also that their lists had been used by the rioters; (b) that the CA had profited from this whole exercise by taking fees from a number of these businesses in exchange for certificates to display and thereby avoid being targeted – i.e. that they had effectively been running a protection and extortion racket. Seen in this light, Beamish's deliberate evasiveness and his abrupt post-riot resignation from the CA take on a much more sinister aspect. However, he was at pains to distance himself from such activity by blaming instead his former associates. Here's his account to the Select Committee:

> All I know is that before the riots the Alliance had no money at all, but during the riots I believe that they made a great deal of money. It was of course legitimate and honest, as far as South African concerns can be honest, but they took this money, in my opinion, absolutely immorally, and I put it in writing at the time. I strongly objected to it.

With Beamish on the defensive, the questioning intensified:

C: How much money did they get?
B: I do not know. I was so utterly opposed to granting these things under stress that I refused to have anything more to do with it.
C: What do you mean by granting them under stress?
B: If a man comes to me with a gun and says I must do something to assist him I take it that is granted under stress. When people are burning places it is near the mark of duress.

Beamish then named two traders – Chudleigh and Herbert Evans – whom he said had complained to him and to the PC that they were being 'practically blackmailed' into obtaining certificates.

C: Then the position in Johannesburg was this: that the merchants and traders had to take out these certificates. They were compelled to do so?
B: I would not say that. I am giving you the names of two men who said that to me.
C: That was for the purpose of protecting their property?
B: That is what it amounted to.
C: Against whom?
B: Whoever were doing the damage, no doubt.
C: Was that after the riots had commenced?
B: During the riots.
C: And before the riots?
B: Not before the riots. Up to that time the people were simply being asked whether they would join the Association the same as they might be asked to join the YMCA or anything else, and if they did not like to join they needn't. Apparently during the riots these emblems saved a lot of people's windows, and then some of the people thought they would join at once.
C: With regard to these lists of traders, were there any lists framed by the Consumers' Alliance?
B: Not that I know of. There was only the list of people who took the emblems. There was no other list to my knowledge. The Petitioners' Committee did not frame any lists. I did not know the German firms then, but I know a good many of them now.
C: Did you ever see a list of exclusively German firms?
B: I have now a fairly good list, because some of the firms who were then trading are still trading. I make a list every day. The Petitioners' Committee was formed at a few hours' notice for the purpose of getting up the meeting.

The Petitioners' Committee was finally dissolved on 10 August 1915.

C: Why was the Committee dissolved?
B: It was only dissolved to be formed into something else. Then it became the British Citizens' Movement.
C: Is this the body which organised these big petitions to Parliament? Is this the British Citizens' Movement?
B: Yes, and I am the Chairman of it.

Beamish had already referred to Mr. Schlesinger being a Jew. Now he seemed to be singling out others. In his evidence, he drew attention to a Mr. Gebhardt, saying:

> I may tell you that this Mr. Gebhardt is so keen on being a Britisher that he has changed his name to Martin. I suppose that you know that. My name is Beamish, my father's name is Beamish, and my brother's name is Beamish, but Mr. Gebhardt is so intensely British that he has changed his name to Martin.

The Select Committee, having been told by a former CA secretary that she had typed out copies of a list of German-owned companies, pressed Beamish further on this question:

C: Are you definite there was no list prepared of Germans who were to be dealt with? There was a list of British subjects. Is it not rather surprising that there was, on the other hand, no list of people who were not to be dealt with in trade?
B: We did not have any list of German firms.
C: The only list to your knowledge was that of people who were to be traded with?
B: Yes.
C: Then if this young lady says she typed copies of such a list, she is not correct?
B: She might have typed a list of people who refused to take that emblem. That was quite another thing. Lots of people were asked to take it and did not, but if a man did not take it it does not follow that he was a German.
C: Were you in the Alliance office at all or did you know what was going on there?
B: Yes.
C: And you mean to say that there was no list actually prepared of German subjects in Johannesburg?
B: Yes.
C: You think that owing to the actions of the mob there was some power behind it and directing it?
B: I think there must have been, but I have no idea as to who it was.[21]

Along these lines, Beamish's testimony drew to a close. It seems that there was no subsequent action taken against him. Soon after this, he again joined up and was commissioned to the 2nd Regiment of the South African Infantry (Overseas Brigade). This was a regiment specifically recruited from Natal and the Orange Free State.[23,24]

Was Beamish innocent? Not according to his friend Arthur G. Barlow. Here's what he had to say about it:

> A few days after the sinking of the *Lusitania* by the Germans Henry Beamish took me into a basement in Commissioner Street, Johannesburg, where we found a small number of men drawing up lists. Two men who were there were D. C. Greig (afterwards a chairman of the Johannesburg Stock Exchange and whom I had known well as a fellow member of the ill-fated 'Young Unionists' Movement) and Harry Lyons, who, at one time, had been editor of *The Star*.
>
> Beamish led a mob of howling Johannesburgers through the streets of that city and the crowd burnt down many valuable properties. I have no doubt at all that Beamish was the arch-villain behind this stupid and criminal rioting.[19]

It's not unreasonable to hazard a guess that, in going off to war and subsequently returning to England, Beamish was making sure that he had no consequences to face.

Beamish, of course – by the simple act of omission – presented a very different version of his overseas life and work between 1891 and 1918. This can be found in a one-page document among the papers of his younger brother Tufton. These now make up the Beamish Collection held in the Churchill Archive Centre at Cambridge University. Typed out by Henry himself, with a handwritten footnote by Tufton which reads 'my brother 1919 TPHB', the sheet is headed 'Experiences of Mr. H. H. Beamish in connection with Land Settlement Work and Employment of Labour'. It reads:

> In early life spent 4 years in Canada, where, in addition to being employed on surveying, took up two farms in the North West Territory.
>
> Proceeded to Ceylon and was Superintendent of second largest factory in the island. Took part in the South African War, was one of the Officers of the Ceylon Contingent, and since that War have lived in South Africa, where, in addition to owning a number of Commercial enterprises have been closely associated with land settlement work. Have been general Manager of the largest land Settlement Company in the Orange Free State, Managing Director of a Farmers Cooperative Business and have been Agent for the Land Department of the Chartered Company for a number of years.
>
> Established a number of Colonial Industries some of which have been subsidised by the Government, and established and own the oldest Agricultural paper in South Africa, (Farmers Advocate).
>
> Established a basket making industry and settled the Workers on irrigated plots, on which the necessary osiers are grown, and in connection with the various industries I control, employ approximately 1,000 workers.[25]

The punctuation, grammar and capitalisations are Beamish's. It's the work of a vain man, overly keen to impress by selectively listing and aggrandising his achievements.

During late February and early March 1918, a special subcommittee of the British Empire Producers' Organisation met in London to examine policy for securing the meat supplies of the empire. This body, made up of almost twenty meat trade representatives from throughout the British Empire, included Mr H. H. Beamish representing Western Canada and Orange River, South Africa. Protectionist and deeply opposed to foreign investment within the British Empire, the committee passed four resolutions designed to restrict trade involving companies which weren't British, allied or neutral.[26]

It seems likely that Beamish then remained in London. Certainly, by the end of 1918 he was living there. His xenophobia was, by this time, focused entirely on the Jews. He was utterly convinced that they operated an organised, powerful and corrupt global network. Having begun with their perceived control of South African mining, he had extended this to their control of finance and banking in general, and thence to global business, the manipulation of governments and the ownership of mass media, the cause of strikes and civil unrest, the instigation of wars and revolutions, the destruction of Christianity, and the creation of communism. All of this and more stemmed, he now knew, from one vast Jewish plot to take over the world. He set about trying to find the proof and make it public.

Beamish's military service led him to start campaigning for the rights of returning combatants. He became a member of the Silver Badge Party (SBP) for ex-servicemen, founded during the Great War. Its leader and co-founder was a naval flying officer, Lieutenant Commander Harry MacLeod Fraser, who had been awarded his aviator's certificate from the Royal Aero Club in 1914. Fraser's naval record lists his three successive appointments as commander of a destroyer: HMS *Boyne* (31 July 1912), HMS *Swale* (7 February 1913) and HMS *Doon* (August 1914). He and Beamish became close friends, with Fraser quickly developing similar anti-Jewish views. When Beamish then embarked on compiling his supposed evidence of the 'hidden hand' of Jewish intrigue – an encyclopaedic index identifying influential Jews – Fraser became his willing co-compiler. This would become *The Jews' Who's Who*, which The Britons would publish as a 255-page book in 1920.

Fraser's SBP took its name from the silver war badge which was issued to servicemen who were invalided out of the forces. It was an organisation which had evolved out of the National Association of Discharged Sailors and Soldiers (NADSS), which had been established following a meeting in Blackburn, Lancashire, in September 1916. Because of the subsequent politics of Fraser and Beamish, the SBP is often presumed to have been right-wing and anti-Jewish from the outset. There is no evidence that it was either of these. Indeed, it was initially a left-wing group linked with the labour and trade union movements.

In April 1917, at the National Liberal Club, the Liberal MP for Edinburgh, James Myles Hogge, sponsored a meeting over the Military Service (Review of Exemptions) Bill which proposed to reclassify those who might be recalled to service. This meeting led to the formation of a splinter group, the National Federation of Discharged and Demobilised Soldiers and Sailors (NFDSS), often known simply as the Federation.

By a curious coincidence, there would soon be another influential ex-servicemen's organisation founded and run by left-wingers, one of whom would go on to become a prominent Jew-hater. This was the National Union of Ex-Servicemen (NUX), founded in 1919 by members of the Independent Labour Party. The activist who was central to NUX was John Beckett, then on the far left of British politics but later to become a leading fascist. He already harboured a paradoxical antipathy to Jews, one he would unleash only in the 1930s after the death of his mother, who was Jewish. Beckett and Beamish became acquainted at this time, primarily through their campaigning for ex-servicemen but also because of shared thinking about Jews.[27]

The NFDSS decided to fight by-elections to promote its cause. Its candidate in the June 1917 Liverpool Abercrombie by-election polled an encouraging quarter of the vote. For the general election on 14 December 1918 (dubbed the 'Coupon' election), the NFDSS executive approved five candidates, with twenty-five more being sponsored by local branches. In three Leeds constituencies, the candidates were jointly nominated by the NFDSS, the NADSS and the Comrades of the Great War. Although many of these secured a substantial proportion of the vote, none won. However, one NADSS-sponsored candidate in Sowerby, the one-time left-wing Liberal Robert Hewitt Barker, having inherited the position of unofficial Conservative Party candidate, did actually win a seat.

A notable maverick figure during this period was the wealthy and flamboyant airman Noel Pemberton Billing (of whom Lloyd George said 'This man is dangerous. He doesn't want anything'). Billing stood in the Mile End by-election on 25 January 1916 and lost, though only by a very narrow margin. On 9 March, he was elected MP for East Herefordshire. He had run as an Independent Air Candidate, securing 4,590 votes to beat the 3,559 acquired by the Unionist candidate, Captain Brodie Henderson. It was Billing who would bring Beamish his one brief stab at British political power.

On 7 October 1916, Billing launched *The Imperialist* as his own Hereford-based 'independent viewspaper', which was published weekly from then until 2 February 1918, a total of seventy editions.[28] Less than a year later, on 29 July 1917, following two large meetings in London, Billing founded a pressure group, the Vigilante Society, to 'promote purity in life'. His stated aim, through this body and his journal, was to 'campaign against and expose corruption, malpractice, underhand tactics and political intrigue'. His main co-founder was Captain Henry Hamilton Beamish, who became a regular contributor to *The Imperialist*. A third founder member who also contributed pieces to *The Imperialist* was Dr John H. Clarke, who would later become vice-president of The Britons.[24]

In the spring of 1918 the society headquarters moved from Hereford to London and *The Imperialist* changed its name to *The Vigilante*. The first issue appeared on 9 February 1918.[28] The industrious Billing needed someone to handle the running of the journal and so appointed a young American, Captain Harold Sherwood Spencer, as his assistant editor. Spencer, who had been in the British Army, claimed that he had been an MI6 agent. In fact, he had been dismissed from the army in September 1917 suffering from 'paranoid delusional insanity'.[29] It was Beamish who, having met Spencer at a National Party meeting, had introduced him to Billing.

Within months, Billing had to warn Beamish that the virulently anti-Jewish tone of his magazine contributions was unacceptable. The same problem soon arose with the extreme anti-Catholic views regularly expressed by Clarke. Despite these reprimands, and with the conspiracy-obsessed Spencer making many of the editorial decisions, anti-Jewish sentiment continued to feature in the journal – as did lurid articles decrying Billing's two personal bugbears. The first of these was a supposedly vast (and Jewish-linked) German spy network. The second was lesbianism and male homosexuality. A scurrilous front-page piece on lesbianism headlined 'The Cult of the Clitoris' resulted in a high-profile court case at the Old Bailey in May–June 1918, with Billing conducting his own defence and eventually, after much mud-slinging on all sides, securing an acquittal for himself. However, evidence suggesting that he had had sexual relationships with two women in the case left Billing, a married man, far from untainted.[30]

During the case, which caused a sensation and attracted vast amounts of newspaper coverage, there was one notable figure among those called by Billing to give evidence in his defence. This was Arnold White. Another was Beamish, who, in his evidence, speaking as the treasurer of the Vigilante Society, said he had risen to the rank of sergeant in the war in the South African Brigade. He testified to the parlous financial state of the Vigilante Society and of its newspaper in particular, stating that it was 'published at a heavy loss'.[31]

There is an interesting aside that demonstrates the power of literature in promoting bigotry. Both Spencer, in the pages of *The Vigilante*, and Billing, during the court case, made much of a so-called *Black Book* said to have been compiled by the Germans. They claimed that it listed 47,000 names of prominent English people who were 'perverts'. The list of names, each followed by details of their sexual activities, was said to include cabinet ministers and their wives.[32] There was no proof of the book's existence then, nor has there been any such proof since. It's a myth, but one people were willing to believe.

When, in Chapter 8, we come to examine the unquestioned existence of *The Protocols*, we'll see how cast-iron proof that it was a forgery didn't stop people believing it to be true – quite the reverse: they defiantly embraced it, and continue to do so today.

The delusional Spencer, who claimed to have seen the *Black Book* himself while on special service in Albania, appears personally to have concocted the story of its existence. The book features in an article by him (probably co-written with Billing) entitled 'The First 47,000', which was published in the 26 January 1918 issue of *The Imperialist*. This article begins:

> There exists in the cabinet noire of a certain German prince a book compiled by the Secret Service from the reports of German agents who have infested this country for the past 20 years, agents so vile and spreading debauchery of such a lasciviousness that only German minds could conceive and German bodies execute...

This *Black Book*, he claimed, contained instructions for 'the propagation of evils which all decent men thought had perished in Sodom and Lesbia'. According to Spencer, the 47,000 English male and female 'perverts' listed in the book included 'Privy Councillors, youths of the chorus, wives of Cabinet Ministers, dancing girls, even Cabinet Ministers themselves, while diplomats, poets, bankers, editors, newspaper proprietors and members of His Majesty's household follow each other with no order of precedence.' The book, Spencer continued, also contained details 'of the unnatural defloration of children who were drawn to the parks by the summer evening concerts.'[33]

The 'German prince' was actually Prince Wilhelm of Wied (26 March 1876–18 April 1945), who, though born and raised in Germany, had been selected to be prince of Albania. Spencer claimed to have served in Albania and that, while there, had acted as ADC to the prince in 1914, during which time the latter had shown him the *Black Book* and had read sections of it to him. All of this was part of Spencer's testimony at Billing's Old Bailey trial. The authorities, however, not only maintained that Spencer had never been ADC to the prince but added that he had never even served in Albania.[24] They were also lying. Spencer is on record as having 'fought bravely in Albamia' in 1914.[34] There is also evidence that in 1914 he was a volunteer on the staff of Prince Wilhelm.[35]

So where do we stand on all of this? Was Spencer mentally unstable and unreliable? Very probably. Would the authorities lie to defend themselves and the establishment? Most certainly. Conspiracy theory thrives where neither side can be shown categorically to be telling the truth or lying. However, with hindsight, we can be fairly sure that the *Black Book* was pure fiction, even though covert homosexual activity in England or Germany – or, indeed, anywhere else – was an obvious and fairly commonplace reality.

Interestingly, we can trace the origins of this obsession with 'perversion' on the part of the Vigilante Society to none other than Arnold White, who, at the end of 1917, published an article in the *English Review* under the title 'Efficiency and Vice', which was reprinted in *The Vigilante*. In it White maintained that most German men were homosexual. Using the German word *Urninge*, meaning gay men, he warned of 'the systematic seduction of young British soldiers by German urnings and their agents', describing this as 'a great cancer made in Germany'. The German troops, he said, were not only raping women but were out to spread homosexuality among Englishmen in order to undermine national efficiency. According to White, one of the prime aims of the German Empire was the legalisation of homosexuality and the restoration of Sodom and Gomorrah. 'Every father and mother in the British Empire should know', he asserted, that their aim was to 'infect clean nations with the Hunnish erotomania.' He further claimed that 'The English conception of their national life is that the home is the unit of the nation ... but if the conception of home life is replaced by the Kultur of the urnings, the spirit of the Anglo-Saxon world wilts and perishes.'[33] As an organisation avowedly established to 'expose corruption and malpractice', the Vigilante Society was now merely a vehicle for fantasised and jingoistic anti-German Jew-hatred and homophobia.

The 23 March 1918 issue of *The Vigilante* carried an article detailing how Germans and Jews were collaborating to spread venereal disease. It asserted that:

> The German, through his efficient and clever agent, the Ashkenazim, has complete control of the White Slave Traffic. Germany has found that diseased women cause more casualties than bullets. Controlled by their Jew-agents, Germany maintains in Britain a self-supporting – even profit-making – army of prostitutes which puts more men out of action than does their army of soldiers.[33]

In June, Beamish, who was by now the treasurer of the society, became the Vigilante-sponsored candidate in the Clapham by-election. In this, he was also part-sponsored by the NFDSS, of which he was now a member. There was also support from some branches of the NADSS, although not from the group's national executive. Beamish's campaign assistant was his friend Harry MacLeod

Fraser. The two men ran this operation from an office in the Silver Badge Party premises at 4 Spring Gardens, Charing Cross. Having together been thrown out of the Albert Hall for calling Lord Robert Cecil a traitor,[29] they rashly displayed a poster in their office window accusing Sir Alfred Mond, a prominent Jewish businessman and politician of German descent, of also being a traitor. The wording of this poster ('Sir Alfred Mond is a traitor, he allocated shares to the Germans during the war') was soon to plunge the pair into a disastrous libel case brought by Mond.

Meanwhile, Billing officially announced Beamish's candidature in a speech he made at the Royal Albert Hall on 15 June. The meeting, which began with a concert of songs and organ music, followed by the speech from Billing, ended with the unanimous passing of a resolution calling on the government to take steps to denaturalise and intern forthwith all enemy-born subjects and to take powers under the Defence of the Realm Act to provide that all aliens should, for the duration of the war, 'exhibit on the lapel of their coats the emblem of their nationality'. Thereafter, Billing campaigned hard in Parliament on this issue – knowing well that 'alien' was perceived by many as a euphemism for 'Jew' and that anti-Jewish campaigners such as Beamish regarded Jewishness as a separate nationality, not a religion.

Beamish, while standing as an Independent, adhered faithfully to Vigilante Society policies, and so the 21 June by-election hinged on his call for the rescinding of naturalisation, the immediate internment of all citizens of enemy countries, the closure of all foreign-owned banks, and the wearing of a badge by all people of non-British origin. These issues, as raised by Beamish's campaign, even occupied the prime minister, Lloyd George, as *The Times* reported that month under the headline 'Hun Influence – New British Policy – Drastic Action Proposed':

> Mr. Lloyd George is determined, in view of public unrest, to intern all enemy aliens, if it is shown their freedom is a menace to the country. He will deal first with Germans recently naturalised, personally examining the departmental information, and dismissing all Government employees and munition workers of German extraction. He is also considering the closing of German banks.
>
> The National Party is organising a petition 'for the immediate internment of all enemy aliens'.
>
> Unusual interest is being taken in the Clapham by-election. The Coalitionist, Mr. Harry Green [a mistake; it was Harry Greer], is opposed by Mr. Hamilton Beamish, a nominee of Mr. Pemberton Billing. Both are giving attention to the enemy alien question. Mr. Beamish recently said that if returned and all the enemy aliens were not interned he would create a pandemonium in the House of Commons.
>
> The Prime Minister's secretary has written to Mr. Green that Mr. Lloyd George is personally examining the whole question of alien enemies in this country and is determined to take whatever action is necessary.[36]

As the most vociferous candidate in the election and a prominent member of both the Vigilante Society and the National Party, Beamish seemed truly to have caught the zeitgeist. This must have seemed as if it was to be his opportunity for the taking. However, he narrowly lost the by-election, Greer securing 4,512 votes against Beamish's creditable 3,331 (43 per cent). Undeterred by this defeat, Beamish stood once more in Clapham in the general election on 14 December 1918, this time running as an NFDSS candidate. Again he came second, but he lost by the much larger margin of 6,706 votes.[37]

Immediately before the 21 June by-election, Spencer had sent a telegram, on behalf of Billing, to the prime minister, Lloyd George, in which he again called for the internment of all enemy-born subjects. Further controversy, stoked by Billing himself, arose when the prime minister's office denied that they had received the telegram.

On 24 June, after a series of persistent attempts to push forward issues related to allegations of covert alien involvement in British politics, Billing was forcibly removed from the House of Commons. The following evening he attended a play, *The Hidden Hand*, at the Strand Theatre. As the curtain fell, he stood up and addressed the astonished audience from his box, outlining what he saw as the play's relevance to the alien situation.

The next day, Billing nominated Spencer as the Vigilante Society's candidate in the forthcoming East Finchley by-election. Another telegram was then sent to Lloyd George offering to withdraw the candidacy if the Vigilante Society's recommendations on the alien question were adopted.

Despite this appearance of unity, all was far from well within the society. On 5 July, Billing received a letter of resignation from all three members of the Vigilante finance committee. The trio – Beamish, Clarke and James Horace Collings – were claiming that Billing was spending large amounts of the society's money without their sanction. From the outset, Billing had personally and extensively funded the impoverished society, providing roughly 75 per cent of its income. However, the financial committee, appointed a year earlier, had tried to regulate outgoings, only to find that Billing ignored them. In particular, they had failed in their attempts to limit his spending on election campaigning.

Billing's reaction to the resignation letter was to express concern that it would damage the good name of the Vigilante Society. He therefore suggested that every member should be informed not only of the committee's resignation letter but also of the origins of the schism – namely that Clarke was 'endeavouring to turn the Society into an anti-Catholic movement', while Beamish was anti-Jewish. It was agreed to call an extraordinary general meeting of the society at Queen's Hall at the end of the month.

In the meantime, the press began attacking Billing's anti-alien campaign by pointing out that his own wife, Lilian Maud Pemberton Billing (née Schweitzer), was German and therefore, according to her husband's campaign, should be interned. The couple initially issued a complete denial of her or her father's German ancestry but were soon proved to have been lying. She was, indeed, born in Germany of a German father.

As the East Finchley by-election approached, Billing campaigned heavily. On the eve of the poll a crowd of almost a thousand, led by Billing and Spencer, attacked a meeting of the other independent candidate, A. S. Belsher. Fighting broke out. Belsher's car was wrecked. Stones were hurled through windows into the meeting hall. Police reinforcements were called and, finding that Billing was using his own car as a platform from which he was speaking out against aliens and military shirkers, ordered him to stop. In response, some of his audience attacked anyone whom they took to be aliens or shirkers. Eventually, the ringleaders were arrested and order was restored. This was the version reported in *The Times*. A very different version, written by Billing, appeared in *The Vigilante*, painting his crowd as the heroes of the whole encounter.

At the extraordinary general meeting on 27 July, Beamish spoke on behalf of the finance committee, outlining their problems with party expenditure and adding that, contrary to their wishes, Billing had refused to allow a collection at the Albert Hall meeting, which had attracted nearly 10,000 people. Had the collection been allowed, it would, Beamish claimed, have raised at least £1,000 of much-needed funding. He added that it was this clash that lay behind their resignations. Billing's response was to point out that he had personally funded most of the society's work and that a collection at a meeting was against the constitution of the society. He then went on to call for strength and unity. When the vast majority of the 400 supporters present sided with Billing, Beamish flatly refused to return as treasurer. The upshot was the damaging departure from the society of a number of leading members, among them Beamish, Clarke and Collins, along with Spencer.

Billing was re-elected to parliament in that December 'Coupon' election and decided to devote his energies to parliamentary work. On 3 February 1919, a four-page *Review and Valediction* was published. Compiled by the Vigilante's former secretary, Euphemia Tait, it announced that both the journal and the Vigilante Society had been wound up.[30] The final issue of *The Vigilante* appeared on 8 February.[28]

The departure of Beamish et al. from the Vigilante Society and its subsequent collapse can be seen as their prime reason for founding The Britons in 1919. And it was the intervening Mond trial that fully persuaded Beamish to establish the society as a specifically anti-Jewish organisation. That Beamish, Clarke and Spencer were three of the fourteen present at the inaugural meeting of The Britons is further proof that the organisation was a product of the collapse of the Vigilante Society.

In March 1919, Beamish and Fraser were taken to court by Sir Alfred Mond, who sought 'an injunction to restrain them from printing, publishing or exhibiting any poster or advertisement alleging that he was a traitor or from publishing any similar libel affecting him in his profession and office'. On 16 March, Beamish wrote to Clarke. In this letter, he detailed his plans to maintain the libel against Mond in court, accusing him (as the poster had done) of selling shares to the 'Huns' during the Great War. Beamish went on to say that he fully expected to lose the case if libel charges were brought, and that he wanted Dr Clarke to handle his affairs in his absence. He wrote:

This will no doubt lead to my arrest for criminal libel, but I am prepared to take the consequences. I have tried every avenue to expose the machinations of the International Jew financial gang who have been selling our dear old England – the head of which in my opinion is Mond – but without success owing to the press and leading politicians, including Lloyd George being controlled by this Jew gang.[38]

Proof that Beamish was far from alone in antipathy to Jews comes from one of the most powerful and influential men in Britain at this time, Alfred Milner (1834–1925).

Milner had held the post of governor of the Cape Colonies and high commissioner for southern Africa (5 May 1897–6 March 1901) before being made responsible for the Transvaal and the Orange River Colony, first as administrator (4 January 1901–23 June 1902) and then as first governor (23 June 1902–1 April 1905). Britain's annexation of South Africa in 1877 had already resulted in the Zulu War and then the First Boer War. Neither had resolved tensions, and Milner, regarded as a moderate Liberal, was sent out there by the colonial secretary, Joseph Chamberlain. As the representative of British empirical might, Milner pitted himself against the Transvaal Boers. He regarded their growing influence in the region as a direct threat to British hopes of establishing control of the whole of Africa, from Cape to Cairo. Boer wealth and power had greatly increased with the recent discovery of gold in the Transvaal. This had attracted thousands of European immigrants to the territory – many of them British. The Boers responded to this influx by instituting legislation denying rights to these 'Uitlanders', thus giving Milner the pretext he needed to precipitate the Second Boer War (11 October 1899–31 May 1902).

Despite arousing much controversy and criticism back in Britain, Milner retained his post in South Africa until forced by ill health to quit in 1905. After returning to England, he remained politically active while pursuing business interests. Now Viscount Milner, he became chairman of Rio Tinto Zinc and, in 1906, a director of the Joint Stock Bank (a precursor of Midland Bank). From December 1916 until November 1918 he served as a highly influential member of Lloyd George's five-strong war cabinet. In January 1917 he led a British delegation to Russia in support of the tsar (who was toppled a few weeks later). That same year he was also a key author of the Balfour Declaration, which stated that the British government favoured the founding of a Jewish homeland in Palestine.[39, 40] This wasn't out of love or even sympathy for Jews, as is clearly illustrated in the letter he sent to his fellow war cabinet colleagues in January 1919. Urging British intervention in Russia to counter the threat to European freedom and civilisation presented by Bolshevism, Milner wrote:

We must not lose sight of the fact that this movement is engineered and managed by astute Jews, many of them criminals, and nearly every commissar in Russia is a Jew, and I have noticed, since I came to this country, that meetings of protest against intervention are largely composed of alien Jews, and that in constituencies where there is a large Jewish vote, it has invariably gone to the extreme Socialist candidate ... For the sake of humanity it is imperative that something be done to put a speedy end to this criminal, bloodthirsty and horrible combination misnamed 'Peasants' and Workmen's Republic'.[41]

Note that this letter was written in the very year that Beamish faced Mond in court and founded The Britons. Note also that Beamish and Milner had very similar South African experiences during the first five years of the twentieth century. That Milner held views remarkably close to those of Beamish is illustrated by Milner's 'Credo', a document found among his papers after his death and widely published. Milner had written:

> I am a Nationalist and not a cosmopolitan ... I am a British (indeed primarily an English) Nationalist. If I am also an Imperialist, it is because the destiny of the English race, owing to its insular position and long supremacy at sea, has been to strike roots in different parts of the world. I am an Imperialist and not a Little Englander because I am a British Race Patriot.[42]

Strangely, not only was Milner's paternal grandmother German. He himself was born in Germany, brought up there, and educated there.

The Mond trial, starting in March 1919, ran for two months and drew extensive press coverage. Further hearings would see the entire proceedings last until March 1920. The statement of claim of the plaintiff, Alfred Moritz Mond, delivered on 11 April 1919, was itemised as follows:

1. The Plaintiff is and was at all material times a member of His Majesty's Government and a member of the Privy Council.
2. On or about the 18th day of March 1919 the Defendants falsely and maliciously wrote and published of and concerning the Plaintiff and of and concerning him in relation to his position as aforesaid the words following, that is to say, 'Sir Alfred Mond is a traitor he allocated shares to Huns during the war.'
3. The said words were written on a large poster which was exhibited to the public view in the window of No. 4 Spring Gardens, Charing Cross, London.
4. The said words meant and were understood to mean that the Plaintiff was a traitor, that he had business relations with an enemy country during the war and that he was unfitted to hold office in His Majesty's Government or to be a member of the Privy Council.
5. By reason of the premises the Plaintiff has been injured in his credit and reputation and has been brought into public scandal, hatred and contempt and has suffered damage.

The Plaintiff claims:—

1. An Injunction to restrain the Defendants, their servants or agents from printing publishing or exhibiting any poster or advertisement alleging

the Plaintiff to be a traitor or any similar libel affecting the Plaintiff in his profession and office.
2. Damages.
3. Further or other relief.[43]

The defence of Henry Hamilton Beamish, signed by him and delivered on 10 May 1919, was trenchant and without a hint of regret or apology:

1. The defendant admits that he wrote the words set out in Paragraph 2 of the Statement of Claim. In so far as the said words consist of allegations of substance and fact they are true in substance and in fact, and in so far as they consist of expressions of opinion they are fair comment made in good faith and without malice upon the facts hereinafter more particularly referred to which are matters of public interest.
2. The said words were contained on a poster exhibited with a series of other posters and the Defendant craves leave to refer to the whole of the said series.
3. The Defendant repeats and adopts the separate Defence of his Co-Defendant Harry MacLeod Fraser as though same were set out seriatim in this Defence.

And as a further Plea this Defendant says:–

4. The Plaintiff (who is an international Jew Financier), by reason of his associations and his said actions, has committed a breach of faith which as a citizen and subject holding a public position he owes to the British Nation to the great scandal and the corruption of the purity of public life and patriotism, and by reason thereof it was for the public benefit that the allegations set forth in the Statement of Claim should be published, and these the said Henry Hamilton Beamish is ready to verify and justify.[44]

The defence (for both Fraser and Beamish) was conducted by Percival Frere Smith, the lawyer with whom Beamish had been associated in South Africa some seven years earlier. Now living back in Britain, Smith wrote an article for the *New Witness* in which he too accused Mond of dealing in shares with the enemy during wartime, Mond responding by suing and won, because what deals he had done had been sanctioned by the Board of Trade and so couldn't be deemed illegal.[45]

Hoping to benefit from this burst of public exposure, Beamish actually conducted a good part of his own defence and used his court appearance to hammer home his message of Jew-hatred. He was determined to convey his belief that Jews were of a separate race and that, as such, their loyalty could not be guaranteed. He told the court that 'A man can't be both a Jew and a German.' And, equally, 'A man can't be both English and Jew.' At this point in the proceedings, there was some applause at the back of the court. Clearly his supporters were present. Mond, however, won his case and was awarded £5,000 damages by Mr Justice Darling, plus costs.

As the trial drew to a close, the press reported that Beamish gave a final speech in which he stated that 'he had spent the most unhappy time of his life in that court. The cost of this trial on the other side was £1000 a day. He would have preferred the plaintiff to come into the court without the help of counsel, so that they could have had it out in the good old English way, like the prize fight the previous night' (this is a reference to a series of championship boxing matches in London marking the birth of British amateur boxing. It drew laughter in the courtroom). Beamish, clearly very bitter about the outcome, is reported to have then said that he 'came over here as a private at great sacrifice, and found the country absolutely putrid. The costs of this case would make him bankrupt.'[46] Beamish, who according to court files was in the early stages of founding The Britons, gave notice that 'he was about to take a sea voyage for the benefit of his health' and then quit Britain for southern Africa without paying the fine.[47]

Faced with an order to pay this large fine, plus his own legal costs, plus the very considerable legal costs incurred by Mond, Beamish lodged an appeal and, on 12 January 1920, was instructed to post £100 as security. He couldn't even afford this relatively small sum. On 23 February, his secretary applied on his behalf for an extension of time for him to pay the £100. She explained that she was representing him because he was in South Africa, 'to which country he had been ordered for the benefit of his health'. This application was very bluntly dismissed, and incurred further costs.[48] Mond then launched a counter-appeal. A subsequent and final hearing was held on 8 March. The press reported that 'Counsel for Mr Beamish now stated he did not feel justified in pressing his notice of motion, and would agree to it being dismissed with costs, and to Sir Alfred Mond's motion being allowed with costs.'[49]

The vast bill (the £5,000 fine, plus costs which ran into many thousands more) must have come as a shattering body-blow to Beamish. In anticipating a prison sentence, as outlined in his letter to Clarke, he had envisaged becoming a political martyr. However, these financial consequences were utterly beyond his means. Furthermore – even if he had been able to afford it – the payment of the fine alone to a Jew, and to Mond in particular, would have been against all his principles. Above all, though, in driving him from these shores, the verdict forced him to rely on others to set up and run The Britons.

The timing, in officially launching The Britons straight after the trial, appears to have been deliberate. As he stated in his letter to Clarke, Beamish saw Mond as the British head of the international Jewish conspiracy, so this trial was to have been the big showdown between Judaism and this self-appointed defender of 'dear old England', with The Britons intended as the phoenix rising gloriously from the ashes of that St George-and-the-dragon clash. In fact, the birth of The Britons was a tiny and almost unrecorded gathering. Beamish and just thirteen others attended that inaugural meeting in July 1919. Clarke, appointed vice-president, took charge of The Britons, while the president, Beamish, was packing his belongings, boarding his ship, and fleeing back to South Africa.

His South African friend, the journalist Arthur G. Barlow, reports encountering a rather frightened Beamish, who seemed convinced that Lord Melchett (the title later adopted by Mond) would pursue him for his £5,000. By his own account, Beamish had no money left at this time and needed to sell his newspaper. Barlow wrote:

> Passing rapidly through Bloemfontein in his haste to escape from Melchett's clutches, he asked me to sell his *Farmer's Advocate*, which I did to *The Friend*, and Beamish told me that his final hiding place 'until the coast is clear would be a cave in a forest in the Congo, somewhere near where the Pygmies live'.[19]

Based in fact in Southern Rhodesia, Beamish would retain the presidency of The Britons for the next three decades. However, apart from a few rare return visits, when he had attempted to inject more life into the society, he had to leave Clarke and a handful of other like-minded Jew-haters to handle the organisation's day-to-day London-based operation.

And what of Harry MacLeod Fraser? After becoming an early member of The Britons, he, like Beamish, went overseas in the wake of the Mond trial. Living in India, he wrote books, pamphlets and articles attacking Jewish influence.[50] His pamphlet *Truth* (1921) provoked outrage in the Indian press, which dismissed him as a racist. In it, he attacked Montagu (Edwin Samuel Montagu, a Jew who was secretary of state for India, 1917–22) and Lord Reading (Rufus Daniel Isaacs, also Jewish and viceroy of India, 1921–5). Montagu, he claimed, had created anarchy across the subcontinent 'to organise Asia's mute millions into a human avalanche to overwhelm Western civilisation and then Christianity'. Jews, Fraser maintained, 'were seeking to discredit and weaken the British connection under the guise of forwarding Indian Nationalism, merely in order to make the Jew control and dominion more complete.' He claimed that 'The British Raj has for a good many years, become less and less British and more a Jew Raj' and concluded that Indian Swaraj (self-government) 'merely means Jew Raj'.[51] After eventually returning to Britain, Fraser continued to write and campaign on the same anti-Jewish platform. However, these activities came to an abrupt end on 15 July 1924, when he was killed in a motoring accident.[50]

In 1920, its inaugural year, the Judaic Publishing Co. (as The Britons' publishing arm was initially known) produced a journal, leaflets, pamphlets and two books. The first of these books was *The Jews' Who's Who*, compiled jointly by Beamish and Fraser. Its stated aim was 'to make plain the garrotte like grip of Finance when dominated by the International Jew and used for exploiting Trusts and Combines against national interests'. Though the book caused an initial stir, it soon sank from view. Not so The Britons' second book, George Shanks's translation of *The Protocols of Zion*. Although they would later opt for another translation, this book was destined to bestow a lasting notoriety on the society.

Beamish, meanwhile, acquired property in Tanganyika.[4]

During October 1920, Beamish and a Mr Salamon, who was Jewish, had a public exchange of views on the Jewish question in the letters pages of *The Spectator*. They continued to correspond privately for a year or so afterwards. Here is Beamish being typically abrasive and condescending in a letter written to Salamon from Johannesburg on 22 July 1921:

Dear Sir, – I am sorry I have been unable to reply to your letter before, but I have been away in Central Africa, and was only able to send you one of my 'Britannia Rules the Waves' postcards in acknowledgement. You are right to surmise that I am the individual who made myself look 'ridiculous', as you so kindly call it, in the Mond Libel Action. Incidentally, and being a Jew, I know how hard it will be for you to understand, I deliberately and openly attacked Mond in order to expose the Jew plot to destroy civilisation and Christianity. In taking the action I did I knew, of course, that I must 'legally' lose the case, as, pending a 'White' revolution against the on-coming Jew-led Reds, I know that it was impossible, under our Jew-controlled laws and lawyers, to win a case against International Jewry and its all-powerful finances. My case was not with Mond – I had never seen this Asiatic before I saw him in court – but was an attempt, and I am glad to say a very successful one, to expose the gigantic International Jew Plot to destroy our (not your) Empire, and with it Christianity and Civilisation. My effort entirely crippled me financially, and as a result I am now forced to live in the wilds of Central Africa. I will, however, not dwell on this, as, being a Jew, it will be impossible for you to understand what self-sacrifice and love of country means. You seem very anxious to know whether I am a Christian, and in so far as I try to follow the ethics of Christ, particularly in regard to his precepts on 'Live and let live' and in 'doing unto others as I would be done by', I am. This is, of course, in entire variance to Jews' precepts, who don't believe in letting others live, except under that all-polluting domination. Your bible, the Talmud, clearly defines what your 'religion' is, namely, materialism in the grossest and meanest form. As I wrote you before, I am *not* an anti-Semite, and I not only say that a Jew has a perfect right to live and enjoy life, but that snakes and other vermin have the same right. What Englishmen and other White races complain of is that Jews pollute all the races they come in contact with, and that they should be forced to live in Palestine in the same way that snakes and other vermin should be forced to live in the jungle and not in people's houses. I am sending you some literature on the subject of your race (*not* religion, please), and you should really study and analyse the reasons for the rising storm against Jew domination of the White races. I quite admit that Englishmen are easily bluffed, and though long suffering you must admit that the ones who see the danger ahead have a perfect right to prevent their Empire – the last one remaining – from being destroyed by the alien Jew.

I trust you will continue this correspondence as you letters interest me.

Yours faithfully,
(signed) H. H. Beamish[52]

Beamish spent the last few weeks of 1922 in America. The passenger manifest of the SS *Tartar Prince* records that he boarded at Port Elizabeth, South Africa, on 29 September and disembarked at Boston, Massachusetts, on 7 November. He was listed as an English miner, aged forty-nine, resident in Sonoia, Rhodesia, and able to read English and Zulu. His nearest relative or friend was given as Mr F. Gibaud of Rosebery Avenue, Port Elizabeth.[53]

Beamish stayed in America for only a few weeks. In late December he boarded the SS *Dominion Miller* in Newport News, Virginia, and sailed for London, where he arrived on 2 January 1923 (in this manifest he is listed as the sole disembarking passenger, travelling first class, a miner, last resident in South Africa, whose UK address is given as the Royal Societies Club, St James Street, London).[54]

Just over two weeks later, Beamish was in Germany. On 20 January 1923, *The Times* reported that 'Henry Beamish, said to be an English miner, addressed a meeting of the Bavarian Fascisti at Munich.' Having declared himself 'greatly impressed with the Organisation', he said he was 'returning to England with the idea of starting a similar movement'. This event, which had taken place on 18 January at the Krone Circus, had been organised by the NSDAP (the Nazi Party, founded in 1920). The speech delivered by Beamish had been in English, with a German translation by Dietrich Eckart. The very fact that a man of Eckart's stature served as his translator shows the level of respect that Beamish already commanded among his fellow Jew-hating racial nationalists in Germany. Eckart, who was to die of a heart attack less than a year later, came to be remembered as the 'spiritual father of National Socialism'. The second volume of Hitler's *Mein Kampf* is dedicated to him. Here is a brief extract from Beamish's speech, said to have been enthusiastically received:

> I also was in the war as a private in the infantry, but it did not take me long to realise that instead of the Christian nations fighting each other, we ought all to turn our guns against the Jew, who brings about all these wars … The magnificent way in which you Bavarians have tackled this Jew problem has filled me with courage, and I hope it may be possible for all the Aryan races to join forces against the common enemy to our civilisation and Christianity.[2]

There were rumours – but no proof – that Beamish went away from this German visit with money to assist his plan of 'starting a similar movement'. That seems unlikely. The new Nazi Party wasn't yet wealthy itself, and very little new cash went into The Britons' coffers at this time. What does seem more than possible – for a man 'crippled financially' by the Mond case – is that, throughout the 1920s and 1930s, he received sufficient German money to fund his globe-trotting as an unparalleled relentless apostle of Nazi-esque Jew-hatred. Thus, for example, from the early 1920s onwards, his ocean voyages were made by first-class ticket.

During January or February, Beamish was also in Rome, where he met with Mussolini. On 7 March he wrote to Henry Ford's Michigan-based *Dearborn Independent* newspaper and enclosed a copy of an earlier letter, written in Italy, which talked about this meeting. In his reply of 31 March 1923 (sent to Beamish c/o the Royal Societies Club in St James Street, the address he used for all correspondence), William John Cameron, the paper's assistant editor, refers to the encounter:

> I see from your letter, and the press, that you have had the privilege of meeting Mussolini in Rome: which I hold to be a great privilege. Inasmuch as it will give you an insight into the mind of one of the most unusual figures of our

time. I was wondering if it would be within your convenience to give us an article sketching the characters of these men and your impressions of them.

During 1922, Cameron had been instrumental in the serialisation in the *Dearborn Independent* of *The International Jew*, their notorious series of articles based on *The Protocols*.[55]

On 1 March 1923, the Vienna newspaper *Wiener Morgenzeitung* published what the *Hidden Hand*, the magazine of The Britons, called 'a gross libel against our president'. Headed 'The English Crown Witness of Adolph Hitler', it read:

> From Munich it is announced: the Social Democratic *Munich Post* has procured in England information about the English friend of Adolph Hitler, Mr Henry Beamish, which is to the effect that Beamish, who appeared on January 18th with Hitler in the Krone Circus in Munich and made an anti-semitic speech in English, is known in London as the leader of a gang of extortioners, and was some years ago condemned before a sworn jury to a punishment of several years in prison. At this meeting [Munich], Beamish stated that he had called the Cabinet Minister Mond a traitor, and in consequence had been in exile for three years in Central Africa. For this remark he was heartily applauded at the meeting, and was introduced as showing the existence of international solidarity on the part of anti-semites. From Nationalist circles it is stated that Hitler has given Beamish a large sum of money for the purpose of founding a Nationalist Party in England.

The claim by this German newspaper that Beamish had been 'the leader of a gang of extortioners' may in fact have been a garbled reference to his anti-German role within the ranks of the Consumers' Alliance in Johannesburg during 1915, when that organisation did indeed appear to have been extorting money from German citizens.

Having returned to Britain after an absence of more than three years, on 5 March 1923 Beamish addressed a 'large and enthusiastic' London meeting of The Britons at the Plane Tree Restaurant, Great Russell Street. In his address, entitled 'Future of the Society', he outlined plans to reorganise The Britons and appointed J. D. Dell as office superintendent, tasked primarily with fund-raising via guarantees of regular donations from members, the aim being to use this income to produce more literature.[56]

Beamish was in Paris in early April. While there, he visited the offices of the right-wing paper *L'Action Française* to place what he termed 'an advertisement', paying 480 francs for its publication. The Britons already worked closely with the fiercely anti-Jewish French journal *La Vieille France*, in which this 'advertisement' had already appeared. It read:

> A Warning from our English friends. Are you aware that the present manipulation of the foreign exchange is entirely the work of the Jews? The Jews wish to Bolshevise France as they have done Russia. The Jews in England are

to be removed. Frenchmen, get rid of your Jews! The Jews are an Asiatic race and do not belong to Europe. All the White People must combine against this world menace or the Jews will destroy us.

The statement was signed 'The Britons'. A letter dated 9 April reached Beamish back in London two days later. It informed him that *L'Action Française* refused to publish such a text. An angry correspondence ensued which ended with the French paper refunding the 480 francs. Enraged, Beamish promptly donated this to *La Vieille France*.[57]

The founding editor of *La Vieille France* was Urbain Gohier (17 December 1862–29 June 1951), a French lawyer, journalist and notorious Jew-hater who had actually started out as a socialist opponent of militarism but had become increasingly anti-Jewish. Having worked on various journals, he had founded *La Vieille France* (*The Old France*) in 1916, and would remain its editor and publisher until its demise in 1924. Throughout its existence, this Paris-based weekly was rabidly anti-Jewish. In 1920, *La Vieille France* published the first French edition of *The Protocols*, entitled *Procès-verbaux de réunions secrètes des Sages d'Israël*.[58] Beamish probably gave Gohier the 480 francs because he knew the journal was struggling, and because the money would have been well spent if it had kept this useful French counterpart of The Britons going. It proved to be of little assistance. Three months later, in the summer of 1923, Gohier announced that, after seven years as a weekly, *La Vieille France* had ceased publication, having 'completely exhausted its financial resources'. Reprinting the announcement, the July–August issue of the *Hidden Hand* described it as 'the only publication to stand up openly against the total conquest of France by the Jewish hordes'. The piece went on to mention Jean Drault as Gohier's co-worker and to say that there had been a total of 344 editions. Shortly afterwards, in a brief reversal of fortunes, Gohier resumed publication. However, due to 'lack of support', it ceased publication permanently in the summer of 1924, after issue 373. This sorry progress was fully reported in successive Britons' journals. In January 1925, Gohier would become a regular contributor of literate but obsessively anti-Jewish articles to The Britons journal, the *British Guardian*, though not for long. A year later, it too would cease publication due to lack of funds.

All this was yet to come. Back in London in the spring of 1923, The Britons briefly reinvigorated by the presence of Beamish – became more active publicly. On 11 May 1923 they met in the council chamber at Hammersmith Town Hall. The 152-strong gathering,[35] chaired by Dr J. H. Clarke, heard a lengthy speech from Beamish on 'The Alien Menace', at the end of which he read out the following 'drastic resolution':

> In view of the fact that there is a very serious shortage of houses for our people, which is largely due to the influx of Jews into these already crowded islands; that Great Britain still has over a million unemployed, which is largely due to the same cause; and believing that unless drastic steps are taken to prevent the influx of a race of people diametrically opposed to Christianity,

> British morals and customs, that serious international trouble will result; this meeting of the citizens of the Borough of Hammersmith, here and now demand from his Majesty's Government that they take drastic steps: (1) To stop the further invasion of our country by these aliens; (2) To deport those already here; (3) That the Secretary of 'The Britons' be authorised to send copies of this resolution to the Prime Minister, the Secretary of State for Home Affairs, all Cabinet Ministers, the Governors of the Dominions, the leading government bodies throughout the Empire, all patriotic societies, the Mayor of Hammersmith, and the Mayors throughout the United Kingdom.

After Beamish had fielded questions from this entirely sympathetic gathering, the resolution was 'put and carried by acclamation'.[59]

The return of Beamish, four years after the Mond case, didn't go unnoticed in Jewish circles. The account of his speech at the Hammersmith Town Hall meeting, as subsequently published in the *Hidden Hand*, was reprinted verbatim in the *Jewish Chronicle* under the heading 'The Alien Menace' and subtitled 'Mr. Beamish's Anti-Semitic Outburst'.[60]

Although he had undoubtedly been driven by his bigotry, Beamish hadn't been entirely wrong in accusing Mond of selling bonds to German nationals during the war. Mond was a wheeler-dealer who knew how to make money for himself and, despite his denials, certainly profited from the war. It seems likely that Mond's anger and indignation was not triggered by the slur itself but by Beamish's anti-Jewish stance.

Indeed, two years later Mond's brother-in-law, the artist Sigismund Goetze, would bring a similar case against Harold Sherwood Spencer. Lord Alfred Douglas had resigned his editorship of *Plain English* in October 1921 after a furious row with Spencer, his assistant editor. Douglas had had enough of Spencer's repeated publication of fictions as factual. Spencer took over the editorship of the journal and, the following month, published a vicious attack on Goetze, who sued him for libel and won. Spencer received a six-month prison sentence. Shortly after being released he was arrested and charged with unspecified 'disgusting behaviour', for which he received a fine of 40 shillings.[24] By then, *Plain English* had ceased publication.

Spencer had always survived by depending on the wealth of others. In his early twenties, he had been briefly married to a wealthy countess twice his age. They had moved to Paris and lived there in style.[61] On 10 November 1917 he had married Ella Shearer Beattie.[62] For the next ten years the pair lived at 52 Eaton Square, the home of her wealthy parents. In May 1927 they began divorce proceedings, each accusing the other of infidelity.[63] That same year Spencer sailed from London to New York aboard the *American Farmer*. The manifest lists him as a 37-year-old American, whose profession was given as 'none'.[64]

In 1925 there was another attempt to prove that Mond was profiting through trickery. And the case may not be unconnected because the main person behind the accusations was the newly elected MP for Gateshead, John Beckett, who had been acquainted with Beamish at the tail-end of the Great War.

Beckett and two other new MPs, Neil Maclean and Hugh Dalton, discovered that Mond owned a lucrative company – Brunner, Mond – that was the only business in Britain efficiently extracting nitrogen from air for use in explosives and fertiliser. This was done by a highly secret method which the Germans had developed during the Great War. At the end of the war, the British government had sent a team of three army officers to Cologne, where they had spent several months discovering precisely how this process was carried out. They then returned to Britain and wrote a report on their findings. This report was never published. Instead, Mond, then a government minister, bought a publicly owned fertiliser factory in Billingham-on-Tees. This factory, which had cost the country £1,100,000 to establish and run, was sold to Mond for just £450,000. Here Mond began using the German extraction method. It further transpired that the senior officer of the team sent to Germany had been made a director of Brunner, Mond, the company running the factory. Furthermore, the other two officers who had gone with him were now both employed by the company. Try as they might, however, Beckett and co. were unable to prove that the wily and well-connected Mond was behind this corrupt profiteering. Tricked out of raising the issue in Parliament, Beckett found no editor willing to carry the story. Eventually, he managed to place it in the leftwing *Labour Weekly*. Ahead of publication, he sent a copy of the piece to Mond to see how the rascal would react. Mond's friendly reply simply thanked Beckett for his letter, adding that he had read the contents with the greatest interest![27] That there was some truth in the slur against him might well explain why Mond doesn't appear to have pursued Beamish for the unpaid £5,000, not even following the latter's return to England in 1923.

Beamish was steadily cultivating useful friendships within the ranks of German Nazism. It was through two of these, the Jew-hating publisher and journalist Theodor Fritsch and the leading Nazi theoretician Alfred Rosenberg, that he had an influential article published in the prominent Nazi newspaper *Völkischer Beobachter* (*National Observer*). In this featured piece, which appeared on 26 June 1926, he outlined his theory that there were just three ways to deal with Jews – extermination, assimilation or isolation. Ruling out extermination on the grounds that all people have a right to exist and assimilation on the grounds that it had been resisted for centuries, he argued for isolation by sending every Jew to Madagascar and keeping them all there.[65]

On 28 August 1926, Beamish boarded the SS *Ceramic* in Liverpool and sailed for Cape Town. His UK address was still given as the Royal Societies Club in St James Street, London, his occupation given as mining.[66] He was visiting the family home in Bloemfontein of his new wife, Frances Winifred Lingard Green. The pair had been married in Belgium at the British Consulate office in Brussels on 28 July. Eighteen years his junior, she was the daughter of Alfred Lingard Green, a retired British army Lieutenant-Colonel.[1] This marriage would be childless and appears not to have lasted. I can find no record of them living together and, by 1940, he was living alone as a mine-owner in Southern Rhodesia.

Beamish's international reputation as a Jew-hater was now spreading. In 1926 the New York-based Anti-Bolshevist Publishing Company (the publishing arm of the Universal Anti-Bolshevist League) published *The Secret World Government or The Hidden Hand*, by Major General Count Cherep-Spiridovich, a White Russian who had fled to America following the overthrow of the tsar in 1917. In this book 'the famous patriot H. H. Beamish' is quoted thus: 'I am prepared to prove that Bolshevism (which is merely a modern word for Judaism), the vicious manipulation of foreign exchanges, and the general 'world unrest' prevailing today, may be summed up in two words, namely, "Jew Finance".'[67]

Beamish was to find a kindred spirit in Arnold Leese, a retired veterinary surgeon, who had been one of Britain's first two elected fascists. Leese and a fellow fascist, Harry Simpson, had served as councillors in Stamford for the British Fascists (see Chapter 6 for a detailed account of Leese's life and career). Their friendship began when Beamish visited Leese in Stamford in the mid-1920s after he had begun buying Britons publications, starting with *The Protocols*.

Having moved to London in 1928, Leese had co-founded the Imperial Fascist League (IFL). By 1932, when the group was actively and increasingly Jew-hating, he had taken over the leadership totally. Beamish was an enthusiastic member, and throughout 1931 he toured southern Britain speaking at a series of public meetings of the IFL, usually sharing the platform with Leese.

On Thursday 21 May he and Leese addressed a meeting held in the Kentish Rooms in Tunbridge Wells,[68] and on Thursday 11 June the pair spoke at an IFL gathering in Sedlescombe Village Hall, Rye, East Sussex, at which they 'asserted that Britain was being fooled by politicians and Jews, and advocated a return to statesmanship by the setting up of a Fascist regime'.[69] On Tuesday 14 July Beamish and Dr White jointly addressed an IFL meeting held in Wadhurst Institute in Sussex.[70] On Wednesday 25 November, in Tunbridge Wells Town Hall, Beamish and Leese were the two ILF speakers debating the resolution 'That the League of Nations is not worthy of trust' with two speakers from the League of Nations Union.[71] The ILF pair easily won this debate.[72] And Beamish seems to have enjoyed this speaking tour. A couple of the reports mention him actually making his audience laugh.

On 28 October 1931, Beamish was the guest speaker at the weekly Wednesday IFL meeting at the society's headquarters, where his topic was 'The Real Causes of Wars'. Just over a week later, on 6 November 1931, the IFL held a public meeting at the Public Hall, Prince of Wales Road Baths, London, NW5. This gathering, under the title 'The Nation in Pawn!' was described by the IFL as a 'Patriotic Demonstration'. The event was chaired by Brigadier General Blakeney and the speakers were Arnold S. Leese, H. H. Beamish and W. W. Drinkwater, supported by N. A. Thompson and Lieutenant H. D. Caslon.[73]

Early in 1932, Oswald Mosley, still leading the remnants his New Party (all but destroyed by disastrous results in the general election of 27 October 1931), set about founding the British Union of Fascists. In doing so, he attempted to court like-minded groups, hoping they would join him. To this end, his representatives approached both the IFL and the British Fascists. Thus, on 27 April 1932, Mosley chaired a meeting of NUPA, the New Party's youth wing. This, its most violent section, founded only the previous September, was the New Party's only remaining intact section. Both Beamish and Leese addressed the gathering. The joint title they allocated to their two speeches was 'The Blindness of British Politics under the Jew Money-Power'.[74]

Negotiations broke down soon after this meeting, with Mosley deciding that association with the virulent Jew-hatred of Beamish, Leese and their few dozen compatriots was too risky. Their views might cost the BUF its hoped-for mass appeal and 'respectable' support. Indeed, the BUF at this time actually set about actively denying that it was anti-Jewish. Leese, disgusted with Mosley's readiness to compromise, never forgave him, thereafter taking every opportunity to deride him as a phoney Jew-hater and a 'kosher fascist'. There would be many violent clashes between supporters of the ILF and the BUF.

Beamish, meanwhile, wasted no time leaving Britain. He sailed, first class, from London on board the SS *Umkuzi* on 18 June 1932, bound for Natal. In the manifest he was listed as a sixty-year-old farmer whose permanent residence was South-East Africa.[75]

In South Africa in July 1934, three leading members of the South African Greyshirts were put on trial for slandering Rabbi A. Levy of the Western Road Synagogue in Port Elizabeth. The accused, who conducted their own defence, were Johannes von Moltke, leader of the South African Gentile Socialists and of the Southwest African Greyshirts; Harry Victor Inch, Eastern Cape leader of the Greyshirts; and David Olivier, editor of *Die Rapport*, the journal of the South African National Socialist Movement.

At a Nazi meeting held in March 1934 in the market square of the small town of Aberdeen, Inch had read out sections of a document that he claimed was signed by Rabbi Levy and had been stolen from his synagogue. The content of this document echoed sections of *The Protocols* and, claimed Inch, proved the existence of a new and local Jewish threat.

Beamish attended the trial as a witness for the defence, arrogantly attempting to use the courtroom as a platform for himself and his own views on Jews. Beamish, who would later be described by the judge, Sir Thomas Graham, as 'the witness in chief', had opened by declaring that he was 'a mining engineer residing in Rhodesia, who had been in South Africa for over thirty years'. He informed the court that he had studied the Jewish question for thirty years, that he knew Hitler and other Nazi leaders personally, and that the German Nazis had consulted him on the Jewish problem because of his friendship with Theodor Frisch, the notorious Leipzig publisher of anti-Semitic books. Beamish went on to assert that practically all the governments of the world were controlled by Jews, while the Soviet government was 90 per cent Jewish. He further offered to prove to the court that *The Protocols* were true in every aspect. Moltke then read out sections of *The Protocols*, with Beamish nodding in agreement throughout. Beamish then claimed that every plan outlined in *The Protocols* had come true. He backed up his assertions by declaring that 'practically all the landowners in England had been forced out of existence and forced to marry wealthy Jewesses'. He further added that 'All political parties in the world are controlled by Jews' and that an integral part of the Jewish plot was the 'demoralisation of the young Christians of the world by Jewish films, jazz music and the sculpture of Jacob Epstein. The Jews', he continued, 'are a menace. They have secured a hold on English aristocracy, parliament and other English institutions.' He then boasted: 'I taught Henry Ford the meaning of the Jewish menace and I followed closely his utterances on the Jewish question', before adding that 'international financiers are Jews and have a stranglehold on the entire world. Rothschild controls gold, the Guggenheimers control copper, and Oppenheimers control all diamonds. That is why the Hitler movement was founded.'

Henry Ford, as we shall see, was an ardent advocate of *The Protocols*, which is the only book mentioned in Hitler's *Mein Kampf*. While Beamish certainly wrote to both Hitler and Ford – and may well have met them – his repeated claims that he deeply and directly influenced and even educated both men seem more than far-fetched. However, they serve to indicate that he saw, in these two powerful individuals, not only justification for his own extremism but some real hope for a world in which he would be deemed to have been right all along in his Jew-hatred.

It was a distant hope. Even in racially segregated South Africa, no such world was yet evident. In a lengthy judgement on 24 August, Judge Graham found in favour of Levi, declared *The Protocols* to be a known and long-proven forgery, and fined Inch £1,000, Moltze £750 and Olivier £25, with costs in each case. Inch was subsequently sentenced to several years in prison after being criminally indicted and found guilty of compiling a forged document, making false statements in affidavits, and committing perjury.[76]

Beamish had blithely believed that his very presence had impressed both judge and court and thereby greatly assisted the three defendants. He could not have been more wrong. In fact, his transparent vanity, posturing self-importance and extremism had the opposite effect entirely. In the course of this judgement, Graham expressed his opinion of Beamish as follows:

> It is difficult to accept evidence of this character seriously. The witness Beamish impressed me as a man profoundly obsessed with the views he enunciated. Intolerant in his beliefs, with an exaggerated idea of his own importance, he regards himself as a modern crusader whose mission it is to reveal to the world the existence of a world plot organised by the Jews since the beginning of their history to overthrow Christianity and to destroy civilisation. He has greedily swallowed every anti-Jewish publication that he has discovered and accepted as facts every anti-Jewish statement they contained, and upon this question he is a fanatic; he has been unable to produce a vestige of relevant evidence in support of his charges.[77]

What Beamish did succeed in doing was repeatedly to demonstrate to the court that he was Hitler's man. Asked if he studied the Jewish question before or after Hitler came to power, he replied: 'I have studied it for well over thirty years, probably nearer forty.' Asked if he knew Hitler personally, he said: 'I do.' Later in his evidence he stated: 'I taught Hitler.' He was then asked if the Nazi leaders had ever consulted him on the Jewish question, to which he replied: 'Yes, very often.'

Beamish went on to tell the court that he had visited Germany, France, England, Italy, America, Romania, Czechoslovakia, Yugoslavia, Austria, Hungary and most of the British Empire and China and India, adding that he had been associated with movements of a similar character to the Nazi movement in France, Austria, Hungary, Romania, Palestine, Belgium, Switzerland, Italy, Spain, Portugal, China, Manchuria, America, Canada, Australia, New Zealand and more.[78]

Asked then if he occupied any prominent position with regard to racial movements in Great Britain, he replied: 'I belong to most of the Fascist movements in Great Britain. I'm also President of the League of Gentiles and President of the Bund Völkischer Europäer.'[74] The nominally pan-European Bund was a Nazi-affiliated Jew-hating organisation based in Germany, while the league was a South African 'secret society' formed in Johannesburg in 1925 expressly 'to boycott Jewish traders and professional men' across the Rand and 'to cast out socially, industrially and economically the Jewish element which is too prominent today'. The similarity between the aims of the league and the founding aims of The Britons six years earlier (see start of Chapter 3) certainly suggests the influence of Beamish. By the end of 1925, the league was extravagantly claiming to have a membership of 10,000.[79]

It is interesting to note that Beamish singularly failed to mention his presidency of The Britons. Why? The fact is that, as the 1930s progressed, he lost much of his enthusiasm for the increasingly moribund society. While retaining his post as their president, and without actually dissociating himself from them, he largely lost interest in their work and got more involved with actively anti-Jewish groups, notably the Imperial Fascist League.

Beamish spent time in America during the second half of 1935. However, this wasn't one of his usual publicity-seeking trips. On the contrary, it was a secretive visit and – as such – offers us a first clear indication that he was now actively working as a representative of the German government as a Nazi agent.

One piece of evidence for this visit was provided by William Kullgren, an Englishman born in Plymouth, Devon, in 1885, who lived in Atascadero, California. He was a professional astrologer and far-right activist. In this latter capacity, he was a former member of the Silver Shirts who had become one of the most prolific distributors of anti-Jewish and related literature on the American west coast, including publications by The Britons and books by Arnold Leese. In 1933 he founded a nationalist magazine, the *Beacon Light Herald*, later shortened to the *Beacon Light*, which he continued to publish until 1960. In 1942 it was deemed so seditious that it was banned from the mail.[80] There is an interview with Kullgren in which he talks about his far-right associates and mentions, in passing, that in 1935 he had had Beamish as a guest in his California home.[81]

Further evidence came from Neil Howard Ness, an American engineer who had been a trusted member of the German-American Bund in Los Angeles and had worked closely with its leadership. In early October 1939, Ness testified in Washington before the Dies Committee. This committee, active between 1938 and

1944 under the chairmanship of Martin Dies, was established by the House Committee on Un-American Activities to investigate extremist groups in America. Ness was questioned by Dies Committee member Mr Rhea Whitley and spoke of having worked closely with Hermann Max Schwinn, who led the Los Angeles branch of the German-American Bund. Schwinn had been born in Hamburg, Germany, on 3 August 1905 and had arrived in America in 1924. He lived for a few years in Ohio, became a naturalised American citizen, and then moved to Los Angeles, where he had got involved with the Friends of New Germany (which later became the German-American Bund). In the mid-1930s he had been appointed western director of the German-American Bund. As a consequence of his pro-German activities, Schwinn's citizenship was revoked in 1940. In 1944, while in custody as an enemy alien, he became one of the defendants in the abortive Great Sedition Trial, which eventually failed in its attempt to criminalise dozens of American anti-Jewish activists.[82] (Incidentally, William Kullgren was similarly arrested and charged, in 1943, but was never tried.)

On 6 October, Whitley asked Ness if, during the latter part of 1935, he had 'had occasion to meet or become acquainted with an individual called Captain Beamish'. Ness replied: 'I recall that Captain Beamish came from South Africa, and was the representative of the German Government in the World News Service.' When Whitley then asked: 'That is what is known as a German organisation known as 'World Service'?', Ness replied: 'That is right.' The questioning then continued as follows:

Whitley: Did Captain Beamish associate or work with Hermann Schwinn and the Bund officials while he was in Los Angeles?
Ness: Yes; he made his headquarters in the German House.
W: Did he wear any insignia of any kind to identify himself with any of the organisations of the German Government?
N: 'Yes; he wore on his left arm a band ... That was a stripe which had an insignia of the German Nazi Party.
W: The Swastika?
N: Yes.
W: Did he attend the meetings or address the meetings of the Bund while he was in Los Angeles?
N: Yes; he attended all the meetings while he was there, and he was also a speaker on one occasion.[83]

So, here was Beamish visiting Schwinn's Bund in Los Angeles. They were based at the Deutsches Haus – what Ness called the 'German House' – at 634 West 15th Street. Beamish was wearing a Nazi armband and claiming to be a representative of the German propaganda machine that was World Service.

It doesn't end there. Talking about Bund activities, Ness told the Dies Committee: 'We frequently discussed plans for blowing up water works, dock and munitions plants. We had a hundred men on whom we could depend to paralyse the Pacific

Coast.' These plans, he said, were discussed at Bund meetings. There's an obvious inference here that Beamish was not simply a passive agent but was actually associating with men prepared – indeed preparing – to fight as mercenaries on behalf of Germany, and this four years before the outbreak of war. Ness clearly saw Beamish as party to this. He went on to name others, including prominent Silver Shirts members Kenneth Alexander and Roy Zachary and the leaders of the American Nationalist Party, as people who had also addressed Bund meetings and worked closely with them. However, first and foremost, he had singled out Beamish.

According to Ness, Schwinn 'outlined a platform for the Bund in Los Angeles based directly upon the policies of Hitler'. He informed the Dies Committee that 'Schwinn told me we would commence with an attack upon the Jews and after we had beaten down the Jews go for the Catholics.' Ness added that the German consulate in Los Angeles had, on several occasions, supplied Schwinn with funds for the Bund. Schwinn, he continued, had cautioned him that they would have to be very careful and guard against any congressional committee discovering that the counsellor of the German consulate gave cash to them.

Ness was very clear on the fact that this German funding related directly to espionage and Nazi propaganda. He told the committee that German espionage agents frequently came ashore in Los Angeles from German ships visiting the port. On one occasion, he said, one of these spies photographed the coast artillery proving grounds 20 miles south of Long Beach, adding that he and Schwinn were with the agent at the time. Ness also said that, in the course of a speech to a meeting of the Los Angeles Bund, the Silver Shirts' leader, William Dudley Pelley, had said that he was proud of being called America's Adolf Hitler, 'because that is what I consider myself'.

Ness additionally asserted that all Bund members, most of whom were naturalised Americans, took an oath of allegiance to Hitler and the National Socialist Party and that the Bund was directed by the Nazi headquarters in Berlin to fight the Roosevelt administration and American Jewry. To this end, a steady stream of propaganda came from Germany to be disseminated to Americans – either by being handed out directly at meetings or by being passed on to other Bund groups and allied organisations. Content would then be reproduced in their journals and other literature. One of the key sources of German propaganda of the kind described here by Ness was World Service, the very organisation which he had said Beamish represented.

Ness apparently startled the committee when he casually mentioned that, until the summer of 1936, Schwinn and other Bund leaders had exchanged documents with the captain of every German ship that put into Los Angeles harbour. He said the captains brought instructions for the Bund directly from Germany and in turn received confidential advice and information from the Bund leaders to take back to Germany.[83]

Interviewed by the journalist John J. Spivak around the end of 1936, Schwinn admitted to little but was very thrown by the detailed research that Spivak had compiled. It seems clear that Schwinn and his associates were indeed meeting regularly with the captains of visiting German ships, taking briefcases with them.

At these meetings they would hand over details of American armaments, bases, etc., all gathered during spying missions by Bund members. Their now empty briefcases would then be filled with instructions and propaganda, including numerous copies of *World Service*, the journal of the organisation of that name, to be distributed to American Nazi sympathisers and to be used as source material for articles in their publications and talks by their members.[84]

A report on the opening sessions of the Great Sedition Trial appeared in the *Salt Lake City Tribune* on 6 September 1944. Schwinn and several of his Bund associates, including 'youthful Nazi leader Hans Diebel', were among the twenty-six defendants. Diebel, who had been paid by the Bund to buy and distribute the work of leading American supporters of Nazism and to disseminate other pro-Nazi literature, had 'maintained a world-wide correspondence with other Nazi leaders'. Some of these letters were produced in court. One was from Beamish, in which he stated: 'Your branch of the German-American bund and the Deutsches-Haus will go down to fame as a rallying point in California of all decent people who do not want to be turned into Jew-soviet slaves.'

Among further documentary evidence against the Bund members was *The Golden Book of the Los Angeles Bund*. This was the record book of their activities. Its final page carried an inscription hand-written and signed by Beamish which read: 'It is better to live for your country than to die for the Jews.'

By November 1935, Beamish was in New York. Emory Carney Burke, a lifelong far-right activist, claims to have met him there at that time and identified him as the man 'who headed England's Fascist League'.[85] Burke, then aged twenty-one, spent just six months in New York and was very specific about this meeting. While there, he had worked closely with Earnest Elmhurst, a key organiser for both the German-American Bund and the American National Socialists. Part of Burke's role was to help publish the *American Bulletin* and to serve on the staff of *The Storm*, both American Nazi journals that carried the sort of propaganda material supplied by the Germans via World Service.

In 1936, Beamish returned to England. Here he joined the Nordic League, a hard-line and covert pro-Nazi Jew-hating body founded with direct German assistance in 1935 and run by a fourteen-man leadership council chaired by the Unionist MP Archibald Maule Ramsay. It was a sinister outfit which met secretly, used passwords for entry to meetings and numbers instead of names for its officers, and fostered very close relationships with other European Nazis, particularly in Germany. In the late 1930s, as war became inevitable, the organisation (briefly before being disbanded) emerged publicly in opposition to the conflict.

Beamish's involvement with both the Imperial Fascist League (ILF) and the Nordic League is telling in itself. Key members of these two British leagues are known to have worked directly with and for German propagandists, just as Bund members were doing in America. We know that Beamish had just returned from America, where he had apparently been representing both the German World Service and the British ILF as a guest of the Bund in Los Angeles and then in New York. Clearly he was acting as a transatlantic go-between for pro-Nazi Jew-hatred.

And it was the Bund which would openly host his subsequent American visits. His relationship with World Service is crucial here. It existed specifically to provide German anti-Jewish stories and propaganda to sympathetic news outlets worldwide. In Britain, the IFL leader, Arnold Leese, worked particularly closely with World Service, supplying them directly with anti-Jewish pieces and reproducing pieces supplied by them in his publications, exactly as the Bund was doing in the USA. Beamish was the link man for this entire network.

Now, his efforts spread further. In September 1936 he visited Tokyo, where he was quoted as saying that, 'Even in Japan, I find something Jewish. Doesn't the Japanese system of foreign trade smell of the Jews?'[86] And he was in Canada in October 1936, when he was a guest anti-Jewish speaker at a rally held in the Winnipeg Auditorium.[87] This event was organised by the Canadian Nationalist Party (CNP), which had been founded in September 1933 by an Englishman, William Whittaker, who was a former Ku Klux Klan leader and a notorious Jew-hater. CNP members adopted a uniform of brown shirts and armbands bearing the swastika emblem. Unsurprisingly this group had faced strong legal and political opposition, especially from the Canadian Jewish community, and was consequently not in great shape. The arrival of Beamish – whose Jew-hating speech urged those in the CNP to act on his words – served greatly to reinvigorate the group. As a seasoned campaigner, Beamish impressed his audience by remaining unruffled when heckled by a small group of around twenty-five Jewish protesters. As fights broke out, he continued to speak.[88]

The December 1936 issue of *Free Press*, the London-based and pro-Nazi Militant Christian Patriot journal, reported Beamish's return to England after a five-year absence. It was a brief stop-off en route to Germany, where he embarked on a major lecture tour starting in mid-December 1936 and continuing into January 1937. He was reported to have been there as the honoured guest of Foreign Minister Ribbentrop. Touring nationwide, wearing his swastika armband, Beamish addressed his audiences on the subject of 'Who Wants War?' His speech at Berlin University on 15 December was reported as follows in Berlin's leading Nazi daily newspaper *Der Angriff* (*The Attack*, founded in 1927 by Joseph Goebbels):

> Professor Dr Kraeger introduced the speaker. Beamish lives in South Africa. He was in the Boer War and in the World War he fought in Flanders. Behind those bloody events he recognised the hand of Jewry and based his life's struggle on that realisation. He founded, in 1918, the 'Britons' Association, which has now become known all over the globe. Beamish gave a picture of the present Jewish activities throughout the world. Specially revealing were his statements on South Africa, where the professions and the economic key positions were even more Jew-ridden than Germany was before the National Socialist revolution ... The speaker warned his younger listeners not to relax in their watchfulness regarding the Jewish world enemy. During his last trip round the world he could observe everywhere how Jewry was working day and night to the detriment of Germany.

Beamish's speech a few days later at Munich University was reported in the 19 December issue of *Der Völkischer Beobachter* (*The National Observer*, the Nazi's national daily newspaper, published under the banner 'The fighting paper of the National Socialist movement of Greater Germany'). He said that he envied German youngsters for being able to grow up in a philosophy which upholds racial purity. During his present stay in Germany he had been able to find out for himself that the vilifications of Germany everywhere in the world were based on foul lies. In Germany he had found nothing but order and humaneness. In conclusion, Beamish admonished the Germans to be ever thankful for what Adolf Hitler had achieved.

The climax of Beamish's tour came in Nuremberg, where he met his German counterpart in publishing rabid Jew-hatred – Julius Streicher, editor and publisher of *Der Sturmer*. There, Beamish addressed a gathering of leading Nazis in the Hotel Deutscher Hof, introduced by Streicher himself, who said: 'Germans and Englishmen are blood relations and must stretch out their hands to each other. A time will come when other nations too will realise the significance of the Jewish question.' He then said: 'Mr. Beamish has already been to Germany, in 1922, when Dietrich Eckart was still alive. Then he spoke to German workers. What he said was of immense importance.' In his opening response, Beamish stated:

> I am happy to be able to speak at the same meeting as Julius Streicher. I have taken special care to see that the anti-Jewish movements in South Africa and Canada no longer work against but with each other. The paper of your Gauleiter, *Der Sturmer*, is read all over the world. I bow before this brave man.[14]

He went on to say that an agitation of the most evil kind and exceeding all bounds had caused him to seek a first-hand impression of the new Germany. During his visit his conviction had been strengthened that Germany desired nothing but peace.[89] Confident that his audience were with him, he then criticised his hosts for not dealing properly with the Jewish menace in Germany, outlining to them the Madagascar Plan, under which, he said, all Jews would be sent to the island off the coast of Africa. His reasoning was that 'Madagascar, being an island, would make the problem of complete segregation a simple one.'[90] Fifteen years earlier, however, in the pages of *The Jews' Who's Who*, Beamish had advocated Palestine rather than Madagascar as the best place for the banishment of all Jews:

> There is only one cure for this world-evil, and that is for all the Christian white races to combine and to repatriate to Palestine and the neighbouring territories every Jew, male and female, and to take the most drastic steps to see that, once they have founded their Zionist state in their own Promised Land, they permanently remain there.[91]

The Madagascar Plan had originally been proposed in 1885 by the anti-Jewish orientalist scholar Paul de Lagarde. In the mid-1930s, Beamish became its most fervent advocate. In this specific instance, Beamish may indeed have influenced Hitler, who initially adopted and advocated the Madagascar Plan. When hostilities then rendered Madagascar impossible, the Warsaw ghetto, then concentration camps (modelled on those instituted by the British during the Boer War) and, finally, extermination camps ensued.

According to another report in *Der Völkischer Beobachter* (24 January 1937), Beamish concluded his Nuremberg speech with the words: 'It is better to live and work for your country than it is to die for the Jews.'

Der Fränkische Tageszeitung (*The Franconian Daily Newspaper*, owned, published and founded in 1933 by Streicher) gave the greatest publicity to Beamish's tour, clearly suggesting that Streicher was delighted with his guest. Its issue of 23 January 1937 stated:

> The great hall of the Hotel Deutscher Hof was packed out by District Leaders, Gau Office Leaders and Local Group Leaders of the Nazi Movement, by representatives of State and Municipal authorities, members of the armed forces, by men from the economic, scientific and artistic spheres. They had all accepted the invitation of Gauleiter Streicher to come to see and hear Henry Hamilton Beamish, the English writer and politician.

This fulsome praise heaped on Beamish wasn't quite what it seemed. The British Embassy reported that there were distinctly mixed feelings about his visit in the German Ministry for Foreign Affairs and in the Auslandsorganisation (the Nazi Party's foreign propaganda section). They were concerned that his extremism made him unrepresentative of Britain and that hosting him would be counter-productive. They were aware that in Britain he was known as an eccentric. British diplomatic staff had informed them that he was a 'Hyde Park orator' and an 'unbalanced and ill-educated propagandist with a bee in his bonnet'. The whole visit went ahead only after Ribbentrop had decided to endorse it,[37] so the high praise gleaned by Beamish may well have been primarily for show, backing up Ribbentrop's decision.

By 1937, Beamish had become the vice-president of the Imperial Fascist League. In this capacity, on 14 April 1937[92] he addressed the weekly Wednesday HQ meeting of the party's core elite, a body known as the Graduates Association. His lecture, described as a Jewish intelligence report, was entitled 'National Socialism (Racial Fascism) in Practice in Germany'. Beamish told the London gathering that Germany was a great country today because Hitler had named the enemy. The IFL, he said, knew of three remedies to the Jewish question: to kill them, sterilise them or segregate them. Questioned after the lecture, he went on to say that the Russian Revolution had killed off the intelligentsia and that the country was now inhabited by 'animal life people', adding that it would be the task of a great leader, preferably Hitler, to march into Russia within the next five years and place one half of the population in the lethal chamber and the other half in the zoo.[74]

In America, the German-American Bund was working hard to unite Nazi sympathisers. Through the Bund, those who shared Beamish's faith in Germanic

Jew-hatred could now find a forum for their views. Indeed, the Bund even organised some large-scale gatherings. On 12 February 1937, Beamish was one of 4,000 who attended a German-American Bund meeting held at the Hippodrome in New York. The speakers included Bund leaders Fritz Kuhn, James Wheeler-Hill and Rudolph Markmann, two representatives of White Russian groups – Colonel P. Kartacheff (for the All Russia Fascist Party and the Russian National Organisation) and Nicholas Melnikoff (editor of the fascist Russian-language paper *Rossiya*) – Luigi Ciancaglini and John Finizio (representing Italian fascist groups) and Russell J. Dunn (of the Common Cause League).[87]

However, such gatherings were rare. Beamish, the globe-trotting preacher of anti-Jewry who had been driven from his own country by his refusal to pay money to a Jew (Mond), still found scant support for his extremism in most countries. Germany seemed his only real hope. Even in his adopted southern African homeland he was widely regarded with contempt. The Johannesburg *Sunday Express* of 4 October 1937 carried a portrait of Beamish by its editor, his one-time friend Arthur G. Barlow, who had clearly lost all patience with his extremism, especially as exhibited in his July 1934 courtroom testimony in South Africa. The piece was hardly flattering:

> A queer fellow is Henry Hamilton Beamish, the South African who taught Hitler to be an anti-Semite.
>
> Henry Beamish has just completed a triumphal tour of Germany, where he was acclaimed by large crowds as one of the original teachers of Nazism.
>
> I have known him for 37 years and always found him interesting, full of knowledge and strange. Son of a British Admiral who was at one time A.D.C. to Queen Victoria, and brother of another British admiral who is a Conservative MP, Beamish left home when quite a boy and has wandered all over the face of the globe. First he tried Canada where he shod horses and ploughed fields.
>
> The Anglo-Boer War gave him his opportunity to come to this country and, after serving as an officer in an Imperial regiment, to settle down and run a first-class night club in Bloemfontein of all towns.
>
> It was successful because at all hours one got champagne at 10 shillings a bottle. And champagne at all hours was at that time a great attraction, for Bloemfontein was packed with young officers commanding the thousands of British troops who were quartered at Tempe.
>
> When this stunt was played out he established a newspaper, *The Farmers' Advocate*, which became a well-known agricultural organ, and with it he made quite a lot of money. He also ran a farmers' supply store, built churches and did everything that came to hand.
>
> The Great War came and he drifted to Johannesburg and was the leader of the little group who organised the burning down of the German shops and

buildings in Johannesburg. That, as will be remembered, was just after the sinking of the Lusitania by a German submarine. He led the crowd from building to building, and had matters so perfectly arranged that the marked out buildings for destruction went up in flames in five minutes after being attacked.

Beamish gloried in this work, which turned thousands of pounds of assets into ashes.

Then he went to Flanders to fight, and after the war visited Germany and fell in with Hitler and his crowd. About that time he was bitten by the anti-Jewish bug and, as in everything else he tackled, he went to extremes.

He propounded his anti-Jewish scheme to Adolf Hitler and his friends and found the Hitler junta to be ready listeners to his extraordinary and stupid tales. Beamish in England and Hitler in Germany started their anti-Semitic campaign and published an enormous amount of literature, some of which Beamish posted to me in South Africa.

It was dreadful stuff. Beamish crossed to London and launched a savage attack on the late Lord Melchett (then Sir Alfred Mond, M.P.).

Mond was not the type of man to sit quiet and he went for Beamish hammer and tongs. It ended in one of the biggest libel actions held in London and lasted for many days, Mr. Justice Darling presiding over the Court. The newspapers featured it and every word was published and the proceedings may still be read in the chronicles of the day. At times the proceedings were most amusing, as Beamish has a dry cutting wit – he spoke with a lisp – and Mr. Justice Darling could use the rapier as well as any politician. It was not long before these two were at it hammer and tongs, and before the case closed Darling gave Beamish a merciless choking-off.

The action brought by Sir Alfred Mond ended in him being awarded £5,000 damages and costs from Beamish; the latter folded up his tent and stole quietly away. He disappeared into the blue – without paying the damages, of course, and on his way to his retreat visited Bloemfontein and sold the *Farmers' Advocate* for a song. I bought the newspaper and sold it to the Friend Newspaper Company.

Beamish for his sins trekked into the interior of Africa, where for many a long day he hid his light under a bushel, and when I again heard of him he was planting cocoa-nuts on a small island in the Indian Ocean.

But that was too quiet for his restless soul and he trekked back to Africa, Southern Rhodesia, and seized the opportunity of once more indulging in his anti-Semitism in giving 'expert' evidence on behalf of Inch in the famous case at Port Elizabeth three years ago.

Now he is overseas and probably linked up with Mosley. As I said before he is 'a queer fellow', and anti-Semitism is his kink.

> Strange as it may be Henry Beamish has quite a number of Jewish friends, some of them close friends, and he never attacks a Jew personally, but when it comes to the Jews on the whole he wants them all put in Palestine and nowhere else.
>
> How one is going to settle 17,000,000 people in Palestine I do not know, but Beamish, like all anti-Semites, would waft that problem airily away with a light wand.
>
> I suppose one of these days he will turn up in my office and again give me a full dose of his stupid anti-Semitism. Outside this particular question he is a man of great common sense and experience, and a delightful and amusing companion. But you know what a kink can do to a man.

Stung by this attack, especially coming from someone who had been a close friend, Beamish responded with a seven-page pamphlet, *South Africa's Kosher Press*, which was published by The Britons. It consisted of the piece by Barlow followed by Beamish's letter of response to Barlow at the Johannesburg *Sunday Express*.[68] That letter reads as follows:

Sir,

I feel it incumbent to reply to the article you wrote about me in your issue of August 29th, 1937, because it contains so many untruths. I am therefore reprinting your article together with my reply, and have only omitted reproducing Adolf Hitler's portrait and the array of the five-pointed stars of Judah with which you have embellished it, since this Ghetto symbol is an insult to all Aryans.

RAN NIGHT CLUB

I presume you are referring to a harmless concern called the 'Empire Tea Rooms' in which I had an interest in 1903, in conjunction with a friend of mine who was killed in the late Jew-won war, and it was such a 'success' that within a month after closing it, I was driving a traction engine for a living! You were born in the Orange Free State yourself, where even to-day it is illegal to fish on Sundays, and knowing Bloemfontein and the Free State laws as well as you do, you must know perfectly well that a night club was an impossibility.

THE LUSITANIA RIOTS

Not only is it totally untrue that the crowd 'went from building to building' and turned thousands of pounds into ashes, but I was the individual authorised in writing by certain members of the South African Cabinet to put down the riots, and, what is more important, did so with complete success. Perhaps, you and your kosher paper will now suggest that I was responsible also for similar riots which broke out simultaneously in practically every town in South Africa?

To prove my contention and to show conclusively the part I took in quelling those unfortunate riots, I challenge you to reproduce the evidence I gave before Parliament in Cape Town when I described the riots as being 'idiotic'. When asked by certain members of Parliament who was to blame for these riots, I replied that the fault lay entirely with a few members of the Cabinet for not interning certain rich merchants, nine-tenths of whom were Jews and who were making themselves particularly obnoxious, while Aryans in Europe were being slaughtered at the rate of thousands every day. The sinking of the 'Lusitania' merely supplied the spark; the origin of the unfortunate riots was a much deeper one. My evidence before Parliament was printed in the Blue Book on Incendiarism which the Government issued after they had taken the proof submitted, and as your statement about myself is quite incorrect, I ask you, if you are a fair-minded man, to reproduce this evidence.

ANTI-SEMITIC CAMPAIGN

Nobody but a fool is 'anti-Semitic', because, by being this one would have to be anti-Arab. The Arabs are members of a manly and courageous race and are having a terrible time in trying to hold their own against the Jews, not only in Palestine but in all parts of North Africa. All good Aryans heartily sympathise with the efforts the Arabs are making to throw off the Jewish yoke.

The expression 'anti-Semitic' was coined by the Jews during the upheavals in Europe in the middle of the last century, in order to prevent Europeans from using the dreadful word Jew, Juif or Jude. You, being an educated man, must know this.

SIR ALFRED MOND (Melchett)

My reason for selecting the rich Jew for attack, shortly after the members of his race had won the late War, was because I realised that they debase the artistic temperament of all who have the misfortune to view them. People like Einstein, Epstein, Litvinoff (Finkelstein), Trotsky (Bronstein), and all the artistic leaders of Jewry will be able to show the non-Jewish world what a refined and cultured race they are, and as a Press will be required, not to mention numbers of theatres, cinemas, insurance companies and orange farms, it will be a simple matter for Theodore Shlesinger to arrange for a complete Jew monopoly amongst his own people, and so release the stranglehold he at present has on South African Gentiles throughout the length and breadth of South Africa. Having been for so many years associated with Judah, you will doubtless make this trek with the 'chosen' to Madagascar yourself, and to this no objection will be made by the Board which will be appointed to deal with such cases.

ADOLF HITLER AND ARYAN CIVILISATION

In conclusion let me say that I taught Adolf Hitler none of his 'monkey tricks', an insolent expression worthy of the Kosher press you edit. The Fuhrer of Germany is a really great man, he has saved our Aryan civilisation, and it is thanks to him that the British Empire, Kosherised though it be, is in existence today. If he had not taken the stand he did in 1933 and honestly stated that 'Bolshevism is Judaism' the entire civilised world would have crashed and followed the example of Russia, which, since the Jewish revolution of 1917, has been absolutely dominated by Jewish anarchists.

South Africa herself is rapidly awakening, and I hope I may live to see the day when National Socialism, headed by some of the present young leaders, will be able to replace the existing system of Judaised Democracy with a type of Government which will not only give every citizen a chance to make good, but will eliminate Racialism and the Kosher press, which had fostered Racialism for many years.

I request you to publish this letter, and I reserve all rights to publish it myself, also.[9]

Barlow, of course, didn't publish Beamish's ranting reply.

His obsession with Jews had deeply changed Beamish. The Mond case had not only hit him financially, its aftermath had left him rootless and alienated. His monomaniacal cause, a lost one from the outset, had brought him few rewards and had demanded much of him. And, along the way, the 'happy-go-lucky, humorous fellow' whom Barlow had known in South Africa in the early years of the twentieth century had become embittered, humourless and – at times – unhinged. Now, however, as if in self-fulfilling prophesy, Hitler and Germany seemed to offer Beamish a true home for his barbed brand of Jew-hatred.

Back in 1882, Germany had hosted the first International Congress of Anti-Semites in Dresden. The idea was revived in the 1920s with similar gatherings in Florence (1923), Paris (1924), Budapest (1925), Springforbi, Finland (1926) and Stockholm (1927). In 1930 the anti-Semites gathered again, this time in Lucerne, Switzerland. Two years later they met twice, once in Munich and once in Paris, and in 1933 they were in Bellinzona, Switzerland. There was a final gathering in Belgium (22–6 September 1934), after which the event found a permanent annual base in the central German city of Erfurt.

Now specifically a Nazi event, each annual gathering was organised by an Erfurt resident, Colonel Ulrich Fleischhauer (1876–1960), a fanatical Jew-hater who, on 1 December 1933, had founded the international Nazi newsletter *World Service*, which he published bimonthly in a variety of language editions. Under his editorship, this became the global organ of Nazi propaganda with which Beamish had been identified in the testimony of Bundist Neil Howard Ness to the Dies Committee. Such was the eventual intensity of Fleischhauer's all-embracing obsession with Jewish conspiracies that it finally became too much even for his fellow Nazis. In 1939 he would be quietly relieved of his post.[93, 94]

Meanwhile, Beamish was an invited speaker at the September 1937 gathering which also featured the Reverend Doctor Stanisław Trzeciak (from Poland), Jean Drault (from France, Gohier's former co-worker on *La Vieille France*), Professor Herman de Vries de Heekelingen (from the Netherlands) and others, including speakers from German and South African fascist groups. Arnold Leese didn't attend but sent a long message expressing his solidarity.[92] The speech by Beamish was again entitled 'Who Wants War?' Talking of his visit to a concentration camp, he told the audience:

> I can frankly say that the treatment of prisoners was in every respect perfectly humane. I even was allowed to speak to all the prisoners and made use of that opportunity to enlighten some of them about the false doctrines that they had formerly embraced. Throughout the whole world, I have done my best to inform the Aryan world about the criminal elements of disorder and

> their Communist accomplices who think that they can incite honest and loyal nations against each other. Everywhere I have delivered frontal attacks against the common enemy and I would remind you of my big law-suit after the war against the Jew Mond (alias Lord Melchett) ... I have helped many anti-Jews in the fight they are leading against the eternal parasite, especially in law-suits brought against them by the eternal enemy; for this I have made journeys of thousands of miles.

After telling his audience that he had paid a visit to his 'militant English comrade' Arnold Leese, he continued:

> All have to thank the German Fuhrer for what he has done for the world: he has not only saved his country from Bolshevism and the sadistic slavery imposed on it by international Jewry, but he has also saved civilisation everywhere from ruin ... Systematic and intense propaganda directed against the sinister activities of Jewry is absolutely necessary and most urgent ... My watchword is: Compulsory segregation! I suggest Madagascar ... The greatest success of the Fuhrer's policy is undoubtedly the pact with Japan, that is the only country of the East which fights Bolshevism effectively. West meets East in the struggle against the common enemy. Communism and Jewry being international, can only be fought in the international field.

On 15 October 1937 Beamish sailed from London to New York aboard the SS *American Banker*. The passenger manifest listed him as an alien passenger and an English miner, aged sixty-four.[95]

In New York Beamish had three speaking engagements, for each of which he appeared wearing a swastika armband. At the first of these, on 30 October, at the New York Hippodrome, he once more addressed a public gathering of the German-American Bund, many of whom gave the Nazi 'Sieg heil!' salute to the speakers. The audience, reported to have numbered 10,000, included members of other American, Canadian and British Empire anti-Jewish groups. Opening speeches were given by James Wheeler-Hill, Rudolph Markmann (in German) and John Finizio (in Italian), before Beamish and then Adrien Arcand spoke.[96]

On 31 October Beamish spoke at a private banquet in the Harvard Club, and on 1 November he was the guest speaker at a private gathering in a prominent clubhouse. Speaking with him at all three events was Arcand, a long-time Jew-hater and the founding leader of the National Social Christian Party of Canada (also known as the Christian National Socialist Party). Arcand, already a firm friend of Beamish, would later declare himself Führer of Canada. In 1934, in a deliberate echo of Beamish's campaign for Jews to be deported to Madagascar, Arcand had advocated anti-communism and the deportation of Canadian Jews to Hudson Bay.

There was a third keynote speaker at the last two events. He was Robert Edward Edmondson, an American Nazi and close associate of William Kullgren. It has since been revealed that Edmondson was believed by US intelligence to have been an agent of Nazi Germany.[97] Introducing Beamish at the Hippodrome, Edmondson, who hosted all three events, announced:

> Captain Beamish, Veteran and Dean of this historic movement of Liberation, REAL representative of the Jew-oppressed people of Great Britain, brings a message of Truth. You will have the priceless privilege of listening to Nestorian words of wisdom from a great-hearted Soldier-Statesman who knows whereof he speaks by the unimpeachable authority of two-score years of unselfish personal service to a world-cause. Ponder well this warning![96]

The three men had together attended the German-American Bund meeting at the Hippodrome back in February. The importance that this triumvirate attached to their combined words is shown by the fact that a booklet was subsequently published by Edmondson containing the main parts of each of the three speeches. This was widely distributed. Here are the highlights of what Beamish had to say. Even to some of his sympathisers it must have seemed cranky:

> We are engaged in the greatest war history has ever known. The last war was a picnic compared to the one we are now fighting. The question is, whether the Jew shall rule the world, or we white men.

> The chairman has said that I was the originator of the racial movement in England. After taking part in three wars, I was tired seeing millions of people wiped out for this race of Asiatics. I started the movement after the Kosher Peace of 1918.

> Communism is Judaism. The Jewish Revolution in Russia was in 1918. I found it out pretty quickly and I put it in writing. Jews are a race and not a religion.

> Jews, being aliens in our midst, they must be segregated. They have debased art, music, architecture, etc. I am glad to say that the Germans have collected together all their pictures left in various parts of the world. If you really like filth, go and inspect some of them. It is so-called Jewish Leaders like Epstein who have ruined art, music, press, architecture, ethics, morals.

> If not I am a lunatic, a criminal lunatic, something is radically wrong in the world today.

> The Boer War occurred 37 years ago. Boer means Farmer. Many criticised a great power like Great Britain for trying to wipe out the Boers. Upon making enquiry, I found all the gold and diamond mines were owned by Jews; that Rothstein controlled gold; Samuels controlled silver; Samuels controlled oil; Baum controlled other minerals; and Moses controlled base metals. Anything these people touch they inevitably pollute.

The life of Henry Hamilton Beamish   53

The world condition up to 1933 was perfect for the Jews. The position in England was perfect for them. At the Kosher Peace there were so many Jews that they had to have Kosher food.

Up to 1933 Russia, France and other nations were politically Kosherized; England was going perfectly – all on complete Bolshevick architecture. Spain, with Prima Rivera, was really Judaized.

Conditions were the same in Germany until the Great Leader came through. It may interest you to know that I met the Fuehrer in 1922. Hitler had named a name in three letters – 'JEW'. When I got there I learned that the whole movement in Germany was for labor. Jews are not laborers. The movement in Germany was and is for the working classes, the one great asset to Germany and the entire world.

What we have to realise today is that the Jews are working overtime to bring another war. The position is serious. They tried their utmost in Spain. The movement having failed there, they have shifted to Shanghai, where there are 7,000 Jews – refugees, doctors and dentists – now working night and day to bring trouble to the far east.

There are very few newspapers not owned or controlled by Jews except in the countries that have named the Bolshevists as the enemies of mankind. The newspapers never attack Kosher France, Belgium and England.

I was in Rome when Mussolini saved Italy. In Germany war really began in 1918. I was there during inflation, before and after. Germany has been reborn. It is a new country. I have never seen such a remarkable difference.

In discussing the Jew question, we must be race conscious of the fact that we are white people. We must not mix race with religion.

The answer to the problem is to be found only in one of three ways:

(1) Kill them, which is out of the question.
(2) Sterilise them, which is out of the question.
(3) Segregate them – and there is only one place, Madagascar.

I have only been here a few days, but a few points strike me. I spent some time in your East side having a look at the ghettoes of this country. I have been in many countries, but must say that the conditions in New York are perfectly appalling to me.

The whole essence of this fight is moral courage. Edmondson is a great fighter. Large numbers of people will die for their country, but few will live for it. It is infinitely better to live than to die, as the leaders have done in Germany.

When Lord Kitchener was asked to go to Russia to reorganise the Russian army, his boat, the S.S. Hampshire was torpedoed, and a meeting was held in

London on the question of how Lord Kitchener met his death. No one dared speak. Not one speaker would tell the audience how Kitchener met his death. Had he lived the whole war would have changed.

At the Kitchener meeting in London three speakers spoke, but not one dared name the enemy. The first two rows of the audience were filled with brass hats. The speakers merely spoke of some mysterious thing. This is what I had to say: That I was a private; that it was against regulations to talk on political matters; that I noticed in the first two rows all were soldiers. I challenged the war office to court-martial me for what I had to say. Anyone would know why Kitchener met his death, if he could spell JEW. Lord Kitchener was murdered by Jews and Jew Finance. I told them that if they wanted to know more they should ask Lord Rufus Isaacs, Chief Justice of England – and then said good night.

First know your subject, and then have the moral courage to say so. In my nine libel actions that was the whole point. I have arrived at the age of 64, and I am still living. You must get at the truth.

I regret that I cannot be here for the Edmondson trial on November 15th. Whether Mahoney on one side or LaGuardia on the other side, wins the election, the telegraphic address for both will be 'Kosher.' Please do not think you have a monopoly on Jew control. England, Belgium, France, etc., are now run by Jews. If you have never read The Protocols, you know nothing about the Jewish question.

Every man should be fined for saying 'anti-Semitic.' The Arabs are Semites and they have been standing up against the Jews. In 1848 the word 'anti-Semitic' was invented by the Jews to prevent the use of the word 'Jew.' The right word for them is 'Jew.' We are not against the Syrians, Armenians and Arabs, all of them Semites let down by the 'kosher' power behind England.

The real war began in Germany in 1918 when they had the 'kosher' peace terms. It is the power behind. The Jews make the wars. The Jews manufactured Bolshevism and inflation. The question of money is only the question of the Jews manipulating it. The Jew will inflate it or deflate it at will. Why is it done? To wipe out the upper and middle classes. It is the Jews who preach Communism for us, and who spread socialism, bolshevism and anarchy. Then the Jew is supreme.

I met Emma Goldman at a Red meeting in New York. I asked her who organised the revolution in 1917, and to tell me whether Jews are behind the Spanish revolution. She answered that the Jews have been persecuted in Spain and are behind the revolution there today. I asked 'Are you a Bolshevist?' She answered: 'I am an Anarchist.' Those are the steps, socialism, bolshevism and anarchism.

Do not allow any religion to cross the trail. In the fifteenth century the King of Spain, Ferdinand said to the Jews: 'You must all leave Spain unless you become Christians.' All doors soon had crosses on them, but after four hundred years they have not become proper nationals in that country, any more than they have in France or any other country. Therefore, do not let any religious questions cross this trail.

I implore all of you to be accurate – call them Jews. There is no need to be delicate on this Jewish question. You must face them in this country. The Jew should be satisfied here. I was here forty-seven years ago; your doors were thrown open and you were then free. Now he has got you absolutely by the throat – that is your reward.

You people must be alive to the race question. I have nothing against negroes, but I don't believe in crossing blood. In Nuremberg the laws say 'don't join the Jew.' I once visited a concentration camp near Munich. I tackled a Jew. Do you belong to a pure race? He answered: 'Yes.' Then I asked 'Why then do you object to the Germans keeping their race pure?' If you ask that question in England they say you are a Communist.

Who rules Russia? How do you account for the fact that out of 550 commissars in Russia only 17 are Russian? The white man's country should be run by white people.

You must have leadership – not dictatorship. In England there is no soul we would follow. You must get a leader and define definitely what you stand for.

If Jews are 6% of the population, they must be allowed only that percentage of lawyers, doctors, etc. There must be no false persecution charge because of religion – that is an absolute lie. I went to church after church in Germany, and to the Salvation Army in Hanover, and found no persecution.

The first time I met Hitler I asked 'In the event you come to power what will you do with the Jews in Germany?' He replied 'I will send them all to the allies.' That will not cure it, nothing but segregation will.

The Jew today is the same as in the days of Pharoah, a microbe in the body politic of any nation. He must be handled accordingly. When people begin to suffer they will collect and ask: 'What are we going to do?' How many countries are not tired of Judaism? The whole world is dissatisfied today.

I have discovered the spot for the segregation of the Jews. It is the only place in the world – Madagascar. The map of the island shows it to be 1,000 miles long, and it will hold 100,000,000 people. Segregation is the solution of our problem, and there is the place for segregation of the Jews.[97]

After the New York meetings, it seems that Beamish visited Arcand in Montreal. We know of this because of evidence given to the Dies Committee in August 1939 by a man simply recorded as Mr Allen, who testified that Beamish was there.[98] Also, the December 1936 issue of the French Canadian magazine *Le Fasciste Canadien* carried a piece entitled 'M. H. H. Beamish à Montreal', in which he is quoted as enthusing about French Canadians, 'who, with their religious, racial and linguistic unity, can form a bloc against the forces of evil'. While there, he took part in pro-Nazi meetings in Montreal and Quebec City, both of which were met with protests by left-wingers.[99]

In January 1938, Beamish was once again in California. The 21 January 1944 issue of the New York-based German-Jewish journal *Aufbau* tells us that 'former Californian Bundists and their pals look upon Beamish as the dean of international anti-Semitism and travelling salesman par excellence of National Socialism. They treasure memories of Beamish's visit in California in January 1938.'[100]

As war loomed, Beamish became increasingly anti-British, campaigning against what he called the 'Kosher War', in which he reckoned Britain was 'the headquarters of the plot for the destruction of our civilisation'.[32]

In the summer of 1938, having returned to Rhodesia, Beamish actually achieved political power. Following the death of the Rhodesian MP Roger Edward Downes, there was a by-election in his Southern Rhodesian constituency of Hartley on 30 August. Beamish, standing as an Independent, secured 144 votes, narrowly beating his rival candidates to be elected to the Rhodesian parliament.[101] In a letter dated 12 October 1938, addressed to Mr Kositzin, a White Russian leader in America, and sent from Box 952, Salisbury, Rhodesia, Beamish wrote:

> It was a tough fight, because I not only had against me three candidates, but all their political organisations, representing the three local political parties which are under Judaic-Democracy, under which we suffer in Rhodesia as in other kosher countries ... I have already had over 100 telegrams and cables, which is a good sign as it shows that there are many people who realise that this election in an out of the way part of the world has much more behind it than appears on the surface ... It is some satisfaction to feel that I am the first Briton to be elected to any Parliament in this kosher British Empire with not only a knowledge of THE subject, but what is far more, with the MORAL courage to name THE enemy and tell the Truth.

In what was a lengthy letter, Beamish later talked of having read – in the latest issue of *World Service* – that his friend George Deatherage (a leading American klansman and Nazi sympathiser during the 1930s) had 'attended the Erfurt Conferences and made a most excellent speech and described most graphically the conditions of affairs in the United States'. Then, commenting on American affairs, he added: 'Racial instincts have practically disappeared or have been submerged under that senseless expression "100 per cent American" as if any animal except possibly a Jew and a skunk could be 100 per cent of anything.' After passing on the contact details of leading Jew-hating activists in Argentina and Chile, Beamish went on to praise Kositzin for his own activities:

The Bulletins you are issuing are splendid and you use the right expressions, such as kosher, continually. I am also delighted to see that both Robert E [Edmondson] and James True [an American Jew-baiter who co-founded America First] openly and squarely name THE enemy and do not camouflage under such senseless words as 'Internationalists' or 'Foreigners' etc. etc. ... I have heard from Klapproth [Johannes Klapproth, a German-American chemist for Shell Oil, who was a klansman and the main American agent for *World Service* until his death in spring 1938] and if you find that you cannot pull through with the American Nationalist Confederation [founded in August 1937 by Deatherage, with whom Kositzin was working], you might do worse than go to Erfurt, as matters all over the world are rapidly moving and a man with your knowledge of THE question is bound to get a suitable position before long ... Princess Karadja [a Jew-obsessed White Russian who founded the Christian Aryan Protection League] of Locarno, is a constant correspondent and considering her age it is wonderful how much useful work she does for the Cause and the tenacity she shows ... Arcand writes in excellent spirits, and there is no question that he is the *par excellence* leader of Canada. If he takes over Canada (as he expects to do within two years), I hope and expect he will ask me to run his propaganda department.

After offering the advice that American anti-Jewish campaigners such as Deatherage and Kositzin should look out 'for some rich industrialist to come forward and finance ... your excellent Movements', the letter ended – referencing the Czech crisis and the international situation – 'It will be interesting to see what the next Jew move will be now they have failed with Prague, and it is quite clear after trying to bolshevize, that is Judaize, all countries having only succeeded in Russia, that they must make a new move quickly or be found out.' As this letter clearly indicated, Beamish now saw himself as some kind of global anti-Jewish guru and overseer.

Beamish sat in the Rhodesian legislature for just eight months, during which time he is on record as having warned Ulster and Rhodesia not to obey the 'be-Jewed' House of Commons.[102] An eccentric and ineffective MP, he lost his seat in the Rhodesian general election of 14 April 1939, coming third of four candidates, with just 196 of the 796 votes cast.[103]

It was a bad year for him. By September, his 'kosher' war had come – and 1940 would be worse. In Britain, many of his fellow Jew-haters were being arrested and interned without trial under Defence Regulation 18b. If Beamish thought that he had been safe in Rhodesia, particularly as, until recently, he had been an MP, he was wrong.

Arrested on 10 June 1940 by order of the Rhodesian minister of justice, R. C. Tredgold, Beamish was taken into custody by 'four white men' who found him living alone at his Windsor mine. He was held in Salisbury Prison, where he confidently expected his case to be reviewed within a month. When this failed to happen, he began petitioning Tredgold and the Rhodesian prime minister, Sir Godfrey Huggins. The full correspondence was subsequently published in two parts under the title *Justice in Rhodesia*. Part I covered his correspondence with Huggins, while part II consisted of his correspondence with Tredgold (only the latter is in this author's collection). On 26 October 1940 Beamish wrote to Tredgold from Salisbury Prison:

> Sir, Several members of the deputation which waited on you on July 4, 1940 on the subject of my internment, have suggested to me that I write to you to review my case again. These gentlemen inform me that you expressed your willingness to review the case at a later date, and presuming that their information is correct, I trust I am adopting the correct procedure in addressing you this letter and requesting you review the case again. Yours faithfully, H. H. Beamish.

On 29 October the reply read:

> Sir, With reference to your letter dated Oct 26 to the Minister of Justice, in which you ask that your case be reviewed, it would be of assistance if you would give an indication of your intentions in the event of your release being approved. The matter will receive the full consideration of the Minister. I have the honour to be Sir, Your obedient servant, T. O. Flynn.

Beamish wrote to Tredgold on 31 October:

> Sir, Replying to your letter of Oct. 29, my letter to you of Oct 26 was written at the request of various members of the deputation which waited upon you on July 4, 1940. These gentlemen informed me that on July 4 you stated that you were agreeable to reopen the case at a later date, and that the period of one month was mentioned. On Nov. 10, I will have been in prison for five months, and during this period no approach has been made to me by yourself. I concluded that it was useless for me to take any steps in the matter. What I would prefer to do, is to petition the Prime Minister and Speaker for permission to appear before the Bar of the House, so that the case can be inquired into and myself examined. As precedents on such matters are often asked for, I would mention that several years ago, I gave evidence before the Union House of Assembly on a summons from the Speaker, and also was closely associated with Mr. Percival Frere Smith who appeared before the Bar of the Union House on behalf of the Labour leaders who were arrested and deported without trial shortly after the Rand strikes in 1912. You ask what my intentions would be if released: If the case had been reopened as I was informed it would be, my intention was to return to the 'Windsor' mine which has afforded me a good living for over five years, and which in the words of my late manager who left the mine on Oct. 15, would have given a 'nice living for a man like you for many years.' As, however, the mine could not afford to pay an expensive

manager and pay me as well, and as month after month went without receiving any word about the reopening of my case, the mine had to be sold on Oct. 18; incidentally, wretched prices were realised, and what is infinitely more important, I have been deprived of an excellent living and home. It is difficult to arrange anything with regard to the future from inside Prison walls, now that I cannot return to my mine, but what I wish to do is to get away as far as possible from enquiring Europeans, and that will take some arranging. I would like to visit my farm north of Sinoia, as I have recently received some information about it which demands my presence there. Unpleasant though this 'oubliette' Prison sentence has been for nearly five months, I visualise none too pleasant a time from inquisitive enquirers, as I am well known, and numbers of people are certain to ask me 'why have you been in prison?' and I would infinitely prefer to escape such enquiries. I am putting the position quite candidly to you, and if you have any suggestions with regard to the future, I am quite willing to entertain them. I shall not do anything with regard to petitioning the Speaker to appear at the Bar of the House until I hear from you, as I fully appreciate the fact that you are the responsible Minister for dealing with internments. Yours faithfully H. H. Beamish.

There was no reply.

On 10 January 1941 Beamish wrote to the prime minister, Sir Godfrey Huggins:

Dear Huggins, I am sorry to have to write to you again about myself, but am compelled to do so as the position daily becomes more impossible. You have apparently written to Mr. Rudman in Natal, a man I have not seen or heard of for over five years, what he describes as a 'cordial' letter and intimated to him that my 'release will soon be authorised'. This letter I received last November, i.e. about two months ago. On Oct. 29 last, your Minister of Defence (Mr. R. C. Tredgold) wrote me asking what are 'my intentions in event of release being approved'. I replied to him on Oct. 31, and inter alia stated that I first wished to visit my farm, and after pointing out that my mine had been sold, and which incidentally was my means of livelihood, asked him for any suggestions he would care to make. I have not had even an acknowledgement, let alone a reply to this letter, which I think you will agree is hardly polite. 'Toujours la Politesse'!! The only other letter I have written to your young Minister of Defence is the enclosed, and you as a medical man will appreciate that this 'Oubliette' existence I have experienced during the last seven months and with nobody to speak to is, if not inhuman, certainly detrimental to any human being. With the exception of a few more volumes of Greville's Memoirs written 100 years ago, I have now read nearly every decent book in this library, and though there are plenty of other books, I have not sunk so low as to be able to read Edgar Wallace and other similar trash. My mail is now entirely confiscated, even to the extent of letters from my relatives in England, but I will not dwell on this and other matters as the purpose of this letter is to ask for a transfer to the internment camps so that at least I can associate with human beings, as the question of my release appears to have been side-tracked, buried and forgotten. I know you will be good enough to take the matter up without delay. Yours sincerely H. H. Beamish.

This letter was confiscated along with much other correspondence and returned only when he was released on 3 July 1943. On the same day (10 January) Beamish wrote to Tredgold:

Sir, I write to request to be transferred from this Prison to the Internment Camp. I make this request for humane reasons, as I contend that it is not humane to lock up any man of intelligence and of my age for nineteen to twenty hours a day and to deprive him from contact with human beings, which has been my lot for the last seven months. I am aware of the fact that large numbers of well known men in Britain and elsewhere have been put in prison for the same reason that I have, but I also know that they associate daily with their fellow internees, which enables them to retain their mental balance and to make the best of a most unpleasant situation. If you consider this 'Oubliette' existence I have been forced to lead for the last seven months is a humane one, I have nothing further to say at the moment, but if you think that my request to associate with human beings is a reasonable one, you may perhaps be willing to consider this application. I ask for the curtesy [sic] of a reply. Yours faithfully H. H. Beamish.

There was no reply, but five days later, on 15 January 1941, after seven months in Salisbury Prison, Beamish was removed to an internment camp.

One week later, on 23 January, Tredgold issued notice that he was prepared to approve Beamish's release on the following conditions:

1. He shall reside on Sunflower Farm, Norton, which shall be placed at his disposal for the duration of the war, by Messrs. Meston and Maitland.
2. He shall not go outside a radius of eight miles from the homestead on Sunflower Farm without permission of the Superintendent, Criminal Investigation Dept., Salisbury, obtained though the Police, Norton. Each application will be dealt with on its merits.
3. He will be required to enter into a written undertaking to refrain from arranging or attending meetings and from conducting or being a party to any form of propaganda by word or by writing.
4. He will be required to enter into an undertaking to transmit all letters written to him through Police, Norton, for censorship by the authorities.
5. Failure to comply with any conditions of release will render him liable to reinternment.

On 26 January Beamish replied from his internment camp to Tredgold's offer:

> Sir, Your Memorandum dated 23 January relating to 'Conditions of Release' regarding myself was handed to me yesterday. I have now had an opportunity of studying the terms you wish to impose which I am unable to accept in view of the fact, that numbers of friends of mine in England, Canada, and elsewhere are still in Prison and have been refused Parole and release. The 'White Paper' recently issued by the House of Commons containing evidence given by Archibald Maule Ramsay, M.P. contains such astounding evidence as to the treatment he and others have received, that I feel, should I accept any conditions which even appear to be preferential, that I would be taking a mean advantage of friends, which is an attitude I could not possibly adopt. This is no question of martyrdom, but of standing by friends, many of whom are also my pupils, and if men like Admiral Sir Barry Domvile, Cpt Ramsay, M.P. and a host of others can stay the course in spite of the treatment they have received, I feel that the least I can do is to do the same. I will not comment at the moment on the 'Conditions of Release' except to say that as at present drafted, I could not accept them. I have written to Messrs Meston & Maitland thanking them for their kind offer of 'Sunflower Farm' and explaining why their offer cannot be accepted. Yours faithfully, H. H. Beamish.

Just over a year later, on 15 February 1942, Beamish wrote again to Tredgold:

> Sir, I am writing you this letter in view of certain information recently published in the African press. I am unable to refer to previous correspondence with you, or to my letters to and from the Prime Minister, Sir Godfrey Huggins, because all of my correspondence and papers when entering this camp, from Salisbury Prison over 12 months ago, i.e. in Jan 1941, were confiscated. Speaking from memory therefore, I last wrote to you in Jan. 1941, asking you to formulate any charges you wished to make against me and requested permission to appear at the Bar of the House so that I could answer those charges. You did not have the curtesy to acknowledge let alone reply to that letter! As all 'Hansards' are prohibited from entering this Camp, I have to rely on 'The Star' for the information that your counterpart in the Union of S.A. (Mr. Lawrence), has stated in the Union House that: A Union National Internee was within a short time supplied with a summary of the charges against him. If he wished to appeal he could reply to the charges in writing. He could also secure statements from persons outside. I realise, of course, that practical conditions and pressures within the Union automatically curbs any super autocratic action on the part of the Ministers, as is also the case in Canada, and that such conditions are entirely absent in Rhodesia, but in spite of this I feel that I am justified in requesting you to formulate any charges you have against me, particularly in view of the fact that the

Prime Minister, Sir Godfrey Huggins, who doubtless has inside secret information, has stated this week that the war will continue for a further four years. As it is quite possible that I will not be in existence in another four years, I would at least like to know before I pass out, WHY I was thrown in prison, completely ignored during the seven months I was there by the Department of Justice over which you rule, and given no opportunity to defend myself against charges, which have NEVER been submitted to me. It is not a question of release, and I am certainly accepting no terms of Parole while friends of mine IN MANY countries are still in prison for the same reason as myself, but purely a question of wishing to know what I am accused of, whether I am entitled to the same treatment as Union Nationals, or whether I am considered as belonging to a special category? I trust you will have the curtesy to reply to this letter. Yours faithfully H. H. Beamish.

T. O. Flynn replied on 26 February:

Sir, with reference to your letter dated 15th, I am instructed to reply that your case was fully and carefully considered by the Tribunal which in this Colony corresponds to the body referred to by the Union Minister of Internal Affairs. Before this Tribunal the grounds upon which you were interned were fully canvassed and the Minister is not prepared to re-open this discussion. You have been offered release on Parole upon perfectly reasonable terms, and this offer still stands. I have the honour to be, Sir, Your obedient servant, T. O. Flynn.

On 28 February Beamish wrote to Tredgold:

Sir, Replying to your letter of Feb. 26, 1942, I must say at once that you have entirely avoided the issues I have raised in my letter of Feb. 15 and in my correspondence with you asking to be furnished with any charges you wished to make against me. I have now been in prison for over 20 months and have never been furnished with any document or written charges stating what crime I am alleged to have committed, proving conclusively, as stated in my letter of Feb 15, that I am under a 'special category' and am not entitled to the same treatment as Union Nationals. I put this on record to avoid any possible misunderstanding at some future date. I have a vague recollection of the Tribunal you mention but looked on the discussions raised at that enquiry, as merely preliminary to the launching of charges you might wish to make against me at some future date. The enquiry took place in June 1940, i.e. 20 months ago!! In my long experience of world affairs which far exceed your own, I have always understood that accused persons were entitled to know beforehand and in writing, what they were accused of before they were condemned, but my experiences under your hand have proved that this elementary principle of Justice does not meet with your approval. I note that you are not prepared to 'reopen this discussion' which I can well believe, as even lawyers would find it difficult to 'reopen' a subject which has never been opened, as is clearly proved in convicting myself without ever attempting to furnish me with any endictment or charges in writing so that I might at least know what I am accused of. The Sword of Justice seems to have become somewhat blunted of late in this country, but now that another lawyer in Max Danziger has joined your Cabinet perhaps it will be resharpened? Parole: I have repeatedly told you, and it should be unnecessary to say it again, that on no account will I accept any form of Parole while friends of mine are in Prison for the same reason as myself. The prospect of remaining in Prison for another four years is not pleasant, but it must be faced, and the Prime Minister, Sir Godfrey Huggins, must know! Yours faithfully, H. H. Beamish.

There was no reply. On 10 June 1942 Beamish wrote again to Tredgold:

Sir, I address you this letter on June 10th as it is the second anniversary of my arrest by you on charges unknown to me, and from your consistent refusal to put any charges in writing against myself for the last two years, apparently unknown to you also. I am not in the least surprised that you did not reply to my letter of Feb. 28 1942, in which I again asked you to furnish me with any charges you wished to make against me. One would have thought that your 'Emergency Act' which covers everything from Espionage to whispering Drives. And possibly even sneezing out of turn, would have enabled you to frame some kind of charge, particularly when you have at your command a bevy of lawyers in the Cabinet, all thoroughly versed in the legal verbiage so dearly loved by members of your extraordinary profession. My remarks in my letter of Feb. 28 about the Sword of Justice, which you are at least supposed to keep sharpened, still apply, though it appears to be as blunt as formerly, and this in spite of the fact that you have recently admitted Mr Max Danziger to your innermost circle. As the war approaches its conclusion, and you have steadfastly declined in two years to formulate any charges against me, I am drafting up an indictment against myself, which I can promise you will be framed in such lucid coherent language, and so free from legal jargon, that any layman will be able to clearly understand why and on whose authority I was arrested, deprived of my living, and kept in prison indefinitely without any charges being preferred against me. This duty I owe to the public, who up to the present have only been regaled by you with the purely Jewish side of the question, and even as a lawyer you must admit that there are two sides to every question. I have now entered my 70th year, which probably does not interest you in the least, but for myself, it is ironical that I should be thrown into prison by a young lawyer with the most rudimentary knowledge of world affairs, simply because for more than 40 years I have openly and steadfastly objected to the Jewish

Domination of everything which every honest citizen should be taught to respect. Furthermore, for many years I have strenuously opposed Bolshevism, which is merely a spurious name for Judaism and today I view with much alarm the grave possibility of a Bolshevik wave sweeping over Europe as an aftermath of this war. These therefore, are my 'crimes', and I may tell you that I am completely unrepentant. In conclusion let me tell you Mr Tredgold, though your knowledge of law far exceeds my own for which I am grateful, your ideas of what constitutes justice are of the crudest description. Do not think I am asking for any favours; I am merely putting certain facts on record. Yours faithfully, H. H. Beamish.

There was, of course, no reply. Beamish wrote once more to Tredgold on 15 January 1943:

Sir, As it is two years since I was dumped in this Camp from the Salisbury Prison, it is a fitting occasion to again remind you that in spite of repeated requests during the last two and a half years, you have declined to put in writing any charges against me, and to furthermore remind you that the Sword of Justice which you are supposed to keep sharpened remains as blunt as ever. 'Fiat Justitia' will soon be a museum exhibit! Though my letters to you of Feb. 28 and June 10 remain unanswered, and in view of the fact that the war is rapidly approaching its conclusion, I feel that I should send you the enclosed Memorandum so that there may be a document on record defining the position as far as I am concerned with regard to my arrest and sojourn in Prison over the past two and a half years without being furnished with any charge of any kind in writing. I commend to your notice my final remark in the Memorandum, stating that we are heading straight for Undiluted Jewish Bolshevism, and if you are ignorant of this, it clearly indicates that you know nothing of the history of Russia since the Kerensky Revolution of 1917 and the perfectly candid statements made since that date with regard to world revolution by the various Jewish Bolshevik dictators of that unhappy country. The Tiflis Bankrobber and murderer, Stalin, openly boasts of his intentions with regard to world revolution, and if he succeeds as seems probable, I can at least say, which is more than you can do, that I did my best to WARN MANKIND of what is in store for them if a Jewish Bolshevik revolution sweeps over Europe. Democracy, if properly handled could be made workable, but today it is merely a Jewish instrument to sustain the Jewish Money Power, and conditions in Rhodesia give a glaring example of this. If there is one thing Stalin hates it is Democracy, and if he launches his world revolution, we may say farewell to 'Atlantic Charters' or any kind of 'Social Security' schemes, which schemes are merely disguised names for the principles of Fascism and National Socialism, because Stalin not only has a charter of his own, but has had in addition many years of practice in operating his bloodthirsty scheme for world domination. We are living in a fools

Paradise and when it is too late, this will be realised. Meanwhile, the Shofar is being continually sounded, and if you do not know what this indicates, ask Mr. Max Danziger. Yours faithfully H. H. Beamish.

The attached Memorandum, dated 15 January 1943, read:

> H. H. Beamish, late member of Parliament in S. Rhodesia, was arrested on June 10 1940, when living alone in his mine, situated 25 miles from Salisbury. Four white policemen, including one Officer, arrested him and took him to Salisbury Prison, where he was locked up for 18 hours a day, his cell being in close proximity to the hanging and flogging places. Two people were hanged while he was in Prison, and on most days he had to listen to the howls of natives being flogged. During the seven months he was in Prison, no single member of the Dept. of Justice visited him to ascertain whether he was humanely treated, or whether the ordinary CONVICT food was adequate for a man approaching his SEVENTIETH (70) year. The head of the Dept of Justice during this period, and he still holds this position (1943), was a young lawyer – Mr. R. C. Tredgold – who in his capacity of MINISTER OF DEFENCE and MINISTER OF JUSTICE signed the document, which from memory read: 'You will arrest H. H. Beamish and lodge him in Salisbury Prison.' No reasons have ever been given for his arrest, and this in spite of the fact that he has made frequent requests to the Minister (R. C. Tredgold) to formulate some kind of a charge against him in writing. In addition, as is seen from the correspondence, he offered to appear before the Bar of the House in order to allow the Minister to make what charges he wished to, but the Minister did not have even the curtesy to acknowledge the letter containing this request, and furthermore, CONFISCATED the letter, the copy, together with other correspondence between the Prime Minister (Sir Godfrey Huggins) and H. H. Beamish. (!) After he had been in Salisbury Prison over SEVEN months he was removed to the German and Italian Internment Camp (Jan 15 1941) and from which camp this Memorandum is written. All his papers were confiscated on entering the Camp, including his Memoirs, which was written in the Salisbury Prison. At his own request, towards the end of June 1940, he appeared before some kind of Tribunal, consisting of a Judge (Sir Fraser Russell), a retired civil servant (Devine) and a Labour Member of Parliament (Lister), the latter having avowed Communistic leanings. What enquiry there was was held in camera, though he had made arrangements to have a shorthand writer as he is anxious for publicity and NOT secrecy. The proceedings were so informal that H. H. Beamish looked upon it as merely a preliminary to the launching of some charges of conspiracy against the State, or having been 'subsidised' by the German or Italian Governments. No charges were made, and the chief complaints appeared to be (1) That he did not approve of Democracy, which is correct, because as present practised, together with its OGPU methods of

throwing people into Prison without trial, it is merely JEWOCRACY, and is the slave of the Jewish Money Power; (2) That he did not approve of the King being a Mason, and furthermore being Grand Master of all British Masonic lodges. He admits his 'guilt' on these charges, and is furthermore of the opinion, that the King of a great Empire should not concern himself in not only International, but secret societies, and particularly so when it is well known that the higher degrees of Masonry, and particularly the 33rd degree are controlled by Jews. So concerned were the Tribunal in this Masonic business, that H. H. Beamish had grounds for thinking that the three members were Masons themselves. A lawyer Member of Parliament (H. Bertin, K.C.) who has known H. H. Beamish for nearly 40 years attended this Enquiry and offered 'Pro Deo' to appear for him, but as lawyers are only useful when a person is guilty, his offer, which was made in an entirely friendly spirit, was declined. Parole on several occasions has been offered to him, but has been refused on the following grounds:-

1. Because he was thrown into Prison without any charges being preferred against him, deprived of his living and treated like a criminal, except that ordinary criminals clearly understand why they are punished and in Prison, And,
2. Because many friends of his, many of whom are distinguished men, are still in Prison in many countries for the same reason as himself, namely for opposing the Jewish Money Power, — The REAL reason for his arrest and detention without trial is because for the last 40 years he has taken an active part in exposing the Jewish menace to European civilisation, and in consequence, is well known to all leaders in most countries who also realise that failing steps being taken to putting an end to Jewish domination of ALL phases of National life, and particularly with regard to Jewish control of finance, that civilisation is doomed, and that the future 'New Order' will be UNDILUTED JEWISH BOLSHEVISM.
H. H. Beamish.[104]

So ends Beamish's prison correspondence. His 1943 claim to have actively campaigned against Jews for forty years is one more of his self-serving lies. A mere twenty-eight years earlier, in 1915, he had actually (and ironically in retrospect) been a fervent anti-*German* campaigner, with no more than the occasional derogatory verbal side-swipe at Jews.

On 21 July 1943 the following report – submitted by a reader, presumably Beamish himself or one of his acquaintances – appeared in the *Rhodesian Herald* under the headline 'Mr H. H. Beamish released':

Mr H. H. Beamish, who represented Hartley in Parliament prior to the 1939 general election, and who was arrested on June 10, 1940, by order of the Minister of Justice, Mr R. C. Tredgold, was released unconditionally on July 3.

> The government have agreed to supply him with furnished accommodation, a maintenance allowance and have or will return to him all papers and documents confiscated from him when he was arrested.
>
> The total period of his internment was three years and 23 days, a total of 1,118 days, of which 215 days were spent in Salisbury Prison.[105]

The 26 July 1943 issue of the *Rhodesian Herald* carried the following statement for the Department of Justice:

> The late Minister of Justice, Mr R. G. Tredgold, offered to release Mr Beamish in January, 1941, provided he undertook to reside on a particular farm and not engage in subversive activities, but these terms Mr Beamish refused to accept 'in view of the fact that numbers of friends of mine in England, Canada and elsewhere are still in prison and have been refused BOTH PAROLE AND RELEASE'.
>
> Mr Beamish's age and the subsequent progress of the war have influenced the Government to the view that his unconditional release is justified.[104, 106]

There were protests from Rhodesian and South African Jewish groups at the wartime release of such a notorious anti-Jewish activist. An editorial in the *Zionist Record* asked: 'Where is the justice, when men like Mosley and Beamish are released, while innocent victims of the Nazis remain in camps, and while hundreds of Jews remain in internment in Mauritius?' A question concerning the wisdom of his release was then raised in the Rhodesian Parliament. As reported in the *Rhodesia Herald* that August, it was answered by Beamish's long-term friend and supporter Captain H. Bertin, who, by then, had become the minister of justice. He is quoted as replying:

> I assume the man referred to is Mr. H. H. Beamish. His Commandant at No. 1 (General) Internment Camp for the best part of a year had opportunities to form an opinion on his political outlook and he says that Mr. Beamish is not, as far as he knows, an avowed supporter of the Nazis – and that is my view. Particular enquiry as to whether persons are supporters of Communism, Nazism or any other 'isms' with a view to emprisoning [*sic*] has not been made.

Whatever that statement was supposed to mean, it wasn't merely obfuscated and evasive, it was quite simply wrong. Beamish hadn't wavered one iota in his support for Hitler and for Nazism. He kept in contact with his fellow Nazis during and after his internment. Even while he was interned, his message of Jew-hatred had continued – via supporters – to reach a public. And his reputation wasn't allowed to fade. Thus, for example, on 11 December 1941, just four days after the Japanese bombing of Pearl Harbor, the American Nazi Elmer J. Garner brought out an issue of his weekly hate-sheet *Publicity*, featuring the text of

Beamish's talk 'Who Wants War?' The piece was the work of William Kullgren, the man with whom Beamish had stayed in 1935 during his time with the Bund in California. In his piece, Kullgren, described by the American German-Jewish journal *Aufbau* as 'a great admirer of Beamish', wrote: 'It took a Christian gentleman to present The Protocols to the English speaking world. It was Captain Henry H. Beamish who I had the honour of entertaining and associating with for a week when he lectured on the Pacific Coast.'

Despite seeing his internment as an 'oubliette' (secret dungeon) existence, Beamish was in fact a conspicuous figure. Not only had he become notorious worldwide for his Hitlerian politics, he had also been the only avowed fascist ever to be elected to the Southern Rhodesian legislature[107] and then the only British citizen to be interned in Southern Rhodesia.[108] Throughout this internment, he had been outraged by the fact that neither Tredgold nor Huggins was prepared to put into writing the charges against him. In truth, had they done so, he might well – like William Joyce – have been executed. It would seem, therefore, that Huggins in particular simply felt sorry for the aging bigot and wanted to protect him from such a fate.

The 8 June 1938 issue of the Southern Rhodesian *Parliamentary Report* offered a very different take on this. A piece concerning a Mr Cowrie, said at that time to be illegally detained in a lunatic asylum, read:

> Through H. H. Beamish he joined the anti-semitic movement. He stated that Mr. Huggins was a member and a strong supporter behind the scenes. He was three years in an asylum, where he was seen by Messrs. Macintyre and Keller (both M.P.s). Many of his friends are of the opinion that he was put into an asylum because he was a danger to the Prime Minister (Mr. Huggins) from a political point of view.

Quoting the above, on 19 February 1944 the *Social Crediter* suggested that Huggins had Cowie put in the asylum and Beamish interned simply to prevent either man from exposing him as a covert Jew-hater. However, that seems an extremely far-fetched conspiracy theory – and one further weakened by being based entirely on the word of an asylum inmate.

To the end, Beamish sought the public platform, remaining not just utterly committed to anti-Jewish campaigning but also unshaken in his faith in himself and his ability to speak persuasively on this issue. Thus, in a long letter to Maule Ramsay in 1947, he wrote:

> ARCAND:- The best news I have recently received is that his organisation known as the 'National Unity Party' intend taking what he calls a 'Hope ration' case against the kosher crowd who put him behind bars for over five years. If this case materialises it means PUBLICITY & this as you know is very urgently wanted. The Montreal GAZETTE has recently interviewed him & published three long articles which you should see. They are dated Feb 22nd,

23 & 24th. If this case comes off, and I was constantly mentioned, plus a bunch of photos, when the Jew M P Rose, really Rosenberg, got Arcand thrown in Prison, I will certainly give evidence & I am now anxiously awaiting details.[109]

Arcand, who was more than twenty-six years younger than Beamish, had put a brave face on his internment, despite suffering health problems throughout. Arrested on 30 May 1940 for 'plotting to overthrow the state', he had faced a trial on 19 June. During this hearing, evidence for the defence included a written message of support sent from Rhodesia by Beamish which was read out in court. In it was the statement: 'After Adolf Hitler, I regard Adrien Arcand as being above all other Nazi leaders I have had the opportunity to meet.'

Once again, evidence in court from Beamish did nothing to help the defendants. The verdict went against Arcand and the eleven others tried alongside him. All were found guilty as charged and were interned, and Arcand's National Unity Party was banned.[99]

Surrounded by sycophants in his internment camp, Arcand took to sitting on a throne which they had built for him and speaking of how he would rule Canada after Hitler had conquered it. In the post-war years, while fellow pro-Nazis worldwide faded from public view, Arcand twice ran for the Canadian House of Commons. Standing as a National Unity candidate in the 1949 federal election in the riding of Richelieu–Verchères, he came second, with 29 per cent of the vote. In 1953, as a Nationalist in Berthier–Maskinongé, he again came second, this time with 39 per cent. Until his death in 1967 he remained a totally committed Hitlerian.[110]

During his own internment, Beamish had written to Arcand and other interned Jew-hating friends, but all such outgoing mail had been stopped by the censor and returned to their senders. The contacts he maintained with his fellow internees around the world and with other Jew-haters were all through covert and unofficial channels. In 1946, however, Beamish and Arcand had resumed a warm and regular correspondence. There was even talk of Beamish crossing the Atlantic to join Arcand on an American tour. It never happened.

Beamish, now approaching his mid-seventies, was a burned-out wreck. His health was failing and he had only a year to live. He still corresponded worldwide with fellow fascists – including the French Canadian Dr Paul Émile Lalanne as always keen to build new networks. Meanwhile, Arcand kept up a similar, albeit more formal, correspondence with Arnold Leese.[99]

Beamish's resignation as president of The Britons in 1947 came very soon after his letter to Maule Ramsay. In quitting, he cited ill health as his reason, but he had also lost all faith in the society. His utter disillusionment was made clear in a letter he addressed to them on 17 January 1948:

> Being a realist, I have to face facts and the latter are that The Britons after being established for over twenty-five years for the one purpose of exposing the Jewish Menace, and which long ere this should have been the rallying centre of all Jew wise people throughout the world, is today practically a

derelict concern. To myself it is a complete tragedy and as you are unable to rebut what I have stated the moribund verdict must stand. En passant, the GID not only searched my house, but took away many sack loads of literature, little of which has been returned, while you state that The Britons office was not even searched and seem proud of it. Comment unnecessary.[2]

This was his last letter to them. Just two months later, on 27 March 1948, Henry Hamilton Beamish died suddenly at the age of seventy-five. He was buried in Salisbury.

Beamish left nothing to The Britons. Instead, part of his estate went to Arnold Leese. After paying succession duty, Leese received an inheritance of £3,350, which he used to help finance his journal *Gothic Ripples* and to subsidise The Britons.

The memoirs which Beamish wrote while in Salisbury Prison have never been published. If they were among the papers returned to him after his release from internment, they seem since to have been lost.

Main sources

Throughout: assorted early literature from The Britons (in the author's personal collection), also Wikipedia and similar internet resources to cross-reference, confirm, amend and embellish details. Documents marked with an asterisk are original copies in the private collection of the author.

1. Nick Toczek, Beamish family tree at ancestry.co.uk
2. Gisela C. Lebzelter (1978), *Political Anti-Semitism in England, 1918–1939*
3. Letter in the Beamish family collection, Churchill Archive Centre, University of Cambridge
4. Vickie Slogrove, Slogrove/Slowgrove family tree at ancestry.co.uk
5. www.historyofceylontea.com
6. International Ceylon Database at www.ceylondatabase.net/military.html
7. *Portsmouth Evening News*, 5 October 1901
8. Passenger list of the SS *Staffordshire*, sailing from Liverpool to Colombo, 14 November 1901
9. Henry Hamilton Beamish (1937), *South Africa's Kosher Press*
10. OCLC Worldcat
11. SS *Briton*, incoming British passenger list, 28 May 1910
12. *Report of the Industrial Commission*, Government of the Orange River Colony, 1904
13. *The Chemist & Druggist*, 27 May 1905
14. James Webb (1986), *The Occult Establishment*
15. J. A. Hobson (1900), *The South African War: Its Causes and Effects*
16. Arnold White (1901), *Efficiency and Empire*
17. *Aberdeen Journal* [Scotland], 26 November 1908
18. Harry Hurt, *The Origin and Early History of Parys*, www.parys.info/index.php/about/history-of-parys

19 Arthur G. Barlow (1952), *Almost in Confidence*
20 Panikos Panayi (2014), *Germans as Minorities during the First World War: A Global Comparative Perspective*
21 *Report of the Select Committee on Incendiarism* (a report on the May 1916 anti-German riots in South Africa, printed by order of the House of Assembly of the South African Parliament)
22 *The Western Australian*, 22 June 1915
23 C. C. Aronsfeld, 'The Britons Publishing Society', *Wiener Library Bulletin*, 20 (1966), 31–5; Panayi (2014), *Germans as Minorities during the First World War*
24 Philip Hoare (1997), *Oscar Wilde's Last Stand: Decadence, Conspiracy, and the Most Outrageous Trial of the Century*
25 Document in the Beamish family collection, Churchill Archive Centre, University of Cambridge
26 *The Press* [New Zealand], 19 April 1918
27 Francis Beckett (1999), *The Rebel who Lost his Cause: The Tragedy of John Beckett, MP*
28 Herefordshire Archives and Local Studies: Herefordshire newspapers list
29 John Simkin (1997), 'Harold S. Spencer', http://spartacus-educational.com/FWWspencerHS.htm
30 Barbara Stoney (2004), *Twentieth Century Maverick: The Life of Noel Pemberton Billing*
31 *Birmingham Gazette*, 4 June 1918; *Manchester Evening News*, 3 June 1918
32 Martin Pugh (2006), *Hurrah for the Blackshirts! Fascists and Fascism in Britain between the Wars*
33 *Jewish Socialist*, no. 16, Spring 1989
34 Duncan Heaton-Armstrong (2005), *The Six Month Kingdom: Albania 1914*
35 T. G. Otte (2014), *An Historian of Peace and War: The Diaries of Harold Temperley*
36 *The Times*, 22 June 1918
37 Gisela C. Lebzelter, 'Henry Hamilton Beamish and The Britons: Champions of Anti-Semitism', in *British Fascism* (1980), ed. Kenneth Lunn and Richard C. Thurlow
38 Copy of letter from Beamish to Clarke, 16 March 1919
39 Adam Hochschild (2011), *To End All Wars: A Story of Loyalty and Rebellion, 1914–1918*
40 Alfred Gollin (1964), *Milner: Proconsul in Politics*
41 Alex Grobman (2011), *License to Murder: The Enduring Threat of the Protocols of the Elders of Zion*
42 *The Times*, 25 July 1925
43 Statement of Claim of Plaintiff, Alfred Moritz Mond, 11 April 1919★
44 Defence of Henry Hamilton Beamish, 10 May 1919★
45 Stephanie Chasin (2008), *Citizens of Empire: Jews in the Service of the British Empire, 1906–1940*
46 *Aberdeen Journal* [Scotland], 6 December 1919
47 Colin Holmes (1979), *Anti-Semitism in British Society*

48 *Sheffield Evening Telegraph*, 23 February 1920
49 *Aberdeen Journal*, 9 March 1920
50 *British Guardian*, 5(7), July–August 1924
51 Yulia Egorova (2008), *Jews and India: Perceptions and Image*; Joan G. Roland (1998), *The Jewish Communities of India: Identity in a Colonial Era*
52 *Hidden Hand*, 2(9), October 1921★
53 SS *Tartar Prince*, List or Manifest of Alien Passengers for the United States of America, 29 September 1922
54 SS *Dominion Miller*, incoming passengers list no. 4, January 1923
55 Letter from William James Cameron, assistant editor of the *Dearborn Independent*, to Henry Hamilton Beamish (dated 31 March 1923, received 16 April 1923)
56 *Hidden Hand*, 4(1), March 1923★
57 *Hidden Hand*, 4(5), May 1923★
58 Alexander Baron (1995), *The Protocols of the Learned Elders of Zion: Organised Jewry's Deadliest Weapon*
59 *Hidden Hand*, 4(6, June 1923★
60 *Jewish Chronicle*, 25 May 1923★
61 *New York Times*, 6 August 1911
62 *Flight*, 18 October 1917
63 *Milwaukee Journal*, 15 May 1927
64 Passenger manifest for the *American Farmer*, sailing from London to New York, 1927
65 Henry Hamilton Beamish, http://memim.com/henry-hamilton-beamish.html
66 SS *Ceramic*, passenger manifest, 28 August 1926
67 Maj. Gen. Count Cherep-Spiridovich (1926), *The Secret Government or 'The Hidden Hand': The Unrevealed in History: 100 Historical 'Mysteries' Explained*★
68 *Kent & Sussex Courier*, 15 May 1931
69 *Hastings & St Leonards Observer*, 20 June 1931
70 *Sussex Express*, 17 July 1931
71 *Kent & Sussex Courier*, 20 November 1931
72 *Kent & Sussex Courier*, 27 November 1931
73 *The Fascist*, no. 29 (new series), October 1931
74 Richard Thurlow (1998), *Fascism in Britain*
75 SS *Umkuzi*, passenger manifest, 18 June 1932
76 Jewish Telegraphic Agency, at www.jta.org, assorted articles about the German-American Bund, 19 July 1934, 8 October 1939, etc.
77 *Grocott's Daily Mail*, 1 August 1934
78 David M. Scher (2004), Grey Shirts Trial, Raleigh Street Shul, Port Elizabeth, South Africa, at http://raleighstshul.blogspot.co.uk/2004/12/grey-shirts-trial.html
79 *Sunday Times* [Perth, Western Australia], 29 November 1925
80 Metapedia, *The Beacon Light*
81 John Roy Carlson (1943), *Under Cover: My Four Years in the Nazi Underworld of America*
82 Metapedia, *Herman Max Schwinn*

83 Full text of *Investigation of Un-American Propaganda Activities in the United States: Hearings before a Special Committee* ..., http://archive.org/stream/investigationofu193906unit/investigationofu193906unit-djvu.txt
84 John L. Spivak (1939), *Secret Armies: The New Techniques of Nazi Warfare*
85 *St Petersburg Times*, 14 November 1946
86 *Hoshi Shimbun*, 17 September 1936
87 Metapedia, List of nationalist conferences and meetings in America
88 Henry Trachtenberg, 'The Winnipeg Jewish Community and Politics: The Interwar Years, 1919–1939', *Historical and Scientific Society of Manitoba, Transactions*, Series 3, no. 35, 1978–9
89 Louis W. Bondy (1946), *Racketeers of Hatred*★
90 *Hidden Hand*, 2(4), May 1921★
91 Henry Hamilton Beamish (with H. M. Fraser) (1920), *The Jews' Who's Who: Israelite Finance – its Sinister Influence* [published anonymously]
92 *The Fascist*, no. 95, April 1937
93 Wikipedia, *Ulrich Fleischhaue*; Metapedia, *Ulrich Fleischhauer*; Metapedia, *World-Service*; *World-Service*, no.11/15, 1 August 1935★
94 Richard Alan Nelson (2009), *Propagandist Ulrich Fleischhauer Welt-Dienst/World-Service*, posting about planned research, at http://forum.axishistory.com
95 SS *American Banker*, List or Manifest of Alien Passengers for the United States of America, 14 October 1937
96 *Canadian Nationalist*, 2(1), January 1938★
97 Robert Edward Edmondson (c.1937), *The Greatest War in History Now On! International Jewish System Against National Patriotism*
98 Americanism Committee (1941) *Report No.1: Subversive Activities in America First Committee in California*, www.ajcarchives.org/AJC_DATA/Files/THR-AF12.PDF
99 Jean-François Nadeau (2011), *The Canadian Führer: The Life of Adrien Arcand*
100 American Jewish Committee, *The Anti-Jewish Propaganda Front*, no. 1, 1937, www.ajcarchives.org/AJC_DATA/Files/TH-1.PDF
101 Wikipedia, *Southern Rhodesian General Election, 1934*
102 Micheal Mac Donncha, 'Watching the Sunset', *An Phoblacht: Republican News*, 16 January 1997
103 Wikipedia, *Southern Rhodesian General Election, 1939*
104 *Justice in Rhodesia: part two* (c.1943) the Beamish correspondence★
105 *Rhodesia Herald*, 21 July 1943
106 *Rhodesia Herald*, 26 July 1943
107 L. H. Gann and Peter Duigan (1977) *The Rulers of German Africa, 1884–1914*
108 *Gloucestershire Echo*, 21 July 1943
109 Photocopy of undated letter (1947) from Henry Hamilton Beamish to Archibald Maule Ramsay
110 Wikipedia, *Adrien Arcand*

2

ARNOLD WHITE AND THE BRITISH BROTHERS LEAGUE

Jew-hatred as expressed by Beamish and The Britons was nothing new. It's had a long history.

Not as communities but individually and in family groups, Jews were very probably present in both Roman and Anglo-Saxon Britain. However, the earliest written records providing certain proof of resident British Jews date back to shortly after the Norman Conquest of 1066. Working mostly as moneylenders, these Jews settled mainly in eastern England, from London in the south to Newcastle in the north. Resentment of their financial power fermented a fast-growing antipathy which was further fuelled by a popular mythology that they worshipped the devil. This was soon embellished with a very widely believed fiction that during the Passover Festival of 1144, in an act of blood sacrifice, Jews had kidnapped and ritually murdered a gentile child. Throughout the 1170s and 1180s, this and similar fallacies proliferated, and prejudice spiralled.[1]

There is graphic evidence of widespread anti-Jewish sentiment throughout Western Europe during the latter part of the twelfth century. Anti-Muslim fervour whipped up during the Crusades (the third and last being in 1189–90) spilled over into hatred of non-Christians in general. And in England, France and Germany the prime recipients of this bigotry were Jews. Thus, for example, laws were passed preventing sexual relationships between Christian and 'Saracens or Jews'.[2] Attitudes in England became more entrenched after the death, in July 1189, of Henry II, dubbed 'the protector of the Jews'. Jews attending the coronation of his successor, Richard I, were violently attacked.[1] In the wake of this upsurge, anti-Jewish rioting broke out in London that same year and subsequently spread throughout the country. Several deaths and numerous injuries were recorded. Particularly violent outbreaks ensued in Norwich, Stamford and Lincoln. Worse was to come in York, where, on 16 March 1190, rioters forced the city's entire 150-strong Jewish community to take refuge in the wooden keep of the royal castle that stood where Clifford's

Tower now stands. A baying mob of citizens laid siege to the keep, and the terrified Jews opted for suicide rather than being murdered. The men killed their own wives and children before setting fire to the keep and perishing in the smoke and flames. These shocking events were well documented at the time. Detailed accounts can be found, for example, in the work of William of Newburgh and Roger of Howden, as well as in the Chronicles of the Abbey of Meaux in East Yorkshire.[3]

On 30 March 1218, English law ratified a papal edict that all Jews had to be identifiable by the wearing of a badge, a law reiterated and reinforced by the diocesan council of Oxford in 1222. Initially, wealthy Jews were able to pay in order to sidestep this legislation. However, in 1253 Henry III made the wearing of this 'Jewish badge' statutory. The law was clarified in 1275 in the 'Statutum de Judeismo', in which Edward I stipulated that the badge should be a piece of yellow taffeta six fingers long and three broad which was to be worn above the heart of every Jew over the age of seven.[2]

Coins at this time contained metal to their exact value. Coin-clippers made money by cutting bits out of coins. This practice, for which Jews primarily took the blame, became so widespread that it drastically reduced the value of the currency, and in 1275 coin-clipping was made a capital offence. In 1278, according to the Bury Chronicle, 'All Jews in England of whatever condition, age or sex, were unexpectedly seized ... and sent for imprisonment to various castles throughout England. While they were thus imprisoned, the innermost recesses of their houses were ransacked.' Around 680 people were detained in the Tower of London alone. More than 300 are believed to have been executed in 1279.[4]

A hundred years of frequent attacks on Jews in England ended in 1290, when, backed by overwhelming public support, Edward I issued an Edict of Expulsion. For the next 366 years, with the notable exception of a handful of wealthy Jewish merchants living covertly in London during the 1640s, there were no Jews in England. It was a period in which lasting Jewish stereotypes found their cultural roots, as exemplified by the portrayals of Jews in Christopher Marlowe's play *The Jew of Malta* (1590) and William Shakespeare's *The Merchant of Venice* (1596–8).[2]

In 1655, following an approach made to Oliver Cromwell by Menasseh Ben Israel, a rabbi and leader of the Dutch Jewish community, Jews were finally readmitted, and by 1690 there were around 400 resident in Britain. The 1753 Jewish Naturalisation Act, although it initially met with trenchant opposition, finally allowed Jews to become British citizens. Thereafter, Jewish communities grew and thrived. In 1868, Benjamin Disraeli, a baptised Christian of Jewish parentage, became prime minister. By 1882 there were 46,000 Jews living in England.[5]

Circumstances were about to change. The Russian Empire – stretching across most of Eastern Europe – was experiencing a savage upsurge in Jewish persecutions. In 1882 this resulted in the May Laws, passed by Emperor Alexander III, which 'temporarily' banned Jews from settling outside towns and boroughs. They also severely limited their property rights and banned them from conducting business on Sundays and Christian holidays. Pogroms and further restrictive laws followed.[6] As a direct consequence, there was a mass exodus of Russian, Austrian, Polish and other Jews from Eastern Europe, many of them leaving with little money and few possessions. While 1.9 million (80 per cent) of these dispossessed and uprooted people settled in America, and only around 140,000 (7 per cent) moved to Britain, this nevertheless meant that, by 1919, the Jewish population of England had risen to 250,000, the majority living in London, Manchester and Leeds.[7]

It was this influx which, in the opening years of the twentieth century, saw the establishment of the most notable precursor to The Britons. This was the intensely xenophobic and specifically anti-Jewish British Brothers League (BBL), with its campaign slogan 'England for the English'.

With no formal British passport controls, entry and settlement went virtually unrestricted and poorly recorded. According to the 1901 census report, London was home to the largest proportion of the nation's immigrant population, though this amounted only to 3 per cent of the total. Immigrants, however, were far from evenly distributed, with 40 per cent of them concentrated in the East London borough of Stepney. It is estimated that 80 per cent of the nation's Jewish population was then living in London. Elsewhere, only thirteen British towns and cities had foreign populations of more than 1 per cent. The highest proportion, 2.2 per cent, was in Manchester and Tynemouth, with significantly smaller percentages in Cardiff, South Shields, Leeds, Grimsby, Hull, Liverpool, Swansea and Bournemouth.

It was in the East End of London in December 1900 that Captain William Stanley Shaw founded the BBL. Shaw, who had served with the Middlesex Regiment, was a quiet man who played a strictly back-room role in the BBL. He did write one letter to the *Jewish Chronicle*, which appeared in its issue 8 November 1901, in which he stated that 'The return of the Jews to Palestine is one of the signs of our times.' However, it was left to Shaw's associate, the flamboyant Major Evans-Gordon, to be the voice of the BBL.

The organisation rose to prominence when it held its first large public meeting at the People's Palace in Mile End on Tuesday 14 January 1902. This demonstration, 'in favour of restricting the further immigration of destitute foreigners into this country', was reportedly attended by 4,000 people. They marched with drummers and a 'Britain for the British' banner through Hackney, which had a sizable Jewish community. The BBL was very specifically anti-Jewish. One local councillor, addressing the People's Palace audience that day, asked: 'Who is corrupting our morals? The Jews', and the audience shouted 'The Jews!' He continued: 'Who is destroying our Sundays? The Jews', which drew the same echoed response, to which he added: 'Shame on them. Wipe them out!' At the end of the gathering, the crowd poured out of the theatre shouting: 'Wipe them out!'[8]

The main poster for this event listed the featured speakers, several of whom were leading figures within the BBL. Those named were Major Gordon (who chaired the gathering), Arnold White, S. F. Ridley, H. S. Samuel, H. Robertson, N. Herman, A. T. Williams, Alderman Silver and D. Hope Kyd. Who were they?

Major Sir William Eden Evans-Gordon was a former Indian Army officer who had been elected Conservative MP for Stepney in 1900 after campaigning strongly against Eastern European immigration, particularly of Russian Jews, many of whom lived in his constituency. While working closely with the BBL, he was also serving as the chairman of the 1902 Royal Commission on Alien Immigration, a body he had been instrumental in establishing. Its report, much influenced by Evans-Gordon's own book *The Alien Immigrant* (1903), resulted in the Aliens Act of 1905. This Act gave government inspectors the power to exclude paupers unless they could prove that they were entering the country solely to avoid persecution or punishment on religious or political grounds or for an offence of a political nature. Although the Act was an ineffective one, its introduction effectively ended the BBL. Evans-Gordon sought re-election in 1906 under a slogan adapted from the BBL: 'England for the English and Major Gordon for Stepney'. He died in 1913, having quit politics after resigning from the Commons in 1907.

Samuel Forde Ridley, a British industrialist and prominent Conservative, was the MP for Bethnal Green South West. While speaking at this BBL meeting, Ridley made the vastly extravagant claim that 90,000 aliens had settled in Britain in the first nine months of 1901. Contrast this with the more realistic estimate of the historian V. D. Lipman, who reckoned that around 100,000 Russo-Jewish immigrants settled in Britain during the entire quarter-century from 1881 to 1905.

Sir Harry Simon Samuel, a former businessman who was Conservative MP for Limehouse, was particularly strident in his promotion of the BBL and its aims.[9]

However, as far as this book is concerned, Arnold Henry White (1 February 1848–5 February 1925), whom we encountered in Chapter 1, is the most interesting character among the speakers. White was an author, journalist and unsuccessful election candidate who married Helen Constance in 1879 and became a relentless and influential campaigner against East European Jewish immigration to Europe and the colonies. His book *The Problems of a Great City* (1886) focused on the East End of London, with its large immigrant Jewish population. That same year he had stood unsuccessfully as Liberal candidate for Mile End. After breaking with the Liberals, he failed again when standing as a Liberal Unionist in Tyneside in 1892, the year in which his book *The Destitute Alien in Great Britain: A Series of Papers dealing with the Subject of Foreign Pauper Immigration* was published.

In 1894 White again failed to get elected in Tyneside and had two books published. One was *The English Democracy: Its Promises and Perils*, the other was *The Modern Jew*. He then began campaigning fiercely against Jewish immigration from Russia. Because his campaign was against pauper migration, he even had some support from wealthy Jews who wanted a Jewish homeland and to see action taken to counter the problem of stateless poverty. So, for example, White travelled to Russia as an agent of the aged Jewish philanthropist Baron de Hirsch in an attempt to persuade the tsar's government to found a Jewish colony in Argentina.

In 1901 White published his most successful book, *Efficiency and Empire*, which, as we saw in Chapter 1, blamed Jews for a decline in British society and for the problems of empire, particularly the Boer War.[9] It was in the wake of this book's popularity that White became a leading light in the British Brothers League. At that People's Palace meeting he anticipated the conspiracy theory of *The Protocols* when he told the gathering that 'these great European financiers hold the fate of nations in the hollow of their hands and are unanimously against any country.'

White wrote an article for *The Sun* in August 1903 on the fraudster Whitaker Wright while the case was *sub judice*. It led to his being found guilty of contempt of court, for which he was sent to Brixton Prison.

In 1904 his *The Jewish Question: How to Solve it* was published. White again failed to get elected in the 1906 general election, when he stood as an independent for Londonderry North. The following year, under the pseudonym 'Vanoc', he became a regular columnist for the popular weekly magazine *The Referee*.[10] He sat on the executive council of the Navy League and on the council of the Eugenics Education Society and would become a member of The Britons.

In 1917 White published another book, *The Hidden Hand*, in which he claimed to have uncovered a plot to Germanise Britain. This book's title, popularly used as a euphemism for Jewish influence, would resurface as the title of the key journal of The Britons. In 1918, at a meeting in Cannon Street, White gave a speech supporting the assertion by Beamish and Fraser that the transfer of shares in the Mond Nickel Company to residents in Germany was unpatriotic.

In the post-war years, White's 'Vanoc' column, called 'Handbook', took on an increasingly vitriolic anti-Jewish tone. As a result, after *The Referee* was bought by Sir Robert Donald, his column was dropped, although it was later reinstated. His own version of events was laid out in a letter to the *Hidden Hand* dated 12 June 1922 and published in the July issue:

Sir,
I observe that you refer to my dismissal by the new owner of the Referee.

Not being an ox to be sold on the hoof and slaughtered at the port of disembarkation I did not apply for employment by Mr. Robert Donald: was not offered employment by him and was, therefore, never in his service so far as the *Referee* was concerned.

It is true that when the Arabs of Palestine were subordinated to the Zionist body and, in my judgement, unjustly treated, I wrote to that effect in the old *Referee*. Shortly afterwards I received a letter from the late Editor of which the following is an extract:

'I do wish you would refrain awhile from introducing the Jews into Handbook. Our publisher tells me they are very peevish about it and that ourselves suffer in consequence. I have reasons for believing he is right and I hope you will be able to humour me in the wish I have expressed.'

I have no grievance and no complaint but should be glad of employment as the late *Referee* was sold over my head and I was only informed by a pencilled note the day after the transaction was complete.

My sin is that I stand as ever for the principle of England for the English.

I am, Sir,
Your obedient Servant,
Arnold White[11]

White was a regular subscriber to the journals of The Britons, and in September 1924, five months before his death, he had another letter published in the *British Guardian*, expressing his support: 'I was indeed glad to receive the July-August number of *The British Guardian*: more especially I concur with you in thinking that the struggle is a spiritual struggle. I have never seen the case better presented than by you.'[12]

Other Conservative politicians shared White's enthusiasm for the BBL. A second poster for that 1902 meeting claimed that Major Evans-Gordon would be 'supported by Members of Parliament, County and Borough Councillors, Members of Boards of Guardians of all shades of politics, and Ministers of Religion of all Denominations'.[13] In fact, all their speakers appear to have been Conservatives. Thomas Herbert Robertson, for example, was Conservative MP for Hackney South, and David Hope Kyd, a barrister and prominent freemason, was also a Conservative Party politician. There was a second BBL meeting at the same venue on 2 November 1903, at which the keynote speaker was David John Morgan, Conservative MP for Walthamstow.

A keen supporter of the BBL was Joseph Banister, whose 217-page book *England under the Jews* first appeared around 1900; further editions were published in 1902 and 1907. Savagely and unremittingly Jew-obsessed, it seethed with an intensity of Jew-hatred matched only by the later outpourings of Joseph Goebbels and his ilk. In it, for example, Banister described all foreign Jews as 'thieves, sweaters, usurers, burglars, forgers, traitors, swindlers, blackmailers and perjurers'.[14] Banister went on to become an important founding member of The Britons and edited their journals the *Hidden Hand* and he *British Guardian* from 1920 until 1926. The Britons would sell his book and go on to publish two equally vitriolic Judeo-phobic pamphlets by him: the twelve-page pamphlet *Jews and the White Slave Trade or Lords of the Hells of Gomorrah* (1923) and the extravagantly entitled *Our Judeo-Irish Labour Party: How the Interests of the British Working Men are Misrepresented and Betrayed by Politicians who are Neither British nor Working Men* (1931).

BBL membership was free, so all that was required of those being invited to join it was that they sign up. It isn't surprising, therefore, that by mid-1903 the organisation was claiming membership of 45,000. It seems more likely, however, that membership peaked at around 12,000. Although new members were invited to make a donation, it appears that the BBL was funded primarily by Evans-Gordon himself.

The two People's Palace meetings and other smaller BBL gatherings throughout the East End were reported to have been rowdy affairs attracting many dock-workers and other disgruntled working people. Patriotic music coupled with rabble-rousing anti-Jewish and anti-immigrant speeches would prompt the now anthemic cry from the audience of 'Wipe them out!' Widespread support among East End pub landlords also helped to promote their grassroots popularity. Soon, local BBL activity consisted mostly of attacks on 'alien' businesses, gatherings, homes and individuals by small strong-arm gangs. Fifteen years later, the Vigilante Society prompted similar activity in the area. These two organisations provided the models for attacks of the same kind in the East End in the 1930s by members of Oswald Mosley's British Union of Fascists. In all probability, some of the families involved in anti-Jewish violence on behalf of both the BBL and the Vigilante Society subsequently provided a younger generation of strong-arm Mosleyites. Prejudices linger and are often passed down the generations, and, while BBL support faded after the passing of the 1905 Aliens Act and the Vigilante Society was equally short-lived, it is no coincidence that the East End was a Mosley power base.[15]

A tiny remnant of the BBL persisted until 1923. It was associated with the distributist movement of Hilaire Belloc and the Chestertons,[16] and at the outbreak of the Great War it received a donation of 10 shillings from Arthur Conan Doyle.[17] Prejudice thrives on the endorsement of writers and the authentication that the printed word lends to bigotry, as Beamish and co. well understood in establishing the publishing arm of The Britons from the outset.

The single literary thread that takes us from Victorian Britain through the BBL and the Great War to the heart of The Britons is that of Arnold White. He picked up the 'Jewish problem' in the 1880s and carried it through to the 1920s. He was a leading light of the BBL and the elder statesman of The Britons. It was his baton which was passed to both organisations, and how they ran with it!

When White died in 1925, he left a will in which he requested a simple wooden cross on his grave which should bear his name, date of death and the words 'for England'.

There is a comparable figure to White in the history of German Nazism. He was Dietrich Eckart, the man who translated Beamish's first speech in Germany, as detailed in Chapter 1. White was twenty-five years older than Beamish, and Eckart, the founding father of Nazism, was twenty-one years older than Hitler. Eckart (1868–1923) died leaving an unfinished manuscript, published posthumously as *Bolshevism from Moses to Lenin: A Dialogue between Adolf Hitler and Me*. He and Hitler were very close friends, and the booklet consists of his recollections of their early political conversations which led to the formation of the Nazi Party. As the title suggests, the two men discuss Jews in history, and the tone throughout is one of sheer disgust. Nor are they put off by any lack of evidence for a global Jewish plot of millennial duration. That is dealt with at the start of the text. Hitler opens their discussion: 'Yes!' he cried:

> We've been on the wrong track! Consider how an astronomer would handle a similar situation. Suppose he has been carefully observing the motion of a certain group of celestial bodies over a long period of time. Examining his records, he suddenly notices something amiss: 'Damn it' he says. 'Something's wrong here. Normally, these bodies would have to be situated differently relative to one another; not this way. So there must be a hidden force somewhere which is responsible for the deviation.' And, using his observations, he performs lengthy calculations and accurately computes the location of a planet which no eye has yet seen, but which is there all the same, as he has just proved. But

what does the historian do on the other hand? He explains an anomaly of the same type solely in terms of the conspicuous statesmen of the time. It never occurs to him that there might have been a hidden force which caused a certain turn of events. But it was there, nevertheless; it has been there since the beginning of history. You know what that force is: the Jew.[18]

There is the 'hidden hand' of prejudice. It's simple. You don't need to prove a thing against Jews. All you do is find an inexplicable political fault, or any fault for that matter, and the cause must be Jews.

This book is being written in 2014. In 2013 there were floods in Britain that left many homeless. One homophobic member of the frequently racist and generally xenophobic UK Independence Party seriously informed the media that the cause of all this flooding was the wrath of God resulting from Britain changing the law to allow gay marriage. It's the same logic, and for the convinced bigot it makes perfect sense.

Main sources

Throughout: Wikipedia and other internet sources to check and cross-check the biographical details of many of the individuals in this chapter. Documents marked with an asterisk are original copies in the private collection of the author.

1. Panikos Panayi (1996), 'Anti-Immigrant Violence in Nineteenth- and Twentieth-Century Britain', in Panikos Panayi (ed.), *Racial Violence in Britain in the Nineteenth and Twentieth Centuries*
2. Robert S. Wistrich (1992), *Anti-Semitism: The Longest Hatred*
3. The 1190 Massacre, www.historyofyork.org.uk
4. David B. Green, 'This day in Jewish history/All Jews of England arrested in "coin-clipping" scandal', *Haaretz*, 17 November 2013
5. Shira Schoenberg (2015), 'The Virtual Jewish World: United Kingdom', www.jewishvirtuallibrary.org
6. 'May Laws', www.jewishencyclopedia.com
7. Andrew Godley (2001), *Enterprise and Culture*
8. Martin Smith, 'London's Radical East End', *Socialist Worker*, no. 2206, 15 June 2010
9. Susanne Terwey, 'British Discourses on "the Jew" and "the Nation" 1899–1919', *Quest: Issues in Contemporary Jewish History*, no. 3, July 2012 [journal of Fondazione CDEC]
10. Arnold White (1911), *The Views of Vanoc: An Englishman's Outlook* (and, throughout this chapter, other titles by White)*
11. *Hidden Hand*, 3(6), July 1922*
12. *British Guardian*, 5(9), September 1924*
13. British Brothers League poster for the People's Palace meeting on 14 January 1902

14 Joseph Banister (1907), *England under the Jews*
15 Martin Pugh (2006), *'Hurrah for the Blackshirts!': Fascists and Fascism in Britain between the Wars*
16 Stephen Dorril (2006), *Blackshirt: Sir Oswald Mosley and British Fascism*
17 Robert Winder (2013), *Bloody Foreigners: The Story of Immigration to Britain*
18 Dietrich Eckart, *Bolshevism from Moses to Lenin: A Dialogue between Hitler and Me*, ed. and trans. William L. Pierce, 1966★

3

THE BRITONS

THE FIRST THREE DECADES, 1919–1949

The lengthy constitution of The Britons was drawn up by Henry Hamilton Beamish, and on 18 July 1919 fourteen 'Jew-wise' men gathered in London to realise his plans. The meeting, chaired by Dr John Henry Clarke, established a 'society to protect the birthright of Britons and eradicate Alien influences from our politics and industries'.[1] Beamish became its president, Clarke its vice-president and A. Toulmin Smith its honorary secretary.[2]

Although I have not been able to find a list of the fourteen founder members, it is reasonable to suggest that, together with Beamish, Clarke and Smith, the other eleven men present may have been George P. Mudge, Joseph Banister, Victor Marsden, Lord Sydenham of Coombe, H. S. Spencer, H. M. Fraser, A. E. N. Howard, A. H. Lane, R. T. Cooper, W. A. Peters and Arthur Kitson. Certainly these individuals, along with one woman, Bessie Pullen-Burry, were prominent early members of The Britons. Another early member who might have been in that founding group was F. D. Fowler.

The Britons held regular monthly meetings. These small semi-formal gatherings seldom attracted more than a few dozen individuals and were usually held either in the society's London offices (Evelyn House, 62 Oxford Road) or at the London home of a member.

An imprint was established, the Judaic Publishing Company, Ltd, based at 28 Milkwood Road in SE24. Operations commenced with a series of leaflets under the collective title of English Order. Published during the latter part of 1919 and the early months of 1920, each sheet carried an individual title. Among them were *The English Birthright*, *The Alien Peril*, *Pride of Race*, *What the Jews Say about Themselves*, *Is a Christian Civilisation Possible in a Nation Influenced by Jews?* and *Can a Jew be an Englishman?*

In February 1920 came the first edition of The Britons' monthly journal, *Jewry Über Alles*, printed and published by the Judaic Publishing Company. Most contributions were anonymous, as was the editorship. However, it is now known that Joseph Banister, whose name appeared against a long article serialised in two parts in March and April 1920, did most of the editorial work. These two issues carried advertising for the journal *Plain English* (H. S. Spencer was its assistant editor) and the latter issue also advertised a new pamphlet, *The Menace to the English Race and to the Traditions of Present-Day Immigration and Emigration*, written and published by G. P. Mudge.

During 1920, The Britons produced two anonymous four-page pamphlets, *The Code of the Jew*, and *Is the Jew to Enslave the World?*, as well as Dr J. H. Clarke's sixteen-page pamphlet *White Labour Versus Red, with a Synopsis of The Protocols* and, as we shall see, two books. *The Code of the Jew*, the first of a plethora of anti-Jewish pamphlets which The Britons would produce, followed the tone of their leaflets in outlining a particular way in which Jews were to be seen as the enemy. It was a four-page anonymous attack on Jews via the Talmud. Using carefully chosen sentences from this book, quoted out of context, it purported to prove that every Jew hated non-Jews, was hell-bent on destroying non-Jewish culture and killing all but their own, and was therefore the sworn and dedicated enemy of every non-Jew. On the final page there was even an attempt to prove that the Jews invented pogroms.[3]

The June journal carried a report on the previous month's meeting. This had been held at the Oxford Street office on Saturday 29 May. Vice-President J. H. Clarke 'spoke on The League of Nations, pointing out that the ideal of Universal Brotherhood was a noble ideal, but this could only be brought about by an internal change taking place in every individual. This was the Christian ideal of self-conquest, symbolised by the Christian Cross. The League of Nations was a purely external sham – it was a Jew counterfeit devised to make the attainment of the Christian ideal impossible'. The Britons thus dismissed internationalism as just another facet of the 'International Jewish plot', and yet they adopted it. This same issue carried on its correspondence page a letter both anti-Jewish and (for the first and last time) anti-German from the English Friends of Denmark League. There was also an advertisement for Urbain Gohier's Jew-hating journal *La Vieille France*, a column of news from around Europe, and a report from a Viennese paper about the anti-Jewish movement in Germany that included the darkly prophetic line 'In the press and in the meetings is proposed as the only way of restoring Germany *the extermination of the Jews*.' The italics were theirs.

This international perspective came naturally to The Britons. As we know, before founding the organisation, Beamish himself had spent more than quarter of a century abroad. Indeed, most of the founding and early members of The Britons were people with extensive overseas experience. Many had military backgrounds and had served throughout the empire. Bessie Pullen-Burry was one of the most-travelled women in Britain. Victor Marsden had witnessed the Russian Revolution first-hand, partly from the inside of a prison. When, in 1920, via the Judaic Publishing Company, they began producing literature, everyone involved was well aware of overseas markets in Europe, the empire and throughout the English-speaking world.

There was clear advantage to be gained from networking and exchanging literature with like-minded organisations outside Britain. Thus, from the outset, The Britons began compiling lists of overseas anti-Jewish organisations and sending them sample literature. Within months, regular international exchanges of stocks of publications were being established. They could broaden their own stock by offering overseas publications for sale alongside their own literature. Likewise, their titles could be made available worldwide. One of the first of many such reciprocal exchanges was rapidly established in the summer of 1920 with *La Vieille France*.

Very quickly after this, The Britons established firm links with German Jew-haters, especially with those within the ranks of the newly formed Nazi Party (the NSDAP, which had been founded in January 1919 and adopted a National Socialist programme in 1920), who were soon describing *Jewry Über Alles* as the 'most important unprejudiced journal in England, next to the Chestertons' *New Witness* and Leo Maxse's *National Review*'.

The July 1920 issue of *Jewry Über Alles* reported on another monthly meeting, on Monday 8 July, at which Clarke 'gave an address on "The Protocols of the Elders of Zion". He sketched the history of the document and analysed the contents of each of the 24 Protocols.' Beneath the heading 'The Jewish Peril', this same issue carried the news that 'Messrs. Eyre and Spottiswoode's edition of this amazing pamphlet having been sold out, another edition is in the press, and will be issued shortly by "The Britons".' Beneath was an advertisement for *The Jews' Who's Who: Israelite Finance – its Sinister Influence*, the directory of powerful Jews which Beamish had compiled with the assistance of Harry MacLeod Fraser. These two books were the crucial titles which Beamish believed put flesh on the bare bones of the Jew-hatred that so possessed him and his fellow Britons. For the next few decades, full-on Jew-obsessed literature would pour from the imprints of The Britons – more than from any other British press – but their flagship publication throughout would be *The Protocols*.

The Jews' Who's Who makes for remarkably dull reading. Really it's nothing more or less than a reference work for the Jew-fixated, providing them with a plethora of details they can use to stalk and victimise – a handbook for a British pogrom. It starts by listing British Jewish families believed to have adopted more English-sounding surnames, giving the original (Jewish) name alongside the current (Anglicised) one. Each is followed by the town or borough in which these families live. The clear intention is to enable to 'Jew-wise' to know who is or isn't Jewish and to seek out the 'hidden hand'. After this list comes general 'information' about Jews in the form of a series of short articles explaining why they are always aliens, that 'Jew' is a race not a religion, that the Jews' religion is money, that they control freemasonry, that they dominate the press, etc. There's then a list of British Jews holding titles followed by a chronological 'history' of Jews. The actual 'who's who' follows, listing influential Jews and giving their wealth, company directorships, posts held, etc. Finally, there's a list of quotes about Jews, together with a couple of pieces on Jewish involvement in Bolshevism.[4]

For the token sum of £30, The Britons purchased a set of printing plates and the publishing rights to *The Jewish Peril: Protocols of the Learned Elders of Zion* from

Eyre & Spottiswoode, who had been heavily criticised for publishing it, had no plans to reprint it, and were probably glad to be seen to get rid of it. The translation was anonymous, but it is now known to have been the work of George Shanks assisted by a Major Burdon.

Shanks's 95-page 1920 translation of the Sergei Nilus's *Protocols* consists first of an introduction by Nilus, in which he explains the supposed theft of the manuscript from a mysterious Judeo-masonic source. The manuscript itself is then presented as a continuous text containing a series of monologues given on different days by an unidentified Jewish religious leader. In these, the unnamed elder outlines the reasoning and the means through which global government by Jews for Jews will be conducted, imposed and maintained. This is to be harsh, dictatorial and brutal.[5]

Out of respect for their new-found German allies, the journal name *Jewry Über Alles* (a skit on their national anthem *Deutschland über alles*) was changed in September 1920 to the *Hidden Hand*. For the first time, too, the back page of the journal was almost completely taken up with the publications that The Britons had for sale. There was their brand new edition of *The Jewish Peril*. There was the *Jew's Who's Who*, now being sold as 'a vital practical commentary on The Protocols'. There was a subscription form for the *Hidden Hand* giving membership details for 'The Britons'. There were two Britons leaflets, *Is the Jew Enslaving the World?* and *The Conquering Jew*, each offered for sale in batches of a hundred. Also, setting the tone for how The Britons would work in future, there were publications from other presses – two from the Boswell Press: *England under the Heel of the Jew* (published anonymously, but by J. H. Clarke) and *Democracy or Shylocracy* by H. S. Spencer; *The Call of the Sword* by J. H. Clarke (first privately published in 1917 as *The Sword* under the pen-name Iatros, reissued later that year by the Financial News under its full title with the author named); and the journal *La Vieille France*. All were available directly from The Britons. They now had a fully fledged mail order book and magazine distribution business as well as a publishing house.

A letter in the October issue came from Kurt Kerlen, a German lecturer writing from Bavaria. After thanking The Britons for sending him 'back numbers of "The Hidden Hand" and other printed matter', he offered to send them 'regularly all the new literature of this country'. He then went on to outline his 'idea about the Jewish question', explaining that this was based on his personal catchphrase 'We must kill the Jew in our own heart before killing the Jew in our people.'

With Kerlen as their contact, both Beamish and The Britons would establish long-term links with German Jew-haters. Kerlen himself provides interesting proof of just how small and intimate the international world of extreme Jew-hatred really was. In 1923 the New York press Beckwith published *Boche and Bolshevik*, a book based on a series of articles that had appeared in the *Morning Post*. Its two authors were Nesta Webster and Kurt Kerlen. The story of this book begins in London on 26 and 27 April 1922, when H. A. Gwynne's *Morning Post* carried two articles by the British conspiracist historian Nesta Webster entitled 'Boche and Bolshevik', in which she examined the part Germany played in the Russian Revolution and accused the German government of collaborating with the Jews. On 10 and 11 June, the same paper carried Kurt Kerlen's response on behalf of Erich Ludendorff, the prominent German general and leading fascist who helped found Nazism. In it, Kerlen denied some of her allegations. A rebuttal by Webster appeared in the issues of 15 and 16 June. These six *Morning Post* articles form the core of the book *Boche and Bolshevik*, in which Kerlen is described as 'the mouthpiece of the Bavarian Hitlerites – the Fascisti of Germany'. The volume, however, was published not in Britain, but in the USA, by the Beckwith Company, and carried an addendum covering 'certain Bolshevik activities in America'. This addendum was written by the publisher and owner of the press, 'Peter Beckwith' – the pseudonym of Harris Ayres Houghton, who, as we shall see in Chapter 9, was responsible for the first American translation (by three expatriate Russians) of *The Protocols*, which he published in 1920 under the same Beckwith imprint and pseudonym.[6]

It was via Kerlen that, by the autumn of 1923, The Britons were selling their own edition of *The Gravediggers of Russia*. This notorious picture book had originally been published in Germany in 1921 by Dr Ernst Boepple's imprint, The German People's Publishing House. It consisted of thirty-two caricature cartoons by Otto von Kursell, each of a leading Russian Jew and purported to illustrate the different kinds of Jewish physiognomy. Each cartoon came with a short text written by Dietrich Eckart, and the book had an introduction written by Alfred Rosenberg. All four men – Boepple, von Kursell, Eckart and Rosenberg – would, in 1922, help found the Nazi Party and go on to become high-ranking party members. The Britons published this book in collaboration with Dr Boepple. He would be hanged on 15 December 1950 after being sentenced to death in a Polish court for the central role he played in the wartime extermination of Jews.[7, 8]

The December 1920 issue of the *Hidden Hand* advertises more books for sale, including Clarke's *White Labour versus Red* and a French-language edition of *Les Protocols*, which was a retranslation of the Shanks version produced by *La Vieille France*. There is also a notice announcing that an 'Aryan Associates' branch of The Britons is to be opened, enabling others to join who, though not British, 'are pure nationals of other branches of the Aryan family'. So ended the first year of the society – one in which, despite the early and abrupt expatriation of its founder and president, it very rapidly and successfully became established as the leading British fount of Jew-hatred.

In the April 1921 issue of the *Hidden Hand* is a note headed 'The "Dearborn Independent"', which reads: 'Henry Ford's paper can now be ordered from our office. The subscription is 12/6. It appears weekly and each number contains an article on "The International Jew", which is of the deepest interest to all who are anxious to see a clean and honest world.' This serialisation, based on *The Protocols*, was to plunge the American motor magnate into a controversy that would outlive him (see Chapter 9).

The Britons, meanwhile, not satisfied with just the Nilus Protocols, found four more: *4 Protocols of Zion* was a fifteen-page anonymous pamphlet which was published in 1921. The first of these protocols, said to date from 1489, was supposed to have been issued by Chemor, rabbi of Arles, in Provence. The second, previously published in the *Morning Post* on 6 September 1920, was dated 1860 and, we are told, was issued by Adolphe Crémieux, Grand Master of the French masonic lodges and founder of Alliance Israélite Universelle. The third, which had previously appeared in the 21 October 1920 issue of *La Vieille France*, was dated 1869, subtitled *The Fatal Discourse of Rabbi Reichhorn* and described as a Russian funeral oration. And the fourth and last, dated 1919, was supposedly found in the pocket of a dead Jew called Zunder who had been 'the Bolshevic Commander of the 11th Sharp-shooter Battalion'. Each urges all Jews to rise up against all non-Jews and take over the world.[9]

The May 1921 issue contained a notice concerning the Patriotic Fund, which was an appeal for financial support that had been launched at the start of the year. It read:

> When the Fund reaches £1,000 per annum we shall be able to recall our H. H. Beamish from exile. And when we have a substantial sum in hand we shall be able to contest any seat for Parliament at which a Jew is standing. The Britons have no party politics, but every Jew should be opposed *as a Jew*.

Here is a clear indication that The Britons, as originally conceived, was intended as a national political force. The draft constitution (see appendix 5) shows that a complete network of regional offices had been envisaged. That the organisation never expanded further than a single office (in London and, towards the end, in Devon) is a measure of its utter failure as a public body. Its sole success would be as a publisher and disseminator of predominantly anti-Jewish literature. However, that realisation would take time to dawn on the members, who pressed ahead with gatherings of the society.

In September 1921, the *Hidden Hand* carried an ecstatic review of a German-language book, *Die Un?schuld der Jenseitigen* (*The Innocence (?) of Those on the Other Side*), exclaiming: 'Every reader of the German language should have this book.' Depicting a future global war between Jews and Christians, this 246-page forerunner of Nazi Jew-hatred was published in 1921 in both Leipzig and Innsbruck by Garma Verlag. It was relentless in its utter loathing of Jews, describing them as a pestilence which needed to be rooted out and openly stating that the world would be better off if the Jews were killed. The book even bore a swastika.

On Monday 3 October 1921, in Caxton Hall, London, The Britons held their first large public meeting. It was well attended, although the hall wasn't full. Vice-President J. H. Clarke chaired the proceedings and gave the opening speech, in which he outlined the objects of the society before expanding on his opinion that there were 'two nations domiciled in this country, the Nation of Britons and the Nation of Jewry'. After that, he spoke about the absent Beamish. H. F. Wyatt then spoke for the motion, moving that

> This meeting of 'The Britons', viewing with intense alarm: the uniform betrayal of our country's welfare by the Coalition Government to the interests of Alien International Jewry; the appointment of Jews to high Administrative posts in the Home Government, in India, in Palestine and Southern Ireland, etc.; the reception at Downing Street of emissaries of the Jew tyrants and exterminators of Russia; and of the Jew leader of the murder gang in Ireland; the landing in this country of vast numbers of Jew aliens; the crushing weight of taxes, therefore determines 'To do all in its power to urge upon the Electorate to demand the overthrow of the present system of Alien-controlled Government; and to this end resolves further to extend the membership and propaganda of "The Britons" and to appeal for funds necessary for these purposes.'

A collection was then taken, and promises were made to pledge money to the Patriotic Fund before R.T. Cooper spoke seconding the motion. Lady Moore then spoke in further support of the motion, as did G. P. Mudge (briefly, because he had a train to catch). The resolution was then passed unanimously. After short closing speeches from H. M. Pimm, Mr Varnals and J. H. Clarke, the meeting ended with the singing of the national anthem.

During December 1921 and throughout the early months of 1922, the women's committee of The Britons organised and ran a series of fairly successful meetings which were addressed by popular speakers such as Lady Moore, Bessie Pullen-Burry and Brigadier General Prescott-Decie.

Meanwhile, in August 1922, the Judaic Publishing Company was renamed The Britons Publishing Company. Herein lay their only real future.

Under the heading 'Ku Klux Klan', the following piece appeared in the January 1923 issue of the *Hidden Hand*:

> This organisation [meaning the Klan] is now being very savagely attacked by the Jew-controlled press in this country. This is sufficient proof that it has high ideals, and is not in any way connected with Jew finance. Our readers will not be astonished at this Jew-press attack when we tell them that the Klan is fighting for (1) White supremacy; (2) No Jew control in politics, and, (3) elimination of corruption from public life. The membership is confined to white Protestant citizens who must be members of the Caucasian Race. Its membership already exceeds one million and we have reason to believe that within the last few days an important official arrived in London with a Mandate for Great Britain. With such splendid ideals it is to be hoped that the Klan will shortly get to work to eradicate the Jew menace from this country, which is as formidable here as it is in the U.S.A. With such ideals there is certainly ample and urgent scope for its activities throughout Europe.

The scale and influence of the Ku Klux Klan in America during the mid-1920s was extraordinary (see early in Chapter 9). Had it succeeded in achieving transatlantic influence, the future for The Britons and other Jew-hating organisations in Europe might have been very different.

Immediately below the Klan piece was another, headed 'Black Jews', which read:

> The impudence of Jews in pretending that they are a white race is graphically illustrated by two portraits of 'Falashas' or Abyssinian Jews in the *Jewish World* 21–12–22, which shows them to be as black as any negro. So are Jews in India, and of other countries. Black elements predominate in the blood of all Jews, of all shades of complexion.

Not satisfied with hating Jews for being Jewish, clearly The Britons wanted also to hate them for being black!

If the Klan in the USA offered hope for haters in Britain, in Europe there was the rise of German Nazism. Early in 1923, very soon after Beamish had been so well received when addressing the Nazis at the Krone Circus in Munich on 18 January, The Britons began to advertise in the Nazi and pro-Nazi German press. In particular, they took space in the *Völkischer Beobachter* and the *Deutsche Zeitung*, announcing themselves and their wares and calling for an Anti-Jewish 'union of all Nordic nations'.

By March 1923 The Britons – who had been selling issues of Henry Ford's *Dearborn Independent* since it had first started featuring anti-Jewish articles in 1921 – were also offering for sale all four volumes of Ford's *The International Jew*, in which these pieces were serialised (see Chapter 9). Meanwhile, European journals as far afield as Denmark and Poland were reviewing Beamish's *Jews' Who's Who* and other Britons publications.

The March 1923 issue of the *Hidden Hand* reported that, after three years at 62 Oxford Street, The Britons had moved 'to more commodious offices at 40 Great Ormond Street, W.C. 1, where they also had the use of a spacious hall for meetings.' With the move done, they issued a new four-page membership leaflet, bearing their motto 'Britain for Britons', which stated that 'Membership is confined solely to Britons, men and women over eighteen, who can prove that their parents and grandparents were of British blood.' Describing The Britons as 'A Society to protect the Birthright of Britons, and to eradicate Alien influences from our Politics and Industries', they listed their twelve objects:

1. To insist that in future Britain shall only be governed by citizens of British blood.
2. That only citizens who are born of parents and grandparents of British blood shall be permitted to vote or sit in Parliament.
3. That only those who are of British blood for at least two generations be permitted to sit on the Privy Council, and that all those who are not of British blood be forthwith removed.
4. That the present inadequate Naturalisation Laws be drastically amended.
5. That the Alien Immigration Laws be made more stringent, thus preventing our Country from being swamped with undesirable Aliens and cheap alien labour.

6   That all positions, civil, naval and military, be filled by Britons, i.e. citizens whose parents and grandparents were of British blood.
7   That our industries be protected against dumping.
8   That all Aliens who have changed their names during the 1914–18 war, be compelled to revert to their original names.
9   That all Merchants and Shopkeepers be compelled to display the Proprietor's name in a prominent position, and that all Companies and Firms publish the names of their Directors and Partners on all communications.
10 That all foreigners be registered and be required to carry an identity card.
11 That in view of the overcrowding of the British Isles, and the necessity of obtaining employment for our own people, every facility be given to remove the Jews to a country more suited than Britain to an Alien Race.
12 That the Act of Settlement of 1700 be restored.

And, on the opposite page, under the heading 'Restore the Act of Settlement of A.D. 1700', was the following text:

OUR GREATEST BIRTHRIGHT.
This Act permitted
'No person born out of the Kingdom of England,
Scotland or Ireland (although he be naturalised,
except such as are born of English parents),
shall be capable to be
OF THE PRIVY COUNCIL,
or
ANY OFFICE OR PLACE OF TRUST,
EITHER CIVIL OR MILITARY
or to have
ANY GRANT OF LANDS, TENEMENTS
OR HEREDITAMENTS
from the Crown or to himself or to any others in
trust for him.'
Three days after War broke out (August 7th, 1914), the
Asquith Government so repealed this Act as to place us
At the mercy of the Alien International Financier.

———

BRITONS!
YOUR ANCESTORS PROTECTED
THEIR BIRTHRIGHT.

REGAIN AND RETAIN YOUR OWN!

> For those completing the membership application there is the pledge:
> I Believe:-
>
> 1 In God in the Christian sense,
> 2 That Bolshevism is essentially anti-Christian,
> 3 That Bolshevism is Judaism,
> 4 That the Jew menace seeks to destroy civilisation,
> 5 That the Jews are a RACE and not a Religion,
>
> That our Country should be governed only by those who are of British blood.
> That the Privy Council should consist only of persons of British blood.
> That our present Immigration and Naturalisation Laws require to be drastically amended, and that the Act of Settlement should be restored.[11]

With The Britons now in new offices, offering a wider range of publications than ever and appearing, on the surface at least, set for even bigger things, Beamish returned, complete with optimistic plans to reinvigorate the whole operation. In reality, money was and always had been the problem. The constant appeal for funds attested to this. Just how bad things were was illustrated by the space that had recently been given in the *Hidden Hand* to celebrating the fact that Lord Cardross had made a 'very generous' donation towards the printing side of the society. What he gave was just £30. However, in the heady optimism that prevailed during the early months of 1923, these problems were ignored and, rather than tightening their belts, the members employed J. D. Dell as their full-time office manager. The plan was that he would reorganise the running of The Britons, sell more literature and bring in more donations. The reality resurfaced in the 'Special Notice To Our Readers' that appeared on the front page of the April 1923 issue of the *Hidden Hand*. It read:

> For your convenience we should like to point out that you can obtain current and back copies from our representatives and publicity agents The Holborn Trading and Distributing Company, 17, Dane Street, Holborn, W.C. 1 Phone – Chancery, 8362. Owing to a boycott you may have difficulty with your newsagent.

In other words, there were strong and effective public objections to their literature. They faced problems with circulation and sales. To make matters worse, they were now reduced to paying an outside company to do the work that their office had previously done. All this came despite having brand new premises and a brand new office manager. Not good! A further indication of just how bad circumstances were when Dell took over the office can be found in his letter to George Shanks (see Chapter 8). This reveals that the only thing that had kept The Britons going before his arrival had been a series of generous donations made by the society's vice-president, Dr Clarke. To make matters worse, these had now ceased.

The simple fact was that the society was actually a tiny organisation with very few active supporters. The evidence for this is to be found in the minute book of The Britons, which records that their meetings were attended by no more than fifty people and sometimes as few as thirty. Also, Special Branch obtained figures for the circulation figures of the *Hidden Hand* – just 150 copies of each issue.[10]

As described in Chapter 1, April 1923 saw Beamish occupied in angry postal exchanges – arguing with staff at two other anti-Jewish journals. First he rowed with those at *L'Action Française* after they had objected to the content of the 'advertisement' he had tried to place on behalf of The Britons. Second, he fell out with Leo Maxse, editor of the *National Review*, over the terminology and parameters of opposition to all things Jewish. Just when they needed to make more friends, here were The Britons losing influential ones. It's typical of the fractious Beamish that, instead of forging alliances, he was making enemies. Indeed, far from trying to smooth out his differences with these two anti-Jewish journals, he went public with the two disputes. He had both exchanges printed in full in the May 1923 issue of the *Hidden Hand* – and then republished the full Maxse–Beamish exchange in a specially issued Britons flyer.[12]

Although the return of Beamish helped to raise the public profile of The Britons, it also focused further hostile attention on their activities. The move from private to public meetings meant they could more easily be monitored, reported and countered. Understandably, it was the Jewish press, especially the influential *Jewish Guardian*, which devoted considerable space to their next public meeting at Hammersmith Town Hall, on 11 May, 'to discuss The Alien Menace' (see Chapter 1).

Smaller meetings – mostly attended by regular members – continued, with attendance peaking at almost sixty – so Dell was working hard! There were fifty-seven present at the 7 May gathering, forty-five at the one held on 4 June, fifty-three on 2 July, and thirty-eight on 12 July. But these four meetings together resulted in a total of just nine new members enrolled, less than £5 income from sales of literature, and less than £15 from collections.[10] The Britons had now been going for four years and were still anxiously counting heads and counting pennies.

The June 1923 issue of the *Hidden Hand* gives us further reason to doubt later claims by Beamish to have 'taught Hitler' during the early 1920s. There is a half-page report on a speech by Hitler to a large crowd of supporters in the Bavarian town of Murnau. Throughout this piece, which quotes his warmongering and Jew-hatred with relish, Hitler's name is spelt 'Adolph Hittler'. We know that Beamish was still in Britain and was therefore present when this issue was being prepared because it's the issue in which his Hammersmith speech is extensively quoted. Clearly, even if he had ever actually met Hitler, it hadn't been a memorable encounter. And he never taught the man. Beamish always strove for accuracy. He would have corrected this spelling if he'd known it was wrong. This article is the product of an editorial group who had heard of the man but had never even seen his name in print before.

In July, further extending their German links, The Britons published an English version of *The Grave Diggers of Russia* – the deeply anti-Jewish slice of Nazi propaganda originally published in November 1921 by Dr Ernst Boepple's Munich-based Deutscher Volksverlag. This English edition came complete with publicity for Boepple's publishing company and carried the original introduction by Alfred Rosenberg.

The issue of November 1923 carried the announcement that The Britons had replaced their George Shanks translation of *The Protocols* (which bore the full title *The Jewish Peril: Protocols of the Learned Elders of Zion* and had gone through five editions) with that by the late Victor Marsden. This is the version that would become the flagship publication in their catalogue for the next fifty years, running to eighty-five editions[13] and being translated (and pirated by other publishers) worldwide. To this day it remains the standard version.

Marsden's 75-page *Protocols of the Meetings of the earned Elders of Zion* (1923) is translated from the same text by Sergei Nilus (which is in the British Museum, deposited there on 10 August 1906). It begins with a partially similar introduction, although this one tries much harder to persuade the reader of the authenticity and pertinence of the text. The actual text itself is presented as twenty-four separate protocols, each headed by a brief summary of what that protocol entails. The actual content is very similar to the Shanks version, so both would appear to be direct and literal translations.[14]

The changes wrought to The Britons by the return of the imperious Beamish, coupled with ongoing financial problems and forceful Jewish-led opposition, brought internal friction. During November 1923 a total of ten members were excluded, further reducing their ranks.

The following month, three executive members – J. H. Clarke, R. T. Cooper and W. A. Peters – took charge of the former Judaic Publishing Company, now the Britons Publishing Company. On 15 December, the trio signed a badly worded memorandum which outlined the purpose of the publishing arm, as

> propagating views in regard to the Jews, the Christian Religion, the Government of the British Isles and the British Empire, and other matters which, in our opinion from time to time, it is in the interests of the British Public should be expressed and distributed and to do anything at all which, in our opinion, equips us for the purpose. The Society to be conducted not for the purpose of making a profit.[1]

The last issue (vol. 5, no. 4) of the *Hidden Hand* appeared in April 1924, as vol. 5, no. 4 appeared in May under the new title of the *British Guardian* (so named as a counterblast to the *Jewish Guardian*, first published in October 1919). Although none of the editorial staff is named in any issue, Joseph Banister remained the main editor.[15] A full page in the June issue was devoted to scolding their friends in the newly formed British Fascisti for failing to be fully aware of the threat posed by Jewish infiltration and for not prioritising opposition to Jews. The article stated that the majority of BF members 'who have been kind enough to call upon us from time to time' were anti-Jewish, and yet the BF itself still failed to 'refuse absolutely to admit any Jew'. A further column in the July–August *British Guardian* expanded on this theme in a belated attempt to mitigate any perceived criticism.

The September 1924 issue of the *British Guardian* carried a piece on the Loyalty League (LL). Although it later moved to another address, the LL began life based at the 40 Great Ormond Street address of The Britons, with George Mudge serving as both its honorary secretary and treasurer.[16] Financial problems were now really dogging The Britons. The whole back cover of the October issue of the *British Guardian* was given over to a piece which began:

> An appeal to those who appreciate the value of the work done by the publication of this Journal is made for financial support. The appeal is made with the greatest regret, but it is unfortunately necessary, for our previous appeal did not result in anything like a sufficient response.

At the start of 1925 the *British Guardian* became a weekly rather than monthly publication, with the price per issue reduced from 6d to 2d.

There had been no further mention of the British Fascisti since June. That The Britons had hoped for so much more from the first fascist party in the country was amply illustrated by a piece on 23 January 1925. Headed 'Mussolini's Critics', it begins: 'The howling, almost shrieking, in which the press has been indulging on the subject of Mussolini's government in Italy is positively disgusting' and ends:

> And what is it that Mussolini has been doing that has so disturbed our journalistic world? He is formulating legislation to suppress the power of Jewry and Jewish masonry in Italy, a power which he has discovered to be the one great danger to the people of his country. In doing this he is naturally coming up against a great deal of trouble, and has had to suppress a number of Jew owned and Jew inspired papers. This is the abominable outrage against 'constitutionalism' which Mussolini committed. Pity it is that we haven't got a Mussolini in this country to smash the power of Jewry and force the suppression of all the Jewish propaganda with which the columns of practically all our newspapers are daily taken up.

Despite their Italianate name, the British Fascisti were and would basically remain ultra-loyalist and just slightly to the right of diehard Conservatism. The real Jew haters who joined their ranks – among them Arnold Lees and William Joyce – wouldn't stay for long and would leave in bitter disgust.

The *British Guardian* of 20 March 1925 reported on a meeting held on Sunday 15 March:

> A group of people at Herne Hill, in the south of London, whose interest in our propaganda has been recently aroused, asked us if we would arrange for speakers to address a meeting which they would promote on the Jewish Question. This we were happy to do and a small but enthusiastic meeting was held.

Tellingly, this tiny event was the first reported meeting, public or private, involving The Britons since those welcoming Beamish back to Britain in the spring and early summer of 1923, almost two years earlier.

The cover of the issue dated 12 June 1925 was given over to a fulsome apology for it being five weeks since the previous issue:

> The difficulty has been, of course, solely a question of finance: simply we had not the money. It is a difficulty we must expect to have to face so long as the Jew is in undisturbed possession of the wealth of the world, which he has illegally and fraudulenty [sic] and by guile appropriated to himself. However, we are out again with this number, and through the generosity of a few friends – especially one very handsome donation – we can see our way to go on for a very considerable time.

Not so. There was one further edition on 19 June 1925, after which, without notice, the *British Guardian* ceased publication.

With the demise of its journal, and in the absence of funds, The Britons drifted into stasis. J. H. Clarke continued to run the society until his death in 1931, after which J. D. Dell ran it, holding the post of secretary until his retirement in 1949. However, in all that time there are records of only two further meetings. The first of these took place in February 1932 in order formally to separate the Britons Publishing Company from its parent organisation. The second was in 1948, shortly after Beamish died.[14]

A new Britons journal, *The Investigator*, was launched in 1936. It was edited by G. E. Thomas and had a swastika on the cover above the words 'for Crown and Country – Blood and Soil'.[17] Short-lived, this 'journal of Aryan defence' ceased publication in 1937.[7]

During 1939, as war approached, Dell wrote regularly to Hitler on behalf of The Britons. One of his letters, dated 5 June 1939, was published in the Militant Christian Patriot journal *Free Press*. Addressed to Herr Adolf Hitler, Berlin, it read:

Sir,

Your speech to ex-Servicemen on Sunday, as published in the London newspapers and broadcast by the British Broadcasting Corporation, fills me with doubts and fears because of the way you referred to the Great War.

For many years this Society has tried to convince people that the Great War was plotted by the Jews, for their own benefit, and that they were able to bring it about through their powerful influence in all countries. It would not appear from your speech that the Jews played any part in the matter at all.

It is fantastic to argue that Germany was the innocent victim before, during and after the War. She was the only country really prepared for war, and not only prepared, but eager for it. Young Germans were being taught the virtues of war, while young Britons were being inoculated with pacifist ideas. The rulers of Germany in 1914 were the principal tools of the Jews.

The only effect your speech can have upon your audience and your people is to fill them with hatred towards the British people and with thoughts of revenge upon this country.

I repeat what I have said in previous communications to you, that the issue of peace or war in Europe rests entirely with you, and if war comes it will constitute proof that you are taking the advice of someone who is an enemy in disguise, and the Jew will prevail after all.

Yours faithfully,
J. DELL.
40, Gt. Ormond Street, W.C.1.[18]

From September 1939 until the Battle of France in May 1940, though Britain was at war with Germany, there was little actual fighting. Churchill called this period the Twilight War; popularly it became known as the Phoney War; cleverly it became dubbed the Bore War. For British pro-Nazis, it was a time of true crisis. If it had ever really existed, the option of siding with Germany, of jointly waging a war against Russia, communism and Jewry, had gone.

Surprisingly few of the pre-war pro-Nazi activists in Britain actually moved to Germany. William Joyce (who became known as Lord Haw-Haw) chose to go, to broadcast from there, and was hanged as a traitor on 3 January 1946 by Albert Pierrepoint, who had hanged John Amery on 19 December 1945. Amery, the son of the MP Leo Amery (who was half-Jewish), lived in France until 1942, when he went to Germany and tried – not very successfully – to recruit British prisoners-of-war for the British Free Corps, a branch of the Waffen SS.

In pre-war Britain, the Anglo-German Fellowship, The Link and, above all, Maule Ramsay's exclusive Right Club had brought together many of those with power and influence who had hoped for a war against Jews rather than against Germany – or at least for Britain to step back and opt for neutrality. At street level there had been Oswald Mosley's British Union of Fascists (BUF).

There are many myths about what Churchill said, but one phrase that is truly his (recorded in cabinet minutes) is 'Collar the lot!' – that being his response when asked at the start of the Phoney War what should be done with Hitler's British supporters. By the end of the Phoney War the overtly pro-Hitler and anti-Jewish organisations in Britain were gone, and many of the individuals who had openly expressed their support had been interned without trial under Defence Regulation 18b. Most of the prime movers – among them Maule Ramsay, Mosley, John Beckett and, eventually, after months in hiding, Arnold Leese – were 'collared'. A few, among them A. K. Chesterton, Barry Domvile and J. F. C. Fuller, along with many of the well-connected, titled and aristocratic British Hitlerites, managed to remain free – probably only through the efforts of influential friends.[19]

The Britons occupied slightly safer ground in that they were fiercely patriotic. This didn't prevent the internment of their overtly pro-Nazi members – notably Beamish himself, of course, who was interned in Rhodesia. Generally, though, The Britons simply went quiet. They published no new books during the years

1939–49. Their short-lived pre-war journal *The Investigator*, with its swastika cover, simply ceased publication. (In his book *Blackshirt*, Stephen Dorril says that its editor, G. E. Thomas,[20] was interned; however, he seems to have confused him with the BUF internee E. J. Thomas).[21]

Throughout the war, The Britons offices at 40 Great Ormond Street continued to function under the guidance of its secretary, J. D. Dell. Remarkably, despite the fact that news was slowly filtering through of the atrocities being committed against European Jewry, The Britons were allowed to continue publishing *The Protocols*. Indeed, a reprint of 1,500 copies was produced in 1941 and another of 1,000 copies in 1943, so there must still have been a British market for the book.

In 1947, Anthony Gittens took on secretarial duties at The Britons, alongside the society's aging mainstay J. D. Dell (who retired two years later, his place being taken by A. F. X. Baron). However, for much of that year, Gittens was out of commission. He, Arnold Leese and several others were each serving most of a year-long prison sentence for the part they had collectively played in sheltering two Dutchmen, both former Nazis, who had escaped from a prison camp (see Chapter 6 for fuller details).

Gittens had long been a prominent pre-war activist in Arnold Leese's Imperial Fascist League. An early and fervent supporter of Hitler, he had been a Jew-finder in the old-school mould of Beamish and Leese. Here's a letter from him which was published in the Catholic journal *The Tablet* in September 1934:

Sir, – Your contributor, Sir George Shee, in his two interesting articles, makes several statements which cannot pass unchallenged.

He implies that, while Mussolini has denounced Freemasonry, Hitlerist Germany has ignored the subject altogether. Yet we find in Hitler's Mein Kampf frequent attacks on Freemasonry as a weapon of the international Jew for the enslavement of the Gentile. (See, among others, pages 345 and 703 of the 70th edition). Furthermore, early last year the German Government actually closed the Masonic Lodges and confiscated some 100 tons of books and papers. We read in Freimaurerie: die Weltmacht hinter den Kulissen, by Engelbert Huber, that on April 7, 1933, General Goring told the G.M.* of the German Lodge that 'In the National Socialist State of Fascist tendency there is no room for Freemasonry.' Certain Prussian Lodges were allowed to remain on condition that they discontinued the use of the words 'Freemasonry' and 'Lodge', severed all international connections, admitted only Germans, and abolished all secret ritual.

Hitler is in fact so anxious to expose the secrets and plots of Masonry that in Erlangen a Lodge has been turned into a 'National Socialist Freemasonic Museum', and is said to have been visited in twelve months by 50,000 Germans and 1,200 foreign tourists. The documents seized by the Nazi Police are even now being sifted for publication in a book appropriately entitled Extinguished Lights, for which an advertisement appears in the German daily paper Frankischer Tageszeitung. On the other hand, Mussolini, who undoubtedly closed the Italian Lodges in 1922, now seems to have 'ratted', for, in the August, 1930, issue of The Rosicrucian Digest, a Californian Masonic Magazine, we read: 'The recent decision on the part of Mussolini permitting Freemasons and Rosicrucians of Italy to hold Lodge sessions and to conduct their work again under a National Council composed of their own members and officers, will result in a rapid revival of the work in Italy.

The Duce's friendly attitude towards the Jews is not so strange as it may appear. Italy has relatively few Jews and practically no anti-Semitic feeling. The High Financial Jews undoubtedly helped the famous march on Rome. Mussolini's own private secretary, for many years, was a Jewess named Signora Saratti, and according to L'Encyclopedie of Mentone for July, 1932, she was associated with the three Jewish sisters of Venice called Tivoli. One of these is the wife of the influential journalist, Senator De La Torre, editor of Il Secolo, another was married to the head of the Commercial Bank of Milan, while the third is the wife of the great industrial magnate, Goldmann. All of these render considerable help to Mussolini's movement. Further, Stalin, the nominal leader of the Soviet, has granted special trading facilities to Mussolini, and among other things we find that the Black Sea traffic is under a monopoly given to the United Company of Italian Navigation directed by Signor Ucelli, of Trieste, a Jew formally called Vogel. Finally, one must challenge Sir George Shee to prove his statement that Hitler has driven thousands of Jews into concentration camps (or even into starvation or exile). Almost any fair-minded visitor to Germany will say that the Jews 'wax remarkably fat' in spite of the 'great persecution' and that the concentration camps are filled almost wholly with Aryans recovering from various forms of 'Red Fever'. The kind of Jews who have suffered from the Nazi terror' are men such as Magnus Hirschfield,** who systematically degraded marriage and the family. This Jew has unfortunately escaped (or been driven into friendless exile) from the 'fanatical' Hitler and is now devoting his attention to a little 'moral uplift' for the British.[22]

Notes: * *G.M. = Grand Master.*
** *Magnus Hirschfeld, a German-Jewish physician, was the first pioneer of homosexual and transgender rights. On 6 May 1933 the Nazis attacked and ransacked his office, burning most of his books and archives.*

There's a tantalisingly curious reference to The Britons in a long and rambling letter written by Beamish in 1947 to Archibald Maule Ramsay. In a brief aside, Beamish types: 'THE BRITONS   I hear that Dell handed over to John Beckett & Carroll & we will now see what we shall see but I don't expect to see much.'[23] If Beamish is correct here, the John Beckett to whom he refers is presumably the former leading Mosleyite, who by 1947 had become the general secretary of the Duke of Bedford's re-formed British People's Party, and Carroll would probably be C. E. Carroll, who, ten years earlier, had founded the Anglo-German Fellowship. Any such planned handover clearly came to nothing. However, had it succeeded, it might have seen The Britons moving in a very different direction, especially if Beckett's involvement had brought with it financial backing from the wealthy Duke of Bedford.

Beamish died on 27 March 1948 and was buried in Salisbury, Rhodesia. Less than three months later, on 22 June, the *Empire Windrush* docked at Tilbury carrying 492 new 'alien' settlers – but these weren't Jewish, they were Jamaican. The focus of British bigotry would soon change completely.

The first edition of a new weekly Britons journal, *Free Britain*, was issued on 25 March 1949. Priced at 1d, it was a single sheet of foolscap printed on both sides, its text typewritten and cheaply duplicated. Topical, anti-communist and anti-Jewish, it trotted out the predictable stuff in a very correct, but slightly flat and lacklustre style. In it we are told that *Free Britain* 'is to lead a resistance movement against the International Parliamentarians; to make it plain that wars and rumours of wars are in fact the blackmailing means by which the Independent Kingdoms of Northern Europe are to be robbed of their sovereignty.' Furthermore, *Free Britain* 'intends to show who are the blackmailers and why they are doing it; why our professional Democrats have caved in – and how much better the ordinary Briton can get along without their services.' The piece that follows lambasts American Jews and their pro-Jewish 'cronies', blaming Jews for the Russian Revolution and the two world wars. At the foot of the page is the slogan 'Bolshevism is Jewish' – all of which leaves little doubt as to the identity of the 'blackmailers'. Appealing for subscribers, the issue ends cryptically with the statement: 'Those in power will do nothing for Britain and it is useless to say what ought to be done until we have enough supporters to do it.'

Issue 2 carried the slogan 'Denounce the Collaborators' beside a circle with a cross in it, which could have been either the crossed hairs of a gunsight or a rounded swastika. The slogan in issue 3 was 'Choose the Path of Most Resistance'. However, it wasn't until issue 16 (17 July) that a range of printed merchandise was offered. Six books and pamphlets were listed as available, all of them about the Jews. They were Marsden's *Protocols*, G. F. Green's edition of *The International Jew*, Fry's *Waters Flowing Eastward*, a Britons' policy pamphlet entitled *The Twenty-Five Points for British Revival*, a booklet (by the Canadian Nazi Adrien Arcand) about the Jewish Question called *The Key to the Mystery*, and Dr A. Homer's *Bolshevism & Judaism*.

The first *Free Britain* feature on black people in Britain came in issue no. 35 (27 November) and offered a taste of attitudes to come. Under the heading 'The Colour Question Has Suddenly Burst On Britain', readers were told that

> Coloured people are ousting the whites not only from South East Asia but also from South East 8 with its colony of West Africans; North London with its 9,000 Jamaicans; Liverpool, Hull, Cardiff; and many places up and down the country where American Negro troops were stationed. Many white families are now being murdered in the genetic sense that the rising generation is not white and the coloured strain may never be bred out.

The piece went on to justify its concern by quoting at length from an American writer, Lothrop Stoddard, the widely read racial anthropologist, eugenicist and white supremacist.

In the final *Free Britain* of the decade (no. 39, 25 December 1949), seasonal greetings were offered to the following British organisations: the Anglo-Saxon Federation, the Birmingham Nationalist Club, the British League, the Gentile Christian Front, *Gothic Ripples*, the *Independent Nationalist*, the National Forum and the National Worker's (*sic*) Movement. Greetings were sent too to

> those working for the same Cause in Canada, Australia, New Zealand and South Africa; to those in Europe, seeking to re-establish Aryan ideas in their own counties; to the pioneers in the same fight in America – particularly *The National American*, *The Cross & the Flag*, *Women's Voice*, and the resurgent Clansmen with their Fiery Cross.

So, who were these new post-war associates of The Britons?

Let's begin with the British ones. The Anglo-Saxon Federation was the tiny and transient UK branch of the much larger Anglo-Saxon Federation of America, founded in 1933. It was British Israelite, believing that the lost tribe of Israel, God's chosen people, was not Jewish but British and Aryan. The Birmingham Nationalist Club had recently been founded by Colin Jordan, soon to join forces with The Britons and become one of their authors. The Gentile Christian Front (also known as the Gentile Action Front) was based in Walthamstow, East London, and was run by Fred Young, a former member of the British Union of Fascists. *Gothic Ripples* was Arnold Leese's post-war magazine, which, following his death in 1956, would be continued first by Anthony Gittens and The Britons and then by Colin Jordan. The *Independent Nationalist*, published from 56 Gloucester Road, New Barnet, Hertfordshire, was produced by G. F. Green, whose abridged version of Henry Ford's *International Jew* was sold by The Britons.[24] The National Forum, probably one of the many attempts to bring together British far-right extremists, appears to have gone otherwise unrecorded. The National Workers Movement had been founded in 1948 by Anthony Gittens, A. F. X. Baron and others loyal to Arnold Leese (using the name of a pre-war outfit run by Graham Seton Hutchison, who had died in 1946).

Of the American organisations, the Klan-linked, white supremacist and anti-Jewish journal *The Cross & the Flag* was run by prominent American racist Gerald L. K. Smith from 1942 until 1977 and claimed to have 25,000 subscribers. Smith was the leader of the Christian Nationalist Crusade of America. *Women's Voice*, which ran from 1941 until 1962, was a widely circulated Jew-obsessed nationalist magazine founded and edited in Chicago by Lyrl Clark Van Hyning, the national leader of the Mothers' Movement and one of the founders of We, the Mothers, Mobilize for America.[25] And, of course, all those 'Clansmen with their Fiery Cross' had almost a century's experience of white on black hatred to pass on to their transatlantic fellow haters in Britain.

102 The Britons: the first three decades, 1919–1949

Main sources

Throughout: a succession of Britons journals: a near-complete set of issues of *Jewry Über Alles*,* the *Hidden Hand*★ and the *British Guardian*★ and the first thirty-nine issues of *Free Britain*.★ Also Wikipedia and other internet sources to cross-check details. Documents marked with an asterisk are original copies in the private collection of the author.

1. Gisela C. Lebzelter (1980), 'Henry Hamilton Beamish and The Britons: Champions of Anti-Semitism', in *British Fascism*, ed. Kenneth Lunn and Richard C. Thurlow
2. H. H. Beamish (1919), The Constitution of The Britons (original part-handwritten, part-typed, part-printed draft copy drawn up by Beamish, alone or with others)★
3. Anonymous (1920), *The Code of the Jew*
4. H. H. Beamish (with H. M. Fraser) (1920), *The Jews' Who's Who: Israelite Finance – its Sinister Influence* [published anonymously]
5. Anonymous [George Shanks, with Major Burdon] (1920), *The Jewish Peril: Protocols of the Learned Elders of Zion*★
6. Nesta Webster and Kurt Kerlen (undated reprint of 1923 edition), *Boche and Bolshevik*
7. Philip Rees (1979), *Fascism in Britain: An Annotated Bibliography*
8. Otto von Kursell and Alfred Rosenberg (1923), *The Grave Diggers of Russia: Is the Jew to Enslave the World?*
9. Anonymous (1921), *4 Protocols of Zion*
10. Gisela C. Lebzelter (1978), *Political Anti-Semitism in England, 1918–1939*
11. The Britons four-page membership leaflet, 1923★
12. The Britons (1923), *Jew or German? Who is Responsible for the World Anarchy Prevailing To-day?* (full text of the exchange of letters between Beamish and Maxse)
13. *Candour*, 25(540, January 1974
14. Victor Marsden (1923), *Protocols of the Meetings of the Learned Elders of Zion* (form given on the title page)★
15. Richard Thurlow (1998), *Fascism in Britain*
16. Loyalty League (*c*.1923), *The Jewish Menace to Christian Civilisation*
17. Louis W. Bondy (1946), *Racketeers of Hatred*★
18. *Free Press*, no. 40, October 1939★
19. Steven Dorril (2006), *Blackshirt: Sir Oswald Mosley and British Fascism*
20. C. C. Aronsfeld, 'The Britons Publishing Society', *Wiener Library Bulletin*, 20 (1966), 31–5
21. Richard Thurlow (1998), *Fascism in Britain*
22. *The Tablet*, 164(4925), 29 September 1934
23. H. H. Beamish in a 1947 letter to Captain Archibald Maule Ramsay
24. G. F. Green (1949), *The International Jew*★
25. *Women's Voice*, 13(8), March 1955★

4
THE BRITONS PUBLISHING COMPANY THROUGHOUT THE 1950s

In post-war 1950s Britain, business was booming and needed cheap labour. The decade would usher in black and later Asian workers. By 1957, Prime Minister Harold Macmillan would be telling us that we'd never had it so good.

The first 1950s edition of *Free Britain* (no. 40, 1 January 1950) urged support for two general election candidates, both Conservatives – Captain Roy Farran in Dudley and Andrew Fontaine (*sic*) in Chorley. Neither man was an average Conservative.

Farran, a much-decorated but renegade wartime SAS hero, had become notorious for his recklessness and excessive violence. While serving in Palestine during the late 1940s, he again ignored frequent reprimands for his use of extreme measures against Jewish resistance fighters. After the much publicised disappearance of sixteen-year-old Alexander Rubowitz in May 1947, Farran was charged with his kidnap, torture and murder. Witnesses stated that he had personally killed the boy with a rock and then had his body disposed of by an Arab associate. Legal loopholes got him off the charge. However, one year later, a reprisal letter bomb was sent to his Staffordshire home. Roy Farran was away at the time, but when the delivery duly exploded it killed his younger brother, Rex.

Fountaine was a vociferous critic of Jews who had already made himself unwelcome in the Conservative Party. He was destined soon to quit the Tory ranks and go on to take a leading role in British racism throughout the 1960s and 1970s. After founding his own short-lived National Front Movement, he would join A. K. Chesterton's League of Empire Loyalists before leading the National Labour Party. He would then become president of John Bean's British National Party. This incarnation of the BNP became notorious for Spearhead, its uniformed Nazi section, with which Fountaine was directly associated, having provided the land on which it ran paramilitary exercises. In 1967 he would be a founder member of the National Front, and later he led his own splinter group, the National Front Constitutional Movement.

According to the piece in *Free Britain*, 'The country's greatest need at the moment is to get just one man into Parliament who will get up on every possible occasion and denounce Communism as a purely Jewish affair.' Sadly for The Britons, both men lost.

During the 1950s, *Free Britain* would become a platform for many leading pre-war pro-Nazi Jew-haters. The first of these, Barry Domvile, already in his seventies, became a regular contributor in 1950. His debut appearance, in issue 79 (1 October), was with a piece which set the tone for his future articles, featuring such phrases as 'scheming foreigners intent on destroying our independence', 'wild-cat adventurers bent on establishing the World Communist State' and 'would-be donors of the national blood to the alien blood-sucker'.

In the following week's issue, mention was made of another notorious pre-war figure, P. J. Ridout, who had been prominent in both the Imperial Fascist League and the Nordic League. He cropped up speaking alongside Anthony Gittens in a report on an 'Anti-Communist Meeting in London', which read: 'A successful meeting organised by the Tottenham Nationalists in conjunction with other Nationalist Groups was held in Trafalgar Square on Sunday 24th September and was addressed by Messrs. Graig, Gittens, Horton and Ridout.'

According to Colin Holmes,[1] The Britons purchased the Boswell Publishing Company during 1950, so acquiring their considerable backlist, including a number of books by Nesta Webster. Given the poor financial state of the society, it seems likely that some of the funding to make this purchase came from supporters such as Arnold Leese and, perhaps, Barry Domvile.

The slightly slow response of *Free Britain* to the growing issue of white–black race relations had a lot to do with the fact that many of its members were rooted in military and empire service overseas. There was a telling tone to the following piece from an issue in November 1950:

> In the treatment of the Coloured races in the White Man's World the choice to-day is between exploitation or segregation. The Racial Agitator inoculated the Coloured peoples with false aspirations whilst worsening their conditions and preaching revolt against 'White Imperialism' ... There will be neither slavery nor exploitation of the Negro in South Africa under Dr. Malan's policy of segregation.

So, for The Britons, while Jews and communists were viewed as scheming figures of hate, there was a take on black people which remained both paternal and patronising. It was all a question of administration. The old colonial view which still prevailed within the ranks of The Britons perceived black people as a broadly uneducated mass whose fate was naturally best determined by their white betters. For The Britons during the early 1950s, segregation of the kind practised in South Africa and the southern US states sufficed; hatred had yet to pass from Jew to black. That would come gradually, ushered in for The Britons by a younger and more street-wise man, Colin Jordan, whose work first appeared in the magazine in November 1950.

At the end of the 1950, however, Satan still supped with Jews and commies in the pages of *Free Britain*. Thus, in the 19 November issue, the two featured pieces were 'Jewish Megalomania' and Colin Jordan's parochial 'Sheffield and the Return of the Israelites', while the following week's issue carried A. Baron's feature 'Blood is Thicker Than Water', which envisaged Anglo-Saxon Europe and America united against Jewish communism. And it is to Mr Baron that our attention now turns.

Anthony Francis Xavier Baron (1913–1974) had become racially active as a supporter of Arnold Leese. It was here that he had first encountered Anthony Gittens, who had long been a Leese loyalist, having served as a key figure in the latter's pre-war Imperial Fascist League. Relationships between the two Anthonys had not been entirely cordial, but, in the small world of London Jew-hatred, they were pushed together. During the late 1940s, both Leese and Maule Ramsay had begun putting money into The Britons, and by the early 1950s the two had joined the growing ranks of pre-war pro-Nazis contributing featured articles to *Free Britain*.

In 1948, with the encouragement of Leese himself, Baron and Gittens, along with other Leese supporters in The Britons, set up an organisation called the National Workers Movement (NWM, also known as the National Workers Party). At its first meeting, a message from Leese was read out which urged them to forget former differences, avoid quarrelling and 'recollect that a "Jew wise" man or woman was a rare and precious phenomenon'. There were even plans to have *Free Britain* become the NWM journal.[2] In the meantime, J. D. Dell announced his retirement as secretary of The Britons, and Baron, who seemed full of enthusiasm, was given the post. From then onwards, relationships between Baron and other members of The Britons began to deteriorate. Tension grew especially between Baron and Gittens.

There's a cryptic note at the foot of the back page of the 14 January 1951 issue of *Free Britain*, which reads:

> After 2 years, Mr. A. F. X. Baron's nominal Presidency of The Britons Publishing Company has ended. It will be remembered that for a time he took over the Secretaryship from Mr J D Dell on his retirement after 25 years of devoted service to the Society. In future all communications should be addressed to the Hon. Secretary at the Society's offices, 40 Great Ormond Street, W.C. 1

This hid traumatic events within the ranks of The Britons. For more than three months there were no further issues of *Free Britain*. When the next issue did finally appear, dated 22 April 1951, the whole of the front page and much of the back were given over to a piece headed 'The Blow from Behind', which read as follows:

> In our last issue dated 14th January we reported the termination of Mr. A. F. X. Baron's Presidency and Membership of 'The Britons' and 'The Britons Publishing Society'. His subsequent behaviour which resulted in the

suspension of 'Free Britain' and many other activities against Communism, compel us to enlarge upon an incident we hoped had closed with his departure.

Shortly after Mr. Baron took over the Honorary Secretaryship of the Society from Mr. Dell when the latter retired in 1949, it became evident that he had neither the time nor the knowledge necessary for this vital work. As soon as other voluntary helpers able to keep the Offices open had been found, Mr. Baron relinquished the Secretaryship and assumed, with the consent of the Society's Executive, the Honorary title of 'President'. His only task was to 'vet' and be responsible for the publication of printed matter. As all such matter was written by experts – some with more than 20 years' experience – there was little risk attached to this simple job.

Unfortunately Mr. Baron seemed to imagine that the title of 'President' called for a general assumption of control, 'tightening of discipline' and 'issuing of orders' although 'The Britons' is a society of voluntary members. Working-men with many years devoted service to the Nationalist Cause found themselves 'sacked' by the President and forbidden entry to the Society's premises because they had objected to being 'ordered' to buy a weekly minimum of 30 copies of 'Free Britain'. Influential and generous donors the Society's funds began to receive unsolicited advice from the President on how to run their own affairs.

His fellow members tried to overlook these mistakes as due to youthful enthusiasm and lack of experience in the handling of men. In fact every tact and kindness was shown to him. Members gave him hospitality and generally tried to entertain him during his numerous week-end visits to London. It was always hoped he would settle down, make friends and finally show some of the organising talents which he and various members of his family felt he possessed. But he never sought advice from more experienced men than himself, and quite failed to take advantage of the numerous introductions to such which he freely received.

Matters came to a head last December when on being requested to pay the money due for his weekly supply of a 100 copies of 'Free Britain' taken since its commencement 2 years ago, he declared that if pressed for payment he would counter-claim for expenses in promoting sales, travelling to London, buying snacks etc. He further proclaimed his intention of closing down the Society in London and running 'the business from my home here in Framlingham'. The Society's Executive immediately met, relieved him of his office and terminated his membership. There we had hoped the matter was ended. We were mistaken. Within a week, the Jews and Reds got the best surprise of their lives. For the first time in 33 years, 'The Britons' (the oldest anti-Communist Society in Europe and the Empire) and 'The Britons Publishing Society' (the 6th oldest publishing house in the country) was closed, its Officers and Members locked out and the 30 year old tenancy of its premises in Great Ormond Street illegally terminated.

The Society was thus forced to take action in the High Courts against Mr. Baron in order to regain the tenancy of its premises and the return of books, records and correspondence. These legal proceedings lasted nearly 2 months and an Agent of the Landlords had to be subpoenaed as witness for the Society before a successful result was obtained and the keys finally handed over.

Apart from all the other considerations, Mr. Baron's political views were causing the Society grave uneasiness. At a time when Nationalist speakers in London were waging a courageous battle against the Jews, the Reds and the Razor Gangsters, he chose to send written 'Orders' to the Secretary of 'The Britons':- 'I would stress upon you most urgently that any meeting in the London area must be conducted in a purely political manner – dealing with Western Union and the Dollar situation only. The Jews must not be mentioned except in as far as it may help to drive home the ruinous nature of Western Union'. Later he practically forbade the co-operation which has always existed between 'The Britons' and kindred Patriotic Societies and Groups. 'All relations,' he wrote, 'of these Groups with the "Britons" should only be on business lines' and the office staff were forbidden to 'take any part whatsoever in any sort of political activity connected with any other parties or groups.'

Later in that same issue was the added information that, on 22 January 1951, Baron had changed the locks on the doors of the Britons Publishing Society offices at 40 Great Ormond Street, closing it down for two months.

The accuracy of the above account and the malign role played by Baron is backed up by a very similar account given in the March 1951 issue of *Gothic Ripples* by Arnold Leese. It seems that Baron did in fact take over the running of The Britons for at least a year and that the NWM was his abortive attempt to create a political wing of the society. This second account also illustrates the extent of Leese's own involvement in The Britons, which he clearly viewed as a complementary organisation to his own Anti-Jewish Information Bureau and one for which he – as the prime benefactor of Beamish's will – felt he had a duty of direct responsibility. With reference to Baron, Leese writes:

> In 1948 we introduced to our readers the name of a Mr A. F. X. Baron as desirous of attempting to take the lead in the stupendous and dangerous task of delivering Britain from Jew control.
>
> He has been a complete failure and the 'movement' never even was born. He proved temperamentally unfitted for this job for a superman.
>
> Mr. Baron also arranged to take over from Mr. Dell the secretaryship of The Britons Publishing Society, 40 Great Ormond Street, London, W.C.1, as the latter wished to retire to South Africa after 25 years service to the Cause. Of course, no political movement could be started at The Britons' offices as the terms of the lease prohibited it, and the premises had to be closed to visitors arriving later than 5 p.m.

> The Britons Society was the work of the late H. H. Beamish and his friends, and exists to do similar work to that of Leese's Bureau of Anti-Jewish Information. The latter gave Baron considerable financial assistance in maintaining voluntary helpers and guaranteeing the rent for one year, actually paying it for nine months. Mr. Leese has had nothing to do with the management of The Britons, and is not a member but has worked with them on a friendly footing for about 25 years.
>
> But Mr. Baron wasn't even a success in this easy post, and, without authority for the Society's Executive (some of whom were founder members), announced that he was going to close the premises and remove The Britons' property to his home-town in Suffolk. He was promptly relieved of his post by The Britons. He then, handed the Jews a gift after their own hearts by closing the premises and giving the landlords 3 months' notice!
>
> Willing anti-Jewish workers had to see these premises, which have been used for nearly thirty years for their Cause, completely idle for two months, whilst legal measures were taken against Baron, to deliver up the keys and property, to say nothing of the correspondence.
>
> Apart from a few minor matters awaiting settlement, we understand that The Britons have won their case and the office is now in full swing again.

Precisely what Baron was trying to achieve in steering The Britons away from open Jew-hatred is difficult to follow. His activities before and after this affair show him to have been unremittingly anti-Jewish, so it seems that his behaviour was simply that of a loner who found team work problematic. Certainly, his fall out with Gittens and co. was only one of several occasions when he alienated co-workers.

Following the legal action that returned The Britons and its premises to Gittens and co., Baron moved on and joined forces with Peter Huxley-Blythe, who had become disillusioned after having been active on the fringes of Oswald Mosley's post-war Union Movement.[3] The two men had been involved with a short-lived (1949–54) post-war fascist group called the European Liberation Front, which had been founded by Francis Parker Yockey (also known as Ulick Varange) and consisted primarily of former Mosleyites. In the early 1950s Baron and Huxley-Blythe founded the Nationalist Information Bureau (also known as NATINFORM), with the ever ambitious Baron at its head. NATINFORM was predictably opposed to Mosley's Europeanism (Huxley-Blythe being jaded and Baron being from Leese's camp), but it was equally damning of The Britons' Catholic Jew-hatred.[4]

Not even Leese had been able to quell the lingering bitterness between Baron and Gittens: whatever he had hoped for from the nascent NWM came to nothing. It managed to convene a handful of meetings and achieve a membership of about three dozen Leese loyalists, most of whom were also associated with The Britons. However, before the end of spring 1951, it was finished.[2]

That Baron made few friends was apparent from another mention of him. A brief note under the heading 'Colleagues' in the 12 March 1953 issue of Leese's journal *Gothic Ripples* read: 'Mr. Hilary Cotter wishes us to announce that he severed all association with Mr. A. F. X. Baron of Framlingham, Suffolk, in April, 1952, and that prior to that held no post or status in the 'Nationalist Information Bureau [NATINFORM]'.[5] Cotter was co-author (with R. De Roiste) of the 1951 book *World Dictatorship by 1955? Why Forrestal Threw Himself out of the Window*. This piece of heavily anti-Jewish American conspiracy theory had been published by the Nationalist Information Bureau from Baron's home address (7 Pageant Place, Framlingham, Suffolk) and distributed by The Britons. They continued to distribute the book after Baron's expulsion, but with Britons stickers covering the NATINFORM publishing details and with masking tape concealing further details on the inside back cover.[6]

Late spring 1951 saw The Britons resume activity. Their president was now Richard T. Cooper (the cartoonist 'Goy'), the post of honorary secretary had been taken by Gittens himself, assisted by Mrs J. Collis-Bird, and the honorary treasurer was the veteran activist H. T. Mills.[7]

Blink and you'll miss it, but Herbert T. Mills (who sometimes used the alias Miller) was yet another pre-war Jew-hating pro-Nazi. Ill-remembered because he led no groups, he had arguably been more immersed in that whole arena than anyone else. He had been an active force alongside Gittens in the inner circle of Leese's Imperial Fascist League, was a key member of Domvile's The Link and was a member Maule Ramsay's Nordic League and of his Right Club. He was also a leading member of the People's Campaign against War and Usury and a regular contributor to the *New Pioneer*.[8] Additionally, as a Nazi enthusiast he played a prominent role in the group of extremists (Maule Ramsay, Domvile, Lymington, J. F. C. Fuller, Lane-Fox Pitt-Rivers, Lady Pearson, Francis Hawkins and others) who held covert meetings in the last three months of 1939 and the first three months of 1940. He was interned for more than three years (May 1940 – June 1943) during the war[1] and was active in A. K. Chesterton's attempt to reunite extremists in the National Front After Victory. They didn't come much more committed than that!

The 13 May 1951 issue of *Free Britain* carried the announcement that the British Empire Party (BEP) was holding regular open-air meetings in London on Sundays at 11.45 a.m. at Hereford Street, Bethnal Green, and at 7.30 p.m. at West Green Road, Tottenham. Further promotion of the BEP and its activities followed in subsequent issues.

Founded by Britons member P. J. Ridout, the BEP was run from The Britons' address with their proactive support. It also received direct financial support from Arnold Leese, Ridout having been another prominent member of his Imperial Fascist League. There's an acknowledgement of a £50 donation from Leese in issue 2 (1 September 1951) of their journal *Bridgehead*, which also carries a piece on the BEP's first Trafalgar Square Rally. Held on Sunday 5 August, it claimed an attendance of 2,000. Speakers E. B. Horton, Trefor David, H. T. Mills, Duke Pile and Fred Coxall were reported to have given talks 'exposing the menace of communism and its Jewish origins'. *Bridgehead*, a monthly edited by Edwin (E. B.) Horton, ran for at least seven issues, with contributions from Horton, Ridout, Leese, Gittens and Domvile.[9]

The presence of Bertram 'Duke' Pile as a speaker at that first BEP rally shouldn't pass unnoticed. Pile, a prominent pre-war fascist, had been active in the National Fascisti before joining the Limehouse branch of the BUF. In 1940 he had been interned under Defence Regulation 18b.[10] In the late 1940s he resumed his fascist activities and was arrested several times, notably after a speech at an open-air meeting in Hereford Street, Bethnal Green, on 20 January 1947, in which he'd urged his audience to burn the synagogues.[11] In March 1950, he and a fellow anti-Jewish activist, John Cook, were put on trial for exploding a smoke bomb in a cinema which was showing *Sword in the Desert*, a film about the Jewish–British conflict in Palestine.[12]

The BEP was a replacement for the abortive Nationalist Workers Movement. Both organisations, instigated by Leese, can be seen as offshoots of The Britons, primarily as vehicles for election candidates. The Britons, being opposed to the party system, didn't field candidates. Both parties were also founded to offer the ailing Leese one last lease of political life. And the BEP did actually field a candidate. He was Trefor David, a former Welsh miner who stood in his local district of Ogmore in the general election of 25 October 1951. Almost the whole of the 30 September issue of *Free Britain* was given over to a detailed profile of David, urging readers to support him. Standing under the slogan 'My Country First – Down With Communism', he gleaned a lot of local support among the mining community, only to lose most of it after local press coverage revealed Ridout's fascist past. In the end, David gained only 1,643 votes (3.5 per cent).

The local press wasn't wrong. On his election leaflet, David had reduced his party's principles to just five seemingly innocuous clauses, and the leaflet even included the line 'I am not Anti-Semitic Still a Christian'.[13] This sounds too moderate to be a Britons spin-off. What the BEP truly stood for is to be found in its twenty-point list of beliefs (none of the following appeared on David's election leaflet). Point 4 read: 'Preservation of our Race and National Character'; 5 read: 'The National Press being in the hands of Britons, and Facts as distinct from Opinions being kept distinct features'; 13 read: 'Stopping all name-changing. All aliens who have changed their names since 1914 to revert to their original names'; 16 read: 'No position of trust or national importance in government, councils or Forces being in the hands of aliens'; 17 read: 'Far greater safeguards being exercised regarding immigration'; 18 read: 'Jewish bolshevism (Communism) being outlawed to ensure the happy continuance of our Christian way of life'; 19 read: 'Recognising the Jew as a nation, and doing all in our power to see them accommodated in a land of their own which can hold them and give them security from persecution, while we are left free to conduct our affair and cultivate our arts in a manner suited to our own race.'[14] Those are more in keeping with The Britons!

A more graphic insight into what Trefor David actually believed is provided by his book *The Bloody Red Streak*, which was published by The Britons in 1951. This is a relentless diatribe against Jews, whom David sees as the evil force behind communism and the left in general. In the front of the book he boasts of having been convicted '7 times for exposing corrupt practices in Local Government', adding that these included a sentence of one year's hard labour in 1938. In all, he had served time in Swansea, Cardiff, Brixton and Birmingham prisons.[15]

A post-election report on the Ogmore campaign that appeared in *Bridgehead* informed readers that 'Trefor David was assisted on his election platform on various occasions by P. J. Ridout, Colin Jordan and E. B. Horton.' It added that he had ended his election-day speech with the words: 'Surely it is the first time in history electors have heard of Jewish ritual murder from the platform!!! Or heard rehearsed the Freemasons' oaths!!!'[9]

For The Britons, links with America were all-important. Not only was there a vast network of like-minded groups and individuals out there, but there was also money to be made. The printing and publishing company sold most of its books, pamphlets and journals overseas. Some went to Europe, the Commonwealth and former colonies, but far more went to America.[16] And bulk quantities of American literature were imported for resale. It mustn't be forgotten that The Britons, such was their influence and importance throughout their half-century of activity, supplied and sustained the worldwide white racist community with its fundamental justifying literature. So even a brand new outfit such as the BEM, hatching as it did from The Britons' nest, immediately inherited these links.

Thus, although *Bridgehead* ran for just seven monthly issues, it offered, alongside copies of Trefor David's *The Bloody Red Streak*, books by Leese, Domvile and Denis Fahey, plus of course *The Protocols* and C. F. Green's *The International Jew*. There were also detailed advertisements for two leading American hate journals – Gerald L. K. Smith's Klan-linked, *The Cross and the Flag* and the communism-is-Jewish *Common Sense*. Finally, there was also a telling sign of transatlantic influence in a plug for Clan-Briton. This tiny Anglicised Klan group was run from his home at 6 Riversleigh Avenue, Lytham, Lancashire, by L. M. Tomlinson, who produced pamphlets and a newsletter. Using the symbol of a cross superimposed on a Union Jack, the group described itself as a 'Family of Britons which believes in "Britain First"'.

In mid-March 1951, the Reverend Fielding Clarke, vicar of Crockham Hill, Edenbridge, Kent, received a letter dated 14 March and headed Clan-Briton. Addressed from 'Secretarial Offices: 220 Ellerdine Road, Hounslow, Middlesex', it came from 'General Secretary: L. M. Tomlinson, M.C.', whose Lytham address was given as Clan-Briton's 'County Branch Office'. The letter, in response to the vicar having recently petitioned Parliament through Sydney Silverman, the left-wing (Jewish) MP for Nelson and Colne in Lancashire, read:

Sir,

I note with the most intense interest that you chose Mr. Sydney Silverman, M.P., to raise the question of privilege in the House of Commons, and wonder what particular qualification the distinguished politician has to cause him to be elected as the spokesman for a professional Minister of the Christian Church, indeed, the English Church. When you made your choice of advocate, you would without the slightest doubt be aware that Mr. Silverman is NOT A CHRISTIAN, NOT A BRITON, AND CERTAINLY NOT A PATRIOTIC BRITISH

SUBJECT INTERESTED IN THE CHURCH OF ENGLAND, NOR ITS MINISTERS.

You apparently considered that Mr. Silverman possessed qualities superior to those of other eminent Sons of Britain, Messrs. Shin-well, Strauss, Mikardo, Stross, Zilliacus, etc., etc., who have all, of course? fought at times with gallantry and valour on the side of this Christian Britain of ours but at the same time avoided getting on to any field of battle in the cause of which they should be so devoted, the cause of the Land which has given them sanctuary and protection from those who would oppress them. You are certainly deserving of great praise for your lack of prejudice regarding the creed and breed of your protector.

Yours in wonderment,
L. N. Tomlinson

An accompanying Clan-Briton leaflet included the paragraph:

> Today our public life is impregnated with the breeders of greed, jealousy, corruption and self gratification, who are too often non-Christians, of alien blood, interested only very superficially indeed in the well being of Britain and Britons. Their loyalties are to themselves alone and the parasite occupations which find them wealth at the expense of the British people who gave them sanctuary.[17]

Leonard Tomlinson, a 57-year-old former major in the British Army had founded Clan-Briton in 1951, proclaiming a programme of 'Britain for the British' and calling for the withdrawal of civil and political rights from all Jews is Britain. Talking to the press that August, Tomlinson said that everyone not 'Christian or of Anglo-Saxon heritage' was a 'foreigner' and that foreigners must not enjoy 'British rights and British privileges'. He added that 'Clan-Briton' would agree to permit Jews to remain in Britain as 'guests' but not as Britons. He then claimed that, in forthcoming general elections, his Clan would come out in force to oppose Jewish candidates for Parliament on whatever party ticket they ran. None of that followed, and within two years, Clan-Briton had disappeared.[18] Tomlinson died in 1960.

One strength of The Britons was the literacy of most of its journalists and authors. These were educated men (and, very occasionally, women), and contributions were usually scrupulously proofread. However, emerging from the stress of the Baron fiasco and with the BEP being set up in their offices, the cracks began to show. Somehow, this chaotically incoherent summary of the current objectives of The Britons found its way into *Free Britain* (no. 104, 15 July 1951):

1) To revive and stimulate a proper national spirit in the British people, which is a quality essential to race and survival, at a time when so many mischievous influences are at work trying to destroy the national character, and transform the British people into some horrid international abortion.

2) To assist this object by exposing the activities of International Jewry, Freemasonry and Communism, which are the most dangerous of those influences, and which could only have reached their present dangerous standard behind a curtain secrecy [sic] achieved by a control of all forms of publicity, and by intimidation.

New blood was needed, and it came in the form of Colin Jordan, who had already contributed to *Free Britain* but was about to join forces with The Britons.

Issue no. 2 of *Bridgehead* (September 1951) carried an advertisement for a magazine called *Defence – Against Alien Control*, which was 'published by the Birmingham Nationalist Club and obtainable from Colin Jordan, Chessetts Wood, Hockley Heath, Birmingham'. Three months later, *Free Britain* (no.120, 9 December) bore a masthead which now read '*Free Britain* incorporating *Defence Against Alien Control*'. There was a new feature headed: 'Newsview: A Nationalist News Service'. Its introduction read:

Under this amalgamation with 'Free Britain' my news bulletin, 'Defence', will henceforth take the form of a regular Nationalist News Service feature in 'Free Britain', entitled 'Newsview', which will be a selection of worldwide news items of nationalist significance with comment thereon, along with reports on nationalist activities and progress. The policy behind 'Defence' remains the policy behind 'Newsview'; a non-party and non-partisan one, based simply on the fundamental nationalist principles of Britain for the British, and British Independence; and seeking to promote friendly relations between all fellow nationalists and anti-communist patriots in Britain the Empire and abroad. Colin Jordan.

Jordan's *Newsview* column in *Free Britain* no. 121 (15 December) included the information that

Andrew Fountaine, who missed winning Chorley for the Tories by only 361 votes in 1950 and who was vetoed by Lord Woolton from trying again in 1951 because of his nationalist views; is giving a lead. He plans to launch a National Front movement with a platform of all-out opposition to the Uno and internationa tei-ups; [sic] all-out support for Empire development; and all-out resistance to Bolshevism; and proposes to contest Chorley again at the next election as a 'British Empire' candidate.

Here was racist newcomer Jordan writing about racist newcomer Fountaine. Post-war racism was taking shape.

The year ended with The Britons moving out of 40 Great Ormond Street WC1, and so the first issue of *Free Britain* in 1952 was published from a new address, 46/48 Princedale Road W11.

Weakly for a weekly, *Free Britain* failed to appear for almost three months between 10 February and 4 May. When it did return, with issue no. 126, it was badly printed in a much smaller format than its previous foolscap sheet. The brief apology blamed a paper shortage (not the Jews!). However, problems continued, and between June 1952 and February 1953 there were just five issues. The whole of Jordan's column in issue no. 130 was given over to stories of 'Negroes' selling 'hemp' to white girls. Interestingly, all of these accounts originated from reports in the *Daily Telegraph*, the *Daily Express* and *The People* – clear proof that our mainstream press can sometimes sensationalise racism even before our bigots get there.

The first issue of 1953 (no. 134, 1 February) came with a red masthead and bore the slogan 'Work for Government of Britons, by Britons, for Britons'. It offered an apologetic insight into how The Britons functioned:

> Free Britain has not been published regularly of late, only because its limited staff has been fully occupied on matters more urgent. The sale of books and pamphlets in the last 3 months has reached a figure exceeding the total sales for the past three years. This has now become a full-time job for two people attending to correspondence, packing parcels and despatching to all parts of the world. The small revenue obtained from this source is essential for covering our overheads. This other literature is reaching new readers, breaking new ground, whereas at present Free Britain circulates mainly amongst those who already know the Jewish menace but like to be assured we are still active.

It went on to assure readers that the society would try to make the journal more regular. This, though, is a problem common to all small publications. Subscriptions get banked and spent, leaving future copies owed to those subscribers. And when money is tight these subscribers become a burden. With bills and wages to pay, new money comes only from new customers, who therefore get served first – at the risk of losing the faithful.

A booklet on the history of The Britons isn't mentioned in any issue of *Free Britain* but is plugged in the 14 January 1953 issue of Arnold Leese's *Gothic Ripples*. Under the optimistic heading of '"The Britons" Ready for Expansion' comes this piece:

> A booklet (called *The Britons*) has been published giving the history of The Britons Patriotic Society and the reasons why it was founded in 1918 [*sic*] by the late H. H. Beamish and others. The Society, with whom we have co-operated for about 25 years, is now firmly established at 46/48, Princedale Road, W.11, a short walk from Holland Park Tube Station. The time has come for its development and growth as an organisation to enlighten public opinion on the Jewish Menace. Apply to the address given above.[5]

Note: From the early 1930s onwards the letterheaded notepaper of The Britons carried the false claim that it was 'Founded 1918'. This booklet about The Britons appears to have been issued in a very limited run solely for loyal supporters – I have never seen a copy.

Around this time there appears to have been a substantial injection of cash into The Britons. This could have come from Arnold Leese, in which case the source would have been the money bequeathed to him by Beamish. However, this was also the year in which (as we shall see in Chapter 5) A. K. Chesterton was in receipt of many thousands of pounds from the Chilean millionaire Englishman Robert Key Jeffrey, some of which Chesterton subsequently used to subsidise other far-right bodies, including The Britons. It is therefore likely that the Jeffrey funds were the source of The Britons' windfall.

Through this cash injection the B.P.S. Printing Co., based at The Britons premises at Princedale Road, suddenly acquired better printing machinery. From issue no. 136 (erroneously numbered 135), dated 15 March 1953, *Free Britain* took on a whole new appearance. Gone was the crudely typed and roneoed copy. Each issue, though still a single sheet, was now professionally typeset and printed, its two pages laid out in newspaper format on foolscap in three columns.

Also in March 1953, Peter Marriott, who had been The Britons' chairman for the past eight months, announced his resignation. He said that he was leaving to start a group 'to reform the Conservative Party'. No name was given for this new group, and there is no record of Marriott influencing Tory policy. His plans, though, were laid out in his 1950 book *Property and the Nation: A New Conservative Philosophy*. During 1953 he entered into a brief correspondence with Enoch Powell, and in the late 1950s he was co-editor (with George Knupffer) of the right-wing journal the *Plain Speaker*.

On 30 June 1953, The Britons moved offices again, just a few doors down Princedale Road to number 74. Announcing that the building would be named Beamish House, they added that 'The new premises are a donation from a friend of the Society ... The name 'Beamish House' commemorates the founder of The Britons in 1918 and its President for 28 years, Henry Hamilton Beamish, who died in 1946.' The 'donor' was Arnold Leese, but the building, as they would later learn to their cost, wasn't a donation, it was merely on loan. Also, just five years after his death, they had forgotten that their founder had died in 1948 and that he had founded The Britons in 1919. The move was also announced in the 28 July issue of *Gothic Ripples*, and in the following issue (22 August) Gittens appealed for 'free and regular clerical help in his office'.[5]

There was a December issue of *Free Britain*. It had doubled to a four-pager which would in future, we were told, appear monthly. At the end of 1953, with their new machinery now up and running in 74 Princedale Road, The Britons had the added income source of jobbing printing. The B.P.S. Printing Co. offered 'General and Commercial Printing, Diestamping, Bookbinding, Rubber Stamps, Stationery, etc.'

In the January issue, alongside contributions from A. K. Chesterton and Archibald Maule Ramsay, was a piece headed 'Colour Comes to Britain', in which Colin Jordan informed readers that 'Thousands of coloured men are flocking to Britain to live off the British taxpayer at the street corner, amusement arcade, and dance hall; while every party in Parliament refuses to do anything to stop them.'

More of the pre-war crowd featured in the February issue: Chesterton again, Barry Domvile and H.T. Mills. And, along with Jordan were two more newcomers, T.V. Holmes and Derek Tozer. Holmes went on to write several pamphlets for the Social Credit Party during the early 1960s. Tozer was a member of Chesterton's League of Empire Loyalists and a regular contributor to the latter's journal *Candour*, for which he wrote features on United Nations agencies.[19] He also contributed an article, 'How Israel Treats Her Arabs', to the August 1957 issue of the racist and anti-Jewish US journal *The American Mercury*. Curiously, quoting Tozer in his seminal book *Bitter Harvest: A Modern History of Palestine*, Sami Hadawi describes him as a Jewish writer. When the conspiracy journal the *Portman Papers* first appeared in 1996, its founding editor and publisher was Derek Tozer, presumably either the same man or his son.

The 29 June 1954 issue of *Gothic Ripples* contained a piece headed 'Breaking the Silence', in which Leese once more sides with The Britons:

> In our opinion, the only useful way of opposing the Jews is by attacking them openly, as Hitler and Beamish did. It sometimes staggers one to find how many people there are who think that it is cunning to omit all mention of them 'because, you see, people will call you anti-semitic'. Senator McCarthy is often said to be 'clever' for employing Jews like Schine and Cohn so that no-one can call him anti-semitic. A book like *Unconditional Hatred* (by Capt. Russell Grenfell) does almost as much harm as good by maintaining silence on the Jewish cause of World War II. Most people who read it will thereafter blame the British for the War, and, when told by some Jew-wise friend that it was a Jews' war will answer 'Rubbish! Grenfell does not even mention the Jews'. That is why we never stock borderline books like his. If Captain Grenfell *had* blamed the Jews, his book would of course not have received the wide advertisement and distribution it has had. But no-one is more Jew-wise than they were before its publication! All that is required to make anti-Jewishness respectable is for about three of our top-drawer public men to announce openly that they are anti-Jewish, and why. They would, of course, have to take due precautions against assassination! In answer to many correspondents, we know of no active anti-Jewish political body in Britain that we could advise anyone to join. The Britons Publishing Society, 74, Princedale Road, W.11, might become the nucleus of such a body, but at the moment it can only function, as its title indicates, as a centre for distribution of literature; it is doing that well, despite short-handedness.

On the front page of *Free Britain* no. 150 (November 1954) was a report on the inaugural meeting of the League of Empire Loyalists (LEL), which was held at Caxton Hall on 16 October. The founder of the LEL was A. K. Chesterton, already a regular contributor to *Free Britain*. Chesterton produced a weekly magazine, *Candour*, subtitled 'the British Views-letter'. This was printed by B.P.S., The Britons' press. The LEL national executive included Captain Arthur Rogers (of the pre-war Liberty Restoration League), a long-standing leading member of The Britons; George Pile, whose book *The Five Races of Europe* was available from The Britons; Lieutenant Colonel John Creagh Scott, whose book *Hidden Government* would be published by The Britons in 1954; and the newly arrived regular *Free Britain* contributor Derek Tozer. A number of the others were active Britons members. So, not wholly, but partially at least, the LEL too can be regarded as a spin-off from The Britons.

As reported in *Free Britain*, the following were elected onto the LEL national executive: Mrs B. M. Attenborough, Mr W. Austen Brooks, Mrs M. Clarkson, Mr Frank Clifford, Elizabeth Lady Freeman, Mr J. R. Holbrook, Mr R. D. Jeune, Mrs Joyce Mew, Mr George Pile, Captain Arthur Rogers, Lieutenant Colonel J. Creagh Scott, Dr Basil Steele, and Mr T. S. Stewart. The chairman was Martin Burdett-Coutts, the secretary was Miss M. C. Greene, and Mr Derek Tozer was co-opted. A. K. Chesterton made the announcement that, thanks to a substantial donation, the LEL was starting with offices and staff at 602 Grand Buildings, Northumberland Avenue, London WC2.

The main importance of the LEL is that, just over twelve years on from its inauguration, Chesterton would combine it with several other far-right groups to produce the National Front, by which time Colin Jordan would be Britain's foremost Nazi at the head of the National Socialist Movement, which later became the British Movement.

1955 was the year Colin Jordan built his power base by exploiting white fear of the growing black and Asian communities in Britain's urban areas. By the end of the 1960s, Enoch Powell from within the Conservative Party and A. K. Chesterton's National Front on the racist extreme right would steal his thunder, but in 1955 he got there well ahead of them. Here he is, stating his case, in the January 1955 edition of *Free Britain* in a piece headed 'Africa Invades Britain':

> The most bizarre invasion in British history is in full swing with the Government intervening every now and again to announce that it cannot do anything about it. Liner-loads of blacks are landing at Southampton, Plymouth and other ports every month. They are making for London, Cardiff, Birmingham, Nottingham, Liverpool, Manchester, Newcastle and other cities. They are swarming the main streets, into cafes, cinemas, parks and public houses, sheltering in the chain stores, filling in the amusement arcades, and lining up at the Labour Exchanges and National Assistance Boards to receive free living and pocket money we provide them with.
>
> They are taking over whole districts in these major cities of Britain where the whites are on the retreat giving up house after house and street after street as the blacks move in. In these rapidly expanding Harlems they are reproducing the conditions of the jungle. They are living as many as 40 to a house, often sleeping on palliasses laid side by side on the floor, with the stench of garbage accompanying the din of hired radiograms.

> Knifings, street battles, drunken disorder, rape, and drug traffic are becoming commonplace. It has come to such a pass that a senior Birmingham police official declared that white women are no longer safe on the streets of the city's black zone in Balsall Heath at night. In Manchester's Harlem in Moss Side and Chorlton-on-Medlock, as elsewhere, back-alley dens are sprouting up where the blacks feed whisky to teen-age white girls and maul them frenziedly round dimly lit dance floors to the blare of juke boxes.

In the same issue, readers were informed that Jordan's previous organisation, the Birmingham Nationalist Club (BNC), was being revived by David Tennant from his home at 15 Melton Road, Kings Heath, and that 10,000 leaflets had been printed for distribution around the city. Approving of this, The Britons announced that they were printing recruitment leaflets which would soon be available for use by anyone wishing to establish similar groups in other cities:

> Order supplies in advance and follow Birmingham's lead by putting them through letter-boxes, house-to-house, handing them out in the street (avoid obstructing the pavement and thereby causing an offence), distributing them at political meetings, and depositing them in reading rooms and other suitable places. A space is provided on the leaflet for groups, or individuals wishing to form groups, to rubber stamp or otherwise insert their particulars.

Here was Jordan turning The Britons into a proactive group spearheading the new British racism, pushing them to become a force on the streets rather than in the comfy living rooms of retired military families. Note, too, that he was drumming up work for B.P.S. Printing (which also happened to make rubber stamps). His zeal wouldn't go unnoticed by Arnold Leese.

Meanwhile, *Free Britain* invited The Britons' old-school supporters to spend 15 shillings each on tickets for the society's annual dinner, to be held at London's New Horticultural Hall 'on the Feast of St George', 23 April 1955.

Jordan had an awkward personality. He wasn't gregarious, didn't make friends easily and was overtly Nazi, factors which would contribute to his marginalisation after the mid-1960s. However, his influence before then was seminal. His language, his terminology and his street-wise approach set the whole tone for post-war British racism and bigotry. Above all, it is his method of playing on fear and ignorance that persists. Listen to the National Front, the British National Party, the English Defence League, the UK Independence Party and right-wing Conservatives since the 1960s, and you will hear Jordan's phrases.

A report in *Free Britain* in March 1955 showed precisely how Jordan's language was spread. After strike action had been taken by West Bromwich bus crews protesting against the recruitment of coloured staff, the revived BNC had 'held well-attended street meetings calling attention to the need for keeping Britain white. Club members have followed up the meetings with the mass distribution of leaflets.' This second BNC leaflet was also produced by B.P.S., which had printed

10,000 copies. It was headed 'Coloured Invasion Threatens Britain' and read: 'The ever increasing influx of Blacks, Negroes, Indians, Hottentots from all corners of the Earth into this country means – less houses for British people, a menace to British jobs and wages, you pay their national assistance, new slums and harlems created, intermarriage with British women.' The leaflet ended with a demand for new immigration laws, and the club's assistant secretary, Mr H. J. Davies, announced that a telegram had been sent to the prime minister calling for legislation against coloured immigration. Much of the wording on that leaflet was culled directly from Jordan's journalism. In the May 1955 issue, it was announced that the BNC, which was now holding regular meetings, was soon to open an office. Meanwhile, its forwarding address for mail was c/o The Britons at 74 Princedale Road – making the revived BNC yet another partial spin-off of The Britons. The front cover of that same May issue of *Free Britain* carried the headline 'Make White Britain an Election Issue!'. Times were changing. Many of the old Jew-haters had died – Beamish in 1948, Blakeney in 1952, the Duke of Bedford in 1953 and, most recently, Maule Ramsay. Even Arnold Leese had less than a year to go.

Meanwhile, business at The Britons was booming – according to Anthony Gittens when he spoke at that annual dinner. One hundred and four members and friends attended the event, which was presided over by Major B. Wilmot-Allistone, the society's chairman. Following Domvile's opening speech, Gittens spoke on the history of The Britons before announcing that 'A most satisfactory feature was the fast mounting total of book sales; doubled since 1953 and more than eight times its pre-war average.' There were two other speakers. Captain Arthur Rogers proposed a toast to The Britons' authors and was responded to by Colin Jordan, whose book *Fraudulent Conversion* was due out from the society's press.

The Britons catalogue now offered around seventy titles, some of which were their own publications, others merely distributed by them. There were books and pamphlets by veteran Jew-haters from Britain (including Maule Ramsay, Barry Domvile, Arnold Leese, H. T. Mills, P. J. Keith, Denis Fahey, the Duke of Bedford and Nesta Webster), from America (among them Gerald L. K. Smith, Lothrop Stoddard, L. Fry and Elizabeth Dilling) and from Europe (notably Rudolf Hess). And soon they would be adding work by some of the rising stars of post-Second World War Jew-hatred and racism in Britain (A. K. Chesterton, Colin Jordan and Noel Stock) and America (Kenneth Goff, Carleton Putnam), as well as bigots and haters from as far afield as New Zealand (A. N. Field) and Russia (Arsene de Goulevitch). There was also an assortment of books and pamphlets by biased conspiracy theorists, anti-Jewish monetary reformers, revisionist historians and religious extremists – oh, and *The Protocols*, of course, now into its eighty-third edition.[20]

In November 1955, The Britons had a bookstall at the Sunday Times Book Exhibition in the Royal Festival Hall in London, prompting complaints from Jewish organisations.[5] The event, opened by the Queen Mother, lasted ten days.

In January 1956, Arnold Leese died. This would have catastrophic repercussions for The Britons, although none – with the possible exception of Jordan – realised it at the time, and half of the February issue of *Free Britain* was given over to his memory.

And, for the time being, Gittens and Jordan remained allied, at least in adversity, as witnessed by a piece in the July issue of *Free Britain*, which also sees both men taking part in a typical piece of direct action by the League of Empire Loyalists (LEL). It reports that Gittens, Jordan and three unnamed LEL members were 'assaulted by Black stewards and subsequently ejected from a meeting of the Movement for Colonial Freedom at the Central Hall, Westminster on the 8th June.' When the five had 'protested against the speaker's insulting references to the British Empire, they were immediately attacked by coloured stewards. One Indian removed his shoe and hit Mr. Jordan over the head. The three League members were knocked to the ground and dragged out by their legs.' What the article didn't tell the readers was that Jordan had been an LEL member for two years and that Gittens had been intimately involved with it from its inception.

With Maule Ramsay gone and Leese's money tied up while his will was being sorted, cash to run *Free Britain* seems to have evaporated by the year's end. The last regular issue came out that December. Over the next eighteen months there were just six more issues, these small in format, A5 instead of foolscap, and published irregularly. A double number (182/183) for May and June 1958 appears to have been the final edition. Two small details hint at a coming split with Jordan. The subtitle on these last six issues has changed from 'Incorporating DEFENCE against alien control' to read simply 'For Defence Against Alien Control'. Also the final issue carries, on its back page, an advertisement for Colin Jordan's new news-sheet, *Black & White News*, which had been printed for him by The Britons.

There was a second likely reason for *Free Britain* folding. Although no editor's name was ever published in the journal, it was clear that the job had been done mostly by Gittens. The sudden death of Leese left his monthly, *Gothic Ripples*, without an editor. Leese had founded *Gothic Ripples* in the late 1940s and usually edited it himself, although others would step in whenever he was absent or indisposed. No editor was ever named in this journal either, just the fact that it was published by the Anti-Jewish Information Bureau from Leese's home address, 20 Pewley Hill, Guildford, Surrey. *Gothic Ripples* no. 134 (4 February) appears to have been put together after his death by his wife, May, and others, but thereafter Gittens took on the job. Issue no. 135 (10 April) had Gittens credited as editor, with the Anti-Jewish Information Bureau now at 74 Princedale Road, The Britons' address. Producing and distributing weekly issues of *Gothic Ripples* as well as running The Britons was probably more than enough work, and the effort needed to keep the small-circulation *Free Britain* going as well may simply have proved too much.

Gothic Ripples no. 135 carried the following slightly off-beat statement from Gittens:

> I have known and worked with Arnold Leese for nearly 30 years and I shall endeavour to carry on the exposure work for the benefit of the *Jew-wise*. This newsletter is *not* for Simpletons but it is to help you to make the Simpleton *Jew-wise*. Anything written here will be without malice and with the desire to remedy a matter of State established, that is, the acceptance of Jews as British citizens, which I believe to be a menace to the nation. Thank you readers for sending in news and cuttings, they are a great help.

Grammar aside, the phrase 'without malice' doesn't quite sit comfortably alongside 'Anti-Jewish Information Bureau'. For at least the next two years, until issue no. 152 (30 November 1958), Gittens kept *Gothic Ripples* going, as a Britons journal, but with its appearance, format, style and content kept just as it had been under Leese's editorship.[5]

By the end of 1958 there hadn't been an issue of *Free Britain* for six months, and it seems, too, that *Gothic Ripples*, which had been produced by the B.P.S. Printing Co., had just ceased abruptly. That brings us to a third possible reason for the demise of *Free Britain*. The Britons were about to be ousted from their offices at 74 Princedale Road.

Jordan had been on good terms with Leese's widow, May Winifred Leese (née King), since he'd first met the couple back in the late 1940s. From the outset he had greatly admired Leese, who became his role model. And Leese came to see Jordan as the man who could best continue his work. With Leese gone and May in control of his estate, the latter took the same attitude. She and Arnold had been a childless couple, and she treated Jordan almost like a son. If Gittens thought that his history as a long-standing Leese acolyte, coupled with his editorship of *Gothic Ripples*, was sufficient to assure The Britons' continued tenancy of 74 Princedale Road, he was wrong. To their dismay, tenancy went to Jordan, who, perhaps out of loyalty, allowed them to stay on for a while. After all, they had published his book and several of his pamphlets. Furthermore, B.P.S. served a valuable purpose. It had printed leaflets and news-sheets for Jordan, and continued to do so. However, during 1959 The Britons had to focus on finding new premises, packing up and moving on. By 1960 they were in a new Beamish House at 111A Westbourne Grove, W2. Meanwhile, 74 Princedale Road had become the offices of Jordan's future ventures and had been renamed Arnold Leese House. When the property was finally sold in 1968, once more it was Jordan, and not The Britons, whom May Leese appointed as the sole selling agent.[2]

Earlier it was mentioned that Chesterton's LEL was important because the National Front (NF) grew out of it. However, there was more to it than that. Other future far-right leaders joined the LEL during the late 1950s. There was Jordan, of course, who would later found the British Movement. Another was John Tyndall, who was to found and lead the British National Party (BNP). Other future prime movers in the LEL were John Bean and Martin Webster.[3] And what made the LEL so influential was that it was street active. It disrupted meetings of every political shade. Its members wrecked almost as many gatherings of Conservatives as it did of Labour Party groups, communists, anti-fascists, anarchists, Liberals or other broadly anti-fascist organisations. And it often did so with eye-catching stunts and headline-grabbing trickery. It made extreme bigotry high profile, an end it achieved by being calculating, clever, unexpected and even funny. An LEL member would jump up in a meeting and interrupt the main speaker until they were ejected, only to be superseded by another, and another, and another – maybe twenty or thirty in all – enough to wreck any meeting. The LEL taught the far right how to eclipse the establishment on its own ground. They would let off fireworks, abseil or jump from balconies, sing, shout, dance – anything to ruin a rival event. And, for a while, it looked like it might work. They got media coverage. Their spokespersons were invited onto radio and TV, but seldom impressed; Chesterton, especially, came across as vain, over-earnest, humourless, bigoted and arrogant. They lacked anybody charismatic or even possessing public appeal. Chesterton, Jordan, Tyndall, Webster and co. turned stone-cold in front of a microphone or camera. They were po-faced, evasive, charmless, eccentric and obsessed. Worse still, they lacked humanity. It's an inadequacy that is common to most of those who preach bigotry, and one which explains why none of them – even apparent front-runners such as Enoch Powell, Nick Griffin or Nigel Farage – ever come close to achieving real power. These wannabe leaders merely linger in the wings until long after their show is over and their audiences have gone home. To his credit, Chesterton – who was flawed but no fool – realised, unlike The Britons, that empire loyalism was outdated, and within a dozen years of founding the LEL he was launching the NF as its modern replacement.

In the late 1950s and early 1960s, British racism was in flux. The war had undone its past and cast the Jew as victim rather than victimiser. Aging old-school bigots could and did opt for The Britons, Mosley's Union Movement, Chesterton's LEL or even the cosy comfort of the Tory right. Younger racists looking for an outlet could also join Mosley or Chesterton or opt for Jordan's more extreme street-active White Defence League by finding Princedale Road and knocking on the door of no. 74. A few did so, but not many. The 1960s were coming, bringing Mods and Rockers, youth culture and pop culture. Jordan would *hate* the 1960s, but he was good at hatred and would continue his increasingly lonely struggle for another fifty years. Later, and in other hands, the British Movement and the National Front would start to appeal to the young and the thuggish. Teenagers would turn to hatred, but by then most of those who had been involved with The Britons would be dead and buried.

Main sources

Throughout: an almost complete set of *Free Britain* (nos. 1–182/3, 25 March 1949–May/June 1958).* Also Wikipedia and other internet sources to cross-check details. Documents marked with an asterisk are original copies in the private collection of the author.

1 Colin Holmes (1978), 'The Protocols of "The Britons"', *Patterns of Prejudice*, 12(6): 13–18
2 Richard Thurlow (1998), *Fascism in Britain*
3 Stephen Dorril (2006), *Blackshirt: Sir Oswald Mosley and British Fascism*
4 Wikipedia, *A. F. X. Baron*
5 *Gothic Ripples*, nos. 78–152 (28 July 1951–30 November 1958)*
6 Hilary Cotter and R. De Roiste (1951), *World Dictatorship by 1955? Why Forrestal Threw Himself out of the Window**

7   C. C. Aronsfeld, 'The Britons Publishing Society', *Wiener Library Bulletin*, 20 (1966): 31–5
8   Robin Saika (ed.) (2010), *The Red Book: The Membership List of the Right Club, 1939*
9   *Bridgehead* (nos. 1–7, 1 August 1951–1 February 1952)★
10 Thomas P. Lineham (1996), *The British Union of Fascists in East London and South-West Essex 1933–1940*
11 Morris Beckman (1993), *The 43 Gang: Battling with Mosleyite Blackshirts*
12 Jewish Telegraphic Agency, 'Britons Go on Trial for Exploding Smoke Bomb at Showing of "Sword in the Desert"', dated 2 March 1950, www.jta.org
13 Trefor David, election leaflet (1951)★
14 British Empire Party Manifesto (1951)★
15 Trefor David (1951), *The Bloody Red Streak*
16 George Thayer (1965), *The British Political Fringe*
17 *Hansard*, 19 March 1951
18 Jewish Telegraphic Agency, 'New Organisation Formed in Britain', dated 16 August 1951, www.jta.org
19 Hugh McNeile and Rob Black (2014), *The History of the League of Empire Loyalists and Candour*
20 The Britons, *Literature for Nationalists and Patriots of all Nations* (catalogue, c.1954)

5

THE BRITONS PUBLISHING COMPANY

THE 1960s AND 1970s

In 1960, Harold Macmillan was warning us all of a 'wind of change'. Bob Dylan and John Lennon were working out hairstyles and guitar licks, and good old British bigotry had swung into baiting and beating black and Asian instead of Jew.

The Britons had just moved into a first-floor loft above a restaurant on Westbourne Road, having lost their lucrative B.P.S. imprint after they left 74 Princedale Road. They anyway needed a new name for a printing and publishing service, one which wouldn't be immediately identifiable with the society. While their controversial reputation served them well when dealing with those sympathetic to their views, in the wider world the notoriety of The Britons was proving problematic. So, it was partly through necessity, partly by choice, that they founded a new imprint to run alongside their publishing and bookselling business. This was the innocuously named Clair Press. Later they would publish Catholic titles under the Augustine Press imprint.

Four people worked at the Westbourne Road office. Anthony Gittens was in charge, helped out by his wife, Joyce, and a young volunteer, Timothy Tindal-Robertson, and there was a printer running Clair Press. Income came partly from book sales and partly from printing jobs, which included restaurant menus, posters and letterheads. Journals were also printed for other far-right groups, among them Colin Jordan's latest magazine, the *Northern European*, and A. K. Chesterton's *Candour*. The Britons' best-selling book by far remained, as ever, *The Protocols*: there had been almost ninety editions in the forty years since its first publication by the society. Half a million copies had been sold in the past twelve years alone.

Another recent best-seller was Lieutenant Colonel John Creagh Scott's Protocols-based *Hidden Government*. Published by The Britons in 1954, it had already sold 7,000 copies. And the press was preparing to publish another winner, *Race, Heredity and Civilisation*, a slim volume by Professor Wesley Gritz George, an American geneticist who argued against the mixing of races and who believed in the superiority of whites. Published in 1961, its sales in the first couple of years would exceed 100,000. However, although they distributed other American titles dealing with race, The Britons' own publications throughout the 1960s would remain focused on the covert power of the Jews – Jews as the cause of wars and conflict, Jews as the power behind communism, Jews undermining Christianity, Jews working through freemasonry, and Jews taking over the world.[1]

Now, however, as the 1960s rolled on, The Britons had no public face beyond their books and the catalogues they produced to advertise these titles. There was no Britons journal. There were no Britons meetings. They just got on with their printing, publishing and book distribution service. And, after four years above a restaurant, Anthony and Joyce Gittens tired of working in London. They moved to Devon, taking Tim Tindal-Robertson and the society with them. In 1964, Beamish House took on its final identity as a five-bedroom detached house (real name South View) in the remote Devon village of Chawleigh. Here, in the late 1960s, The Britons assumed a Catholic identity. Joyce and Anthony Gittens were both Catholics, and Timothy Tindal-Robertson – a convert to Catholicism – was ardent about it. The press began to reflect this.

Starting in 1969 with two titles – the Reverend P. J. Gearon's *The Wheat and the Cockle* and Hugh Ross Williamson's *The Modern Mass* – Gittens and co. began to publish and to distribute Catholic books as well as their usual anti-Jewish fare. Thus their other new publications included Bernard Lazare's *Antisemitism: Its History and Causes* (1967), Major General Richard Hilton's *Imperial Obituary: The Mysterious Death of the British Empire* (1968) and Nesta Webster's *World Revolution: The Plot against Civilisation* (1971). This last title, incidentally, was a new edition, revised, edited and brought up to date by Anthony Gittens himself, proving that – to the last – he remained faithful not only to the Pope but also to *The Protocols*.

On 22 August 1969, the *Catholic Herald* published an article about The Britons which was strongly critical, pointing out that their books were distributed by the National Front and that Gittens himself 'had his name linked with certain non-Mosleyite Fascist tendencies in the 1930s and 1940s. He was later concerned with the League of Empire Loyalists.'[2] On 26 August, Tindal-Robertson responded with a defensive letter. Signing himself secretary of the Britons Publishing Company and heading his letter 'Traditionalist Publishers', he wrote:

Dear Sir,
It is a little difficult to see the reason for the story by your Special Correspondent, 'Traditionalists Find a Taylor-made Publisher', referring to the Britons Publishing Company, unless it was written to embarrass those Catholic authors defending the time honoured glories of our Faith. One cannot help thinking that labels such as 'Fascist', 'Traditionalist', 'Extreme Right-Winger', etc., are used to-day as substitutes for intelligent argument as were 'Christian', 'Papist' and 'Jacobite' in former times.

It is quite absurd, for instance, to label the opponents of Fluoridation 'extreme right wingers' for the anti-fluoridation movement includes people of all parties and religions and many of its leading lights are Socialists and Liberals.

The Wheat and the Cockle was by no means the first Catholic 'traditionalist' book to be published by this Company. In 1948 we re-published Humanum Genus, Pope Leo XIII's Encyclical against Freemasonry, and I am sure The Catholic Herald would not suggest that this sovereign Pontiff was titlting [sic] at an 'extreme right-wing target'. This was followed by Monsignor Dillon's famous lectures against Freemasonry which had been acclaimed by the entire Catholic press.

The policy of this company for the last 20 years has certainly not been as 'extreme right wing' as your Correspondent suggests for in fairness to the other side we have published a book by a Freemason answering critics of the Craft. We have recently re-published Antisemitism by the learned Jewish writer, Bernard Lazare. As for the famous Protocols of Zion, we took over publication from Eyre & Spottiswood [sic], Ltd, in 1920 and to-day we list the scholarly work of exposure by Professor Norman Cohen – Warrant for Genocide.

One could hardly accuse John Murray of favouring 'Fascist themes' because they published Mein Kampf before the war or Hutchinsons because they are about to republish it.

Your Correspondent is concerned that some of our books are purchased by the Nationalist Book Centre which he states is associated with a party called the National Front. As members of the Publishers Association we are only concerned that our customers abide by the provisions of the Net Book Agreement, not with their political or religious views. Our customers include the Catholic Truth Society, the Protestant Book Centre, the S.P.C.K., the Lutheran Book Room, the Lenin Library in Moscow and the Kirjath Sepher Bibliographical Quarterly in Jerusalem.

I prefer to pass over the uncharitable innuendoes against our Founder and present Chairman, but if, as your Correspondent suggests, we are the sole firm prepared to publish traditionalist views, then we are glad that you have drawn attention to this fact, and that we are in a position to offer this service to the Church.[3]

Clearly, The Britons had grown sensitive to criticism. Moreover, in Tindal-Robertson they had shed every visible trace of their trademark aggressive and unrepentant Jew-hatred. Beamish would have loathed the whole defensive tone of this letter, especially its apparent denial of an anti-Jewish stance. And Tindal-Robertson's dilution of The Britons' Jew-hatred wasn't the only change he had wrought. It is to be remembered that even before The Britons formed, when Beamish and Clarke were together in the Vigilante Society and Billing tried to rein in Beamish's anti-Jewish views, he had also to criticise Clarke for his anti-Catholic extremism. This had carried over into The Britons, which as an organisation was also trenchantly anti-Catholic through the 1920s and 1930s. Tindal-Robertson was now slowly turning it into a doctrinal Catholic publishing house.

However, the above letter has been quoted in full for another reason. In it, Tindal-Robertson is actually being far from honest. The Britons, and in particular their press, now the Clair Press, had a long and intimate relationship with A. K. Chesterton and his National Front. Indeed, where Chesterton himself is concerned, this close relationship can be traced right back to the early 1950s.

Following its 1953 takeover by the Staples Press, the journal *Truth* had been revamped and given a much more mainstream Conservative tone, dropping all the openly anti-Jewish content of which it had previously been unashamed. Chesterton had promptly resigned as deputy editor, as had the editor, Collin Brooks. And The Britons had then published Chesterton's bitter response, the pamphlet *Truth Has Been Murdered*. On 30 October 1953, Chesterton published the first edition of his replacement for the 'murdered' journal.[4] Named *Candour* (being a synonym for *Truth*), this four-page weekly was printed by the Clair Press. In appealing for funds for this venture, Chesterton had struggled until winning the enthusiastic support of a Chilean-based millionaire Englishman, Robert Key Jeffrey (3 August 1870–22 April 1961), who had sent a start-up cheque for £1,000, followed within months by two further cheques, for £5,000 and then £10,000. These were vast sums, sufficient for Chesterton to offer direct financial assistance to other far-right organisations,[5] among them The Britons and Jordan's Birmingham Nationalist Club[6] (as well as less remembered reactionary organisations such as the Christian Campaign for Freedom, the National Crusade and the Magna Carta and English Constitution Protection Association).[5]

By paying the Clair Press to print the weekly issues of *Candour*, Chesterton further assisted the continued existence of The Britons. It didn't end there. To this printing job was soon added a steady stream of books, pamphlets and leaflets as the Candour publishing company expanded operations to become both an active press and an energetic campaigning body. When Chesterton then went on to found the League of Empire Loyalists (LEL) in October 1954, vastly more printing jobs came to Clair Press. In the first fifteen months alone, LEL members distributed half a million pamphlets and leaflets, most of which had been printed by Clair Press. And when in 1966–7 Chesterton founded the National Front, the Clair Press was given much of their printing as well.

Although the LEL had some passing contact with right-wing Conservative MPs such as Sir Harry Legge-Bourke and Captain Henry Kirby, its members generally had a very low opinion of all three mainstream parties, particularly the Conservatives, for lacking 'true patriotism'. Writing in the 10 June 1956 issue of *Candour*, Chesterton stated that the only bodies left to organise 'the defence of our national integrity' were the LEL, *Candour* and the Britons Publishing Society.[5]

As we saw in Chapter 4, the roots of the LEL lay, in part at least, in The Britons. Indeed, many members of The Britons were simultaneously members of the LEL, with Gittens, Jordan and others becoming directly involved in their protests and their other high-profile public campaigns.

Further proof of the close and long-lasting ties which had developed between Chesterton and The Britons came in 1968. In March of that year, five members of the Racial Preservation Society (a small group which would later form part of Chesterton's National Front) were in court in Lewes, Sussex, facing charges under the new Race Relations Act. This was a landmark case which hinged on whether or not the content of issue no. 5 of the group's journal, *R.P.S. Southern News*, contravened the new Act. Those charged – Alan Hancock, Sidney Hardy, Geoffrey

Dominy, Edward Budden and Thomas Jones – had published and/or distributed it free through letterboxes. Chesterton organised their defence, working in close collaboration with Gittens and Tindal-Robertson.[7] All five defendants were eventually found not guilty. Chesterton then wrote the introduction to an account of the trial, which was printed by The Britons (as B.P.S. Printing Co.) and published simultaneously in separate editions by the Britons and *Candour*. The text of this pamphlet, *Not Guilty: Historic Race Relations Trial, Lewes Assizes in March 1968*, appears to have been the joint work of Chesterton, Gittens and Tindal-Robertson.[8]

Rural Devon may have been relatively timeless and unchanging, but in urban Britain, and in London in particular, racism was on the move again. In 1969, Symarip, a black British ska and reggae band – one of the first in the country – released a single on the Treasure Island label. Black youths danced to it. One year later, a white DJ and record label boss called Judge Dread re-released it on his own Trojan label. Black and white youths danced to it. It was called *Skinhead Moonstomp*. The youths shaved their heads. They bought Doc Marten boots to be able to stomp better. They rolled up their jeans to show off their boots. They couldn't stomp on the moon so they went out onto the streets and found Asians to stomp on instead. They called it 'Paki bashing'. Black and white youths did this. And then the white youths split from the black youths. The white youths joined the British Movement (founded in 1968) and the National Front (founded in 1966–7) and learned to be proud – of their race, the colour of their skin, their country, their flag and their violence. The irony is that this seminal skinhead anthem – which helped to kick-start a movement that became (and remains) identified worldwide with white racism – was composed, recorded and performed by black British youths with Jamaican roots.

Back in Devon, the literary activity of The Britons – consisting of an increasingly Catholic publishing output together with the steady selling of their extensive back catalogue – was now handled primarily by Tindal-Robertson. The aging Gittens devoted most of his time and energy to correspondence – much of it either in pursuit of the manuscript of Nesta Webster's unpublished second autobiography or in trying to counter the pirating of Britons titles.

Nesta Webster, who had died in 1960, wrote two biographies – *Spacious Days* and *Crowded Hours*. The Britons had been sent the manuscript of the latter, which they had kept on file in the hope of one day publishing. Then they were visited in Devon by a shady Jewish man called Paul Pulitzer. Here is an extract from a letter written by Gittens to the American revisionist historian and white supremacist Revilo Pendleton Oliver (in which 'Mr. P.' refers to Paul Pulitzer; *Common Sense* was a prominent American anti-Jewish and anti-communist journal, 'Desert tread' is a euphemism for Jewish, and the ADL is the Anti-Defamation League – a leading Jewish defence organisation):

> My reason for writing is to discuss our mutual friend, Mr. P. who has recently become 'world expert' for Common Sense. I enclose a snap we took of him while he was in Devon. You will observe the typical 'Desert tread'. Our dealings with him lasted about 8 months and we watched him

like a hawk. By a brilliant bit of three-card trickery he tried to hook us for £2000 which didn't come off but he stung his Swiss Bank for £1000. Someone should warn Common Sense. I have quite a fat File on him. However I am sure he did one fast one on us while here, and this is where you may be able to help in a small way. It is common knowledge that Nesta Webster left an unpublished MS. This is our property and copyright. When he was here, he had access to it and was, seemingly, so impressed that he said he could get immediate finance in the USA to have it published at once. He wrote glowing accounts from America saying he had just the man to back it and could we send it to him for a week. We said no it must be examined here. When he returned he sat at a desk and took notes and then put it back in the file. About 6 months ago when I went to consult it, it was missing and another MS from another part of the building was in its place! Now I can't say for sure that P. is responsible but I would bet he was. He can't very well have sold it in the States but he may well have sold it for quite a tidy sum to the ADL.

Gittens went on to ask for Oliver's help in looking out for any attempt to publish the book in America and in trying to trace any American publisher which might have a copy. As the correspondence continued, it became clear that neither Gittens in the UK nor Oliver in the USA was having any success in locating either the stolen manuscript or any other copy of it. Gittens may well have been correct in his assumption that Pulitzer sold it to the ADL, who, he says in a later letter, 'would give quite a price to suppress it'. To this day, no one has found the manuscript, and *Crowded Hours* remains an unpublished mystery.

And Gittens was absolutely right when he said that 'Someone should warn *Common Sense*'. Exactly two weeks after he wrote that letter, on 16 June 1972, an advertisement appeared in the *New York Times* announcing that the May issue of *Common Sense* had been the last and that the journal was 'now defunct'. Founded by its long-time editor Conde McGinley (13 October 1890–2 July 1963), *Common Sense* had lasted twenty-five years. And it would seem that its demise was engineered by Paul Pulitzer. According to a report in the 20 November 2004 issue of the American neo-Nazi journal *National Vanguard*:

> All the assets of *Common Sense* were liquidated and publication stopped when the proprietoress who had inherited the operation after McGinley's death, and who had published the paper for a decade, up until 1970, had a 'religious experience' stimulated by a Jewish con-man named Paul Pulitzer, who convinced her to devote her life to a 'true Pope' who ran a 'Vatican' in Quebec at that time but which apparently, like McGinley's life's work and fortune, had evaporated as surely as the dews of Spring long past. Thereby a truth-telling publication annoying to the Zionists was terminated and many valuable files were destroyed; and those were probably the aims of Pulitzer's bosses from the beginning.

In July 1973, James Warner, a leading American Nazi, visited The Britons' Devon offices. In his last letter to Oliver, dated 1 August 1973, Gittens (referring to Warner as 'Dr' W.) wrote: 'According to "Dr" W., Pulitzer cleaned up quite a nice little racket selling the Common Sense Property and only gave a small mite to the Canadian Pope as a commission!'

At the same time, Gittens was strenuously striving to counter American publishers who were producing pirate editions of Britons titles. Among them was a press called Omni Publications run by Philip C. Serpico. Omni had just published a pirate edition of a Britons book by the veteran Judeo-communist conspiracy theorist Comte Léon de Poncins. In that same letter to Oliver, Gittens also wrote:

> Comte de Poncins is furious at Serpico's re-printing his Secret Powers Behind Revolution and as his publishers he would like us to take action. We wrote a very strong letter to Serpico, asking what he intended doing as the author wanted full royalties. The Reply: 'Oh heck I didn't know the little guy was still alive.'

Accompanying Gittens's letter was a leaflet concerning other pirated books. Headlined 'The Works of the English Historian Nesta H. Webster' and subheaded 'WARNING!', it read:

> As the Publishers of Nesta Webster's famous and authoritative works on the Revolutionary movements, it has come to our notice that some cheap and worthless imitations of her books have been printed by an American firm. Intended readers are warned against these pirate editions as being out of date and without the authority of the copyright holders. In the case of WORLD REVOLUTION, Mrs. Webster has completely revised the text and brought the subject up-to-date, leaving her Publisher to write the later chapters since her revision. The American edition is allegedly a copy of the 1st Edition of 1921 which is now completely valueless.
>
> All Nesta Webster's works, unpublished manuscripts, articles, Charts and political correspondence are now the exclusive copyright of the Britons Publishing Co., by Deed of Assignment, dated the 29th. day of June 1967 and legal action will be taken against anyone offering pirated editions for sale.[9]

In truth, Gittens's protestations and threats were themselves valueless. Transatlantic legal action would have been prohibitively expensive and so fraught with problems that it would almost certainly have failed.

The company in question was Angriff Press, whose pirated edition of *World Revolution* had come out in 1972.[10] Angriff was run by William Morrison, a man with a long police record as both a child molester and a homosexual. His partner at the time was James Warner,[11] who had been a founder member of George Lincoln

Rockwell's American Nazi Party and, in 1971, had established the New Christian Crusade Church. His own Sons of Liberty Press would later issue pirated editions of numerous racist books. A prime mover in American racism, Warner would go on to become a Grand Dragon in David Duke's Knights of the Ku Klux Klan.[12]

The Britons produced a range of catalogues to suit different readers. Some of these catalogues were numbered and almost like magazines. Their Catholic catalogue, for example, was called *Right Angles: Christian & Catholic Book News* (the author has copy no. 5, which came out in 1972). An indication of the service they offered to customers is to be found under the heading 'Other Lists', which reads

> When ordering, please indicate if you have special interests in any of the following subjects: Africa, British Empire, Common Market, Communism, Fluoridation, International Finance, Palestine, Political Philosophy, Race Problems, Student Revolution, United Nations and World Wars I & II. We have separate leaflets for a number of other titles covering these subjects, and a general list embracing them all which will shortly be available on request. Also ask for our second hand books, lists of which will be issued at regular intervals.[13]

They weren't. Anthony Gittens died on 17 November 1973[7] and The Britons effectively died with him – except for one last anti-Jewish title published in 1975. This was *State Secret: A Documentation of the Secret Revolutionary Mainspring Governing Anglo-American Politics*. It was written by Count Léon de Poncins and translated by Timothy Tindal-Robertson, who took over the Devon property.

There was one final attempt to keep The Britons going as an anti-Jewish operation. A. K. Chesterton had been a friend and close campaigning associate of Eric Butler (7 May 1916–7 June 2006), a prominent Australian right-wing and anti-Jewish agitator and pamphleteer who ran the Australian League of Rights. One of Butler's keenest followers, Don Martin, moved to Britain in 1970 and, the following year, established the British League of Rights. On 15 February 1975, Martin wrote a letter to his supporters. In it he stated:

> I am happy to be able to announce to you an entirely new and unique scheme of co operation between the League and Britons Publishing Company – neither of us is surrendering or altering our identity in any way, since we both operate complementary services which will be to the advancement of the common cause – to give you and the general public a steady improvement in our services, and the prospect of a firm base for future expansion.
>
> Britons Publishing Company under the direction of Mr Timothy Tindal-Robertson will give us access to a sympathetic publisher who can help us with certain printing and at the same time provide a co-operative service with respect to our general list of books.

132   The Britons Publishing Co.: the 1960s and 1970s

But the planned tie-up came to nothing, and Don Martin, who was already setting up Bloomfield Books as his own publishing and distribution business, went on rapidly to establish it as the leading UK source of right-wing, anti-Jewish, anti-communist and other such literature, with a catalogue offering hundreds of books and pamphlets, including most of The Britons' back catalogue. Effectively, then, from the mid-1970s onwards, Bloomfield Books replaced The Britons. Indeed, after 1975, any enquiries concerning political or conspiracy theory publications received by Tindal-Robertson at the old Britons address were referred to Don Martin's Bloomfield Books.[14]

In 1976, Tindal-Robertson and his wife, Andrea, officially established the Augustine Publishing Company as an orthodox Catholic imprint and distribution service producing and supplying books on religious doctrine. It continued for twenty years, ceasing to trade in 1995.

Since the early 1990s, Tindal-Robertson has established himself as an authority on 'the vision of Fatima' (in which the Virgin Mary is said to have appeared in 1917 to three children in the Portuguese town of Fatima).[15] His key book on the subject, *Fatima, Russia & Pope John Paul II* (1992, since revised) tackles the role of the apparitions, together with papal influence in defeating Russian atheism(!).[16] He has since produced two booklets, *Message of Fatima* (1998) and *Fatima in the Third Millennium* (2001), both published by the Catholic Truth Society.[17, 18]

Revilo P. Oliver wrote the following about The Britons:

> Anthony Gittens eventually became the manager of it, and during his incumbency Britons was forced to leave Beamish House in London; he elected to move it to Devon, as far as possible from the increasing squalor and corruption of a metropolis in which Englishmen were already being displaced and harassed by racial enemies imported from their lost colonies. At his death in 1974 [*sic*], he was succeeded by his pale young assistant, who promptly scrapped the patriotic enterprise and converted it into a house that published pious Christian tripe.[19]

Main sources

Throughout: Wikipedia and other internet sources to cross-check details. Documents marked with an asterisk are original copies in the private collection of the author.

1. George Thayer (1965), *The British Political Fringe*
2. *Catholic Herald*, 22 August 1969
3. Letter from Timothy Tindal-Robertson to the editor of the *Catholic Herald*, 26 August 1969★
4. *Candour*, no.1, 30 October 1953
5. Kevan Bleach (2005), *Unending Battle: A History of A. K. Chesterton and the League of Empire Loyalists*

6 Hugh McNeile and Rob Black (2014), *The History of the League of Empire Loyalists and Candour*
7 Timothy Tindal-Robertson, 'Death of a Briton', *Candour*, 25(540), January 1974 [obituary of Anthony Gittens]*
8 A. K. Chesterton (ed.) (1968), *Not Guilty: An Account of the Historic Race Relations Trial at Lewes Assizes in March 1968**
9 Correspondence between Anthony Gittens and Revilo P. Oliver, 1972–3
10 Nesta H. Webster (Angriff Press edition, 1972), *World Revolution*
11 Jeffrey Kaplan (ed.) (2000), *Encyclopedia of White Power: A Sourcebook on the Radical Racist Right*
12 Metapedia
13 The Britons (1972), *Right Angles: Christian & Catholic Book News**
14 Derrick Knight (1982), *Beyond the Pale: The Christian Political Fringe*
15 John de Marchi (1952), *The Immaculate Heart of Mary*
16 Timothy Tindal-Robertson (1992), *Fatima, Russia & Pope John Paul II*
17 Timothy Tindal-Robertson (1998), *Message of Fatima*
18 Timothy Tindal-Robertson (2001), *Fatima in the Third Millennium*
19 Revilo P. Oliver, 'Postscripts', *Liberty Bell*, 15(6), February 1988

FIGURE 1 Archibald Maule Ramsay

FIGURE 2 Arnold Leese

FIGURE 3 Part of the author's collection of literature from Arnold Leese (including handwritten draft of his letter to the home secretary and personal notes, both written during his wartime internment; above and to the right of these are typed and handwritten notes for a speech)

FIGURE 4 The controversial Britons Publishing Society stall at the Sunday Times Book Exhibition held at the Royal Festival Hall, London, in November 1955

FIGURE 5 All three Britons journals: *Jewry Über Alles* (also known as the *Hidden Hand*), the *British Guardian* and *Free Britain*.

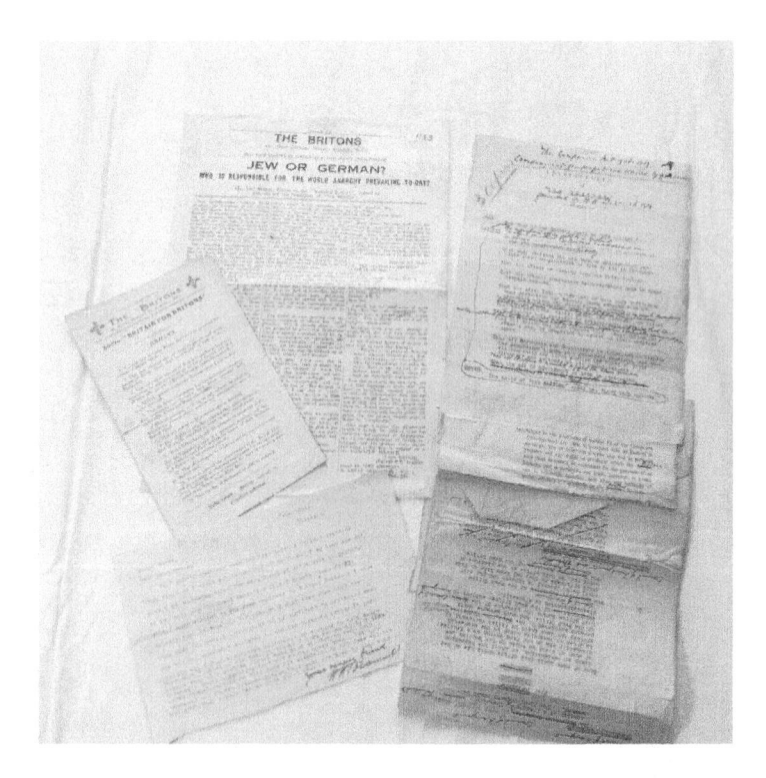

FIGURE 6 Early Britons documents, including part of the draft constitution (right of picture), a letter from Beamish (bottom left) and their objectives (centre-left)

FIGURE 7 The London offices of The Britons at 74 Princedale Road

FIGURE 8 Some of the author's copies of *The Protocols of Zion*; the first edition (by Eyre & Spottiswoode) is at the bottom, second left

FIGURE 9 Barry Domvile

FIGURE 10 German Nazi propaganda in English: Fichte-Bund leaflets (left) and World Service publications (right)

FIGURE 11 Henry Hamilton Beamish

FIGURE 12 Henry Hamilton Beamish leaving the rostrum after speaking in Nuremberg, Germany, in January 1937: note that he is wearing his swastika armband. Behind him, in uniform, is his host, Julius Streicher.

FIGURE 13 Henry Hamilton Beamish, wearing his swastika armband, speaking at the Hippodrome, New York, 30 October 1937

FIGURE 14 Henry Hamilton Beamish

FIGURE 15 Letter from Mrs Colin Jordan (Françoise Dior) and photo of Jordan

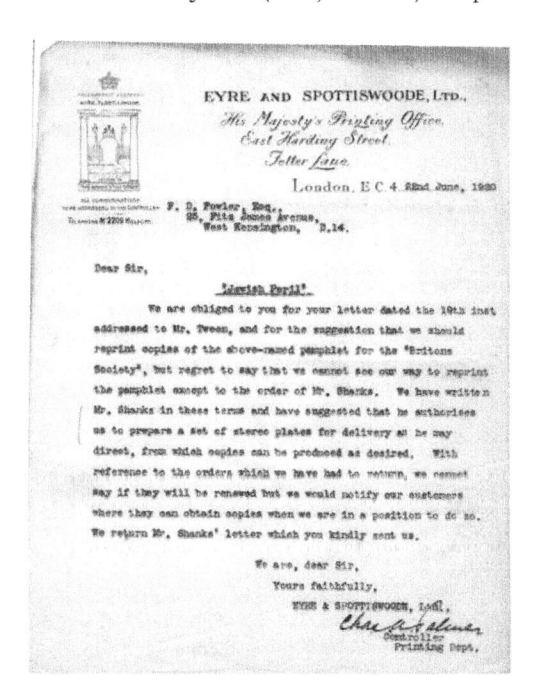

FIGURE 16 One of the letters in the correspondence between Eyre & Spottiswoode and F. D. Fowler which led to The Britons taking over publication of *The Jewish Peril* (i.e. the translation by George Shanks of *The Protocols of Zion*)

FIGURE 17 The *National Socialist*, Vol. 1, No. 3, January 1963, with cover photo of Colin Jordan

6

ARNOLD LEESE AND THE BRITONS

Although he was never officially a member of The Britons, Arnold Leese played a crucial role in the life of the organisation and in the spread of Jew-hatred in Britain and overseas. Indeed, his utterly obsessive anti-Jewish campaigning easily matched that of Henry Hamilton Beamish, with whom he formed a long and close working friendship. No account of Beamish and The Britons would be complete without examining the life of Leese.

Arnold Spencer Leese was born in October 1878 in Lytham, Lancashire, the last but one of eight surviving children, five girls and three boys, of Spencer Leese and Mary Ellen Hudson. His father was a professional artist who died just before Leese began his final term at school. His education had begun at a dame school, continued at a boys' day school and was completed at Giggleswick School in Settle, Yorkshire. Arnold Leese wasn't academic, didn't enjoy school and didn't do particularly well. At fifteen, he became articled to a chartered accountant and spent what he described as 'three rather miserable years in the City', working at Messrs Craggs, Turketine & Co. While there, he lodged with a family in Hampstead. Their youngest daughter, May Winifred King, who was six years his junior, was just a child when Leese moved in but would eventually become his wife.

Aged eighteen, Leese enrolled as a student at the Royal Veterinary College in Camden Town. A lifelong animal lover, here, at last, he excelled. He loved the four-year course and spent his vacations working in veterinary practices, first as a pupil, then as an 'improver' and finally as assistant. Later, working as a locum for a vet at Seaham Harbour, he daily went down the Seaham and Silksworth pits to tend their 400 pit ponies. Having won a childhood bet made with his sister Nora that he wouldn't drink or smoke until he was of age, he maintained that pledge, abstaining from both alcohol and tobacco for the rest of his life.

Having graduated in the summer of 1903 as a member of the Royal College of Veterinary Surgeons, Leese took up a post as an assistant with a veterinary practice in North London (Messrs Batt & Sons of Oxford Street). A year later he took a better post in the East End, managing a practice for the estate of a vet who had died. Much of his work during this period was with horses. He then took a two-month postgraduate course before securing a post in the Indian Civil Veterinary Service.

Leese worked for six years throughout North-West India, and it was during this time that he began treating camels. In 1909 the first of many articles he would write on the maladies of camels appeared in the *Journal of Tropical Veterinary Science*. He soon became a recognised authority on these creatures. There is even a camel parasite, *Thelazia leesei*, which is named after him.

In February 1912, Leese left India and sailed back to England, where he spent two months, during which time he visited the King family and he and May Winifred announced their engagement. He then joined the Veterinary Department of the East Africa Government as a camel officer, based in Marsabit, in what later became Kenya. It was a tough, Spartan existence. Leese lived by shooting, butchering and cooking his own food, mostly birds and small deer. He didn't much enjoy the eighteen months spent there, and his health suffered.

At the start of the Great War, Leese took a commission as a captain in the East Africa Veterinary Corps, again working with camels, and served for two gruelling months in the Serengeti before returning to England. There he joined the Royal Army Veterinary Corps, was made a captain after nine months' service, and was sent to serve in the trenches in France. A year later, while he was on his first home leave, he and May Winifred were married. They didn't have long together: he returned to France to work in a veterinary hospital at Abbeville. After a while there, he was transferred to Somaliland with instructions to buy a herd of camels and ship them to Egypt, which he did, picking up a dose of malaria en route. Following a brief period of leave in England, Leese returned to the front in France, where he served until the end of the war. Here, in his own words, are the details of one particular experience:

> One night, the depot suffered an intense bombing, 320 horses being hit, of which about 180 were killed outright or had to be slaughtered. I was on continuous duty for 48 hours; in some sections, the dead horses were piled one on top of the other to the height of one's shoulders; perhaps the ones at the bottom of the heap were still breathing, some with their legs blown right off. I had to get them out how I could, and my revolver was almost too hot to hold. One poor fellow, I remember, had both hind legs blown off at the hock and was standing on the stumps, looking like a bewildered rocking-horse; I could not get his head down for the usual brain shot, and I shot him just in front of the ear and leapt quickly to one side as he came crashing down dead, nearly on top of me. All that first night I was doing this grizzly work, shooting the hopeless cases and extricating the others. All next day I was doing first-aid on the wounded ones, getting the milder cases off on the one-mile march to hospital before they had time to get too stiff to move off under their own power, and loading the worst cases into ambulances. Right

into the second night I was still extracting splinters from wounded horses where the missiles had not penetrated deeply enough to require special facilities for their removal. I knew the beastliness of war, that night.

Leese was a man who didn't make human friendships easily and he didn't like children. Even his devoted wife, May Winifred, received scant attention. There are few mentions of her in his slim autobiography, and she appears in none of the eleven photos, most of which are of Arnold on his own or of his favourite animals or of him with an animal. And there is one photo of Beamish, also alone and unsmiling. Both were lonely individualists, toughened by war and empire service, who would channel their acquired grim determination into obsessional bigotry.

By 1919 Leese was in private veterinary practice in Stamford. In his spare time he wrote and eventually, in 1928, self-published a book on the care of camels, *The One-Humped Camel in Health and in Disease*, which became the standard textbook on this subject for the next fifty years, especially popular in India and Somaliland. That same year, after nine years' work without a holiday, he took retirement, and he and May Winifred moved to Guildford in Surrey, where he would live for the rest of his life. By then, however, he had had his political awakening. He wrote:

> The deflation of 1926, which was the real cause of the general strike, had hit every business in the town of Stamford, my own practice included … I knew little of politics and politicians, but detested Socialism in any form, because it seemed to me to be a system which would level down the body politic to a state in which the least enterprising and the least deserving would benefit at the expense of the better elements of the people. … I suppose I was vaguely Conservative, just as I had been vaguely Liberal before I went out to India and found that one man was not half as good as another … I could not understand how it was that, although we had won the war, we seemed to be losing every yard of the peace which followed. Something, I felt, must be acting like a spanner in the works…

– or a hidden hand, perhaps. Here was a man ripe for that conspiracy theory, and he was about to encounter it, via Arthur Kitson and The Britons. In his autobiography we are told:

> I heard Arthur Kitson speak at one or two political meetings of various complexions. Kitson had worked about 35 years for Monetary Reform, a subject of which I knew nothing; he owned a factory in Stamford for the manufacture of 'Kitson's Lights' which were used for illuminating lighthouses and large railway stations. He was not popular in town, but I felt that he knew something, goodness knows what, which others didn't, including myself, and I asked him one day to drop in and tell me what it was all about. That started our friendship which lasted until his death … Apart altogether from Kitson's influence, I had watched with interest the bloodless revolution of Mussolini who, by sheer determination had ended the chaos into which Liberalism

> (disguised) had brought his country; it appeared to me that here was a movement which might end political humbug, and his declaration 'My Aim is Reality' appealed to me strongly. I wrote a little pamphlet *Fascism for Old England*, suggesting that only those should have a vote who were willing to pay for the privilege ... I also joined an organisation called the British Fascists.

Leese continued:

> Arthur Kitson had introduced me to the Jewish Menace, of which hitherto I had no real knowledge. He was very nervous about the Jews because of threats and injuries received, and would never speak of them at his meetings, but he knew all about them. He introduced me to a little Society called 'The Britons', in Great Ormond Street, W.C.1, founded by the now well-known anti-Jewish pioneer, the late H. H. Beamish. From them I got a copy of The Protocols of the Elders of Zion, in which is concentrated the main outline of the Jewish Plot for World Domination. Everything in this little book rang true; I simply could not put it down until I had finished it. When I came to investigate further, I realised how little information was available for detailed study of the subject; want of knowledge among the public was the result of a deliberate conspiracy of Jewish silence; I determined to break that silence and to make the knowledge public property. Beamish lost no time; he appeared outside my door at Stamford on a motorcycle side-car within two days of my application to 'The Britons' for information.

This is glaring example of Beamish's crusading zeal. He gets a keen letter of interest and responds with a 180-mile round trip from London by motorbike to meet its author. It turned out to be a crucial encounter for both men. They became firm friends who would spend the rest of their lives singing loudly from the same Jew-hating song-sheet.

In 1924, Leese and a local friend, Harry Simpson, jointly decided to run as fascist candidates in the municipal elections. Leese wrote:

> we put in a lot of hard and sickening work canvassing our wards and the result was we both got in. ... when canvassing ... it was impressed upon me what utter humbug the democratic vote really is; many people, I knew, voted for me because I had cured their pigs or pets and without the slightest idea what I stood for ... I was a Councillor for three years, but found it dull work. Simpson served his three years and then put up again as Fascist and was re-elected: I did not try again as I knew I was leaving the town. We were the first constitutionally elected Fascists in England.

Leese stood in St George's Ward and Simpson in All Saints Ward in the Stamford council election on 7 November 1924. The results were, in St George's: G. Chapman (Con) 469, A. S. Leese (BF) 449, S. Bassendine (Lab) 413; and in All Saints: A. Cliff, who was the mayor (Lib) 702, H. L. Simpson (BF) 552, J. Harvey

(Lab) 535. So both men came second in their respective wards, in each of which seats went to the top two candidates. Three years later, when Simpson ran again in the same ward, he came first. The results were: H. L. Simpson (Fasc) 528, A. F. Denning (Con) 512, L. Large (Lab) 301.[1]

In 1927, disillusioned with their adherence to Conservatism and utter lack of true fascist zeal, Leese quit the party he had begun calling 'the BFs' (meaning Bloody Fools).

Shortly after this, he joined the Centre International d'Études sur la Fascisme (CINEF), an international study group based in Lausanne, Switzerland. Its secretary-general (1927–9) was Major James Strachey Barnes, who was British but had been raised in Italy and was the foremost British advocate of Mussolini's fascism. By 1929, Leese had become CINEF's British correspondent.

In 1928, the Leeses left Stamford and moved into the White House, 20 Pewley Hill, Guildford. That November, Leese, Brigadier T. Erskine Tulloch, Major J. Baillie and L. H. Sherrard, all four of whom had seen military service in India and Africa, together with a fifth (but unremembered) individual, founded the Imperial Fascist League (IFL).

Tulloch had been a prominent member of the British Fascists until joining the 'Loyalist' contingent who quit during the 1926 General Strike. Sherrard became the leader of the IFL's paramilitary section, the Fascist Guard, which had to be disbanded following the 1936 Public Order Act. There are MI5 files on the early days of the IFL. These claim that it was also known as the Imperial Guard and that initially, under Tulloch's leadership, it wasn't anti-Jewish. That came with the growing influence of Leese, whom the files describe as 'a fanatical anti-semite'.

Leese, Baillie and Sherrard became the ILF's three-man directorate. And, when, in 1932, the other two resigned, Leese readily took charge, adopting the title of director-general.[23] Simultaneously, he took over the editorship of its magazine, *The Fascist*. Initially, the IFL functioned along the same lines as CINEF. However, within months the group adopted overtly anti-Jewish overtones. Much of this stemmed from the fact that both Beamish and Kitson had become active and highly influential IFL members. Leese was the first person in Britain specifically to link fascism with Jew-hatred.[2] He wrote: 'our first headquarters was a poky little room in Chandos House, near St. James' Park Tube Station. After six months or so, I was made Director-General of the organisation and remained in that position until the first day of the second world war when we closed down.'

Throughout its existence under Leese's leadership, the ILF remained a small extreme Jew-hating body which was financed mainly by Leese himself. With the help of one of his uncles, he had been steadily investing surplus income since the Great War. And, because he was a non-drinking and non-smoking man who was anything but gregarious, this pot had steadily grown. As a result, Leese had a reasonable income over and above his military and state pensions. He wrote that

> after about a year, we were able to move to bigger offices, first at 16, Craven Street, Strand; later at No. 30. All help was purely voluntary and unpaid. There was nothing to pay anyone with. During the first year, a lot of political crooks and

most of the cranks went through my hands, but my policy was to entrust no new member with anything important until we had had the chance to try him out, they were never able to do us any harm and were all slung out in due course. We ran a monthly paper, *The Fascist*, and published our pamphlets as funds permitted. It was my rule that no liability should be incurred until we had the funds to cover it.

Money was always a problem for the ILF. There was never the influx of members that might have made the organisation more legitimate. And there was never the kudos of having wealthy or titled members. Surprisingly, this bothered its members, who, of course, blamed the power of the Jews. Leese wrote:

I had imagined, when I started, that it only needed the initiative of a few pioneers to get the support of influential people, but I had underestimated the power of Jewish money; the fact was that influential people would at once lose their influence as soon as it was known that they were anti-Jewish.

He was wrong, of course, as Mosley's BUF and even Maule Ramsay's Right Club would prove. The truth was much more a matter of image. With their swastikas, black paramilitary uniforms, rigid discipline and obsessive Jew-hatred, the IFL fanatics simply marginalised themselves. In contrast, Mosley's movement was glamorous, image-conscious, broad-based in its range of policies, and both populist and party-political. And it had money.

Although the ILF obsessed about Jews, there was, on paper at least, a broader eight-point political programme, which appeared on the back page of *The Fascist* along with a list of publications for sale. Beside its own literature was offered selected titles from The Britons, the Boswell Press and the Militant Christian Patriots. The eight policy points were:

1 Provision of adequate protective forces to secure the safety of the Empire.
2 Preservation of the National Character, particularly of the priceless and world-wide reputation of the BRITON for *Honesty*.
3 Elimination of evil alien influences, especially that of the Jews.
4 Deliverance from the fraud of the Gold Standard; adoption of a Scientific Monetary System.
5 Upholding Agriculture, for the Nation's sake.
6 Federation of the Empire's foreign policy.
7 Protection of our Industries, as requisite.
8 Compulsory Arbitration in industrial disputes and cessation of industrial civil war.[3]

The IFL, outraged by the support that Mosley's British Union of Fascists got from both the masses and the establishment, strove desperately to unearth evidence of their Jewish links. Here's the wording of one leaflet which, in IFL style, carried a swastika in the top right-hand corner:

Now You Anti-Jew Mosleyites! In the 'Blackshirt' of the 29th November appeared a half-page advertisement for Superla Cigarettes. Coupons from same could be exchanged for B.U.F. Publications and Uniforms. Superla Cigarettes are manufactured by the Premier Tobacco Co., Ltd., who are attached to the independent tobacco trade association, whose directorate is as follows:- Chairman: B. Guissin; Vice-Chairman: M. Bendel; Treasurer: R. L. Guissin; Secretary: Maurice Orbach. Committee of Management: S. S. Abelson, Mr. Guissin, A. Orbach, I. Straskin, J. Redman, L. Saipe, J. Solin. B. Guissin is Director of Premier Tobacco Manufacturers, Ltd. Are these the Englishmen the B.U.F. expected us to support? Don't be side-tracked any longer by a Kosher Party! Join the only 100% Anti-Jew Organisation: The Imperial Fascist League.[4]

And the antipathy was returned. The following is a November 1933 report headlined 'Uproar at Fascist Meeting':

A free fight, in which chairs were used as weapons, broke out last night at a meeting organised by the Imperial Fascist League and held at Trinity Hall, Great Portland Street. Uproar broke out when a man exclaimed that he objected to another man, on the platform, cleaning his finger nails in public. Half the audience stood up, shouting 'Apology.' Men in black shirts moved to eject the interrupter, and soon afterwards men were striking each other with chairs, and women were beating off attacks with umbrellas. Chairs were thrown by supporters of the interrupters at those on the platform, and there were broken chairs all over the hall. The interrupters tore down from the walls a Union Jack on which was superimposed a black swastika; a standard bearer was attacked and his flag torn to pieces; windows were broken; and one man had part of his clothing torn off. After the fight had lasted quarter of an hour, a strong body of police forced their way into the hall, and some of the more violent men were forcibly removed. Two men were taken to a police station. The hall was cleared up, the smashed chairs were put in a pile, and the meeting proceeded in an orderly manner. There were cheers when Major [sic] A. S. Liese [sic], the leader of the movement appeared with his head bandaged, and his torn clothes pinned together, to address the meeting. It was announced that the collection boxes had disappeared, and hats were passed round for a collection. The interrupters are alleged to belong to the British Union of Fascists. Brigadier-General Blakeney had spoken before the trouble began.[5]

Despite their efforts to rival the BUF, the IFL remained a small organisation with very few supporters and even fewer active members. Their office easily held everyone who came to their regular Wednesday evening meetings. They worked long hours, often past midnight, to produce and distribute their literature. Here is Leese again: 'For years, I went out every Friday evening, for 2½ hours, to sell *The Fascist* on the kerb of Coventry Street; sometimes alone, sometimes with as many as five others ... We were sometimes attacked, and once a blow over the eye paralysed one of my eyelids for a week.'

The content of the July 1936 issue of *The Fascist* resulted in Leese and the printer, Walter Whitehead, who was also an ILF member, appearing in court. They were charged on two counts, one of which was that they had created ill will between Jews and non-Jews. Two passages in particular were cited. The first alleged that Jews practised the ritual murder of Christians in order to obtain fresh blood for Passover. The second read:

> Jews are not wanted anywhere on earth. Unfortunately they are on the earth and all over it destroying everything good and decent by their dominating influence. The alternatives are (1) to kill; (2) to sterilise; (3) to segregate. Our policy is the last one, conducted and maintained at their expense.

Also cited in court was an advertisement for a swastika badge 'by which you commit yourself: (1) never to buy from Jews; (2) never to employ Jews; (3) to do all you can to stop the Jewish invasion of your country.' The two men conducted their own defence and lost. Whitehead was fined £20. Leese got a six-month jail sentence, which he served in Wormwood Scrubs, though he got out in February 1937, 1½ months early, for good behaviour.

Speaking at a reception held on 17 February 1937 immediately following his release, Leese was utterly unbowed in his Jew-hatred:

> If I am killing a rat with a stick and have him in a corner, I am not indignant if he tries to bite me and squeals and gibbers with rage. My job is, not to get angry, but to keep cool, to attend to my footwork and to keep on hitting him where it will do the most good.[6]

To prove his point, he defiantly wrote (or co-wrote with Charles Gore) and published another book, *My Irrelevant Defence: Meditations Inside Gaol and Out on Jewish Ritual Murder*, for which he expected another prosecution. It didn't come.[7] That same year, he also published, as a companion volume, *Gentile Folly: The Rothschilds*. On the frontispiece were these words: 'This book is dedicated, with permission, to H. H. Beamish, the pioneer, who set my feet upon the way.'

During the 1930s Leese worked tirelessly. He wrote and published at least twenty pamphlets for the IFL. He wrote, co-wrote, edited, produced and distributed regular issues of *The Fascist*. He ran the organisation, arranged and chaired meetings, gave speeches, wrote for other journals worldwide, endlessly networked and corresponded, etc. – all in his obsessively fastidious and controlling way. He wrote: 'We of the Imperial Fascist League did all we could to prevent the outbreak of war between Britain and Germany. We foresaw that whoever won such a war, Britain would be ruined. We knew that the Jews, assisted by the Freemasons, were resolved to destroy Hitler.' Leese now viewed both the government and the impending war as Jewish. He applied a manic zeal to flogging the dead horse of the IFL. 'I was greatly overworked, attempting the impossible by having to administer an organisation and do a lot of research and writing our paper, all at the same time. One evening, when addressing a meeting, I collapsed; it was sheer exhaustion of nervous energy.' On the day that war was actually declared, he was bedbound with a gastric ulcer from which it took him two months to recover.

By the end of May 1940, many of Leese's fellow fascists had been interned under Defence Regulation 18B. He went into hiding, staying with friends or slipping home under cover darkness. A detention warrant was issued for his arrest on 28 June.[8] Several times, police called at his home looking for him, but he was never there. Eventually, though, he became careless. On 9 November, the police found him at home:

> I was doing some indexing in my bedroom about noon, when my wife came running in to tell me that detectives had burst into the house and were half way up the stairs! I seized a thick stick, which I always had close to me throughout the time I had been 'on the run', and crept out onto the landing. There I saw a plain-clothes detective looking into the linen cupboard. I crept up behind him and could have brained him, but I simply said: 'What the hell are you doing in my house?' He turned round quickly with his hand in his pocket and just then a uniformed man came along the passage behind me, so I backed into a corner and there followed a sort of parley. I told them the facts and pointed out the dirty work they were doing for pay. They replied that they were ignorant men who had been ordered to make this arrest and if anything happened to them, others would follow to do it. Reasonable enough, that, for morons! Eventually they rushed me and a long struggle ensued; I did what I could, but there were two of them, each as strong as I was, and twenty years' younger. My wife tried to help me and was, afterwards, fined £20 for it! At last they got me to the head of the stairs and then uniformed men came rushing up the staircase, the first one waving a revolver. This made the force against me overwhelming, which I took to be the only excuse for calling off resistance. Then I was taken down to Guildford Police Station, where, after searching, I was placed in a filthy cell, below ground, with stinking W.C. complete; I smashed everything breakable and tore the noisome blankets into strips and stuffed them down the W.C. This I did because I did not intend to be spirited away into detention without the people of Guildford, at least, getting to know. The Superintendent charged me at the Police Court with the damage, for which I was fined, but, of course, would not pay; and I was given one month's imprisonment instead.

Leese served his month's sentence in Brixton Prison, where he remained as imprisonment became internment. There was much published about him in the press, some true, some not. On 24 January 1941 he and some of his fellow internees were transferred to a camp at Ascot and, six weeks later, by train to another camp in Huyton, Liverpool. Here, on 4 March, he went on hunger strike and also did all he could to be disruptive. On 18 March he was consequently transferred back to Brixton. His hunger strike lasted for almost fifty days with a brief ten-day break on minimal food. He eventually called it off on the evening of 22 April, but only after he had been held down and force-fed through a tube that had been thrust down his throat.

On 30 May 1941, Leese wrote to the home secretary. His original pencilled draft, headed H. S., reads:

> I am under detention under Section 18B, Defence Regulations, & your Under-Sec^y stated in the House of Commons on 23rd April 1941 that you were 'satisfied that it was necessary to exercise control over' me. I therefore request to be supplied with a statement of the precise grounds for my detention signed by yourself, so that I may take action in my defence. Please do not send me the usual unsigned (& therefore worthless) indictment form, as I am not interested in the Advisory Committee & have no intention of appealing before it, particularly since you yourself have now decided on grounds unknown to me that my detention, especially ordered by Sir John Anderson, is 'necessary' – You will recollect that the PRIVATE Secretary of HM the King passed to you my wife's letter protesting in my name against my detention. ASL.[9]

The reply on 21 June[5] gave him 'no more information than I already had'. A second letter, written over a year later, on 12 June 1942, received no response. So Leese employed a lawyer to write (on 28 August). The reply to this (on 12 September) stated that the said A. S. Leese was director-general of the Imperial Fascist League, 'a pro-German and Fascist organisation, and in that capacity was responsible for the propaganda produced and disseminated by the League against the prosecution of the War and the Allied cause.' Leese then got his lawyer to send another letter (on 17 December) demanding 'what specifically was objected to in the "propaganda" mentioned'. Five weeks later (on 20 January 1943) came the response. Leese was dismissive of its content:

> Then it appeared that it was pretended that the items which had caused my detention were: (1) publications made since the war by Angles News Service for which I had no responsibility (although I thoroughly agreed with everything that the Service did); (2) a leaflet which I published called *Leese for Peace*, in which I advocated peace and quoted Lord Halifax's statements as to *Why* we were at war, criticised them piece-meal and pointed out we were simply fighting for the Jews; (3) a printed poem – ONWARD CHRISTIAN SOLDIERS, which I did not write and did not disseminate, nor do I know to this day who the author was!

Leese replied in person, dismissing the accusations. Of that reply he later wrote: 'As to being pro-German, I made it clear that I was against the return of former German colonies captured in the first World War; I admitted that I was anti-Jewish, and that I considered Hitler was right in the main, as I do now.' This brought one last letter from the home secretary's office (around 11 February), which 'made it clear by his evasive replies to my lawyer's letters that it would be a waste of time to pursue the matter further'.

A curious distinction arises here. While Leese was definitely pro-Nazi, collaborating with German and other European Jew-haters, contributing to German Nazi journals and publishing their literature in *The Fascist*, he was less of a Hitler fan. He had never been to Germany and, according to MI5 files, had turned against Hitler for invading Scandinavia (in April 1940). Indeed, on 19 April 1940, speaking at a meeting of the IFL, Leese upset his audience when he told them of his disgust at the German action in Norway. He was also upset that Hitler had made a pact with Russia. In his opinion, Hitler should have been retired and replaced by Goering.[10]

In mid-December 1943, suffering from an enlarged prostate gland, Leese was transferred, still in detention, from Brixton Prison to Horton Emergency Hospital, where he underwent a successful operation. Finally, after three years and four months' imprisonment without trial, he was released on 2 February 1944. He was sixty-five years old. The prison regime had been tough on him, as it had been on many internees, and he was in poor health.

Leese offered 'to testify about the Jewish menace' in the trial of William Joyce, a man whom he had met only once. The offer was refused, as was a subsequent offer which he and 'my old friend H. H. Beamish' made to 'give evidence on the Jewish issue in defence of the Nuremberg accused'.

Shortly after this, despite great difficulties in finding a willing printer, Leese managed to publish a poor-quality first edition of his book *The Jewish War of Survival*. It was subsequently (in September 1945) properly printed and published in America.[11] Also in 1944, Leese began publishing a new occasional journal, *Gothic Ripples*, its declared purpose being 'to keep watch on every important move of Jew and Mason "pieces" on the vast chequerboard of world-wide Judaeo-Masonic intrigue for Jewry over all'.[12]

The magazine, like much of Leese's post-war publishing, seems to have sold mostly in America. Certainly the content of *Gothic Ripples* under his editorship reflects this, from its numerous references to the activities of American (and Canadian) anti-Jewish individuals and groups to the number and range of American publication that it offered for sale – often obtained in exchange for copies of his own publications The Britons worked in this way too. It was a cashless (apart from postage) way of promoting and disseminating work. Although one or two of the organisations involved in this widespread literary and political network worked on a significant scale, most were small-scale bodies or even one-man bands which could, through such networking, appear much more influential than they were. And thus an entire international network of essentially insignificant organisations can created the illusion of a global mass movement.

In 1946, the lord chancellor revealed in the House of Lords that there were five people in the country who would not be allowed passports. Out of mere curiosity (he had no intention of going abroad), Leese applied for one – and was refused.

That same year, two Dutch prisoners of war, Herman Meyjer and Henry Tiecken, who had been captured in December 1944 while serving in the German armed forces, escaped from Kempton Park prison camp by wearing British uniforms. Having read about Leese, they turned up at his home on 13 June and stayed with him for two days before moving to the East End home of some of his friends. Before they left, he advised them to contact a person in the Argentine Embassy in the hope of getting smuggled onto a ship heading for Argentina. They had promised Leese that they would surrender if this didn't work out. However, when this plan failed, they changed their minds and stayed on with his friends instead, and they were eventually rearrested in Worthing on 15 December. Subsequently, Meyjer gave the names of Leese and six others who had sheltered them and then testified against them in court. Each of the seven accused received a one-year prison sentence. They were Alfred MacCarthy, John Robert MacCarthy, Emanuel John William Alford, Leslie Raymond Alford, Frederick Tom Edmunds, Anthony William Gittens (of The Britons) and Leese himself.[13] Because of his previous convictions, Leese was sent to the toughest of prisons, Pentonville, from which he was released for good behaviour after eight months, on 17 November 1947. Almost seventy by now, he had fared badly psychologically, fellow prisoners having ostracised and threatened him because he had aided enemy soldiers. His physical health had suffered too.

On 27 March 1948, Beamish died, having promised Leese two years earlier that he would leave him what money he could. Once the legal process was completed, Leese received £3,350, which, they had both agreed, would be used as the latter saw fit to 'fight against the Jewish Menace'.

Leese began immediately by putting money into a new political party, the National Workers Movement (also known as the National Workers Party), which was an off-shoot of The Britons. As we saw in Chapter 4, the whole organisation rapidly fell apart following clashes between Anthony Baron and Anthony Gittens.

The 14 August 1950 issue of *Gothic Ripples* carried an article claiming that 'Police in the East End of London appear to be instructed by their Jewish Chief to knock off any street-corner orator who dares to mention the word Jew in any derogatory sense. I take a hard view of Police Officers who, to earn pay, carry out such vile orders'. The wording of the article saw Leese up in court once more, on 12 December 1950, charged with criminal libel against Sir Harold Scott, commissioner of the Metropolitan Police. This time, conducting his own defence, he actually won. The case is detailed in his book *Rex versus Leese*.[14]

In 1951 Leese published his autobiography, *Out of Step: Events in the Two Lives of an Anti-Jewish Camel-Doctor*. All his books were slim volumes. The thickest, *The Jewish War of Survival*, was only 124 pages; his autobiography, just 74 pages of text; *Gentile Folly*, 68 pages; and *My Irrelevant Defence*, 64 pages. That same year, too old to found a new party of his own, and disillusioned with the National Workers Movement, he helped fund another non-starter, the British Empire Party, also a spin-off from The Britons (this was covered in Chapter 4). Throughout all of this, Leese remained extreme and unremitting in his preaching of hatred. Here is a typical piece from *Gothic Ripples* of September 1951, headed 'This Nigger Stuff':

One of the weapons of the Jews for the purpose of breaking down the White Races, the Nordic in particular, is the popularising of race-mixture among the ignorant. Perhaps the most blatant article of this sort which we have seen of late is that in the *Sunday Pictorial* of 26th August, in which the marriage of a white girl 'Peggy' with a negro 'Gene' is made the subject of a plea for social recognition. The author is the Jew journalist Sidney Jacobson; it is the Editor who should hang.[15]

In 1953 Leese gave The Britons the free use of 74 Princedale Road for their offices. It's possible that he did this simply to honour the memory of his old friend Beamish. However, a more likely motive is that he was conscious of having inherited from Beamish money that The Britons, now run by his former IFL colleague Anthony Gittens, had hoped to receive. Also, working alongside Gittens was Leese's young protégé, Colin Jordan. In the February 1955 issue of *Gothic Ripples*, Leese wrote that 'The best recognition of our work we ever had was when the late H. H. Beamish made us a bequest of most of his estate.'[16] That year, the old man stumped up more money so that The Britons could publish Colin Jordan's first book, *Fraudulent Conversion*, thereby helping to pave the way for Jordan to become his successor.

And here is Leese again, in a piece simply headed 'The Britons', which appeared in *Gothic Ripples* a month later:

> All friends of *Gothic Ripples* should be thankful that The Britons Publishing Society at 74 Princedale Road, London, W.11 (nearest tube station, Holland Park) has, after a desperate struggle for continued existence, been developed into a dynamic organisation for the dissemination of racial, anti-Jewish and anti-Masonic knowledge the world over. This is chiefly due to the efforts of its Secretary, Mr. A. W. Gittens, and his small staff of devoted workers. One hopes that the Society may find the necessary funds and strength to become the basis of an activist movement of the younger generation. Its monthly organ, Free Britain, is of high calibre. If it had not been for the existence of The Britons Society in the nineteen-twenties, the Editor of *Gothic Ripples* might have remained in the ranks of the Mugs much longer than he actually did; the Imperial Fascist League always had close contact with 'The Britons'; the late H. H. Beamish, The Britons' most active chief, often spoke from our platforms; and when he died, left the greater part of his estate to the Editor of G.R. to be used for anti-Jewish work, and about half of it has already gone to aid The Britons in their time of greatest need. Mr. J. Dell, for many years Secretary of The Britons, traded with us for books in both directions throughout the I.F.L.'s existence, whilst their President of today, Mr. R. T. Cooper, M.B.E., the best anti-Jewish artist in the world, gave us freely his services as such over the years. No one can buy The Britons although several have tried. Thank God for them.[17]

Some ten weeks before his own death, in one of the last issues of *Gothic Ripples* that he was to edit (5 November 1955), Leese commented on the passing of a man every bit as extreme as himself. Under the headline 'A Casualty of 18B', he wrote:

> The body of James Laratt Battersby was washed up by the sea at Formby, Lancashire, on 4th October. Interned in the War as a Mosleyite, the experience proved too much for his mental stability, and although his moral courage was great, his judgement was hopeless; he was wealthy, and on release from prison travelled about trying to organise a World Aryan Union, which might have been a god [*sic*] thing if Battersby had not fallen into the hands of undesirables and abandoned sound Aryan standards himself; but he and his three-men-and-a-boy actually attacked the ancient Aryan institution of marriage! Needless to say, Battersby failed completely to convince anyone, although he was dead right in maintaining that Race is the basis of politics and that Adolf Hitler was a great statesman. Battersby was statesman material gone wrong; had he joined the Imperial Fascist League in the nineteen-thirties he would not have gone all hay-wire under the stress of detention in 18B.[18]

Leese could almost have been looking in a mirror and writing his own obituary. Battersby had been out on the same limb as him. Having been interned in June 1940, Battersby was released three years later. Possessed by a religious mania, he believed that Hitler had been Christ returned to earth. In 1947 he founded the League of Christian Reformers, published their magazine, *Kingdom Herald*, and brought out his first book, *The Bishop Said Amen*. In 1951 he published *The Book of Aryan Wisdom and Laws*. Finally, in 1952, he brought out his most notorious volume, *The Holy Book of Adolf Hitler*. On 29 September 1955 he committed suicide by jumping into the paddles of the Mersey ferry. On his body, washed up five days later, was found a suicide note, which read: 'Through the sacrifice of the Aryan martyr the world victory is assured. Heil Hitler.'[19]

Arnold Spencer Leese died on 18 January 1956 at the age of seventy-seven. A Leese Memorial Fund was set up, which by the end of December had reached just under £84. *Gothic Ripples* reported:

> If the memorial takes the form of a book dealing with the joint life and work of Beamish and Leese a sum of at least £400 would be needed. The Trustees, Messrs. Royston Knott, H. T. Mills and George Pile will review the problem in the light of donations received within the next three months.[20]

All three trustees – Knott, Mills and Pile – had been active pre-war fascists interned during the Second World War.[21] However, the appeal for funds failed. No more donations were forthcoming, so three months later readers were told:

> For the time being it has become necessary to postpone the plan to produce a book combining the biographies of Arnold Leese and H. H. Beamish,

because the Leese Memorial Fund will not cover the cost of such a publication and subscribers to that fund are asked to submit alternative suggestions. The intention is to use the £80 odd, so far subscribed, for a fitting memorial and later to publish the proposed book, which is regarded as a priority on the list of future publications.[22]

The penultimate issue of *Gothic Ripples*, edited and published by Anthony Gittens, appeared in mid-April 1958. The final issue, no. 152, followed more than seven months later, at the end of November. There would be no more editions until the title was relaunched twenty-one years later by Colin Jordan. It seems that, during 1958, there was a final breakdown in the cooperative relationship between Gittens and Jordan. Soon after this, The Britons moved out of 74 Princedale Road and into 111a Westbourne Road, leaving B.P.S. Printing and its machinery with Jordan at Princedale Road.

That final issue of *Gothic Ripples* (printed – apparently as a final concession – by B.P.S) contained the following report:

> Shortly after the production of the last issue of *Gothic Ripples* we received the following letter from the printers who had been typesetting and machining this and certain other publications for The Britons Publishing Society:
>
> 'Dear Sirs, This letter gives formal notice that we will be unable to print any further issues of Gothic Ripples, or any other publication sponsored by your Society.'[23]

Books and pamphlets by Arnold Leese

Those published during his lifetime include *Fascism for Old England* (self-published, c.1923); *The One-Humped Camel in Health and in Disease* (self-published, via Stamford, Haynes & Son, 1928); *The Growing Menace of Freemasonry in Britain* (24 pp., Imperial Fascist League, early 1930s); *Bolshevism is Jewish!* (12 pp., Imperial Fascist League, 1933); *P.E.P. (Political and Economic Planning) or Sovietism by Stealth* (16 pp., Imperial Fascist League, 1934); *Freemasonry* (22 pp., IFL Research Department, 1935); *The Destruction of India: Its Cause and Prevention* (12 pp., Imperial Fascist League, 1935); *Jewish Press-Control* (8 pp., Imperial Fascist League, 1936); *Our Jewish Aristocracy: A Revelation* (8 pp., Imperial Fascist League, 1936); *Disraeli the Destroyer* (8 pp., Imperial Fascist League, c.1937); *Money No Mystery: Mastery by Monopoly* (16 pp., Imperial Fascist League, c.1937); *Devilry in the Holy Land* (16 pp., Imperial Fascist League, 1938); *My Irrelevant Defence* (64 pp., Imperial Fascist League, 1938); *The Mass Madness of September 1938 and its Jewish Cause* (16 pp., Imperial Fascist League, 1938); *Race and Politics: A Counter-Blast to the Masonic Teaching of Universal Brotherhood* (12 pp., Imperial Fascist League, 1938); *The Jewish Method of Cattle-Slaughter: Legalised Cruelty of Shechita* (8 pp., Imperial Fascist League, c.1939); *Gentile Folly: The Rothschilds* (68 pp., self-published, 1940); *The Jewish War of Survival* (124 pp., self-published, 1945); *Chinese Communism? Yes, but it was Jewish when it*

Started (4 pp., self-published, 1949); *Rex versus Leese* (16 pp., self-published, 1950); and his autobiography, *Out of Step: Events in the Two Lives of an Anti-Jewish Camel-Doctor* (80 pp., self-published, 1951).

Also undated, but probably from the 1930s: *Racial Inequalities in Europe* (8 pp., Imperial Fascist League); *Agriculture Comes First* (12 pp., Imperial Fascist League); and *The Era of World Ruin! (The Era of Democracy)* (8 pp., Imperial Fascist League).

Main sources

Throughout: Arnold Leese, *Out of Step: Events in the Two Lives of an Anti-Jewish Camel-Doctor*, plus copies of some two dozen booklets and pamphlets by Leese (in addition to those given below), as well as Wikipedia and other internet sources to cross-check details. Documents marked with an asterisk are original copies in the private collection of the author.

1   *The Fascist*, no. 95, April 1937
2   George Thayer (1965), *The British Political Fringe*
3   *The Fascist*, no. 123, August 1839*
4   IFL leaflet, *Now You Anti-Jew Mosleyites!* (n.d. [c.1933])*
5   *The Times*, 25 November 1933
6   Arnold Leese (1940), *Gentile Folly: The Rothschilds*
7   *The Times*, 15 August 1936, 10 September 1936 and 22 September 1936
8   Handwritten personal notes by Arnold Leese in pen on a torn scrap of brown paper headed 'Essential dates' with, in print on the reverse, 'A. S. LEESE, ESQ, No … / DETAINED UNDER RE … / BRIXTON PRISON / C WING / BRIXTON'*
9   Handwritten draft copy in pencil on scrap of brown paper (could be toilet paper or part of a paper bag) of Leese's first letter to the home secretary – much amended with many corrections and crossings out – originally dated 29 May 1941, but subsequently corrected in pen to 30 May*
10 MI5 files on the Imperial Fascist League
11 Arnold Leese (1947), *The Jewish War of Survival**
12 *Bridgehead*, no. 3, 1 October 1951
13 *The Times*, 25 February 1947
14 *Gothic Ripples*, no. 81, 15 October 1951*
15 *Gothic Ripples*, no. 80, 26 September 1951*
16 *Gothic Ripples*, no. 123, 8 February 1955*
17 *Gothic Ripples*, no. 126, 19 April 1955*
18 *Gothic Ripples*, no. 132, 5 November 1955*
19 Joseph Anthony Amato (2002), *Rethinking Home: A Case for Writing Local History*
20 *Gothic Ripples*, no. 142, 17 December 1956*
21 Friends of Oswald Mosley (2008), *The Defence Regulation 18B British Union Detainee List*
22 *Gothic Ripples*, no. 143, 12 March 1957*
23 *Gothic Ripples*, no. 152, 30 November 1958*

7
COLIN JORDAN AND THE BRITONS

Just as no full account of The Britons is complete without reference to Arnold Leese, the same can be said for Colin Jordan. He was directly involved with The Britons throughout the 1950s, and, as a devoted disciple of Arnold Leese, he went on to become a leading international figure in racism and the one British individual who most obviously picked up the baton of Jew-hatred after the deaths of Beamish and Leese.

John Colin Campbell Jordan, the son of a postman, was born in Smethwick, Birmingham, on 19 June 1923 and was educated at Warwick School from 1934 to 1942. During the war he tried but failed to get into the Fleet Air Arm, failed again to get into the Royal Air Force, and finally enlisted successfully in the Royal Army Educational Corps. In 1946[1] he became a history student at Sidney Sussex College, Cambridge, served on the staff of the university newspaper, *Varsity*, and became a front-bench speaker in Union Society debates. He graduated with second-class honours in 1949.[2] After working briefly as a door-to-door soap salesman, Jordan became a teacher, first in Leeds and then, folowing a non-teaching job in the highlands of Scotland, as an English and Maths master at Stoke Secondary Modern Boys School in Coventry. He held this post until July 1962, when he was dismissed and disqualified as a teacher after his hard-core Nazi politics had finally brought him to national attention.[3]

Jordan's political life had begun almost two decades earlier, towards the end of 1945. When still serving in the army, he found himself based at a military hospital in South-East London. While there, he started going to meetings of the British League of Ex-Servicemen and Women (BLESW), which had been set up in 1937 as an alternative to the Royal British Legion. Although it had been founded by James Taylor to fight for better pension rights for military veterans,[4] by 1944 it was being run by Jeffrey Hamm and Victor Burgess, both of whom had been interned as leading members of the British Union of Fascists.[5] At its first meeting, held in

Hyde Park on 4 November 1944, it drew hostility from the crowd by being openly fascist, preaching racial purity and calling for 'Britain for the British'.[6] The BLESW was represented at a June 1945 meeting of the National Front After Victory, which was A. K. Chesterton's attempt at a post-war regrouping of the British far right. By 1946, Hamm had gained full control of the BLESW by ousting his rival, Burgess, together with the public relations officer John Marston Gaster, whose overt Nazism had become an embarrassment even to Hamm. Despite these changes, the BLESW retained a reputation for both violence and extreme Jew-hatred.[4] On 15 November 1947, Oswald Mosley held a meeting in the Memorial Hall on Farringdon Road to announce his return to politics. Four key groups attended. They were Anthony Gannon's Imperial Defence League, Victor Burgess's Union of British Freedom, Horace Gowing's Sons of St George and Hamm's BLESW.[6] And when Mosley's Union Movement (UM) was formed the following year, despite some objections from moderate Mosleyites concerned about the extreme reputation of the BLESW, most of the latter's members were allowed to join the UM, and the BLESW was consequently wound up.[5] The young Jordan's involvement with this organisation demonstrates that, from the outset, he was drawn to the extremes of Nazism and Jew-hatred.

After being demobbed in 1946, Jordan began his direct involvement in far-right politics. During the late 1940s, while still a student, he founded and ran the Cambridge University Nationalist Club (CUNC).[7] In 1946 he wrote to Arnold Leese, then visited him and May Winifred in their Guildford home, where he soon became a regular house guest. After John Beckett, the general secretary of the Duke of Bedford's British People's Party (BPP), had been a guest speaker at a meeting of the CUNC, Jordan became a BPP member and began contributing to its journal, the *People's Post*; he was soon invited to join its national council. Meetings, chaired by Beckett, were held at the Duke of Bedford's Woburn Abbey home. Here, Jordan gained a reputation for fiercely attacking what he saw as the BPP's settled moderation.

By the end of 1949 Jordan was living in Birmingham, and in late 1950 or early 1951 he formed the Birmingham Nationalist Club (BNC), which he ran, together with its journal, *Defence – Against Alien Control*, from his home in Hockley Heath. At the end of 1951 this journal became incorporated into The Britons' journal *Free Britain*. From then onwards it carried a sizable section penned by Jordan, who became active both as a member of The Britons and as one of their authors, an involvement that would last until the end of the 1950s. His BNC ceased when he moved briefly to Leeds to teach.

Jordan wrote pamphlets for The Britons and, in 1955, had his first book published by them. *Fraudulent Conversion: The Myth of Moscow's Change of Heart* was a 143-page volume which had been written under the guidance of Arnold Leese, who also financed its publication.[8] Leese and Maule Ramsay were both putting money into The Britons during the first half of the 1950s. The aging pair had seen in Jordan a young Jew-hater who would carry the banner of their bigotry after they'd gone – which wasn't far away. Both would be dead within a year. Shortly before Jordan's book was published, Leese printed the following announcement in the 22 September issue of *Gothic Ripples*:

> *Fraudulent Conversions* by Colin Jordan: the publishers are being sabotaged at almost every stage of the process and we are sorry that our customers who have ordered this book are kept waiting so long. The fact that the book is so treated by the enemy agents is itself a testimonial to the book, which will cost 8/10d., post free.

Jordan was now living and teaching in Coventry but spending much time also in London. Towards the end of 1955 he joined the League of Empire Loyalists (LEL) and became their Midlands organiser. However, after having been a prominent LEL activist for a year, he fell out with Chesterton over membership policy. Jordan wanted LEL admission restricted to white gentile Britons. Chesterton wanted it extended to include what he termed 'loyal coloured subjects of the Empire', envisaging an empire-wide movement. Jordan lost out and resigned from the LEL at the end of 1956.[9]

By 1957, thanks to May Winifred Leese, Arnold's widow, Jordan found himself in control of 74 Princedale Road. He and May Winifred soon renamed it Arnold Leese House, which, in 1958, became the headquarters of his next organisation, the White Defence League (WDL). With The Britons still there, Jordan had access to their printing facilities, enabling him to have the new WDL journal, *The Nationalist*, printed on site.

Arnold Leese House was close to Notting Hill, where, in the late August and early September of 1958, there were race riots triggered mainly by fights between Teddy Boys and black residents. It was against this background that the WDL came into existence.

The start of the 1960s brought more change for Jordan. He had a new magazine, the *Northern European*, which promoted his faith in the purity of a white Aryan race of Northern European origin. By then he had split with Bedford's BPP, and the brief flare of publicity which the WDL had gained by playing on fear generated during and after the Notting Hill race riots was over. By February 1960 the WDL had amalgamated with John Bean's National Labour Party (NLP) to form the British National Party (BNP), a name John Tyndall would later revive. From the outset, Bean and Jordan didn't get on well, their alliance being created by circumstance rather than design. Jordan had needed to move on from the WDL and Bean's NLP had been taken to court by the Labour Party over its name.

Based at Arnold Leese House, this early BNP had Andrew Fountaine as its president, May Winifred Leese as vice-president and Jordan as national organiser, while Bean edited the group's magazine, *Combat*. John Tyndall was a founder member. So the importance of this short-lived group is that it brought together the foursome of Fountaine, Jordan, Tyndall and Bean, all four destined to become leading figures in the tiny world of British racism during the 1960s and after. Although direct links with The Britons had been severed by Jordan, the BNP, based in their former premises, drew on The Britons for members and supporters, used their printing service, and sold their books. And much of their Jew-hatred drew directly on that of The Britons. Predictably, the BNP wanted to free Britain from 'the domination of the international Jewish-controlled money-lending system' and to 'send those coloured immigrants already here back to their homelands'.

In the summer of 1960, Jordan founded the BNP's 'elite corps', Spearhead, the party section which organised and ran their own neo-Nazi paramilitary summer camps on Andrew Fountaine's land.[7] They invited fellow Nazi revivalists from Europe and America to attend these gatherings and were photographed wearing Nazi-style uniforms. They carried out exercises, gave rousing speeches, sang racist songs and got drunk together. Despite these apparent displays of unity, the BNP was torn by factionalism. It had too many leaders and too few followers – no more than 350 at best. There was little public action by the BNP – a couple of public meetings in Trafalgar Square in 1960, some demonstrations at railway stations where new immigrants were arriving, demonstrations against a new (Jewish) lord mayor of London, and counter-demonstrations against the Anti-Apartheid Movement, but little else. Attempts to oust Jordan failed due either to procedural hitches or to threats from the motherly May Winifred Leese to take back 74 Princedale Road.[7] However, by February 1962 it was over. Bean, Fountaine and about 80 per cent of the members moved out. With them went the name BNP and the journal *Combat*.

On Hitler's birthday, 20 April 1962, Jordan held a birthday party, complete with swastika cake, and launched his next venture, the National Socialist Movement (NSM). John Tyndall and another future racial activist, Martin Webster, were founder members.[10] The highlight of the night was a phone call to George Lincoln Rockwell, leader of the American Nazi Party. Jordan was the NSM's 'leader', May Winifred Leese retained her vice-presidency, and Tyndall became national organiser. The old Britons' bookshop at 74 Princedale Road now became the Phoenix Bookshop, the printing press became the Phoenix Press, and both the upper outside of the building and inside of the bookshop were decorated with large swastikas.[11]

On 1 July 1962, the NSM held a London rally in Trafalgar Square. Here 800 fascists fought violently with more than 4,000 anti-fascists in what developed into a full-scale riot. Amid all of this, Jordan, wearing a brown shirt, boots and a pagan sun-wheel armband, gave a deeply racist and viciously anti-Jewish speech. Behind him were banners which read 'Free Britain from Jewish Control' and 'Britain Awake'.[12] Jordan and other speakers were arrested, and his speech subsequently earned him a two-month prison sentence (later reduced to one month) and cost him his teaching job in Coventry. In a wonderful legal understatement, his speech was deemed by the court to contain 'insulting words likely to cause a breach of the peace'.[3]

In August, a four-day Spearhead camp near the Gloucestershire village of Temple Guiting was attended by Rockwell and a former SS officer, Colonel Friedrich Borsch. Here the attendees ratified their 'Cotswold Agreement', which established the World Union of National Socialists (WUNS) as a wholly Hitlerian organisation, with Jordan as its World Leader or Führer. More a publicity stunt than an organisation of any significance, the WUNS issued sinister proposals for a global revival of Nazism. It was, for example, to be 'a monolithic, combat-efficient, international political apparatus to combat and utterly destroy the international Jewish-Communist and Zionist apparatus of treason and subversion'.[7] The members got the publicity they wanted, but it led to police raids on Jordan's Coventry home and on 74 Princedale Road, which yielded weaponry, uniforms, and the ingredients to make explosives. There was even a can of rat poison that had been labelled 'Jew killer'. It was sufficient to have four men – Jordan, Tyndall and two associates, Ian Kerr-Richie and Denis Pirie – charged under the Public Order Act. All four were tried at the end of 1962, found guilty and imprisoned – Jordan for nine months, Tyndall for six, and the other two for three months each. In the meantime, public opinion had turned against the far right and its freedom to march and hold public meetings. Anti-fascists turned out in force to oppose action by any such organisations, and meetings of Mosley's Union Movement in particular were ended violently.

The French perfume heiress Françoise Dior had strong far-right leanings. In 1962 she had turned up at 74 Princedale Road and a relationship had developed between her and Jordan. However, while Jordan was serving the final months of his prison sentence, she and Tyndall became engaged. On his release Jordan reclaimed her affections, and the two were married in a bizarre Nazi blood-mingling ceremony on 6 October 1963. The battle for her fickle affections drove a permanent wedge between Jordan and Tyndall. As with so many of Jordan's ventures, this marriage was short-lived. The couple separated in January 1964, with Dior claiming that Jordan had become 'bourgeois', and their union was officially dissolved in 1967. During 1964, due partly to the rift over Dior and partly to a disagreement over whether the NSM should be Germanic (as Jordan wished) or British (as Tyndall believed), the majority of the NSM membership quit, along with Tyndall and Webster. That year, Tyndall launched his own new party, the Greater Britain Movement, leaving Jordan, Dior (albeit briefly), May Winifred Leese and a handful of others to struggle on with the NSM, its Princedale Road premises and its magazine.[8]

1964 was a bad year all round for Jordan. It saw the launch of the anti-fascist magazine *Searchlight*, which, for the rest of his life, would work to thwart any and every political move he made. It was also the year that The Britons quit London. Going into semi-retirement, the sixty-year-old Gittens took the society with him to a remote new Beamish House in the Devon village of Chawleigh. This signalled a complete end to The Britons as a publicly active body. From then on, until it was wound up following the death of Gittens in November 1973, the organisation would be nothing more than a small publishing house.

★★★

Though not strictly relevant to this book, here is a postscript on Jordan just to complete his life story.

There was one last small success for Jordan and his NSM. This concerned the Labour government's foreign minister Patrick Gordon Walker, who had famously travelled to Germany at the end of the Second World War. He had broadcast about the German atrocities and then written a book, *The Lid Lifts*, about the Bergen Belsen concentration camp. Such a background hardly endeared him to Jordan. Walker, who was shadow foreign secretary at the time of Labour's win at the 1964 general election, was MP for Smethwick (Jordan's birthplace). However, in that election, he controversially lost his Smethwick seat to the Conservative candidate, Peter Griffiths. There was racial tension in the constituency, and Griffiths' party was accused of racism after his pre-election campaign material carried the slogan 'If you want a nigger for a neighbour, vote Labour'.

Despite the fact that he was no longer an MP, Walker was controversially appointed foreign secretary by Prime Minister Harold Wilson. Walker needed to win a seat. He was therefore put up as candidate when a by-election arose in January 1965 in the safe Labour seat of Leyton. Jordan saw his chance and, knowing a change of tactics was necessary, adopted those he had learned while in the League of Empire Loyalists. The NSM, along with some members of both Bean's British National Party and Mosley's Union Movement, set about wrecking Walker's campaign and making the election an immigration issue.

When Walker held his opening press conference on 4 January, there was a large swastika daubed on the front of the Leyton Labour Party HQ. At Walker's first public meeting, on 7 January at Leyton Town Hall, he was drowned out by racists with chants of 'Send the blacks back!', and Jordan had to be dragged from the stage. Fights ensued. On 11 January the NSM arrived outside the town hall with one of their members dressed as a black-faced minstrel, carrying a placard saying he was 'Walker Gordon, the race-mixing candidate' and declaring that his policy was to 'make Britain black'. On 16 January another NSM member, Gerald Lawson, turned up outside Walker's HQ dressed as a gorilla and carrying a placard that read 'We immigrants are voting for Gordon Walker'. The campaign earned the NSM much publicity and succeeded in turning the whole election into one about race. When Walker then lost to the Conservative candidate, the NSM claimed it as their victory. If so, it was a short-lived victory. Walker won the seat in the 1966 general election.[10]

In 1967 Jordan was prosecuted and convicted under the Public Order Act and received an eighteen-month jail sentence for 'peddling racist literature' – namely, writing, producing and distributing a four-page leaflet entitled *The Coloured Invasion*. In this he claimed that a million non-white people were living in Britain and that 'The presence of this Coloured million in our midst is a menace to our nation for the following reasons', which he then listed under the headings 'Housing Shortage', 'New Slums Created', 'Disease', 'Burden on Taxpayer', 'Crime', 'Threat to Employment', 'Blood Transfusion', 'Racial Mixture' and 'The Problem Grows'.[13] It was actually an updated version of a piece he had originally published in the *National Socialist* two years earlier.[14]

In 1968, following an internal split,[1] Jordan reorganised the NSM and renamed it the British Movement (BM), which he also led. Seven years later, in June 1975, he was arrested for stealing three pairs of red women's knickers from a Tesco supermarket in Leamington Spa, for which Warwick magistrates later fined him £50.

Having been made a laughing stock by the ensuing publicity, he stood down as BM leader[15] and quit the organisation, citing declining health and personal circumstances.[1] His place at the head of the BM was taken by Michael McLaughlin.

In December 1979, from his North Yorkshire home in Greenhow Hill, Harrogate, Jordan relaunched Arnold Leese's journal *Gothic Ripples* as 'an occasional report', which he continued for a quarter of a century. He had moved to Yorkshire because it was where his father's family had had their roots. From the outset, his *Gothic Ripples* oozed bitterness and resentment, printing blistering tirades against Michael McLaughlin ('this man has pursued a campaign of lying denigration and disparagement against me, impelled by a frantic and delirious vanity which enjoins him to belittle others in order to enhance himself'), against the National Front for accepting Jewish members, against fellow Nazis who were gay, against young Nazis for being 'yobs', 'cretins', 'punks', 'skinheads', 'mods', 'teds', etc., against 'political soldiers' Joe Pearce, Nick Griffin and Nick Wakeling for being Strasserite ('Bolshevism in a brown shirt'), against all popular music as being 'substantially negroid in influence and performance', and, of course, against *Searchlight*, other anti-fascists, the police and the courts for having persecuted 'true' Hitlerites like himself.

Jordan, who made too many enemies and very few friends, was then living an isolated existence in a remote Yorkshire village. For the rest of his life, like Beamish in Southern Africa or Mosley in France, he would be driven to live in a self-induced exile which placed him beyond the easy reach of those determined to oppose him and his activities. Throughout the 1980s, via *Gothic Ripples* and through letters, stickers, leaflets, journalism in other publications, pamphlets and interviews, Jordan campaigned single-handedly against immigration, modern culture, Jews in British politics, Israel, multi-faith projects, and his enemies on the far right.

A police raid in 1991 on Jordan's Harrogate home, prompted by his persistent and provocatively outrageous attacks on the Jewish MP Gerald Kaufman, was found to have been carried out on an invalid warrant. This resulted in his being awarded £10,000 in damages and £4,000 in costs but earned him enemies among those who believed he had won the money on a mere technicality – particularly the police.

On 4 August 1998, seven Harrogate police officers carried out a four-hour raid on Jordan's home and seized 8,831 items, including books, pamphlets, printing materials, broadcast material, videotapes and audiotapes. Having eventually been charged on 19 April 2000, Jordan was up in court in Harrogate on 3 August, when he denied all eleven charges brought under the Public Order Act. There were six charges connected with the content of issues of *Gothic Ripples*, one each for leaflets entitled *Election Special*, *Only a Change of Management in the Regime of Ruin*, *Jack Straw's Jewish Justice* and *Our Steven Lawrence Report*, and one for his booklet *Merrie England 2000*. Charged alongside him was the notorious printer and publisher of racist material Anthony Hancock, who denied two offences of aiding and abetting Jordan by printing *Merrie England* and the Jack Straw material. Jordan complained loudly throughout the proceedings that this was all just in revenge for his payout after the 1991 raid. The case was referred to the Crown Court. On 31 March 1999 Jordan was arrested while out shopping and held for ten hours at Harrogate Police Station while his car and home were searched. More material was seized.[8] In November 2001 he appeared in Leeds Crown Court, only for the case to be deferred due to his age and a heart condition. However, he was ordered to take no part in politics. A month later, on 5 September, also in Leeds Crown Court, a jury found Anthony Hancock not guilty.[8] (Incidentally, his father was Alan Hancock, who had been similarly charged and found not guilty in the 1968 trial in Lewes Assizes which was described towards the end of Chapter 4).

Jordan had, by this time, remarried and was living with his second wife, Julia.[1] In the spring of 2002 he 'retired' to a small croft (which he had bought four years earlier and named Thor Nook) in the tiny remote village of Diabaig in the north-west highlands of Scotland.[15] He died, following a massive heart attack,[1] on 9 April 2009, aged eighty-five.[16]

Books and pamphlets by Colin Jordan

Those published during his lifetime include: *Fraudulent Conversion: The Myth of Moscow's Change of Heart* (144 pp., Britons Publishing Society, 1955); *White Power for Britain: Speech at Wolverhampton, 15th May, 1971* (12 pp., British Movement, 1971); *Britain Awake! Speech at Wulfrun Hall, Wolverhampton, 17th October, 1971* (20 pp., British Movement, 1971); *National Socialism: World Creed for the 1980s* (16 pp., Gothic Ripples, 1981); *A Train of Thought* (Gothic Ripples, 1989); *Merrie England 2000* (40 pp., Gothic Ripples, 1993); *National Socialism: Vanguard of the Future* (selected writings, 136 pp., Nordland Forlag, 1993); and *The Uprising* (108 pp., NS Publications, 2004).

Main sources

Throughout: Wikipedia and other internet sources to cross-check details. Documents marked with an asterisk are original copies in the private collection of the author.

1 *Heritage and Destiny*, no. 37, July–September 2009
2 Colin Jordan (2004), *The Uprising*
3 Martin Walker (1977), *The National Front*
4 Graham Macklin (2007), *Very Deeply Dyed in Black*
5 Peter Barberis, John McHugh and Mike Tyldesley (2000) *Encyclopedia of British and Irish Political Organisations: Parties, Groups and Movements of the 20th Century*
6 Stephen Dorril (2006), *Blackshirt: Sir Oswald Mosley and British Fascism*
7 George Thayer (1965), *The British Political Fringe*
8 *Gothic Ripples* (ed. Colin Jordan), nos. 1–46, December 1979–December 2002★

9. Kevan Bleach (2005), *Unending Battle: A History of A. K. Chesterton and the League of Empire Loyalists*
10. Nigel Fielding (1981), *The National Front*
11. *National Socialist*, no. 9, April–June 1965★
12. *The Guardian*, 13 April 2009 [obituary]
13. Colin Jordan, 'The Coloured Invasion', *National Socialist*, no. 9, April–June 1965★
14. Ray Hill with Andrew Bell (1988), *The Other Face of Terror: Inside Europe's Neo-Nazi Network*
15. *The Guardian*, 12 April 2002
16. *The Times*, 16 April 2009 [obituary]

8

THE PROTOCOLS

ORIGINS, CIRCULATION AND INFLUENCE

The story behind the *The Protocols* is an international one based on serial plagiarism. Versions of how this undoubted forgery came into existence differ in their details, but there is broad agreement on the basic facts.

In 1864 a political satire on Napoleon III, *Dialogue aux enfers entre Machiavel et Montesquieu* (Dialogue in Hell between Machiavelli and Montesquieu), was published in Geneva, Switzerland (and later in Brussels, Belgium). It was written by a Frenchman, Maurice Joly (1829–1878), and purported to be a discussion between the damned spirits of the Italian political intriguer Niccolò di Bernardo dei Machiavelli (1469–1527) and the French philosopher Charles-Louis de Secondat, Baron de La Brède et de Montesquieu (1689–1755). When they meet in Hell, Machiavelli outlines to Montesquieu how he would turn a republic into a tyranny. Copies being smuggled into France were seized by the police, who tracked down and arrested Joly. The book was banned and, on 25 April 1865, its author was tried and sentenced to fifteen months' imprisonment. Joly appears to have plagiarised a section of his book from a popular 1850s novel, *Les Mystères du peuple*, by Joseph Marie Eugène Sue (1804–1857).

Joly's book was, in turn, plagiarised by the German writer Hermann Ottomar Friedrich Goedsche (1815–1878) in his 1868 anti-Jewish novel *Biarritz*, written under the pen-name of Sir John Retcliffe. This book contains a chapter entitled 'At the Jewish Cemetery in Prague and the Council of Representatives of the Twelve Tribes of Israel', which describes a secret night-time meeting of rabbis. This fictional council, said to meet once every hundred years, gathers to discuss the progress of a supposed Jewish plan to gain global political dominance through infiltration of high office, control of the press, acquisition of land, ownership of business and industry, manipulation of workers, and so on. At midnight, the Devil appears to contribute his advice. This setting and the plot are themselves lifted from a scene in an 1848 novel entitled *The Queen's Necklace*, by Alexandre Dumas, père.

By 1871, versions of this story were circulating in France as historical fact. In 1872, a Russian translation of *The Jewish Cemetery at Prague* appeared in pamphlet form, also purporting to be non-fiction.

The actual text of *The Protocols* appears to have been fabricated between 1897 and 1899 under the direction of Pyotr Rachkovsky, chief of the Paris branch of the Russian secret service (known as the Okhrana). One of his Paris agents, Matvel Golovinski, is credited with having actually written it, while another agent, Yuliana Glinka (1884–1918), is believed then to have taken the text from France back to Russia. The daughter of a diplomat and a follower of the anti-Jewish occultist Madame Blavatsky, Glinka is an interesting figure who also supplied the Okhrana with another anti-Jewish document, *The Secret of the Jews*, which blamed Jews for the Illuminati and freemasonry and portrayed the whole as a Satanic plot against civilisation.

A version of *The Protocols* first appeared in Russia in 1903. It purported to be the actual minutes of a late nineteenth-century meeting of world Jewish leaders, the 'Elders of Zion', gathered to plan a Jewish global takeover. Consisting of twenty-four protocols, it laid down brutal methods to gain and maintain control over banks, economies and the press, to subvert the morals of non-Jews, to destroy their civilisation and to establish world Jewish government. From the outset, it was presented as a genuine document, often accompanied by elaborate explanations as to how it fell into the hands of the translator and/or publisher. Many readers believed it to be true. And it gained particular popularity with those who wanted it to be so, those seeking an excuse to be actively anti-Jewish. During August and September that same year it was serialised in Pavel Krushevan's ultra-nationalist and anti-Jewish Black Hundreds newspaper *Znamya* (*The Banner*).

In 1905, the Protocols reappeared as a final chapter in the second edition of a book published in Tsarskoe Selo, near St Petersburg, entitled *The Great within the Small and Antichrist: An Imminent Political Possibility: Notes of an Orthodox Believer*, by the Russian mystic Sergei Aleksandrovich Nilus (1862–1929), and again in later editions, of which there was one in 1911, perhaps another in 1912 and finally one in 1917 published under the title *It is Close at Hand: At the Gates*.[1] Another version was published in St Petersburg in 1906 and 1907, when it appeared as an added section of the third and fourth editions of G. Butmi's book *Enemies of the Human Race*.[2]

These three separate, though very similar versions circulated widely around the Russian Empire and served as tools to blame and persecute Jews for defeat in the Russo-Japanese War (1904–5) and for the 1905 Russian Revolution. However, their influence throughout this period remained relatively small. Vast amounts of such literature circulated in Russia at this time. Between 1905 and 1916 the Russian government allowed 2,837 specifically anti-Jewish titles to be published. In all, these amounted to more than 14 million books, and the tsar was said to have contributed more than 12 million roubles towards their publication and circulation.[3]

The first British version of the Protocols, entitled *The Jewish Peril*, appeared in the spring of 1920. This was an anonymous translation of the Russian text by Nilus which was published and paid for by private order at the expense of the translator through Eyre & Spottiswoode. That translator was George Shanks. There was just the one edition of 30,000 copies.[4]

The Britons then expressed an interest in taking on responsibility for a second edition. A meeting was held on 4 June 1920 at the home of J. H. Clarke. Among those present were Shanks, who still held the copyright on his translation, a man called F. D. Fowler, who had been asked to be The Britons' negotiator, and Clarke himself.[5] The Britons then met on 6 June and, in Fowler's absence, agreed to go ahead. That evening, Clarke (whose handwriting is far from easy to read) wrote as follows to Fowler:

> We were very sorry to miss you this afternoon. It was an extraordinarily interesting meeting – Re 'Peril'. It was thought so urgent that it should come out that we should be glad if you would ask E. & S. what their terms would be for say 2000 copies. We don't propose to make any alterations at present, but if we pay for the edition [we] should like 'The Britons' to be the publishers. Will you please undertake this? Congratulate you on your letter in Spectator. The editor [illegible word] of the title of mine 'Britain for Britons'. The editor's notes are quite fair especially the one on the Samuel tribe.
>
> Peters was here today & Mr Robt. Saunders who gave a quite plain account of underground Ireland.
>
> John H. Clarke
> We agree to Shanks 3d a copy if we can arrange with E & S.[6]

Notes: E. & S. is clearly Eyre & Spottiswoode; Peters is probably W.A. Peters of The Britons who, in 1923, would – with Clarke and Cooper – found The Britons Publishing Company; 3d was the royalty per sold copy to be paid to Shanks as copyright holder.

Fowler clearly agreed to undertake this task because, on 12 June 1920 he wrote to Shanks as follows:

> At our meeting at Dr Clarke's on the 4th you told us that the Jewish Peril edition was nearly exhausted and that you did not propose to venture any more money on bringing out another edition. We had a meeting yesterday evening to discuss the question of bringing out another edition either through the agency of Eyre and Spottiswood [sic] or the Judaic Pub. Co. and it was arranged that before taking action either way I should go to Eyre and Spottiswood [sic] and find out the conditions on which they would be prepared to bring out a reprint: but we agreed that before doing so we ought to make sure that we were not trespassing on any rights – that you have in the translation. We understood you to say that you had no further concern in the matter and that as far as you were concerned we had a free hand to publish another edition either through Eyre and Spottiswood [sic], the Judaic Pub. Co. or other publishers. If we understood this correctly I should be much obliged if you would confirm.

Replying from Dalehurst, Sidcup, Kent, on 16 June, Shanks confirmed that Eyre & Spottiswoode still possessed the type of *The Jewish Peril*. He stated that they would probably be willing to come to an agreement regarding a reprint, adding that they had an unfulfilled order for 500 copies, and restipulated his claim of 'a royalty of 3p per copy sold'.[5]

On 19 June, Fowler wrote to Eyre & Spottiswoode asking whether they would print 2,000 copies and guaranteeing to pay Shanks his royalty.[5] Their reply, dated 22 June and addressed to F. D. Fowler, Esq., 25 Fitz James Avenue, West Kensington, W.14, reads:

Dear Sir,

'Jewish Peril'

We are obliged to you for your letter dated the 19th inst addressed to Mr. Tween, and for the suggestion that we should reprint copies of the above-named pamphlet for the 'Britons Society', but regret to say that we cannot see our way to reprint the pamphlet except on the order of Mr. Shanks. We have written to Mr. Shanks in these terms and have suggested that he authorises us to prepare a set of stereo plates for delivery as he may direct, from which copies can be produced as desired. With reference to the orders which we have had to return, we cannot say if they will be renewed but we would notify our customers where they can obtain copies when we are in a position to do so. We return Mr. Shanks' letter which you kindly sent us.

We are, dear Sir,

Yours faithfully,
EYRE & SPOTTISWOODE, Ltd.,
Charles Palmer
Controller
Printing Dept.[7]

Eyre & Spottiswoode later sold their publishing rights and the above-mentioned printing plates to The Britons for just £30. The second edition, under the imprint of The Britons, appeared in August 1920.

Clarke's choice of F. D. Fowler as the intermediary between The Britons and Eyre & Spottiswoode prompts a look at Fowler's background. Clearly he and Clarke were already acquainted. Indeed, Fowler appears to have already been associated with The Britons and must have shown Clarke some correspondence about his letter to *The Spectator* (referred to by Clarke in his letter of 6 June letter) because it was yet to appear (it was printed in the issue of 18 June 1920). In it Fowler attacks the Labour Party for being 'so enamoured with the Russian Terror' despite 'the fact that 90% of the Soviet commissaries are Jews'. The letter ends by stating that 'it is surely time that all to whom the honour of their country is dear should join with the Society for Upholding Political Honour in registering their protest.'[8] Fowler was the honorary secretary and treasurer of this society (SUPH), which he had founded in 1917 'to expose the abuses of Government by Party'.[9] It operated from his address at 25 Fitz James Avenue, W14 (where he is listed in phone directories from 1915 until 1926 – once as F. D. T. Fowler).[10] In 1918 the SUPH published (anonymously) *Political Corruption and How to End it*, which was described as 'A pamphlet showing how the Standard of Political Morality has been lowered and political freedom lost to the Electorate, investigating the reasons for this deterioration and suggesting remedies'. The SUPH chairman was a retired British diplomat and ambassador, Sir Henry George Outram Bax-Ironside. The one pre-condition for SUPH membership, very like that of The Britons, was to be British-born of British parents.[8]

Towards the end of 1920, Fowler had a book published in London by Grant Richards Ltd entitled *Socialism Explained*. Near the beginning, he informs his readers that

> The anti-patriotic and internationalist bias of Socialism has been largely due to the teaching of philosophers of Jewish race, who have in most cases repudiated all religion. It is therefore not surprising to find that the leaders of the Russian Soviet are practically all Jews, or that the notorious Bela Kun is of the same Asiatic race. Of a total of 556 high-grade officials of Soviet Russia 458 are Jews. Thirty-five per cent of the remainder are Letts, of whom about 90 per cent are camouflaged Jews.

These statistics come directly from Beamish's *Jews' Who's Who*. Fowler continues:

> The tendency of modern finance is increasingly international and modern finance is largely controlled by Jewish firms or individuals. It may be that the Jews whose national instinct is as strongly developed as that of other races but who are not, and see no prospect of being, a nation in the ordinary acceptance of the term – conceive that their interest lies in the destruction of nationalism and the substitution of a world-commonwealth in which they would be on the same plane as other races. They would then, by their industry and talent for organisation and money-making, be in a position to dominate the world. That extraordinary book, The Jewish Peril, originally published by Messrs. Eyre and Spottiswoode, and now by 'The Britons' (62 Oxford Street, 3s. net.), purports to show that this is in fact the deliberate aim of the leaders of a secret society of Jewish freemasons, an aim of which the general body of English Jews are doubtless entirely unaware. In this connection Mrs. Webster's monograph on the French Revolution adduces evidence to show that the French, like the Russian, Terror was engineered by a secret society and carried out mainly by Aliens, and not as generally supposed by the French people.[11]

It would therefore seem reasonably likely that Fowler had first come into contact with the newly formed Britons while researching his book. He may even have been a founder member.

The Jewish Peril initially sold well for The Britons. They first published it (the second edition) in August 1920, and the third edition followed a month later, in September 1920.[12] By August 1921 the fifth edition was being printed. Thereafter, however, sales diminished. Also, by that time The Britons had become embroiled in a bitter dispute with George Shanks, who was demanding the royalties due to him as translator. Documents concerning this dispute and revealing Shanks as the anonymous translator came to light only in 1978.[13, 14]

George Shanks was born in 1895 in Moscow, where his father, Henry Shanks, was a well-known British merchant who ran the family firm, Shanks and Bolin, Magasin Anglais. It was a company that had been founded by Henry's father, James Steuart Shanks, in 1852. The family lost both the business and their home as a result of the 1917 Russian Revolution and returned to London, virtually penniless. It was only when he was back in London that Shanks translated *The Jewish Peril* from a copy of the Nilus version of the Protocols that was in the British Museum. He did this with the assistance of a Major Burdon.

The actual identity of Major Burdon proves elusive. Most accounts refer to an Edward G. Burdon. However, in the Gwynne papers, held by the Bodleian Library in Oxford, there is a private letter dated 11 February 1920 written by the art historian Robert Henry Hobart Cust (1861–1940).[15] It is addressed to H.A. Gwynne, the editor of the *Morning Post*, which had that same day published a lengthy review of *The Jewish Peril*. In his letter, Cust identifies the anonymous translators:

> I notice your reviewer suggests that the translator is a Russian ... The actual translator is a Mr. George Shanks, son of a well-known and highly respected ENGLISH merchant till recently established in Moscow – a sort of Debenham and Freebody. His mother is of French extraction belonging to one of the well-to-do French penniless settled in Russia for some generations. Of course the entire family are now ruined and refugees in London.
>
> Mr. George Shanks was at one time employed in the Russian Mission in Kingsway. He made an exact transcript of what, I believe, is the only copy, actually known of definitely of this work at that time – as he says in the Preface – in the British Museum (It seems to have been 'borrowed' since). He then, with the assistance of Major Howard G. G. Burdon of the Northumberland Fusiliers, a most accomplished linguist, made the translation before you. Major Burdon is a very old friend of mine, and I am not betraying confidences when I say that he showed me the M.S. last November and asked me to help his friend to find a publisher. I did my best: and I believe that, in the end I was the means by which it eventually found a publisher, although not quite so simply as I had hoped. But the really strange thing is that quite independently of either Mr. Shanks or Major Burdon the existence of such a pamphlet was known; and the enclosed leaflet, a copy of which was given to me many weeks after Major Burdon had shown me his friend's M.S. by – you may as well know – General Spiridovitch – tells its own tale. Neither of these parties

knew anything about the other and as you will observe the compiler of the leaflet did not know for certain that the British Museum copy even existed.

It was the accident of my being able to bring these two parties together, that in the end led quite independently of me to the publication of the Pamphlet. I am writing this in order to vouch for the bona fides of the authors of the translation since in my opinion the pamphlet is of such serious import that its genuineness should be supported and guaranteed by every evidence that can be brought forward for that purpose.[16]

From this letter, it is clear that Robert Cust was himself enthusiastic about *The Protocols*. His revelations raise more questions than they answer. He claims 'Major Howard G. G. Burdon of the Northumberland Fusiliers' as a 'very old friend'. Strangely, no record of any such major, or of a Major Edward G. Burdon, can be traced. And Cust adds spice to the origins of this translation by mentioning the involvement of 'General Spiridovitch'. This is Alexander Ivanovich Spiridovich (1873–1952), who was a key figure in the Moscow branch of the pre-revolutionary Russian intelligence service, the Okhrana. In 1902 he was appointed head of its Kiev section. Then, in 1906, he was appointed head of the personal guard of Tsar Nicholas II (1868–1918). Having held that post for ten years, he was arrested during the revolution, escaped after being released by mistake, and settled in Paris in 1920.[17] This was where, just over twenty years earlier, Pyotr Rachkovsky (1853–1910), chief of the Paris branch of the Okhrana, is believed to have directed the fabrication of the original text of the Protocols. In 1905, Rachkovsky had returned to Russia to take up the post of overall head of the Okhrana. The direct involvement of Spiridovich – if Cust is to be believed – would suggest that the rump of the Okhrana (which disappeared in Russia in 1917) was instrumental in that first English translation of *The Protocols* by Shanks. Also, as we know that the Shanks family arrived in Britain with nothing, having fled Russia during the 1917 revolution, it is reasonable to assume that Spiridovich's role – if not assisting translation – must have been financial. The money to pay Eyre & Spottiswoode to produce the book had to have come from somewhere, and not, it seems, from the Shanks family, as they were 'ruined and refugees in London'.

We can be certain that the Shanks translation was done at the British Museum. The introduction (dated 2 December 1919) to that Eyre & Spottiswoode first edition tells us that 'A copy of the original may be seen at the British Museum Library, under No. 3926 d 17, stamped British Museum, 10th August, 1906.' This Russian-language copy carries an introduction written in 1905 by Sergei Nilus, followed by notes from a series of lectures he delivered to Jewish students in 1901. There is also an epilogue by Nilus.[18] The book is stamped with the words 'Passed by the Censor Moscow, 28th September, 1905'.[19]

Shanks, it seems, had justifiable misgivings about whether The Britons would honour their promised royalty payment. He therefore put the issue in the hands of the Authors' Syndicate, who, on 7 September 1920, wrote to The Britons to ask whether the second edition of *The Jewish Peril* had been published. It had, on 15 August. Fowler, who dealt with the enquiry, was offended and wrote to Clarke:

> I enclose a letter received this morning and copy of my reply. I should think that quarterly payments would be most convenient – but why Shanks should put the matter in the hands of the Authors' Syndicate Ltd. beats me altogether: does he think that we are going to play him a Jew trick, or is he of the trick! I suppose the real explanation is that he is in such a mortal funk of being identified with the J. P. for fear that it might do him harm with the authorities that he thinks it safer to make his communication through a third party. I noticed quite a stock of J. P.s at Mudie's Library in Kensington and they told me it was selling well: they informed me that it had been suppressed!

Fowler then passed the details on to A. Toulmin Smith, the honorary secretary of The Britons, for him to deal with. Toulmin Smith informed the Authors' Syndicate that the second edition had been published. This organisation responded on 20 September, enclosing a formal contract which had been drawn up between The Britons and George Shanks.

Meanwhile, on 17 September, Eyre & Spottiswoode, having seen a copy of the new edition, wrote to The Britons complaining that in the preface it was stated that 'Messrs Eyre and Spottiswoode have disposed of their rights in this work to the present Publisher'. They wanted this removed, as 'This imputes a right which we at no time possessed and which we had no desire to claim.'[5] Clearly, the controversy surrounding the book was already of great concern to them, to Shanks, and to some of the book's sales outlets.

Despite these problems, sales continued and, initially, Shanks was duly paid. By the end of 1922 he had received £54.16.6, but there was no subsequent payment. Eventually, in 1930, the Authors' Syndicate wrote again to The Britons. J. D. Dell, by then the secretary, replied, claiming that The Britons now believed that Shanks 'did not wish to be associated or concerned or connected with the book any longer … [and] did not wish for any further payments in the way of royalties.' He was wrong. Furthermore, although another £6.2.5 was outstanding, The Britons no longer had sufficient funds to pay, as illustrated by Dell's candid personal note sent to Shanks (at 10 Great Stanhope Street, Park Lane, London W1 – his home address, listed as such in his phone book entry for that year):

> I should like to add these few unofficial remarks for your consideration.
>
> I used to attend this office pretty regularly to help the late secretary and when he died rather suddenly it was clear to me that this Society would have to close down if I did not undertake the running of the office, and in an honorary capacity; it would not stand a salaried secretary. Dr Clarke used to finance the society very generously, but the time came when he decided he could do no more, and without his support, withdrawn before I took over, I

have had the greatest difficulty in keeping the office open; and I cannot really afford to do what I am doing.

Under the circumstances of financial stringency the Society is in, I wish to ask you as a favour to accept copies of 'The Jewish Peril' in lieu of cash. This would mean 40 more copies, as you have had five recently, if the figures in my official letter are accepted. Or, if you could not see your way to do this, your acceptance of some copies in lieu of cash would be appreciated.[5]

So here are two extremely revealing details. First, had it not been for Clarke's considerable personal expenditure, The Britons would not have survived its first four years. Second, once Clarke stopped that funding, in or around 1923, Toumlin Smith and then Dell worked as unpaid secretaries to keep the office running – and the whole operation was still barely viable. They desperately needed a book which would provide them with a steady income.

With sales of *The Jewish Peril* falling away, plus resistance to its provocative title as well as its content, plus hassles from both Shanks and Eyre & Spottiswoode, continued publication of this version by The Britons was becoming highly problematic. Knowing that, in itself, *The Protocols* was a marketable proposition, The Britons looked round for an alternative translation. They didn't have to look far. There was an obvious version translated by the late Victor Marsden, a Russian scholar who had been a founder member of The Britons. The fact that he was now dead meant that they would be spared the inconvenience of needing to pay him royalties. Some accounts suggest that The Britons might have commissioned Marsden to translate *The Protocols*, others that he had simply offered it to them before he died. It has even been suggested that, since he was dead, his name was used as a cover for some other translator. None of these are true.

Marsden was the Russian correspondent for the *Morning Post*. In July 1920, this populist daily paper carried a series of eighteen articles under the collective title 'The Cause of World Unrest'. The first was published on 10 July. Two further pieces appeared in the issue of 12 July, five more on 13 through 17 July, a further six on 19 through 24 July, and the last four on 26 through 29 July. They were written predominantly by Ian Colvin with the assistance of the paper's editor, Howell Arthur Gwynne (usually known simply as H. A. Gwynne) and several other members of his staff. The articles, together with contributions from Gwynne and Nesta Webster, were subsequently published in book form by Grant, Richards, Ltd, under the same title. The precise extent of the contributions by each of the seven writers involved was made plain in a letter written by Gwynne to Colvin on 17 August 1922 in connection with a payment of royalties:

The shares, as you know, are divided up as follows, according to the average length of the contribution of each person:

Yourself 91
Mr. Grant 48

Mr. Faulkner 28
Mr. W. Allen 26
Mrs. Webster 17
Mr. Meldrum 8
Editor 32[16]

In the book *The Cause of World Unrest*, before presenting a series of quotes from *The Protocols*, Gwynne discusses their origins in the work of Nilus and then writes:

> An English translation of these protocols has now been published (Eyre and Spottiswoode, 2s. 6d. net). This translation which we have compared with the Russian 1905 edition in the British Museum, is substantially correct, but in a work of such importance we have preferred to use our own translation.

The quotes which then follow throughout the articles are taken word for word from the Marsden text first published by The Britons three years later.[20] In other words, Marsden specifically translated *The Protocols* from the same British Museum copy which Shanks had used, so that they could be used by Gwynne, his editor at the *Morning Post*, in the World Unrest articles and subsequent book. And it was this translation, entitled *The Protocols of the Learned Elders of Zion*, which was first published by The Britons in November 1923.[21] It has since become the standard version. Not only would there be more than eighty Britons editions over the next fifty years, but the vast majority of editions published since by other presses, whether in English or translated into another language, have used this version, a fact that greatly upset The Britons, who seemed to think that they, rather than the estate of the late Victor Marsden, were entitled to claim copyright.

By the end of 1920, conscious of their international market, The Britons were already offering for sale a French translation of *The Protocols*.[22] In the preface to the 1921 popular edition of *The Jews' Who's Who*, we are told that 'The Zionist Protocols have been published in England, America, France, Germany, Sweden, Finland, and are now being translated into Italian and Portugese [sic]'.[23] Scandinavian, Italian and Japanese renderings were published in the summer of 1925, as was an Arabic translation, which was published in Damascus and widely circulated.

The first German-language version of *The Protocols*, published at the end of 1919, was *The Secrets of the Elders of Zion* by Gottfried zur Beek (the pen-name of Captain Müller von Hausen), which went on to sell 120,000 copies. By 1922, a subsequent German-language translation of Shanks's *The Jewish Peril*, edited by Theodore Fritsch, had already reached its twenty-first edition. Then, in 1924, Fritsch published a German translation of The Britons' Marsden *Protocols* under the title *The Zionist Protocols – The Program of the International Secret Government*. Hundreds of thousands of copies were printed and distributed. And Wilhelm Meister's *The Account Book of Judah*, which was based on *The Protocols*, sold a further 120,000, while Alfred Rosenberg's 1923 commentary on *The Protocols*, published as *The Protocols of the Elders of Zion and Jewish World Policy*, ran to three printings in the first year and sold 50,000 copies.[24]

In Britain, initial reactions to *The Protocols* were very mixed. Unsurprisingly, H.A. Gwynne of the *Morning Post* described them as 'a most masterly exposition'. One correspondent for *The Times*, while admitting they might be a forgery, claimed that they offered a credible account of Jewish influence in Russia since 1905.[4] However, in the same paper, on 8 May 1920, under the headline 'A Disturbing Pamphlet: A Call for Inquiry', the paper asked 'What are these Protocols? Are they authentic? If so, what malevolent assembly concocted these plans, and gloated over their exposition?' A week later, *The Spectator* dismissed them as 'moral perversity and intellectual depravity'.[25]

Soon, however, the solid evidence against their authenticity began to mount up. As early as 1920, the British journalist and diplomat Lucien Wolf wrote and published *The Jewish Bogey and the Forged Protocols of the Learned Elders of Zion*. However, it was during 1921 that *The Protocols* were widely and publicly revealed as forgeries. Their origins had always been too vague for comfort, and serious doubts had already been cast on the reliability of Nilus and others who had claimed they were authentic. The first solid proof in Britain came in *The Times* in a series of pieces by the journalist Philip Graves, published on 16–18 August 1921. Publishing parallel texts, he was the first to show that, far from being the authentic records of some meeting, whole sections had simply been plagiarised from works of fiction. That same year, in the *New York Herald*, reporter Herman Bernstein published *The History of a Lie: The Protocols of the Wise Men of Zion*, proving the same fact to Americans.[26] And Macmillan published a slim book, *The Myth of the Jewish Menace in World Affairs; or, The Truth about the Forged Protocols of the Elders of Zion*, by Lucien Wolf – based on essays he'd written for the *Manchester Guardian*, *The Spectator* and the *Daily Telegraph*.[27]

Then, in 1924, Binjamin Segel, a German Jewish journalist, published a detailed book, *The Protocols of the Elders of Zion, Critically Illuminated*, itemising the proof that they were false and forged. In theory, this damning evidence alone (and there was much more published) should have put an end to any suggestion that the protocols were genuine documents.[28] However, the fact is that too many people simply wanted either to believe them or to make use of them to fool others. Thus, the same year as Segel's book appeared, Joseph Goebbels wrote in his diary: 'I believe that *The Protocols of the Wise Men of Zion* are a forgery … [yet] I believe in the intrinsic but not the factual truth of The Protocols.'[29]

Legal opinion on *The Protocols* was determined by two trial sessions held in Berne, Switzerland, in the mid-1930s. A case was brought against two Nazis, Theodor Fischer and Silvio Schnell (and three others, later acquitted) by representatives of Swiss Jewish groups. The charges were based on a law in Berne which made it illegal to produce and distribute improper literature. Fischer was the former Führer of the Swiss National Socialists and the editor of the newspaper *Der Eidgenosse (The Confederate)*. Schnell led the National Front of Switzerland, which was closely allied to the Swiss Nazis. The two men were accused of having circulated *The Protocols* and related writings and of laying claim to their authenticity.

The first trial session (29–31 October 1934) dealt directly with the question of whether *The Protocols* were genuine or forgeries. A series of experts was called, including several Russians able to provide first-hand or second-hand factual knowledge of the origins of *The Protocols*. Other evidence came from various journalists, historians and authors who had studied them in detail. The prosecution argued strongly that *The Protocols* were both improper and forged literature. The defence argued mostly about the definition of improper literature rather than that they were genuine.[2] One of the crucial submissions was written evidence from Philip Graves, the *Times* journalist who had convincingly proved that whole sections of *The Protocols* were virtually identical to sections from Joly's book. The second session (from 29 April to 13 May 1935) included evidence for the authenticity of *The Protocols*. A key witness here was Colonel Ulrich Fleischhauer, the Erfurt-based publisher of *World Service* and organiser of the International Congresses of Anti-Semites, testifying on behalf of the accused. On 14 May 1935, Judge Walter Meyer found Fischer and Schnell guilty. Token fines of 50 (Fischer) and 20 (Schnell) Swiss francs were imposed, although the two men had to pay considerably more in court costs, plus some of the costs of the plaintiffs. Judge Meyer ruled that *The Protocols* were forgeries and 'Schundliteratur' (improper literature) which might instigate crimes by agitation against a minority. However, on 1 November 1937 Fischer and Schnell were acquitted on appeal – though only on the technicality that the 'Schundliteratur' of Bernese law applied only to obscene publications, not political ones.[30] Contrary to subsequent misinterpretations by some anti-Jewish writers, the judgement that *The Protocols* were forgeries remained unchallenged.

So what actually prompted both George Shanks and Victor Marsden to translate *The Protocols* into English? The question is a valid one simply because the two translators shared one glaring personal motive. The Shanks family had lost a well-established and successful business, their home, and their possessions when the Russian Revolution drove them out of Moscow and back to England. Marsden had endured jail, torture and neglect before he too was expelled from Russia, and he returned to England so weakened that he would be dead within a couple of years. The pair therefore had every reason to hate the revolution and to look for a scapegoat – and, of course, like so many refugee White Russians, extreme anti-communists and Jew-haters in general, they resorted to equating communism with Judaism and directing their spleen at Jewry and Jews everywhere. And how better to spread that message across the English-speaking world than by translating *The Protocols*?

Nowadays, despite the overwhelming proof that they are completely concocted, *The Protocols* continue to be circulated worldwide as if they were true. Many editions are available via the internet. One ambitious example is *Protocols of Zion: Trilingual Spanish, English, Arabic*, a weighty 400-page tome edited by Dr Hasan Yahya and published by the Lansing-based print-on-demand company DYTV. The English version is Marsden's, while the Spanish and Arabic versions are direct translations of it. Not only is the book passed off as the truth, there is also an attempt to lend it quasi-academic credibility in the back cover blurb. Marred by its semi-literate English, it reads:

Dr. Hasan Yahya is the Dean of Arab writers in North America. Graduated from Michigan State University with two Ph.D degrees, Dr. Hasan Yahya is a highly educated person. Trained as a social scientist, in sociology, psychologist, and education. Generally he was working in Educational institutions. Involved in the development of human brains socially and psychologically. He experienced too many types of work in Jordan, Kuwait, United Arab Emirates, and the United States of America. This is the first edition in three languages in one book. Arabic, English and Spanish. It was composed to serve readers of the world in these languages.[31]

Main sources

Throughout: Wikipedia and other internet sources to cross-check details. Documents marked with an asterisk are original copies in the private collection of the author.

1 Anonymous, *The Mysterious Protocols* (1945 Australian edition of the Marsden translation)
2 John S. Curtiss (1942), *An Appraisal of the Protocols*
3 Salo Wittmeyer Baron (1976), *The Russian Jew under Tsars and Soviets*
4 Martin Pugh (2006), *Hurrah for the Blackshirts! Fascists and Fascism in Britain between the Wars*
5 Colin Holmes (1978), 'The Protocols of "The Britons"', *Patterns of Prejudice*, 12(6): 13–18
6 Photocopy of original letter
7 Photocopy of original letter
8 *The Spectator*, 18 June 1920
9 *Flight*, 14 June 1917
10 British phone books, 1880–1984, via ancestry.com
11 F. D. Fowler (1920), *Socialism Explained*
12 Alexander Baron (1995–6), *Infotext Manuscripts: Protocols Bibliography*
13 Sharman Kadish (1992), *Bolsheviks and British Jews: The Anglo-Jewish Community, Britain, and the Russian Revolution*
14 Robert Singerman, 'The American Career of the Protocols of the Elders of Zion', *American Jewish History*, 71, September 1981
15 *Dictionary of Art Historians*, https://dictionaryofarthistorians.org
16 Colin Holmes (1977), 'New Light on the "Protocols of Zion"', *Patterns of Prejudice*, 11(6): 13–21
17 Richard Pipes (2011), *The Russian Revolution*
18 Anonymous [George Shanks, with Major Burdon] (1920), *The Jewish Peril: Protocols of the Learned Elders of Zion*★
19 Victor E. Marsden (1923), *The Protocols of the Learned Elders of Zion*★
20 Howell Arthur Gwynne (2009 reprint of original 1920 edition), *The Cause of World Unrest*

21 J. Findlater, letter to the editor, *West Australian*, 30 November 1933
22 *Hidden Hand*, 1(11), December 1920
23 H. H. Beamish (with H. M. Fraser) (1920) *The Jews' Who's Who: Israelite Finance – its Sinister Influence* [published anonymously]
24 Binjamin W. Segel (trans. c.1935), *The Protocols of the Elders of Zion: The Biggest Lie in History*
25 Neil Baldwin (2003), *Henry Ford and the Jews: The Mass Production of Hate*
26 Henry Makow, 'Is "Secret of the Jews" another "Forgery"?', www.rense.com/general79/secret.htm
27 Lucien Wolf (1921), *The Myth of the Jewish Menace in World Affairs; or, The Truth about the Forged Protocols of the Elders of Zion*★
28 Binjamin W. Segel (trans. and ed. Richard S. Levy, 1995), *A Lie and A Libel: The History of the Protocols of the Elders of Zion*
29 Alexander Baron (1996), *The Protocols of the Learned Elders of Zion: Organised Jewry's Deadliest Weapon*
30 Imperial Fascist League, *A Brief Report on the Libel Action at Berne, May 1935*
31 Hasan Yahya (n.d., print-on-demand copy, 2013), *Protocols of Zion: Trilingual Spanish, English & Arabic*

9
HENRY FORD AND *THE PROTOCOLS*

The story of the arrival of *The Protocols* in America begins with Harris Ayres Houghton (1874–1946), a doctor who had given up medicine to work instead for American military intelligence. There, he had become obsessed with the idea of a Jewish threat to America's war effort. In 1918 his assistant, a young woman called Natalie de Bogory, whose parents had been White Russians, gave him as a present a rare book, the 1917 Russian edition of *The Great within the Small and Antichrist* by Sergei Nilus, which contained *The Protocols*. She had obtained the book from a fellow White Russian, Boris Brasol.

Brasol (1885–1963) had been a lieutenant in the tsar's Russian Army who, in 1916, had been sent to America to work as a lawyer for an Anglo-Russian purchasing company. For tsarists like him, returning to Russia after the 1917 October Revolution was an extremely dangerous proposition. He therefore decided to stay in the USA, where he soon became established as a prominent anti-Bolshevik journalist and speaker.

Houghton paid Brasol and de Bogory to work on an English-language translation of *The Protocols*, assisted by another White Russian, General G. J. Sosnowsky. They finished their work in early June. Houghton and Brasol shared a deep antipathy for Bolsheviks and for Jews, and *The Protocols* provided them with the necessary ammunition to pursue these targets. Separately, they set about trying to interest editors and publishers in their new English-language version.[1] They would have to hurry if either was to be the first to inform America, as others were already discovering *The Protocols*. In October 1919, a Philadelphia daily newspaper called the *Public Ledger* had published a series of articles headed 'The Red Bible'. Written by an American journalist, Carl William Ackerman (1890–1970), these articles included a first English-language version of *The Protocols*. However, throughout, Ackerman had replaced every reference to Jews with Bolshevists, thus turning it into an anti-communist rather than an anti-Jewish hoax.[2]

It took until 1920, following the publication of *The Protocols* in Britain by Eyre & Spottiswoode, for Brasol and Houghton to find a publisher for their own annotated editions, both of which were entitled *The Protocols of the Wise Men of Zion*. Small, Maynard agreed to publish Brasol's book, while Putnam & Son accepted Houghton's. However, following discussions with an anxious Louis Marshall, president of the American Jewish Committee, Putnam withdrew, so Houghton bought the printing plates from them, found a backer and published the book privately under the pseudonym Peter Beckwith and the imprint the Beckwith Company. It didn't sell well. And the Small, Maynard edition of the Brasol version fared little better, as bookstores refused to stock it, although mail order sales went quite well. Brasol, however, was ambitious for the ideas contained in *The Protocols* to reach a much wider market. This wish was granted when he sent a copy to the office of the automobile manufacturer Henry Ford (1863–1947) in Detroit, Michigan.[1]

In an interview published in the 17 February 1921 issue of the *New York World*, Henry Ford said: 'The only statement I care to make about The Protocols is that they fit in with what is going on. They are sixteen years old and they have fitted the world situation up to this time. They fit it now.'[3]

Ford, however, was anti-Jewish well before he encountered *The Protocols*. The naturalist John Burroughs, a close friend, was one of the invited guests at a 1919 camping holiday organised by Ford. On the evening of 5 August they had a dinner party round a table in a large tent. Ford was not in a good mood and began attacking Jews. Burroughs jotted down in his notebook that he was 'saying the Jews caused the War, the Jews caused the outbreak of thieving and robbery all across the country, the Jews caused the inefficiency of the Navy.'[4] Such thoughts had been with Ford for a while. In 1915 he had scribbled a pencilled note in a small pocket jotter that he kept for ideas. In part, it read: 'people who profitt [sic] from war must go … War is created by people who have no country or home except Hadies [sic], Hell and live in every country.'[5] And here he is again, later that same year, at a meeting with Hungarian (Jewish) pacifist Rosika Schwimmer: 'I know who caused the war, The German-Jewish bankers. I have the evidence here. Facts. The German-Jewish bankers caused the war.'[4]

Ford was far from being a lone voice. Bigotry was on the rise on America. Nothing illustrated this more than the Ku Klux Klan, an organisation that was often as rabidly anti-Jewish (and anti-Catholic) as it was anti-black. In 1915, two events prompted William J. Simmons to revive the organisation. The first was the instant popularity of D. W. Griffith's 1915 film *Birth of a Nation*, which glorified the Klan. The second was the lynching of a Jewish businessman, Leo Frank, near Atlanta, Georgia, after the commuting of his death sentence to life imprisonment for the murder of Mary Phelan, a young white factory worker. The rise of this 'second' Klan during the first half of the 1920s was meteoric. Conservative estimates put its American membership by 1925 at between 3 and 4 million. One-fifth of the adult white male population was in the Klan.[6] And membership went right to the top. There is evidence that US President Woodrow (in office 1913–21) was a klansman, albeit an inactive one. His successor, Warren G. Harding (in office 1921–3), was sworn in as a klansman by Simmons himself (as Imperial Wizard) in a full Klan ceremony which was actually held in the White House. And Calvin Coolidge (in office 1923–9) was a noted klansman who was openly active in the movement, allowing cross burnings on the Capitol steps and reviewing the giant Washington, DC, Klan parades of 1925 and 1926.

In 1910, Henry Ford had hired a former bank employee, Earnest Gustav Liebold, who was born in Detroit of German Lutheran stock, as his personal assistant. Ford, who distrusted bankers and believed that they controlled the press, wanted his own bank and his own independent newspaper. In 1911 he bought D. P. Lapham Bank, a failing enterprise based in Dearborn, and put Liebold in charge of its management. Acquiring a newspaper took a little longer. Meanwhile, in 1916 Ford ran for the presidency on a Republican Party ticket and again in 1918 for the US Senate. He did well in both but failed to win election. At the end of December 1918, Ford resigned as president of Ford Motors 'to devote my time to building up other organisations with which I am connected'. Foremost among these was his dreamed-of newspaper, for which plans were already well in hand. He had hired an experienced newspaper man, Edwin G. Pipp, to be its editor, and Pipp had brought with him a skilled Detroit-based Canadian journalist called William John Cameron. The two had been working closely together on the *Detroit News* since 1904. And Liebold, acting on Ford's behalf, had purchased a struggling local paper, *The Independent*, from its owner, Marcus Woodruff, who stayed on as a journalist. The paper's future business manager, Fred Black, bought a second-hand printing press, and they were ready. The first issue of the *Dearborn Independent*, described as 'The Ford International Weekly', appeared early in 1919.

Poor sales in the paper's first year led to losses of around a quarter of a million dollars. Seeking experienced advice, Ford was told to take one clear issue and keep working at it. He was more than ready to act on such advice. He knew which issue to go for: his paper would attack the Jews. Liebold, himself no fan of Jews, was in complete agreement. They wanted Cameron, because of his great skill with words, to write the pieces. At first Cameron, like Pipp, was against the idea, although he was already anti-Jewish. As a member of the religious group the British-Israelites, he believed that white Anglo-Saxons and not Jews were descended from the ten lost tribes of Israel, and that they, not the Jews, were God's chosen people. His resolve weakened. In the end, Pipp quit in disgust, but Cameron capitulated. He not only wrote the pieces, he also stepped into Pipp's editorial shoes, a post he retained until Ford sold the paper in 1927.[4] As the paper's owner, Ford was president of the Dearborn Publishing Company, while Liebold served as its vice-president.[7]

Although the paper had already carried some articles that were critical of Jews, the first full-on attack came with the issue of 22 May 1920, which carried the front-page headline 'The International Jew: The World's Problem'. It was the first of a series of ninety-one successive articles dealing with 'The Jewish Problem'.

It is too easy simply to blame Ford and his staff for promoting this bigotry, but they weren't operating in a vacuum – far from it. In a national climate more than susceptible to anti-Jewish opinion, Ford's paper simply latched onto the zeitgeist. Sales soared. Circulation rose from a figure of just 72,000 in 1920 to 300,000 by 1922 and continued to expand. In 1924 the print run of each issue peaked at around half a million copies,[4] with a total readership of around 700,000 – just 50,000 fewer than New York City's *Daily News*.[8] Such sales figures, alone, suggest that some of Ford's critics were right to claim his publishing efforts did more than any other to promote belief in *The Protocols*.

Circulation of these articles, however, went well beyond the pages of the *Dearborn Independent*. That autumn, a 250-page bound collection of the articles from 22 May to 2 October, with a preface dated October 1920, was published by Ford's company under the title *The International Jew* and subtitled *The World's Foremost Problem*. Estimates of the print run range from 200,000 to 500,000. It was just the first of four volumes to appear under the title *The International Jew*. The three subsequent volumes were published over the next eighteen months, subtitled respectively *Jewish Activities in the United States* (1921), *Jewish Influence in American Life* (1921) and *Aspects of Jewish Power in the United States* (1922). All four volumes frequently cited and quoted from *The Protocols*.

And it wasn't just in America. A four-volume issue of *The International Jew* was published in Germany by Theodor Fritsch. It was widely read and led to Ford earning the dubious distinction of being the only American mentioned in Hitler's *Mein Kampf*. In 1922, the *New York Times* reported that there was a large framed picture of Henry Ford in Adolf Hitler's office, and after the war a well-thumbed copy of *The International Jew* was found in his personal library.[9] At the Nuremberg Trials, Baldur von Schirach, who had been in charge of the Hitler Youth, testified that he and his young friends had been deeply impressed by *The International Jew* and that reading it had been a primary influence in their conversion to anti-Semitism. And Ford himself had impressed these young Nazis, as von Schirach went on to explain, telling the court that

> we saw in Henry Ford the representative of success, also the exponent of a progressive social policy. In the poverty-stricken and wretched Germany of the time, youth looked toward America, and apart from the great benefactor, Herbert Hoover, it was Henry Ford who to us represented America.[10]

In 1925, Aaron Sapiro, who was a San Francisco lawyer and organiser of a Jewish farm collective, sued Ford for libel. This concerned anti-Jewish remarks made about him in the *Dearborn Independent*, which had mounted a series of fierce attacks on him and his farming campaigns. Sapiro said that his million-dollar libel suit for defamation of character was 'to vindicate myself and my race'.

After much preparation, the case finally came to court on 15 March 1927. During the trial, the newspaper's editor, William Cameron, testified that he never discussed the paper's content with Ford and that the editorials, though published under Ford's byline, weren't written by him or even shown to him prior to publication.[4] However, James M. Miller, who had worked on the paper, testified that

Ford had told him that he intended to expose Sapiro. Later, Mrs Stanley Ruddiman, who was a friend of the Ford family, told the court: 'I don't think Mr. Cameron ever wrote anything for publication without Mr. Ford's approval.'[11] With the case looking unwinnable, Ford eventually agreed to a distinctly unfavourable settlement, which included his making a full retraction and formal public apology. That December, he sold the *Dearborn Independent*.

Ford's apology was drawn up by the lawyer Louis Marshall in consultation with Ford's representative, Joseph Palma. On 30 June, Palma passed a draft copy of the proposed text of the apology to another Ford man, Arthur Brisbane. He, in turn, took it to Harry Bennett in Ford's New York City offices. Bennett, in the presence of Ford's New York business representative, Gaston Plantiff, then phoned Henry Ford. After telling Ford that it was 'pretty bad', he began to read out the wording of the apology. Ford didn't want to hear it. He stopped Bennett, saying, 'I don't care how bad it is, you just settle it up.' He then added: 'The worse they make of it, the better.' Palma reiterated how bad it was, only to be told by Ford to 'Go to it.' Bennett claimed later that Ford didn't even sign the document but simply instructed him (Bennett) to forge his signature and send the completed document to Marshall, who was astonished to receive the signed item without a single deletion or amendment.

Worldwide publication of Henry Ford's 'apology' followed on 8 July 1927. The full text reads as follows:

> For some time past I have given consideration to the series of articles concerning Jews which since 1920 have appeared in *The Dearborn Independent*. Some of them have been reprinted in pamphlet form under the title, 'The International Jew.' Although both publications are my property, it goes without saying that in the multitude of my activities it has been impossible for me to devote personal attention to their management or to keep informed as to their contents. It has therefore inevitably followed that the conduct and policy of these publications had to be delegated to men whom I placed in charge of them and upon whom I relied implicitly.
>
> To my great regret I have learned that Jews generally, and particularly those of this country, not only resent these publications as promoting anti-Semitism, but regard me as their enemy. Trusted friends with whom I have conferred recently have assured me in all sincerity that in their opinion the character of the charges and insinuations made against the Jews, both individually and collectively, contained in many of the articles which have been circulated periodically in *The Dearborn Independent* and have been reprinted in the pamphlets mentioned, justifies the righteous indignation entertained by Jews everywhere towards me because of the mental anguish occasioned by the unprovoked reflections made against them.
>
> This has led me to direct my personal attention to this subject, in order to ascertain the exact nature of these articles. As a result of this survey I confess

that I am deeply mortified that this journal, which is intended to be constructive and not destructive, has been made the medium for resurrecting exploded fictions, for giving currency to the so-called *Protocols of the Wise Men of Zion*, which have been demonstrated, as I learn, to be gross forgeries, and for contending that the Jews have been engaged in a conspiracy to control the capital and the industries of the world, besides laying at their door many offenses against decency, public order and good morals.

Had I appreciated even the general nature, to say nothing of the details, of these utterances, I would have forbidden their circulation without a moment's hesitation, because I am fully aware of the virtues of the Jewish people as a whole, of what they and their ancestors have done for civilisation and for mankind and toward the development of commerce and industry, of their sobriety and diligence, their benevolence and their unselfish interest in the public welfare.

Of course there are black sheep in every flock, as there are among men of all races, creeds, and nationalities who are at times evildoers. It is wrong, however, to judge a people by a few individuals, and I therefore join in condemning unreservedly all wholesale denunciations and attacks.

Those who know me can bear witness that it is not in my nature to inflict insult upon and to occasion pain to anybody, and that it has been my effort to free myself from prejudice. Because of that I frankly confess that I have been greatly shocked as a result of my study and examination of the files of *The Dearborn Independent* and of the pamphlets entitled 'The International Jew.' I deem it to be my duty as an honourable man to make amends for the wrong done to the Jews as fellow-men and brothers, by asking their forgiveness for the harm that I have unintentionally committed, by retracting so far as lies within my power the offensive charges laid at their door by those publications, and by giving them the unqualified assurance that henceforth they may look to me for friendship and good will.

It is needless to add that the pamphlets which have been distributed throughout the country and in foreign lands will be withdrawn from circulation, that in every way possible I will make it known that they have my unqualified disapproval, and that henceforth *The Dearborn Independent* will be conducted under such auspices that articles reflecting upon the Jews will never again appear in its columns.

Finally, let me add that this statement is made on my own initiative and wholly in the interest of right and justice and in accordance with what I regard as my solemn duty as a man and as a citizen. – Henry Ford, June 30, 1927, Dearborn, Michigan.[4]

The apology is longwinded and patronising, but – of course – Ford neither wrote it nor read it. It genuinely didn't matter to him. He was a rugged individualist whose towering wealth and power made him feel virtually invulnerable. However, as a businessman, he was a pragmatist. When the tide so turned that it threatened his sales figures, he would act. And if a thing needed doing, he would do it. Also, it is worth noting that his hatred was of 'the Jews', not individual Jews. Indeed, he had many Jewish employees and friends. His hatred of 'the Jews' stemmed from his dislike of all cabals, those power groups that succeeded through mutuality rather than individuality: banks, unions, political movements, politicians and the law. Like many of his generation, he too easily identified these with 'the Jews' collectively. His prejudice fell on a particular Jew only when, as in the case of Sapiro, that person appeared to represent other Jews. This is not in any way to defend his brand of Jew-hatred, more to distinguish it from that of someone like Leese or Beamish who focused obsessively on proving the Jewish ancestry of individuals and believed that Jewish blood was of itself a pollutant.

So, publicly, with the issuing of this abject apology, Ford was a changed and shamed man. Privately, he was unchanged, unbowed and simply pursuing business as usual. In his book *Reminiscences*, Liebold wrote:

> I don't know as Mr. Ford ever apologised for anything. Of course, he was supposed to have apologised to the Jews, but I think everybody knows about that. He never even read that or never even knew what it contained. He simply told them to go ahead and fix it up.[4]

In 1934, less than seven years after Ford's personal abdication from active public Jew-hatred, the Patriotic Publishing Company of Chicago produced a 300-page expanded edition of *The Protocols*, which was published under the title *United We Stand, Divided We Fall: The Protocols of the Meetings of the Learned Elders of Zion*. This was The Britons' Marsden translation with extensive notes, most of which consisted of complete articles from the *Dearborn Independent* culled from Ford's *The International Jew*.[12] And in 1949, in England, George F. Green published his one-volume abridged version of *The International Jew*.[3] Like the Marsden translation of *The Protocols*, the Green abridgement has since become a widely republished standard text.

In July 1938, in celebration of Henry Ford's seventy-fifth birthday, Hitler's Nazi government awarded him the Grand Cross of the German Eagle, the highest medal Nazi Germany gave to any foreign citizen. The fact that he didn't refuse it but chose instead to publish photos of himself having the award bestowed on him by the German consul speaks volumes.

Main sources

Throughout: Wikipedia and other internet sources to cross-check details. Documents marked with an asterisk are original copies in the private collection of the author.

1 Wikipedia, *Boris Brasol*
2 Wikipedia, *Carl W. Ackerman*
3 G. F. Green (June 1949), *The International Jew*★
4 Neil Baldwin (2003), *Henry Ford and the Jews: The Mass Production of Hate*
5 Barbara S. Kraft (1978), *The Peace Ship*
6 Marty Gitlin (2009), *The Ku Klux Klan: A Guide to an American Subculture*
7 *Dearborn Independent*, various issues, 1921–7★
8 Alex Grobman (2011), *License to Murder: The Enduring Threat of The Protocols of the Elders of Zion*
9 Timothy W. Ryback (2008), *Hitler's Private Library: The Books that Shaped his Life*
10 Max Wallace (2003), *The American Axis: Henry Ford, Charles Lindberg, and the Rise of the Third Reich*
11 Michael Barkun (1996), *Religion and the Racist Right: The Origins of the Christian Identity Movement*
12 Victor E. Marsden (1934), *United We Stand, Divided We Fall: The Protocols of the Meetings of the Learned Elders of Zion*

POSTSCRIPT

The legacy of Henry Hamilton Beamish and The Britons

Henry Hamilton Beamish, who died in 1948, and Arnold Spencer Leese, who died in 1956, were Britain's two most influential preachers of extreme Jew-hatred. Both are now virtually forgotten except in neo-Nazi circles. Little is known of either man even there, although they are accorded respect through their reputations – Leese for his extensive writings on all aspects of extreme Jew-hatred and for being Colin Jordan's mentor, Beamish for having founded Britain's most significant and enduring anti-Jewish publishing company.

A measure of their personal insignificance is to be found in the fact that there isn't a single known sound recording of either man. Although both spoke extensively in public and lived through an age of radio, tape recording and acetate discs, it seems that no one thought it worthwhile to record a single word by either of them – not one speech, not one interview. Their more moderate racist contemporaries, such as Oswald Mosley and A. K. Chesterton, can each be heard on dozens of recordings, but the voices of Beamish and Leese appear to have been lost. And, while Mosley and Chesterton were much photographed, there are a mere handful of photos of Beamish and Leese.

Likewise, Mosley and Chesterton both wrote numerous books and pamphlets, many of them still available via frequent reprints. Although Leese wrote and published dozens of obsessive tracts and a slim, little-read autobiography, these are more rarely republished, and it requires some effort to trace copies of most of them. Beamish, by contrast, was much less literate, preferring to leave the writing to others. Indeed, he published virtually nothing except for some of his letters and speeches, a few articles for journals, and the extremely rare *Jews' Who's Who*, which, in all probability, was his personal research written up by his assistant, Harry MacLeod Fraser.

Ironically, Beamish, who attacked the Jews as belonging to no nation, became equally stateless precisely because of his Jew-hatred. Thus he was driven out of his

British homeland in 1919 by the Mond court case and jailed during the early 1940s by his adopted country, Rhodesia. And, also because of his views, he spent most of his life globe-trotting, living a nomadic existence more wandering than that of any Jew – but here was a man who lacked the vision or intelligence ever to see himself as he really was.

His one memorable achievement, The Britons, succeeded only by becoming something Beamish never even envisioned. When, in the early months of 1919, he drew up his plans for the organisation (see appendix 5), he imagined a society with a nationwide membership of many thousands, an anti-alien pressure group with active branches throughout the country. Had his envisaged network of Jew-hatred become a popular reality, it might have seen Britain blaming the Jews during the General Strike of the mid-1920s and the slump of the mid-1930s. It might even have brought to fruition his vision of Anglo-German unity in a second world war against Judeo-Bolshevism. In that endeavour, Beamish could hardly have been less successful. With its single small London office, the perpetually impoverished Britons remained a tiny club with a membership that never went beyond a couple of hundred fanatics. By the mid-1920s, even this had declined to a mere handful of dedicated and dogged extremists. It was only in establishing the Judaic Publishing Company, primarily to publish his own *Jews' Who's Who*, that Beamish happened upon The Britons' saving grace – publishing. Likewise, it was less by design, more as a result of his prosecution and resultant departure from Britain, that he became an influential global networker and disseminator of Jew-hatred, relentlessly hammering home the same message, in the same words, in every country he visited throughout the 1920s and 1930s – forever the blinkered one-trick pony.

And yet, from this unprepossessing apostle of bigotry came lasting achievements in his own terms. These were twofold. The first was that Beamish succeeded, through that global networking and dissemination of literature, in spreading Jew-hatred and lending it a façade of pseudo-factual, historic, academic and cultural legitimacy. He believed it to be real and played a part in persuading others to share that faith. The second was in taking an obscure forged document, *The Protocols of Zion*, and turning it into the global handbook of Jew-hatred that it has remained ever since.

APPENDIX 1

PRECURSORS OF THE BRITONS: 1900–1919

In the introduction to this book I suggested that readers might like to start by look through this appendix. For those doing so, here is a brief preamble.

The armistice of 11 November 1918 ended the Great War and allowed undistracted international attention to focus fully on the dramatic changes under way in Russia. Its 1917 revolution had toppled the tsar and initiated a ferocious and bloody civil war between the Bolshevik 'Reds' and the anti-Bolshevik 'White Russians'. This was resolved only in 1922, when Red victory led to the establishment of the Union of Soviet Socialist Republics (the USSR).

One very widespread slant on these events held that Bolshevism, and therefore communism, was Jewish in both leadership and origin. Though simplistic, this interpretation provided a tangible and – for many – a credible scapegoat. Jews, like Gypsies, had long been blamed for human woes. Both were stateless cultures, nomadic people with their own languages and ways of life that left them perpetually alienated. And, indeed, 'alien' became the key word used against them. What stigmatised Jews even more was their association with wealth. Even in poverty they were perceived as acquisitive and manipulative – hence Shakespeare's Shylock. The mythical 'hidden hand' of Jewish power is an ancient concept, popular among the Romans and a recurring Christian/biblical theme.

In the wake of the Norman Conquest, two hundred years of increasing persecution had culminated in 1290 in Edward I's Edict of Expulsion banning Jews from England. This edict remained in force for more than three and a half centuries, ending only in 1657, when Oliver Cromwell allowed Jews to return in exchange for finance.

If, in the twentieth century, Jews were to be shown to be behind communism, proof was required. To this end, Jew-haters simply sidestepped the awkward fact that communism was antithetical to the wealth, commerce and banking with which they directly associated Jewish power. One book in particular seemed to provide the very evidence they sought. This was *The Protocols of the Learned Elders of Zion*, which purported to detail a genuine Jewish plot to gain global control. First serialised in a Russian newspaper in 1903, it was subsequently published there in book form in 1905. A German-language edition came out in January 1920, and George Shanks's English-language translation appeared later that same year, first printed by Eyre & Spottiswoode and then published by the newly established Britons.

To clarify the post-war British climate and context within which Henry Hamilton Beamish could create The Britons as an expressly anti-Jewish organisation, we need first to look at some of its precursors. Most of these crop up again in the course of this book, as do some of their members. Listed chronologically according to date of founding they are:

1 the Tariff Reform League
2 the Eugenics Education Society (later the Eugenics Society)
3 the Anti-Socialist Union (later the Anti-Socialist and Anti-Communist Union)
4 the National Political League
5 the National League for Clean Government
6 the British Empire Union
7 the British Workers League
8 the Vigilante Society
9 the National Party
10 the British Commonwealth Union
11 the Order of the Red Rose
12 the Reconstruction Society
13 the People's League
14 the Middle Class Union
15 the Economic League
16 the People's Defence League

The Tariff Reform League (founded 1903)

This ultra-Conservative protectionism pressure group was founded by Sir Harry Brittain and Sir Cyril Arthur Pearson. The latter became its first president and was succeeded by Viscount Ridley. Sir Henry Page Croft became chairman of its organisation committee. Campaigning against 'unfair' foreign imports and in favour of imperial produce, it gained wide support in the run-up to the First World War. However, having proved both divisive and electorally disastrous to the Conservative Party, it was disbanded after the war, and its mantle of xenophobic and imperial protectionism passed to a variety of other groups, some of which are listed below.

The Eugenics Education Society (later the Eugenics Society) (founded 1907)

The Eugenics Education Society (EES) was founded in 1907 with the elderly Sir Francis Galton as its honorary president. An influential early member was George

P. Mudge, a lecturer at the London Medical School who wrote the widely read and still popular *A Textbook of Biology* (1901); he later became a founder member of The Britons. Other active EES members were Arnold White (also of The Britons) and George Lane-Fox Pitt-Rivers (later to be in the British Council Against European Commitments and a signatory of the Link letter). In 1926 the EES changed its name to the (British) Eugenics Society. From 1909 to 1968 it published the *Eugenics Review*. The society changed its name again in 1989, when it became the Galton Institute.

The Anti-Socialist Union (later the Anti-Socialist and Anti-Communist Union) (founded 1908)

Supporting free trade and opposing socialism, the Anti-Socialist Union (ASU) was set up in 1908 by R. D. Blumenfeld, the editor of the *Daily Express*. Although it claimed to be non-political, its membership came almost entirely from the Conservative Party, and it campaigned against the social reforms of the Liberal Party governments under Henry Campbell-Bannerman (1905–8) and Herbert Henry Asquith (1908–16), whose changes it denounced as socialist initiatives.

There were two general elections in 1910, one in January, the other in December. The ASU was active in both, some of its rallies and meetings ending in violence. Around this time, its journal, *Information*, claimed a circulation of around 70,000. During these early years ASU members included a young Stanley Baldwin, William Hurrell Mallock, Walter Long and Samuel Hoare.

The ASU went into abeyance during the Great War, after which it was revived as the Reconstruction Society 'to oppose and expose the doctrines of anarchical Socialism and Bolshevism' and 'to defend the Monarchy, the Constitution, the rights and liberty of the individual, the rights of private property, and the sanctity of the home and family life'.[1] Another name change then saw it become the Anti-Socialist and Anti-Communist Union (ASACU). As such, it attacked such left-wing figures as Harold Laski and Maurice Dobb and also strove to prove links between the Labour Party and the Soviet Union.[2]

During the mid-1920s the ASACU established links with the British Fascists (BF), then effectively under the leadership of Brigadier General Blakeney. Several ASACU members, particularly those with military backgrounds, actually joined the BF. Others, including leading ASACU figures such as George Makgill, John Baker White and Blumenfeld himself, became closely associated with the BF.[3] The ubiquitous Nesta Webster, herself a leading figure in both the BF and the Boswell Publishing Company, was an active ASACU member who wrote and researched a number of its publications. The ASACU chairman, Wilfred Ashley, would later serve as chairman of the pro-Nazi Anglo-German Fellowship.

During the Spanish Civil War (1936–9) the ASACU fervently supported Franco's nationalists while attacking the republican opposition, whom it accused of being both brutal and Marxist. At the same time, it remained fiercely critical of the British Labour Party.[4]

The ASACU was wound up in 1948, when it turned its assets over to the Economic League.[2]

The National Political League (founded 1911/12)

The National Political League (NPL) was co-founded as a 'non-Party organisation' by Margaret Milne Farquharson and Mary Adelaide Broadhurst (1860–1928), who became its president. Broadhurst was an agricultural reformer and radical who had been the Women's Freedom League organiser in Liverpool.[5] The organisation's offices were in Lloyd's Bank Buildings, 16 St James Street, London.

In 1917 the NPL changed its name to the National Political Reform League (NPRL). In the post-war years between 1918 and 1922, it campaigned to 'wake the Nation to the dangers of Bolshevism' via meetings, leaflets and the national press, claiming to stand for 'the unity of the British Race'. It also, notably, campaigned for Arab rights in Palestine, working closely with the Muslim–Christian Alliance of Palestine. Together, they pushed for changes to the principles of the Balfour Declaration in order make the terms more favourable to Arabs. At this time, the NRPL was also active in its support for the establishment of a Muslim centre in St James. A package addressed to Major Rich and sent to The Britons during July 1927 contained three NPRL leaflets – *Blasphemy & Hatred of Parents*, *British Communists* and *The Red Pioneers* – and two circular letters signed by Adelaide Broadhurst. All five were both anti-Jewish and anti-Bolshevik.[6]

The National League for Clean Government (founded 1913)

Demanding the removal of all Jews from public office, the National League for Clean Government (NLCG) was founded in 1913 by the group of writers working on Cecil Chesterton's journal the *New Witness*.[7,8] John Scurr (also an active member of the National Political League) was the secretary of the organisation, which was initially established to promote the candidature of independent Members of Parliament.[9]

In 1913 the NLCG sponsored meetings attacking Jewish influence on public morals.[10] Carrying placards, groups of NLCG members/*New Witness* subscribers also mounted protests outside the offices of several organisations to which they were opposed.[11]

One of the NLCG's main speakers was Frank Hugh O'Donnell, who contributed a relentlessly Jew-hating column, 'Twenty Years On', to the *New Witness*. The whole *New Witness* circle – which included Hilaire Belloc and G. K. Chesterton – was anti-Jewish, though only Cecil Chesterton (G. K.'s brother, who died in France in 1918) matched O'Donnell for unbridled hatred. Others associated with the league were Arnold White (of The Britons), Lord Auckland, Thomas Burt MP, Rowland Hunt MP, two leading educationalists –Mary Jane Bridges Adams and Sir George William Kekewich – the US inventor Hiram S. Maxim (naturalised British and a member of the British Empire League), T. Miller Maguire (a lawyer and military author), Walter Morrison and J. E. C. Weldon (a bishop, author, and former headmaster of Harrow School).

In 1918 the NLCG changed its name to the New Witness League. It ceased to exist when the *New Witness* ceased publication in 1923.

The British Empire Union (founded 1916)

This organisation was actually founded as the Anti-German Union in April 1915, but changed its name to the British Empire Union (BEU) the following year. Sir George Makgill was its honorary secretary, Lord Edward Illiffe its treasurer.

George Makgill, a powerful and influential ultra-Conservative, was a keen supporter of the right-wing journalist Leopold James Maxse, who edited the *National Review*. The two men shared a xenophobic aversion to all things German and a dislike of Jews. Leo Maxse, for example, wrote that 'the international Jew ... is an enemy of England and a more or less avowed agent of Germany.' During his time with the BEU, Makgill was crucially involved with two other noteworthy organisations. These were the Industrial Intelligence Bureau (IIB) and the People's League (PL).

Makgill set up the IIB and ran it until his death in October 1926. Financed by the Federation of British Industries, the Coal Owners Association and the Shipowners Association, its purpose was to gather intelligence on industrial unrest due to the activities of communists, anarchists, the IRA and other subversive groups in the UK and overseas.[12] For this work, Makgill recruited agents drawn mostly from far-right organisations, notably from British Fascisti (BF), among them Maxwell Knight and John Baker White. Knight, who served as the BF's intelligence director, would later become a leading figure in MI5. White, a friend and admirer of the Judeo-communist conspiracy theorist Nesta Webster, was part of a group within the Anti-Socialist Union which had long worked closely with the BF. At one point, the IIB employed six BF members to masquerade as communists at Maxwell Knight's bidding in order to infiltrate the Communist Party of Great Britain.

Makgill was also the vice-chairman of the People's League, a party founded in May 1919 by the thoroughly roguish MP Horatio Bottomley, who was also the founding editor (in 1906) of the populist right-wing patriotic journal *John Bull*. A number of other small groups were soon incorporated into the PL to form 'a union of men and women of the nation as citizens, consumers and tax-payers'. Among them were the British Constitution Association, the National Security Union and the National Unity Movement. The PL, which Bottomley proclaimed would be 'a great Third Party' to represent 'the People' against organised labour and organised capital, was in fact defined much more clearly in its policy statement. This declared that 'Socialism and Syndicalism, Communism and schemes of Nationalisation are to be uncompromisingly opposed' and that the league stood for 'The encouragement of good relations between employers and workmen, and the discouragement and prevention of lightning strikes and direct action'.[1]

The British Empire Union had no shortage of wealthy and powerful backers. On 26 July 1916 Lord and Lady Bathurst, vice-presidents, placed a full-page advertisement in the *Morning Post*, the paper they jointly owned, stating the organisation's objectives. The first clause read: 'To consolidate the British Empire and to develop Trade and Commerce within the Empire and with our Allies'. However, it was the second clause that indicated that the BEU was aligning itself with those opposed to 'alien' Jews in Britain. Ostensibly aimed at Germans, it read: 'To alter our existing naturalisation laws to render it impossible for aliens seeking naturalisation to become British citizens so long as they remain subjects of other countries. This is to apply to existing cases.'

Throughout the war, with anti-German feeling running high, the BEU led the field, organising large-scale anti-German demonstrations. By the end of 1918 it claimed to have 10,000 members across fifty branches. What is memorable about the BEU is just how extreme its views actually were. This is seen most clearly in the notorious post-war BEU poster headed 'Once a German – Always a German'. With illustrations by David Wilson, it featured a German soldier carrying a firebrand aloft, with a dagger in his other hand, next to an identically posed figure of the same man, now besuited, doffing his hat and carrying a suitcase of sample merchandise. Around these two figures were other striking images: a German soldier bayonetting a baby, another drunkenly mauling a woman, a third having just executed a man, a U-boat sinking a ship, and a cross marked 'Edith Cavell' (the English nurse executed by the Germans). Underneath these were the words '1914–1918, Never Again! Remember! Every German employed means a British Worker idle. Every German article sold means a British article unsold. British Empire Union, 346 Strand, London, W.C.2.'.

In the interwar years, the BEU's stated aim was

> to encourage and develop patriotism, love of Empire, appreciation and thankfulness for being citizens of the most wonderful Empire which has ever existed, and a determination to prove worthy of our heritage and to add lustre to the British name, so that posterity shall feel our generation, by its deeds, has added to the prestige of the British Empire.[13]

When the Russian Revolution brought anti-communism to the fore, the BEU moved smoothly and swiftly from anti-German to anti-Bolshevik rhetoric that was no less trenchant. The pages of its journal, the *British Empire Union Monthly Record*, were filled with dire warnings as to the consequences of succumbing to the socialist menace, complete with emblazoned slogans such as 'British workers, read this warning! Help the British Empire Union to keep out Bolshevism!'[14] And, while claiming to be non-partisan, it warned the working classes that the Labour Party would 'Bolshevise Britain'.

Funded by industry, the BEU had a board that consisted almost entirely of landed gentry, wealthy businessmen and retired military figures. So its members had every reason to fear the spread of Russian-style communism. However, combine anti-Bolshevism with opposition to the naturalisation of aliens and you have the reason why the BEU came to be associated with anti-Jewish sentiment during the 1920s and 1930s.

The BEU was later incorporated into the like-minded British Commonwealth Union (BCU). Soon after this, in April 1926, the BCU was itself absorbed into the Economic League (EL). The EL had been founded in 1919 under the name National Propaganda, its declared objectives being 'to diminish unrest', to prove by economic propaganda 'the vital necessity of increasing production', and 'to combat all activities directed against constitutional government'. Furthermore, its work 'must be the measure of the activities of the extremists, whose widespread and intense propaganda it is our duty to fight'. And its subscribers were offered a regular *National Propaganda Bulletin*, 'being a record of extremist activities'.[1]

The founder of National Propaganda was Sir William Reginald 'Blinker' Hall, a former wartime head of naval intelligence, who had just been elected a Conservative MP. He was funded in this endeavour by a group of powerful industrialists spearheaded by George Makgill. The first director of the EL was John Baker White. For almost seventy-five years, until forced to close down in 1993, the EL controversially continued to compile blacklists of political and trade union activists for various employers.[1, 15, 16]

The British Workers League (founded 1916)

In 1915 an anti-pacifist faction of the British Socialist Party led by Victor Fisher broke away and formed the Socialist National Defence Committee (SNDC) to support 'the eternal ideas of nationality' and promote 'socialist measures in the war effort'. Notable SNDC members were the writers H. G. Wells and Robert Blatchford. The following year the SNDC became the British Workers National League, which later shortened its name to the British Workers League (BWL). Under the chairmanship of James Andrew Seddon, the BWL became anti-socialist, describing itself as 'patriotic labour'. The chairman of its London and Home Counties branch was the Reverend A. W. Gough, who would later join The Britons. Another former left-winger who joined was Edward Robertshaw Hartley, while two MPs – Stephen Walsh and Leo Chiozza Money – both became BWL vice-presidents. During the Great War, BWL members threatened to break up pacifist meetings. Part-funded by Viscount Milner, the organisation had links with the British Commonwealth Union, and from 1921 until it was wound up in 1927[17] it published a newspaper, the *Empire Citizen*.

The Vigilante Society (founded 1917)

See Chapter 1.

The National Party (founded 1917)

Reacting to what they saw as the discrediting of the old party system, Henry Page Croft, the MP Sir Richard Cooper and Lord Ampthill co-founded the National

Party (NP) in September 1917. In 1919, Ampthill was elected its president. An anti-German party, it campaigned against tolerating the presence of aliens in Britain. In a wide-ranging ultra-conservative programme, it also called for

(i) complete victory in the war and after the war
(ii) robust diplomacy
(iii) increased armaments
(iv) the eradication of German influence
(v) an end to the sale of honours
(vi) maximum production along with fair wages and fair profit
(vii) the safeguarding of industry and agriculture
(viii) Empire unity through mutual and reciprocal aid in development of the natural resources of the Empire
(ix) a social policy that will ensure a patriotic race
(x) demobilisation and reconstruction.

Though the party briefly won over some right-wing Conservatives, it fared badly in elections. Of the twenty-seven candidates it fielded in the 1918 general election, most lost their deposits and only two, Croft and Cooper, secured seats. It was at an NP meeting in late 1917 or early 1918 that Henry Hamilton Beamish met Harold Sherwood Spencer and afterwards introduced him to Noel Pemberton Billing and the Vigilante Society. Spencer would later become a Britons author. The NP was disbanded in January 1921, and in April that year Croft and Cooper quietly returned to the Conservative Party fold.[18]

The British Commonwealth Union (founded 1917)

Founded as a protectionist body in October 1917, the British Commonwealth Union (BCU) rapidly shifted its position under the directorship of Patrick Hannon to actively oppose socialism by engaging in covert operations against organised labour. Hannon, a former vice-president of the Tariff Reform League, would later sit on the Grand Council of the British Fascisti (BF). He was a Conservative MP from 1921 to 1950. Another prominent BCU member, Major General T. D. Pilcher, was also active in the BF as one of its London officials.[19] Having absorbed the British Empire Union (see above), the BCU was itself absorbed into the Economic League.[1]

The Order of the Red Rose (founded 1917)

Hostile to finance capitalism, this small but influential overtly anti-Jewish body was founded by William Sanderson (later of Imperial Fascist League and English Mistery), George P. Mudge (of the Eugenics Education Society and later of The Britons) and Arthur Gray (Master of Jesus College, Cambridge).[18]

The Reconstruction Society (founded 1918)

See the Anti-Socialist Union (above).

The People's League (founded 1919)

See the British Empire Union (above).

The Middle Class Union (founded 1919)

The Middle Class Union (MCU) was founded in March 1919 'to withstand the rapacity of the manual worker and profiteer' and thus to protect the middle classes from those economically above and below them. It also planned to protect the needs and interests of its members by providing essential services during a general strike. If that was its intended purpose, its stated aims were more blatantly right-wing – indeed, they were remarkably similar to those of Horatio Bottomley's People's League. The MCU was there 'to resist the menace of Bolshevism which is insidiously invading our country, to oppose nationalisation of industries, to support measures for the prevention of lightning strikes and direct action and to organise workers to conduct public utility services in an emergency'.[1]

One of the MCU's founding members, who became its first chairman, was John Pretyman Newman, a company director and right-wing Conservative MP who openly expressed his admiration for fascism. Another prominent member was Sir Harry Brittain, who had also been instrumental in the formation of the Reconstruction Society and the Tariff Reform League.

In 1921 the MCU became the National Citizens' Union (NCU) with, as its president, Lord Askwith, whose book *Industrial Problems and Disputes* had been published in 1920. Speaking at the meeting at which the MCU became the NCU, Askwith stated that the organisation supported the maintenance of representative government and would oppose direct action for political purposes. On 9 July 1922, having given up his post as chairman, Newman was elected vice-president, and the NCU went on to become closely associated with British fascism. Indeed, two Conservative MPs, Charles Rosdew Burn and Robert Burton-Chadwick, were members of both the NCU and the British Fascists.[20]

In 1927, just a year before the publication of his notorious book *The Alien Menace*, Colonel A. H. Lane (of The Britons) was appointed chairman of the NCU,[18] which became openly anti-Jewish under his leadership. Lane went on to found the Militant Christian Patriots in 1929 and became an active member of Arnold Leese's Imperial Fascist League and of Oscar Boulton's Unity Band. Another member of The Britons, the Reverend Prebendary Gough, also joined the ranks of the NCU. By the late 1930s the NCU, which would disappear around the outbreak of war, had become very closely associated with Lane's Jew-hating Militant Christian Patriots.[19]

The Economic League (founded 1919)

See British Empire Union (above).

The People's Defence League (founded 1919)

In response to the mass strike on the Clyde in January 1919, the National Party leader, Henry Page Croft, founded the People's Defence League as a blackleg and strike-breaking organisation.[19]

Main sources

See list following appendix 2.

APPENDIX 2
PEER GROUPS OF THE BRITONS: 1920–1939

Here, again listed in order of inception, are some of the political peer groups of The Britons.

1. the Boswell Publishing Company
2. the National Citizens' Union
3. the Loyalty League
4. British Fascisti (later British Fascists)
5. National Fascisti (later the National Fascists)
6. the Fascist League
7. The Distributist League
8. Centre International d'Études sur la Fascisme (CINEF)
9. the Imperial Fascist League
10. the Militant Christian Patriots
11. Unity Band
12. the New Party
13. English Mistery
14. the British Union of Fascists
15. the National Workers' Movement
16. the British Empire Fascist Party
17. the United Empire Fascist League
18. the Anglo-German Fellowship
19. the Nordic League
20. the Anglo-German Information Service
21. the White Knights of Britain (also known as the Hooded Men)
22. English Array
23. the National Socialist League
24. The Link

25 the British Council Against European Commitments
26 the Right Club
27 the British People's Party
28 the British Council for a Christian Settlement in Europe.

The Boswell Publishing Company (founded 1921)

This influential and overtly anti-Jewish press was founded by Alan Percy, eighth Duke of Northumberland. The Boswell press published books by many anti-Jewish writers, among them Nesta Webster, Admiral Sir Barry Domvile (of The Link), Lord Sydenham (of The Britons, the Liberty League and CINEF), George Lane-Fox Pitt-Rivers (of the Eugenics Society and The Link), Dorothy Crisp and Oscar Boulton (of the Unity Band). It also published its own journal, *The Patriot* (1922–50). The company ran in parallel with The Britons, and the two organisations distributed each other's publications, promoted each other and generally played complementary roles. Following the death of the duke in 1930, control of the press passed to Lady Lucy Houston, the millionaire owner and editor of the popular magazine the *Saturday Review*. From 1924 until her own death in 1936 she was also responsible for publishing *The Patriot*.[30] She put £2,500 into the publishing venture, which was also maintained by an anonymous bequest of £6,750.[22]

The National Citizens' Union (founded 1921)

See The Middle Class Union (appendix 1).

The Loyalty League (founded 1922)

Overtly anti-Jewish, the Loyalty League (LL) was formed in October 1922. This short-lived off-shoot of The Britons operated initially from The Britons' 40 Great Ormond Street address. It had three founders: George P. Mudge (of The Britons), who served its honorary secretary and treasurer,[23] the Hon. Miss E. Akers-Douglas (a daughter of Viscount Chilston who appears to have been the LL's main organiser) and Brigadier General Cyril Prescott-Decie (later of National Fascisti and already a prominent member of The Britons).

Prescott-Decie became the LL's president[19] and H. P. Dyer was appointed its honorary secretary.[24] Modelled on Mussolini's fascism, the league it saw itself as essentially representing right-wing Conservatism[19] and operated under the slogan 'For God, King, Country and the Right'.[23] In November 1922, a month after the formation of the LL, Prescott-Decie stood in the general election as an Independent Conservative candidate against the (Jewish) Conservative MP Samuel Samuel. Although he beat Henry Higgs, the Liberal candidate, by 239 votes; he polled only 5,556 votes (27 per cent) against Samuel's 9,739 votes (47.2 per cent).

Like Mudge, Prescott-Decie made no secret of his anti-Jewish views. This made him a popular speaker at meetings of The Britons. He was, for example, the main speaker at their London meetings held on 14 December 1921[25] and 2 January 1922,[26] and he chaired a third meeting, on 23 February 1922, during the course of which he gave an address that included the statement 'the country must be purged of the foul miasma of the alien Jew who has recently flooded England.'[27]

The first issue of the LL's journal, *Loyalty News Debate* (July 1923), was published from its new offices at 14 Ennismore Gardens Mews, SW7.[28] Given the track records of Mudge and Prescott-Decie, the aims and objectives of the organisation as laid out in *Loyalty News Debate* are unsurprising. Under the slogan 'For God and the Right', they begin:

> To form a Society where membership is confined solely to men and women of British race and blood, which will work primarily for the benefit of that race, its Country and its Empire and which recognises, to obtain this end, alien races must be eliminated from all our Councils and National Institutions.

A later clause calls for 'The drastic control of alien immigration and the compulsory deportation of undesirables'.[29]

In 1924 the LL mounted an extensive speaking tour of towns and villages throughout the west of England. This campaign, organised by Akers-Douglas, featured Prescott-Decie, Mudge and Akers-Douglas herself as its three main speakers. A flavour of these meetings can be gleaned from the fact that Prescott-Decie told his audience there was 'a plot on foot to ruin the British Empire and the three dominating factors were the Jews, the Germans and the Irish Sinn Feiners'. His recurrent anti-Jewish theme during this tour led to him being accused of having 'Jews on the brain'.[30]

The LL appears to have ceased to exist during 1925.

British Fascisti (later British Fascists) (founded 1923)

Rotha Lintorn-Orman, the founder of British Fascisti (BF), was born Rotha Beryl Orman in Kensington, London, in 1895. She came from a military family. Her father, Charles Edward Orman, was a major in the Essex Regiment, and her maternal grandfather was Field Marshall Sir John Lintorn Arabin Simmons; she adopted the name Rotha Lintorn-Orman in the latter's memory.[31] In her teens (1909) she became an enthusiastic member of the Girl Scouts and formed its first Bournemouth troop; later she used elements of its hierarchy for the BF. During the early months of the Great War she served as a member of the Women's Reserve Ambulance and then joined the Scottish Women's Hospital Corps (WHC).

The WHC was founded in 1914, at the outset of the war, by two former militant suffragists, Flora Murray and Louisa Garrett Anderson. Notably, it organised the first group of all-women doctors, who ran two military hospitals in France from September 1914 until January 1915. At the invitation of the War Office, the WHC then founded and ran (from May 1915 until December 1919) the Endell Street Military Hospital in former workhouse premises in London's Covent Garden. This 573-bed hospital, staffed and administered entirely by women, was the first in the UK in which women medical staff cared for men (notching up a total of

25,000 patients and 7,000 major operations). As such, it was a key feminist organisation during that period.

With the WHC, Lintorn-Orman sailed in 1916 to Serbia, where she served as an ambulance driver on the Drina front. While in Salonika (now Thessalonika) she was twice awarded the Serbian Cross of Mercy (Croix de Charité) for gallantry in rescue. This was for her actions during the 1917 Great Thessaloniki Fire, which burnt out of control for thirty-two hours and destroyed two-thirds of the second largest city in Greece, gutting 9,500 houses, mostly in the Turkish and Jewish quarters. Later that year, Lintorn-Orman was invalided home with malaria. Deemed too ill to return, she joined the British Red Cross Society and continued in the field of military medicine as commandant of the Red Cross Motor School at Devonshire House, which had been established to train drivers in the battlefield. Her post-malarial infirmity caused relapses for the rest of her life and contributed to her later problems with drugs and alcohol.

In the course of her war work, Lintorn-Orman became a staunch monarchist and imperialist with a strong sense of British nationalism. Seeking others who shared her views, and concerned in particular by the growth of the Labour Party, she placed a series of advertisements in *The Patriot*, inviting anti-communists to contact her. This led directly to the foundation on 6 May 1923 of the British Fascisti (BF), Britain's first nominally fascist group. Lintorn-Orman's wealthy mother bankrolled the organisation with a £50,000 start-up donation plus a monthly allowance for her daughter. By the end of 1923 the BF claimed to have a membership of 100,000. However, throughout its existence the organisation grossly exaggerated its true membership figures, which only ever amounted to a few thousand at most, as revealed by the BF accounts when it went bankrupt in 1935. These showed that its membership had peaked in 1925–6 with subscriptions of £6,848 in 1925; this sum dropped to £604 in 1928 and less than £400 annually thereafter.[22]

The first BF president was Lord Garvagh. He was superseded by Brigadier General Robert Blakeney. Another leading figure handling much of the BF's early media publicity was Vice-Admiral Thomas Webster Kemp.[32] Other notable members included the historian and conspiracist Nesta Webster, the novelist and naturalist Henry Williamson (author of *Tarka the Otter*), the future spy-master and naturalist Maxwell Knight (placed there by MI5) and the future Imperial Fascist League founder Arnold Leese. There were also three members – Neil Francis Hawkins, E. G. Mandeville Roe and H. J. Donovan – who went on to be key figures in the British Union of Fascists. The American William Joyce worked closely with the BF, although it is understood that he never actually joined the organisation. He later became notorious for his Nazi broadcasts from Germany (late 1939–30 April 1945), which earned him the nickname Lord Haw-Haw. He was executed as a traitor on 3 January 1946.

Hawkins (Neil Lanfear Maclean Francis Hawkins, 1907–1950), who sat on the BF's three-strong headquarters committee, was a popular BF member and sometime contender to replace Lintorn-Orman. He and Mandeville Roe jointly strove to have the BF adopt true fascist principles – and, in particular, to support the creation of a corporate state and to oppose all things Jewish.

Although Lintorn-Orman had named the British Fascisti in admiration of Mussolini's fascism and organised it along military lines, she seemed to know little about what fascism actually meant, and the BF, as she formulated it, was designed more for public service than hard-line revolutionary politics. So, initially at least, the organisation was surprisingly moderate. Its members embraced patriotism and adopted a blue uniform but were middle-class and conservative rather than radical. Thus, for example, Lintorn-Orman proposed reducing taxes on gentlefolk so that they could employ more servants and thus ease unemployment.[33]

However, there was already a hint of things to come in the BF's programme of proposed reform, which included the clause: 'civil servants and parliamentary candidates would be of British birth and race'. By the 1930s, this would harden into the overt xenophobia of 'Jews and aliens would be barred from public posts, from voting and from "controlling" the financial, political, industrial and cultural interests of Great Britain.'[22]

Meanwhile, as others in the BF ranks began pushing for the party to be more fascistic, Lintorn-Orman strove to keep its activities within the law and to keep the party identified with the fringes of the Conservative Party. At street level, members were already engaging in direct physical attacks. Initially, their violence was often directed against individuals and organisations identified as communists. Increasingly, however, those targeted were either Jewish or pro-Jewish.

William Joyce's dramatic facial scar, which ran the length of his right cheek, from the ear-lobe to the corner of his mouth, was the result of a razor slash which he received while the British Fascists were stewarding a Conservative meeting at the Baths Hall in Lambeth. His belief that his attackers were Jewish communists was to colour his future politics. Ironically, the Tory Party candidate he was defending at the time from left-wing agitators, Jack Lazarus, was Jewish.

The administrative structure of the BF was complex and cumbersome. There was an executive council and a nine-strong grand council. Below this were county and area commanders, then district commanders and committees, under each of which were troops, each troop being divided into three units of seven members under a unit leader. This was laid out in the BF's original command structure (dated 30 April 1924), which established it as a paramilitary organisation run predominantly by people drawn from the upper classes and the privileged upper middle classes, many of whom were either ex-military or titled (or both). This extended pyramidal structure served only to dilute policy and further distance the BF from fascist principles. Instead, it campaigned on issues which concerned its wealthier members, such as the decline of the landowning agricultural sector, high death duties and estate tax, and the lack of suitably high-ranking civilian occupations for former military officers.[34]

On 7 May 1924, in order to sound less foreign, the party's name was anglicised to become the British Fascists and, with typical orthodoxy, it also became a limited company. However, the conscious move away from Italianate fascism led to the first schism, with around a hundred members leaving to form the short-lived National Fascisti.

Despite their Conservative leanings, the BF did occasionally run candidates in local elections and, shortly after this name change, successfully gained two local council seats in Stamford in Lincolnshire. Arnold Leese and Henry Simpson were elected as Britain's first fascist town councillors, and Simpson went on to retain the seat in 1927.

Once again, the BF published highly exaggerated membership figures. In 1925 it claimed to have 800 branches, each with between 200 and 500 members, giving a total national membership of around 160,000, of which roughly one-sixth were women. However, the BF accounts reveal that membership was actually, at the very most, merely one-tenth of that total.

In March 1925, five members of the BF 'kidnapped' the leading British Communist Party activist, Harry Pollitt, while he was en route to the Liverpool conference of the National Minority Movement (of which he was secretary). The five were charged by the police, but they were all acquitted after claiming that they meant only to 'take him away for a pleasant weekend'! They added that, when they released him, Pollitt had accepted a payment of £5 to cover his costs and inconvenience.[33]

That same year, a network of fascist children's clubs was set up to rival church Sunday schools. Leaflets were published asking: 'Are you content to let British boys and girls be brought up in "Sunday Schools" where Anti-Christ, Anti-King, "religion" is taught?'[34] A patriotic song league was established a year later, and the children in these clubs were all taught to sing:

> We are all anti-Red and we're proud of it,
> All Britons, and singing aloud of it.
> If Red, White and Blue aren't good enough for you,
> And if you don't like the Empire – clear out of it.

There were three BF magazines: *The Fascist Bulletin* (13 June 1925–12 June 1926, edited by Blakeney), *British Lion* (June 1926–June 1930, edited by Roe) and *British Fascism* (June 1930–May 1932, also edited by Roe). As the BF then slid into decline, issues of *British Fascism* appeared in October 1932 and February 1933 (edited by Mrs D. G. Harnett), August 1933 (edited by Harnett and G. E. Eyre), autumn 1933 (edited by Eyre) and, finally, March, April, May, June and July 1934 (bailed out and edited by Col. H. C. Bruce Wilson).[35]

During the 1926 General Strike, the Conservative government's Organisation for the Maintenance of Supplies (OMS) was established as a voluntary group to counter the worst effects of disruption. The structure of the OMS was in fact based on that of the BF. However, when the BF offered its assistance, the government declined it, apparently wary of its unpredictable renegade element. A compromise was arrived at whereby its members could join in as part of the National Citizens' Union (NCU) contingent, but only on condition that the BF's constitution was altered by incorporating a declared belief in parliamentary government. Blakeney and his supporters were all in favour of this, but Lintorn-Orman opposed it and rallied sufficient support within the ranks of the BF to win the day. It was a Pyrrhic victory, precipitating a second serious defection from BF ranks. Led by Blakeney, a sizable faction left the BF and formed the short-lived Loyalists in order to be allowed to work with the NCU and OMS. Among these departees were General Ormonde Winter, Brigadier General T. Erskine Tulloch, Admiral John Armstrong and the Conservative MP Colonel Sir Charles Rosdew Burn, all of whom had been influential figures in the BF. In the meantime, in order to play its part, the BF formed its own Q Division, which, without official government approval, was allowed to carry out similar work to the OMS during the strike.[36]

When the strike proved fairly orderly and failed to evolve into the predicted British Bolshevik revolution, the BF lost much of its purpose, and its membership and support went into slow terminal decline. The *Fascist Bulletin* became the *British Lion* and went from weekly to monthly to intermittent. To make matters worse, Lintorn-Orman was battling a serious alcohol problem and the BF was riven by in-fighting. Lady Downe headed a conservative faction bitterly opposed to those led by James Strachey Barnes and Sir Harold Elsdale Goad, who still advocated a move to true fascism.[3]

Meanwhile, during 1926, the BF moved offices from 71 Elm Park Gardens to 297 Fulham Road, SW10. Under the slogan 'For King and Country', a new leaflet was issued stating its 'Objects'. These were threefold:

1. To oppose Communism and any movement that is calculated to endanger the Throne, the Constitution and the Empire by all means in our power.
2. To endeavour to keep all Members who shall so pledge themselves, physically and mentally fit, by means of exercise, games, debates, etc.
3. To foster Pride of Race, the feeling that anything British should stand a world-wide test, and the knowledge that Country is greater than self, Religion greater than sect, and practical help in time of trouble is the greatest power against the forces of Communism.

It further stated that 'The British Fascists have no connection whatever with any other Fascist movement either at home or abroad' and that 'It strictly forbids its members to be armed with any kind of firearm, or to indulge in any kind of aggressive action.'[34]

Activities continued with large-scale meetings around London during the early months of 1927. There was a much publicised and well-attended series of lectures on 1 and 15 February and 1 and 16 March at Chelsea Town Hall. These were given by the historian and Jewish-masonic conspiracy theorist Nesta Webster, who was active in the BF at the time as 'Country Commander (Staff) Women's Units'. She was also the main speaker at a meeting on 24 February at Kensington Town Hall. Admission was free, and there was a collection 'in aid of Fascist Children's Clubs, and Special Anti-Red Propaganda Fund'.[37] Another meeting, on 2 March at the town hall in Canning Town, was 'called to demonstrate the Red Menace to British Children and the need for Fascism in Great Britain'.[38]

In 1928 the BF moved again, this time to 99 Buckingham Palace Road, and Arnold Leese, who had been one of its two councillors, formally quit the group, disgusted with its lack of real fascist principles and its reluctance to adopt a firm anti-Jewish stance. He described its stance witheringly as 'conservatism with knobs on'.

1929 saw the BF setting up a fascist dogs' club. Meanwhile, Arnold Leese took charge of the Imperial Fascist League, which lured away more of the BF membership.

By the early 1930s, the BF finally opted for Italianate fascism rather than any British conservative hybrid. In 1931 it fully adopted the programme of Mussolini's National Fascist Party[31] – but it was all too late. Two men who should have been pleased with this change, Hawkins and Mandeville Roe, had already had enough. When Oswald Mosley invited them to join his New Party (formed that same year), they did so, quitting the BF for good. Others followed suit. And when, in 1932, Mosley abandoned his short-lived New Party and launched the British Union of Fascists (BUF), the BF lost the majority of its remaining members.

There was no love lost between the BUF and the BF, which Mosley dismissed as 'three old ladies and a couple of office boys'. In 1933 the BF's London office was stormed and wrecked by a BUF gang in reprisal for BF members having loudly demonstrated outside the BUF offices.[22] Later that year, probably as a result of this attack, the BF office was again moved, to what would be its final address, 22 Stanhope Gardens. With membership now perilously close to Mosley's description (actually around 300), Lintorn-Orman ludicrously claimed that this move had been made to cope with growing membership, which she put at around 400,000. A subsequent fund-raising appeal for £25,000 was so unsuccessful that it actually cost more money to run than it brought in.[22]

Dependent on alcohol and other drugs, enduring scandalous rumours about her private life, including stories of her alleged involvement in drunken orgies, Lintorn-Orman grew too unreliable and then too ill to work. Her concerned mother stopped her allowance and she was sidelined by the party, with effective control passing to her close friend and long-time ally Mrs D. G. Hannett, who sought to revive the failing party by aligning it with Ulster loyalism. This plan failed, as did a succession of unsuccessful merger attempts with other tiny groups. Now desperately lacking funds, the BF was finally forced into bankruptcy in 1934, when Colonel Wilson demanded repayment of the £500 loan with which he had briefly bailed out the group.

Rotha Lintorn-Orman died, aged forty, in Las Palmas in the Canary Islands in March 1935.[22]

National Fascisti (later the National Fascists) (founded 1924)

This was the first splinter group from British Fascisti, launched following the departure of around a hundred BF members who had quit in order to found an organisation which adhered more closely to Italian fascist principles. Its members adopted black shirts like Mussolini's followers and were militaristic, marching with drawn swords, much to the derision of their detractors. They ran boxing and fencing clubs and were strongly anti-communist and stridently anti-Jewish. In 1925 they hijacked a lorry which was carrying copies of the left-wing *Daily Herald*. That same year, a meeting held in London's Hyde Park ended with individuals fighting pitched battles with members of the Communist Party of Great Britain. However, for the most part, they were more show that action, and prone to the ridiculous. One of their leading members was Colonel Victor Barker, who became secretary to the group's leader, Lieutenant Colonel H. Rippon-Seymour. Barker also served as a leading trainer in both the boxing club and the fencing club. It then transpired that, unknown to his fellow fascists, 'he' was in fact Valerie Arkell-Smith, a female cross-dresser.

Like the BF, the National Fascists (NF) contacted the home secretary in the run-up to the 1926 General Strike and offered to act as strike-breakers supporting the work of the Organisation for the Maintenance of Supplies. The organisation's offer was turned down when it refused to renounce fascism and insisted on its members working as NF units. However, many individual members volunteered and were quietly allowed to join the Special Constabulary during the short-lived strike.[36]

The NF published a journal, the *Fascist Gazette*, but the party was riven by petty internal squabbles, some of them violent, as when one member, Colonel Seymour, brandished a sword and pointed an unlicensed gun at fellow member, Charles Eyres. Due mainly to this in-fighting, the NF fell apart within three years of its founding. Its only lasting importance was that two members, William Joyce and Arnold Leese, went on to become significant figures on the extreme right.[3]

The Fascist League (founded 1926)

See Imperial Fascist League (below)

The Distributist League (founded in 1926)

Distributism as an economic ideology operates on Catholic principles and argues that the right to own property should apply equally to all people, one of its slogans being 'Three acres and a cow'. The Distributist League was founded by G. K. Chesterton and was based on ideas he and others (notably Hilaire Belloc and Arthur Penty) had been developing for years. These ideas are explored in Belloc's *The Servile State* (1912) and Chesterton's *The Outline of Sanity* (1926).

The league, arising from the circle of people associated with Chesterton's journal *G.K.'s Weekly*, held its inaugural meeting on 17 September 1926 in Essex Hall, Essex Street, Strand, London. At its first committee meeting, held the following week, G. K. was elected president, Captain Went, secretary, and Maurice Reckitt, treasurer. G. K. later summed up the organisation in seven words: 'Their simple idea was to restore property.' Another definition came from Francis Bacon, who said that 'property is like muck, it is good only if it be spread.' And from Chesterton again: 'the landlord and the tenant should be the same person.'

Chesterton's original 1926 outline of distributism (as reprinted in Aidan Mackay's distributist journal *The Defendant*, 1(1), 1953) reads:

> Distributism stands for the restoration of liberty by the distribution of property. Its two primary principles are:-
>
> 1   That the only way to preserve liberty is to preserve property; in order that the individual and the family may be independent of the oppressive systems, official or unofficial.
> 2   That the only way to preserve property is through the better distribution of capital by the individual ownership of the means and instruments of production. This can only be done by breaking up the great plutocratic concentration of our time.
>
> The commercial and industrial progress which began by professing individualism has ended with the complete swamping of the individual. The concentration of capital in large heaps controlled by little groups has now become equally obvious to those who defend and those who deplore it. But even those who deplore it seldom try to reverse it. The problem of centralised wealth has produced proposals that what is centralised should be centralised even more, by State ownership or nationalisation, but it has not produced the perfectly simple proposal that what is centralised should be decentralised by the voluntary co-operation of small owners.
>
> Distributism recognises that not only has this idea to be explained and defended, but that the measures necessary for its application require to be worked out. Its objects therefore include not only propaganda, but study, inquiry, and the provision of full opportunities for discussion.
>
> Distributism advocates and will work to secure the break-up of plutocratic concentration in agriculture, industry, and finance not only by the distribution of tangible assets (Lands and Tools) but by obtaining for all of a participation in the natural and accumulated wealth of the community.[7,8]

Centre International d'Études sur la Fascisme (CINEF) (founded 1927)

Known simply as CINEF, this organisation was created by the Swiss Catholic historian Herman de Vries de Heekelingen as a body intended for the study of fascism and to dispel the idea that fascism and Catholicism were incompatible. There was a strong British involvement: its general secretary, J. S. Barnes, was the main CINEF representative in Britain, but three others – Lord Sydenham, the authority on Italian literature Professor Edmund Gardner, and the Spanish expert Professor Walter Starkie – were members of its governing body. One of its occasional correspondents was Arnold Leese.[18]

The Imperial Fascist League (founded 1928)

See Chapters 1 and 6.

The Militant Christian Patriots (founded 1929)

Effectively an offshoot of The Britons, the Militant Christian Patriots (MCP) was founded by a prominent Britons member, Colonel A. H. Lane, shortly after the publication of his anti-Jewish book *The Alien Menace*. The organisation was then revitalised in 1935 under the leadership of Mrs Leslie Fry, the American author of *Waters Flowing Eastward*. Her vigorous and thoroughly Jew-hating reincarnation, while relatively small-scale in Britain, developed into a much larger and more influential body in America.

In the UK, this MCP produced two journals. The first, edited by Fry, was *Free Press*, which she launched in 1935. The second, *The Britisher*, published 'to rouse the country into fighting bolshevism, pacifism, Judaism, internationalism and all other subversive movements', first appeared on 15 September 1937. It was edited by the MCP secretary, J. F. Rushbrook, who was the former assistant secretary of the Imperial Fascist League (IFL). Among its contributors were Joseph Banister, A. H. Lane and H. H. Beamish. Throughout its existence, the MCP collaborated closely with The Britons and with other Jew-hating organisations, including the IFL and the National Socialist League, but most notably with the Nordic League. Based at 93 Chancery Lane, London WC2, it also ran the M.C.P. Club at 88a St George Square, SW1, which offered weekly political lectures, boxing instruction, propaganda drives, and a free reference library of 'books on the Jewish-Masonic questions'.[21]

Overtly pro-Nazi, the MCP used a flag modelled on the swastika of Hitler's Germany. While its members were deeply critical of the government and of Anthony Eden in particular, they supported Neville Chamberlain in his efforts to keep Britain out of the war during the Munich Crisis, predictably blaming the Jews when he failed. The orgaisation published a couple of pamphlets: the seven-page *The Jews and the British Empire*, by L. Fry, and a sixteen-page edition of the anonymous *The Grave-diggers of Russia*, previously published by The Britons.

In later years, the MCP was run by Rushbrook but effectively controlled by the Nordic League. Like many other extremist groups, it fell apart in 1940. Regular monthly issues of *Free Press* continued to appear at least until April 1940 (no.46). Curiously, during 1939–40, although its members remained fiercely anti-Jewish and anti-communist, they became very anti-German. They were particularly disillusioned with Hitler himself and blamed him personally for Germany having allowed the Russians to invade Poland. Thus the issue of *Free Press* no. 40 for October 1939, just after the outbreak of war, carried the headline 'Communism Invades Europe!', with the subheading 'Hitler's Dire Treachery'. The ensuing article began:

By a piece of the blackest treachery which has besmirched modern politics, two-thirds of Poland has been handed over to Bolshevism. Herr Hitler, who rose to power on the strength of his resistance to Communism in Germany, has crushed the Polish Army, only to hand over 16,000,000 Poles to Soviet Russia.

This abrupt change of attitude was a drastic one. Immediately before this, the Jewish Board of Deputies had identified the MCP as the main distributor of German propaganda in Britain.[3] Here, then, was the dashing of its hopes for a united Western Christian and fascist war against Jewish Bolshevism, a failure which was blamed on Hitler far more than on the Jews or the Russian communists.

Meanwhile, back in America and based in Glendale, California, in the autumn of 1936 Mrs Fry had launched her American branch of the MCP, issuing a newsletter called *Christian Free Press*. Working closely with the German-American Bund, the stated prime purpose of this MCP was 'Exposure of subversive movements ... such movements as Socialism, Communism, Fabianism and International Jewry and Zionism'.

It would be interesting to know why Fry, having revived the British MCP, left Britain almost immediately, departing as abruptly as Beamish had done after founding The Britons. His reasons for going were clear. Hers were not. It is possible that she simply made few friends. Certainly, Beamish thought she was widely disliked. In a lengthy letter of 12 October 1938 to M. Kositzin, the leading White Russian in America, he writes: 'I am being continually written to about the Glendale female and thanks to her unusual behaviour am unable to give her the "all clear" record I would like to give anybody who is prominent in this great fight.' His reservations appear to amount to more than mere misogyny.

The MCP, as an organisation intimately linked with Beamish and The Britons, provides us with further reason to see the latter as active pre-war arms of Nazism. MI5 named two American-linked organisations in Britain as fronts for the Nordic League. One was Fry's revitalised MCP, the other was a Ku Klux Klan-style outfit called the White Knights of Britain (see below).[22] Both shared premises with the Nordic League. Given that the Nordic League was itself a front organisation for German Nazism in Britain, it would seem that all three organisations served as London conduits through which intelligence, propaganda and more flowed between Germany – and most of the prime movers in the MCP were also active in The Britons.

Unity Band (founded c.1930)

Set up to provide a forum to unite fascists and right-wing Conservatives, the Unity Band (UB) was committed to 'order in politics' and 'freedom in economics'.[18] Its founder and leader, Lieutenant Colonel Oscar Boulton, had been educated at Harrow and Oxford and was the director of a firm of timber merchants.[19]

Being independently wealthy, he was able to fund and maintain the organisation, which he did throughout the 1930s. From 1930 to 1932 the UB worked in tandem with the British Fascists (BF), holding joint meetings and having representatives from each body on the policy-making council of the other. Throughout this period, Boulton had his own column, 'Unity Band Notes', in the BF journal, the *British Lion*. This relationship broke down in July 1932, apparently after Boulton fell out with the BF leader, Rotha Lintorn-Orman. Given the latter's increasingly erratic and dissolute behaviour, this schism was a predictable one. Boulton was a moral Christian who believed strongly in 'duty, sacrifice, honour, generosity and self-restraint'. He deplored progress and change and railed against modern culture and the loss of empire, seeing paternal Western Christianity as the one path to a civilised world. Crucially, however, he loathed feminism, women who dressed like men, and women who strove for sexual equality, wanting, as he put it, to 'make themselves as far as possible into the semblance of men' and to imitate 'all the male attributes and activities'. In this vein, he was, for example, utterly against female constables and female MPs.[19] In all of these attitudes, he could hardly have been more distant from Lintorn-Orman and her associates. Both homosexuality and lesbianism formed a thinly veiled facet of the BF. Curiously, Boulton was not anti-Jewish. Indeed, he spoke out actively in favour of Jewish enterprise and of British Jews.

Following the split, Boulton bought the *British Lion*, which thereafter was published by and for the UB, with Boulton contributing the lion's share of the content. In addition, the UB produced books, pamphlets and leaflets, most of them penned by its leader. The prolific Boulton had also long been a regular contributor to *The Patriot*, with which the UB became increasingly associated. Throughout its existence, the UB was essentially a one-man band, although a Captain Smith was its secretary until 1938, when his place was taken by Frank Wheatley. Another prominent member was the ubiquitous Lieutenant Colonel A. H. Lane.[19]

Boulton published two collections of poetry, *Poems* (1916) and *The Ballad of Life & Death, and Other Poems* (Kegan Paul, Trench, Trübner, 1924), as well as two books of collected journalism from the Boswell Printing & Publishing Company. The first, published in 1930, was *Fads and Phrases – a Prophetic Retrospect of 193_*, compiled from his contributions to *The Patriot*; the second, *The Way Out* (1934), was a collection of his pieces for the *British Lion*.

The New Party (founded 1931)

Oswald Mosley (16 November 1896–3 December 1980) entered Parliament in 1918 as a Conservative and, aged twenty-one, was the youngest MP ever elected. In 1922 he quit the Conservative Party and became an Independent, and in 1924 he joined the Labour Party. However, in 1930 his proposed reflationary programme (contained in the Mosley Memorandum) was rejected by the cabinet. He then tried, but narrowly failed, to convince the Labour conference of these plans and, as a consequence, resigned from the party along with six other MPs. Together, they then formed the New Party early in 1931, campaigning on a revised version of the memorandum, which was dubbed the Mosley Manifesto. At the general election on 27 October that year, the Conservative Party gained a landslide victory. The New Party failed totally, with not one of its seven MPs retaining his seat.[22] These results effectively finished the party, which staggered on for a while, although little remained apart from NUPA, its youth wing. In December 1931, after just twelve issues, the New Party journal, *Action*, was closed down.[32]

Abandoning democratic principles, the remnants from the New Party began adopting fascist principles. At a meeting in Glasgow in September 1931, Mosley was hit on the head with a stone and attacked with a life-preserver. His response was to expand his personal bodyguard, the so-called Biff Boys, originally made up of undergraduates trained in pugilism by the Jewish boxer Ted 'Kid' Lewis. Now, however, a more violent and extreme element was added from the expanded ranks of NUPA. In August 1932, a nineteen-year-old New Party member was convicted of putting up stickers in London's Oxford Street urging the expulsion of Jews from Britain. Two months later, Mosley replaced the New Party with his British Union of Fascists.[22]

English Mistery (established 1931)

This was a small quirky Nietzschean ultra-Conservative fringe group which was both ruralist and anti-democratic. While it might not have been overtly anti-Jewish, English Mistery (EM) brought together a bunch of people who most certainly were. William Sanderson, a freemason and author, who founded the organisation in the summer of 1931, had been a co-founder of the Order of the Red Rose during the Great War. Since then, he had joined the Imperial Fascist League. Other prominent EM members were Viscount Lymington, Anthony Ludovici, Rolf Gardiner, the MP Michael Beaumont (later a supporter of the British Union of Fascists), the MP Reginald Dorman-Smith and Collin Brooks (later the editor of *Truth*). EM never really recovered from the acrimonious departure in 1936 of Viscount Lymington together with most of its leading members, who formed English Array.[18]

The British Union of Fascists (founded 1932)

Having left the Conservative Party in 1922 and the Labour Party in 1930, Oswald Mosley founded his short-lived New Party (see above) in the first few weeks of 1931. Utter failure in the October 1931 general election effectively rendered this venture stillborn. Already attracted to fascism, Mosley visited Benito Mussolini in Italy in January 1932. That October he launched his next party, the British Union of Fascists (BUF).

Initially, the BUF met with some success, supported particularly by Lord Rothermere, whose paper, the *Daily Mail*, notoriously ran the headline 'Hurrah for the Blackshirts!'.[36] As a result the party grew rapidly, attracting strong support in the East End of London. Within a year it had become by far the largest far-right group in Britain. A London rally in the Albert Hall on 22 April 1934 drew an audience of 10,000. However, anti-fascist opposition to the BUF was also growing, especially from the Jewish community and the political left. On 7 June 1934, at London's Olympia Stadium, Mosley held the biggest political rally ever seen in Britain. It drew an audience of 12,000. Outside were 2,000 anti-fascists, though there were others inside among the audience, which also included 2,000 black-shirts. Fights broke out everywhere, and many were injured and hospitalised. The extreme violence at this event marked a change in the nature and reputation of the BUF. Membership declined sharply from a claimed peak of 50,000. The party ran no candidate in the 1935 general election, when it urged supporters to abstain and vote for 'Fascism Next Time'. There would, however, be no next time for British fascism, and no general election for the next ten years, by which time the BUF was long gone.

By the end of 1935, membership had fallen to below 8,000. The violence and extremism associated with Mosley and some of his leading members had become more obvious, especially at larger public events. Crucial among these was the 'Battle of Cable Street' in October 1936, when the BUF attempted to march through that part of the East End of London. The government subsequently responded by banning uniforms and regulating political marches and meetings under the Public Order Act 1936.

That year, the BUF changed its name to the British Union of Fascists and National Socialists, but a year later – responding to growing British antipathy to European Nazism and fascism – it became simply the British Union. It ran candidates in the county council elections of March 1937, when it gained reasonable support in the East End but failed to get any candidate elected.

By campaigning for peace in the late 1930s, the BUF regained some of its lost support, and by 1939 it had around 20,000 members.[22] Some of this resurgence will have been helped by substantial secret donations from Nazi Germany, amounting to around £50,000.[3] In 1940 the British Union was proscribed and its leader was interned along with many of the party's more prominent members.[39]

NB: For the sake of clarity, throughout this book the name changes have been ignored, and the party is referred to simply as the BUF.

The National Workers' Movement (also known as the National Workers' Union, later the National Socialist Workers' Party and then the National Workers' Party) (founded 1933)

This was one of several ventures founded by Lieutenant Colonel Graham Seton Hutchison (1890–1946), an interwar author of popular espionage novels and books on military history, who had won both a Distinguished Service Order and a Military Cross for his activities during the Great War. During that war, he had been instrumental in the formation of the Machine Gun Corps. He also liked to boast that, in March 1918, he had personally shot as cowards all but two of a group of forty British soldiers who were fleeing from German troops.

In the immediate post-war period, Seton Hutchison set up the Old Contemptibles Association for ex-soldiers and became its first chairman. He then took a leading role in the founding of the British Legion. In 1920–21 he served in Germany as a member of the Upper Silesia Plebiscite Commission. Later he published a book, *Silesia Revisited* (1929), for which he was secretly paid by the German government.

Seton Hutchison ran unsuccessfully as the Liberal candidate for Uxbridge in the 1923 general election. Disillusioned, he then began to move to the political right, first in 1930 with his own Paladin League, which promoted male comradeship. As co-editor of its journal, *The Superman*, he called for more eugenically fit men 'who possess in the blood and bones, the matchless tradition of the English, Scottish and Welsh countryside ... Supermen!' The homo-erotic magazine was filled with photographs of naked men posing in comradely physical contact. Both Nietzschean and Nazi-esque, the magazine echoed the German Youth Movement's Männerbund and Karl Pearson's mission to produce 'ideal eugenic man'.

Around this time (1930–31) Seton Hutchison joined William Sanderson's newly formed English Mistery (EM), which attracted several individuals who would go on to play leading roles in the British anti-Jewish far right. In 1931 he headed a fascist organisation (unnamed) that went into merger negotiations with the ailing British Fascists. However, these foundered when Rotha Lintorn-Orman realised that, contrary to his claim that the group had thousands of members ('20,000 in Mansfield alone'),[12] it was in fact little more than a one-man operation. Small wonder that the report on Seton Hutchison by a Special Branch officer described him as a 'braggart and overweening'.[11] He then briefly joined Oswald Mosley's recently formed British Union of Fascists (BUF) but was expelled for 'improper conduct'.

In 1933 Seton Hutchison founded the National Workers' Union (NWU) as a fanatically pro-German and Jew-hating organisation. However, such was his admiration for Hitler ('incorruptible, courageous ... devoted to his people as they are to him') that the NWU soon became the National Socialist Workers' Party. In 1936, its name was again changed, to the National Workers' Party (NWP). It was a truly tiny organisation. Its only other known member was Commander E. H. Cole (of the Imperial Fascist League, the White Knights of Britain and the Nordic League), and its only recorded action was an anti-Jewish meeting in south Hackney in 1936, apparently organised as a direct challenge to the BUF, which Seton Hutchison now believed to be too moderate and under Jewish influence.[19]

In 1936, the NWP published Seton Hutchison's *Truth: The Evidence in the Case*, in which the author praised Nazi Germany as 'a classless community working in harmony for the national welfare', having 'destroyed the Jew-owned brothels and the State of the prevertions [sic] and grotesque impurities and corruption which Jewish finance had imposed.'[41]

What makes this insignificant Nazi group of interest here is that it was based at 40 Great Ormond Street, the address of The Britons. Moreover, Seton Hutchison was regularly visiting Germany, passing information via Rosenberg directly to Hitler, and attending Nuremberg rallies as a guest of the German government, and was paid by Rosenberg for sympathetic pieces which he wrote about them. These were duly published in German and Austrian magazines. So, here was a man working in The Britons' building who was receiving payment from the German government – another example of direct Nazi-funded collaboration that is clearly linked with The Britons.

In 1938, disgusted with how little support he had, and seeing more and more of his associates drifting into the growing ranks of the BUF, Seton Hutchison wound up the NWP.

The British Empire Fascist Party (founded 1933)

This was another minuscule organisation founded by Seton Hutchison (see National Workers' Movement, above). As part of its 24-point plan, the British Empire Fascist Party called for a corporate state to replace the party system, for strikes to be outlawed, and for the creation of an aristocracy based on merit, not class. The plan was also anti-communist and anti-Jewish, demanding the disenfranchisement of Jews and their removal from positions of influence in economic and cultural affairs.[19]

The United Empire Fascist League (later the United British Party) (founded 1933)

This tiny group was founded in December 1933 by C. G. Wodehouse-Temple, who was the director of an engineering company. One of its most prominent members was Serocold Skeels, formerly of the Imperial Fascist League and later of the Nordic League, who would be exposed as an agent for the Nazi government in Germany. As an extreme Jew-hater, he even went as far as suggesting genocide. The party became the United British Party (UBP) soon after its formation. Skeels planned to stand as a UBP candidate in a parliamentary by-election in Cambridge but was prevented from doing so by Wodehouse-Temple, who was worried about his Jew-hatred. Not overtly anti-Jewish, the UBP supported a 'British Empire for British people' and talked about 'the menace of a socialist dictatorship'. With just two branches, one in London, the other in Edinburgh, it was still active at the end of 1936.

The Anglo-German Fellowship (founded 1935)

Ernest W. D. Tennant, a cousin of Margot, Lady Oxford, was a merchant banker who, during the 1930s, spent much of his time on business in Germany. In the course of this work, highly impressed with Germany, he formed a friendship with Joachim von Ribbentrop, who, as a close confidant of the Führer, was appointed ambassador to Britain in 1936 and then foreign minister in February 1938. Tennant began defending Nazi brutality by suggesting that communism would have been worse. As for the Nazis' treatment of Jews, while claiming to deplore it, he thought 'our Press should pay more attention to the constructive side of the Hitler movement'.

In 1934, Tennant joined a trade delegation to Germany. Others in the delegation shared his enthusiasm for developments within the country. Together with German delegates, this group decided to form and finance the start of the Anglo-German Fellowship (AGF). It seems that Ribbentrop played a key part in the planning, and the AGF came into being late in 1935, alongside its German counterpart, the Deutsch-Englische Gesellschaft.

From the outset, the intention was for the AGF to be a club for the rich and powerful in Britain. As such, it declared itself non-political, its aims being simply 'to foster political, professional, commercial and sporting links with Germany'. Membership, it claimed, did 'not imply approval of National Socialism', although the fellowship 'does ask of its members co-operation in the work of establishing contacts and removing causes of misunderstanding'. So, while many members were in no way pro-Nazi, the seeds were sown from the outset for it to promote Nazi ideology and attract those who shared such views. Its president (cum chairman), Lord Mount Temple (who, as Wilfrid Ashley, had been minister of transport in the late 1920s), was described as 'an officer and gentleman of the old school, who regarded socialism as subversive'. He made clear in his speeches to the AGF that he admired Germany and hoped that, when a second war came, the two countries would find themselves on the same side. Many others gave similar speeches at AGF gatherings, and the organisation was very successful in moderating the views of the British establishment towards Germany during the latter half of the 1930s.[41]

In addition to Tennant and Mount Temple, there were several prominent apologists for Nazism who became active in the AGF. Among them were Lord Londonderry, Admiral Sir Barry Domvile, Lord Wellington, Lieutenant Colonel Sir Thomas Moore MP and Lord Sempill.

Londonderry, who had been on the council of the Anti-Socialist Union in the 1930s, had met and befriended Hitler. Domvile, who became increasing anti-Jewish as he aged, visited Germany in 1935, attended the September 1936 Nuremberg Rally as a guest of von Ribbentrop, and in 1937 became chairman of The Link (see below). He was arrested and interned as a Nazi sympathiser from 7 July 1940 until 29 July 1943. Wellington, president of the Liberty Restoration League, was also a member of the Right Club. Moore, who had spoken in support of the BUF in 1934, was associated with the *Anglo-German Review*, the journal of both the AGF and of The Link. Sempill, who was openly pro-fascist and another friend of Ribbentrop, was associated with the BUF and became a council member of The Link.[18]

As war loomed and Nazi policies became more extreme, views even within the AGF changed. Thus, for example, Lord Mount Temple resigned as AGF chairman in November 1938 because of the treatment of Jews in Germany.

The Nordic League (founded 1935)

This would-be umbrella group for key members of British ultra-right and pro-Nazi organisations was founded in 1935, when Nazi representatives of its German counterpart, Alfred Rosenberg's Nordische Gesellschaft, arrived in Britain to promote the idea. The Nordic League (NL) met privately and organised no public events (except during 1939, when it held a handful of public meetings in response to the Munich Crisis). It was run by a fourteen-strong leadership council, with Archibald Maule Ramsay MP, as its prime mover. Ramsay was apparently offered the role of Scottish Gauleiter in the event of a Nazi invasion.[40] Rabidly anti-Jewish, the NL described itself as an 'association of race-conscious Britons'.

MI5 believed that the NL was actually directed from Berlin and served as the centre of German Nazi operations within Britain.[3] An idea of its importance to British Nazism can be gleaned from the fact that its meetings – in a room decorated with swastikas – drew audiences of between 200 and 400 people, as opposed to the maximum of around fifty who would attend meetings of (say) The Britons or the Imperial Fascist League.

The NL members' badge showed an eagle attacking a snake accompanied by the letters P. J. (standing for their unofficial and anti-Jewish motto, 'Perish Judah'; this was attributed to P. J. Ridout, who apparently based it on his own initials).

Members included representatives from a wide range of far-right and anti-Jewish groups. Among them were H. H. Beamish (The Britons), Arnold Lees (Imperial Fascist League), Captain E. R. Serocold Skeets (United Empire Fascist Party, Imperial Fascist League), Brigadier General Robert Blakeney (Imperial Fascist League, ex-president of British Fascists), Commander E. H. Cole (Imperial Fascist League, White Knights of Britain), Major General J. F. C. Fuller (British Union of Fascists), P. J. Ridout (Imperial Fascist League), Oliver Gilbert (British Union of Fascists, Right Club), T. Victor Rowe (White Knights of Britain, Right Club), Jock Houston (British Union of Fascists), Captain Elwin Wright (Anglo-German Fellowship), E. G. Mandeville Roe (British Union of Fascists), A. K. Chesterton (British Union of Fascists) and William Joyce (British Fascisti, National Fascisti, British Union of Fascists, National Socialist League).[22]

In the two years before the outbreak of war, the NL thus brought together a true cross-section of British right-wing extremism. It also forged particularly close working links with the White Knights of Britain, with whom it shared premises, and the Militant Christian Patriots. In addition it worked quietly with and through two less controversial (though still anti-Jewish) establishment bodies, the Liberty Restoration League and the National Citizens' Union.

With these bodies and others, Maule Ramsay formed the United Christian Front Committee and later the Right Club, both intended as more low key and therefore as suitable bodies for his more privileged supporters, in the same way that Mosley's January Club catered for those wary of being seen directly to support the British Union of Fascists. Nonetheless, NL membership remained strong until early in 1939, when it fell away sharply.[22] The organisation officially folded at the start of September 1939, just as war was about to break.

The Anglo-German Information Service (founded 1936)

The Anglo-German Information Service (AGIS) was founded on 1 July 1936 by Rudolph Gottfried Rosel, a German journalist born in Weimar who had arrived in England in 1930. Here he had become the London correspondent of the German newspaper *Deutsche Textil Zeitung* and the diplomatic correspondent of Goering's Essen-based paper *Nationalzeitung*. In fact, it now seems clear that Rosel was working in England for the German government in two key capacities. The first was to disseminate Nazi information and propaganda. The second was to pass back to the Gestapo in Germany information gleaned in Britain, especially concerning anti-Hitler activity. All of Rosel's reports were apparently sent direct to Hitler and read by him personally.[42] Among the information he sent back to Germany were the 'white lists' he compiled, which contained the names of Nazi sympathisers in Britain – 4,000 in all. Rosel's next-door-neighbour in London was Barry Domvile of The Link and the Anglo-German Fellowship, both of which worked closely with Rosel, as did Mosley's British Union of Fascists.[3]

The AGIS was run by Rosel and two female secretaries (one of them Mrs Margaret Rose) from offices at 58–59 Parliament Street, Whitehall, London SW1. From this address he sent out typed and stapled AGIS English-language information sheets, such as the five-page *The Women's Movement in Germany* (sent out March 1939),[34] the seven-page *Speech by the Führer and Chancellor of the German Reich before the Reichstag on January 30, 1939*,[44] the seven-page *Herr Hitler's Avowals of Peace (A Collection of Extracts from his Speeches)*,[45] the eleven-page *Art in Modern Germany*,[46] the ten-page *German Labour Service: Lecture given by General Tholens, Deputy Chief of the German Labour Camps to the Anglo-German Fellowship in London on October 19th 1938*,[47] the two-page *Hitler's Speech to the Diplomatic Corps at the New Year Reception on January 11th, 1937* (sent out on 14 January 1937),[48] and the four-page *Address to the German Führer and Reich Chancellor by the Apostolic Nuncio, Monsignor Cesare Orsenigo, Doyen of the Diplomatic Corps, at the New Year Reception in Berlin on January 12, 1939*.[49] These information sheets, containing recommended quotes (what we would now call sound-bites) were thus designed not merely to inform but specifically for use by their British recipients in journals, articles, speeches, debates and conversations.

In addition to his AGIS work, Rosel was the editor and British distributor of *Deutsche Zeitung in Grossbritannien*, a German-language 'paper for the German community in England', which he founded in January 1938. The first issue was distributed free at a meeting of German nationals held at the Seymour Hall, London, on 29 January 1938 to celebrate the anniversary of Hitler's accession to power. On the front page of this issue was a message from Joachim von Ribbentrop, the foreign minister of Nazi Germany. Headed 'A Bridge to the Thousands Abroad', it read:

> If the Germans living abroad, in the midst of a strange world, are to keep in touch with the German nation and the happenings in their native land, there must be a vivifying and common bond. The *Deutsche Zeitung in Grossbritannien* is intended to create and maintain such a bond. It will strengthen and help

the cohesion of German nationals by building a bridge reaching out to the widely distributed thousands living outside Germany. It will become the spiritual centre of a loyal German colony in England from which the individual may draw new strength to do his part for our Third Empire and its leader Adolf Hitler. I wish our new *Deutsche Zeitung in Grossbritannien* all success and good fortune in this responsible task.

This first edition was printed at the offices of the *Nationalzeitung* in Essen dated 29 January 1938. Three thousand copies of each subsequent issue were printed in Berne, Switzerland, and sent to Rosel's London office.[35] Order forms were sent out with AGIS publications offering to supply free of charge as many copies of this paper as were requested.[44]

Material for the AGIS sheets was sent to its Whitehall office directly from Germany. In 1936 there were reported to have been 275 subscribers in Britain, among them the Conservative Party in London, Edinburgh and Glasgow, several MPs, members of the British Legion and members of the British Union of Fascists.[42] Copies were certainly also sent to the Anglo-German Fellowship, with which Rosel worked very closely, and to The Britons (those in the possession of the author were acquired directly from their library) and therefore certainly to members of like-minded groups such as the Imperial Fascist League, the Nordic League and The Link.

As well as being a propaganda agent and journalist for the German government, Rosel held two posts of real importance in the Nazi Party's organisation in Britain. First, he was the Schulungsleiter of the NSDAP (i.e. the person responsible for the education of Nazis in Britain). Second, he was the Ortsgruppenleiter of London (i.e. the Nazi's London representative). In this latter capacity, he served as the link between the British Union of Fascists and Germany;[42] presumably he acted in the same capacity with other British pro-Nazi groups such as those mentioned above.

Pushy, self-seeking and highly ambitious, Rosel had been unpopular with many of his German associates, so this relatively isolated London posting was an excellent way to make use of his enthusiasm and talents. He also spoke near-perfect English, with little trace of an accent, and so was able to tour England, speaking in particular to the NSDAP support groups that existed in most towns and cities.

British intelligence watched Rosel closely for several years. As early as February 1938 he was being described as Himmler's chief agent in England, and in the summer of 1939 he was expelled from Britain as a suspected Gestapo agent. It was later reported that he had admitted that his express purpose for being in the country had been to organise a reliable 'Fifth Column' or group of people who would secretly undermine Britain from within.[42]

The White Knights of Britain (also known as the Hooded Men) (founded 1936)

Operating from the same premises as the Nordic League and working very closely with it, this British klan lasted barely a year. Commander E. H. Cole served as its chancellor, while T. Victor Rowe ushered in newcomers for their elaborate initiation ceremony modelled on the rituals of freemasonry. Like the American klans, this British incarnation used invented language, codes and passwords and the whole hokum, including the 'death penalty' for those who divulged their secrets. Their declared aim was to 'rid the world of the merciless Jewish reign of terror', and their initiates had thus to swear a bloodcurdling oath to its patron saint, King Edward I, the English king who had expelled the Jews.[22] A precursor of sorts of the Right Club, the organisation folded in 1937.

English Array (formed in 1936)

This small ruralist organisation was formed by Viscount Lymington after he and the other members quit William Sanderson's English Mistery (EM, see above). It was more strongly and openly pro-Nazi and anti-Jewish than EM. Leading members of English Array (EA) were Anthony Ludovici, Rolf Gardiner, the MPs Michael Beaumont and Reginald Dorman-Smith, Collin Brooks, Richard de Grey, Hardwicke Holderness, A. K. Chesterton, J. F. C. Fuller and John de Rutzen. Most of these men were also associated with the *New Pioneer*, the magazine launched by Lymington in December 1938. Many EA members went on to become active in the British Union of Fascists and the British Council Against European Commitments.[18]

The National Socialist League (founded 1937)

William Joyce, John Beckett and John Angus MacNab formed the National Socialist League (NSL) after they left the British Union of Fascists (BUF). Their claim was that they formed the group because they were tired of Oswald Mosley's over-enthusiasm for European fascism. Mosley's counter-claim was that he had simply sacked the three men on 11 March 1937 as part of a BUF cost-cutting exercise. Either way, there was bitterness between them, with the NSL trio accusing Mosley of being more interested in personal glory than in fascism.

Amply financed by a wealthy stockbroker, Alex Scrimgeour, the group began confidently, launching a journal, *The Helmsman*, under the party motto 'steer straight'. Although the NSL was fiercely pro-Hitler, its policy was to develop a distinctly British Nazism, as laid out in the pamphlet *National Socialism Now*, written by Joyce.[3]

The NSL formed close ties with Archibald Maule Ramsay and his Nordic League. A. K. Chesterton, having resigned from the BUF in April 1938, joined the group, addressed its meetings and wrote for its journal. It also attracted the clandestine involvement of the Conservative MP Jocelyn Lucas. However, one of its founder members, Vincent Collier, was in fact a spy for the Board of Deputies of British Jews.[22]

Initial ambition and enthusiasm soon waned. Following contact with Lord Lymington's British Council Against European Commitment, Beckett, attracted by the latter's pacifism, quit the NSL in 1938 and was soon active in the British People's Party. There were also regular attacks on NSL gatherings by BUF gangs.[3] And, to wrap up a bad year for the NSL, Scrimgeour died, leaving not a single penny to its coffers.

Joyce was now drinking heavily. As he became increasingly alcoholic, his talk became more Hitlerian. According to Chesterton, he took to shouting 'Sieg Heil!' at the end of each meeting. In 1939, with public opinion swinging strongly against Hitler, the NSL re-registered as a drinking club rather than a political party. The irony of this was brought into sharp focus that May, when one of the last of the NSL's meetings ended chaotically after Joyce drunkenly punched a heckler among a section of his audience who had begun objecting to the overly Jew-hating and pro-German content of a speech he was giving. On 25 August, just before he left for Germany, Joyce passed control of the NSL to MacNab, instructing him to wind it up, which he duly did.[41]

Joyce and his second wife, Margaret, left for Berlin on the morning of 26 August, though not from choice. He had been tipped off on 24 August by an MI5 agent, possibly Maxwell Knight himself, that he was about to be arrested and detained under the new defence regulation 18b, which came into effect on 26 August.[51] Although mass internment of Nazi sympathisers didn't start until the spring of 1940, by 14 September 1939 there were already fourteen 18b detainees, most of them pro-Nazi fascists. They included Oliver Gilbert and Victor Rowe of the Nordic League, Quentin Joyce (William's brother) of the Imperial Fascist League, and E. Fawcett, William F. Craven and E. J. Thomas, all of the British Union of Fascists.[3] These early arrests were of fascists with proven links with Germany. Had Joyce stayed, that number would have been fifteen. Unlucky to the end, Joyce escaped internment only to earn post-war execution as a traitor.

As arrests began, a wave of panic passed through the ranks of British Nazi sympathisers. Public statements of support for Germany and open opposition to war virtually ceased, and most of their organisations either closed down or continued only covertly. Their panic was well founded. By the end of 1940, more than 700 people had been arrested and interned. Some were held for weeks or months, while others – among them Beckett, Leese, Mosley and, in Rhodesia, Beamish – would not be released for several years.

The Link (founded 1937)

More openly anti-Jewish than its close cousin the Anglo-German Fellowship (AGF), The Link was established in September 1937 by C. E. Carroll, a badly wounded Royal Flying Corps pilot who had edited the paper of the British Legion and then the *Anglo-German Review*. The chairmanship of its council went to Admiral Sir Barry Domvile. Other council members were Professor A. P. Laurie and Sir Raymond Beazley, both pro-Nazi. Prominent too were Major General J. C. R. Fuller, the Duke of Westminster and Lord Tavistock.[3] Its office was run by H. T. Mills and Richard Findlay. Its secretary, Margaret Bothamley, was herself deeply anti-Jewish and pro-Hitler.

The Link's initial claim was to be an 'independent non-party organisation to promote Anglo-German friendship'. Like the AGF, its leadership was more extreme than its declared policies, and it soon attracted a core membership of blatantly pro-Nazi and anti-Jewish activists. The organisation rose to prominence with the publication of the 'Link letter' in *The Times* on 12 October 1938. Written in support of Neville Chamberlain's policy of appeasement with Hitler, it read:

> We the undersigned, who believe that real friendship and co-operation between Great Britain and Germany are essential to the establishment of enduring peace not only in Western Europe but throughout the whole world, strongly deprecate the attempt which is being made to sabotage an Anglo-German rapprochement by distorting the facts of the Czechoslovak settlement. We believe that the Munich Agreement was nothing more than the rectification of one of the most flagrant injustices of the Peace Treaties. It took nothing from Czechoslovakia to which that country could rightly lay claim and gave nothing to Germany which could have been rightfully withheld. We see in the policy so courageously pursued by the Prime Minister the end of a long period of lost opportunities and the promise of a new era compared to which the tragic years that have gone since the War will seem like a bad dream.

There were twenty-six signatories, fifteen of whom were active pro-Nazis. Six were members of the council of The Link – Raymond Beazley, C. E. Carroll, A. E. R. Dyer, Lord Redesdale, A. P. Laurie and Barry Domvile himself. Two – Captain Ramsay and Admiral Wilmot Nicholson – were key members of the Right Club. Captain George Pitt-Rivers was a member of the Council Against European Commitments. Nesta Webster of *The Patriot* was a veteran fascist and Jew-hater. Five others were well-known supporters of Germany – Lord Londonderry, Lord Mount Temple, William Harbutt Dawson, Lord Arnold and John Smedley Crooke MP. Most of the rest were military men – Captain Arthur Rogers (of The Britons) and Major General Arthur Solly-Flood were army, while Captain Bernard Acworth, Admiral Vincent Molteno and Admiral Sir Edward Ingfield were right-wing naval men who probably signed simply because they knew Domvile. The remaining signatories appear to have put their names to the statement not so much out of pro-Nazi or anti-Jewish sentiments but because they favoured compromise to conflict. These included Douglas Jerrold (editor of the *English Review*), a Baltic Exchange shipping man, Sir John Latta, the landowner Lord Halifax of Cameron, the retired diplomat Lord Hardinge of Penshurst, F. C. Jarvis and Bernard Wilson.[41]

Early in 1939, The Link took over the *Anglo-German Review*, which was under the editorship of C. E. Carroll, himself a member of both The Link and the AGF. However, shortly after the outbreak of war on 3 September 1939, The Link faded from view. Some members continued to meet covertly with fellow pro-Nazis, but not for long. Carroll, Domvile and others were soon arrested and interned as suspected Nazi sympathisers.[18] The records show that Domvile was regarded as someone who might 'endanger the safety of the realm'.

The British Council Against European Commitments (founded 1938)

Behind its pacifist façade, the British Council Against European Commitments (BCAEC) was closely associated with the magazine the *New Pioneer* and served as a gathering point for Jew-haters and pro-Nazis who wanted a war against Jewry, not Germany.

Thus the core of the BCAEC consisted of two thoroughly Jew-hating groups – Viscount Lymington's English Array and William Joyce's National Socialist League – plus one less overtly anti-Jewish outfit – the Liberty Restoration League – as well as a strong contingent of departees from the British Union of Fascists. What brought them all together was the growing threat of war in 1938 as a result of the Czech crisis (which would end with capitulation to Germany and Neville Chamberlain returning from Munich with 'peace in our time').

Lymington became the BCAEC president, Joyce its vice-president and John Beckett its honorary secretary. Among its most active members were George Lane-Fox Pitt-Rivers, Captain Archibald Maule Ramsay, Major J. F. C. Fuller and A. K. Chesterton.[18]

The Right Club (founded 1938)

The overtly pro-Nazi Right Club (RC) was established in May 1938 by Captain Maule Ramsay MP. It brought together titled, business and government figures who, despite the changing climate of opinion in Britain, remained pro-Hitler and deeply anti-Jewish. Among them were Lord Redesdale (fanatically pro-Nazi, like his daughter Unity Mitford), the Duke of Wellington (Anglo-German Fellowship and president of Liberty Restoration League), Professor Charles Sarolea, Colonel Charles Teviot, William Le Poer Trench, Major Francis Yeats-Brown, Lord Charles Carnegie, Princess Blücher von Wahlstatt, Sir Samuel Chapman, Sir Earnest Bennett, John Milner Bailey, Lord Colum Crichton-Stuart and Sir Peter Agnew. Rubbing shoulders with them were numerous stalwarts of far-right extremism, including William Joyce, Arnold Leese, Serocold Skeels, A. K. Chesterton, E. H. Cole, H. T. Mills, Richard Findley (The Link, Nordic League), Oliver Gilbert, H. T. W. Luttman-Johnson (founder and secretary of the January Club), Anthony Ludovici and Aubury Lees (The Link, Nordic League).[53]

Officially, the RC folded as war commenced at the start of September 1939. In fact, meetings continued quietly at the home of Oliver Gilbert until he and T. Victor Rowe were arrested and interned on 22 September.[22]

The British People's Party (founded 1939)

Set up in March 1939 as 'an anti-war party' by John Beckett and the Marquis of Tavistock (Hastings William Sackville Russell, later the twelfth Duke of Bedford), the British People's Party (BPP) was based at 13 John Street, near London's Victoria Station.[51] Tavistock, a committed Christian pacifist and supporter of social credit, may not have been pro-Nazi, or even wholly right wing, but many of his BPP co-workers most certainly were. An indication of his naivety was his visit to the German legation in Dublin during the Second World War in an attempt to broker a peace deal.

John Beckett, the BBP's organising secretary, was a former Labour Party MP who had moved to the far right, having until 1937 been a leading member of Mosley's British Union of Fascists (BUF). He then co-founded the National Socialist League with William Joyce before taking up his post in the BPP. Beckett was later accused by others of rashly overspending Tavistock's money. Two curious facts about Beckett: first, his mother was Jewish and, second, he would have had a good education, but was forced to leave school at fourteen after his father lost everything by twice investing in the bogus schemes for which Horatio Bottomley (see People's League, above) was eventually jailed and expelled from Parliament (parliamentary expulsion and jail – internment – later came Beckett's way too).[51]

The BPP's treasurer was Ben Greene, another former Labour Party MP who had quit the party in 1938 having decided that it was in the grip of communists. Believing that Britain should cooperate with Nazi Germany, he joined the Peace Pledge Union and published a newsletter called *Peace and Progress Information Service*. Much of its content was supplied to him by Ernst Wilhelm Bohle, head of the Foreign Organisation of the Nazi Party (the NSDAP/AO). Greene was the anonymous author of the pro-Hitler BPP pamphlet *The Truth about the War* and, as a regular speaker at anti-war gatherings, spoke of the 'danger of Jewish and American capitalists'.[41]

On the BPP's executive committee, which was chaired by Tavistock, were Beckett, Greene, Viscount Lymington (who was the president of British Council Against European Commitments) and John Scanlon (a former left-wing journalist who been in the BUF and who wrote for *New Pioneer*). Two prime movers in the BPP, both involved with Lymington's *New Pioneer*, were Anthony Ludovici and Philip Mairet. Ludovici (as 'Cobbett') was the pseudonymous author of *The Jews, and the Jews in England* (1938). Mairet was a former editor of *New English Weekly*.

After the war the BPP was relaunched (in London at a meeting in December 1945 held in Holborn Hall) by Beckett and Tavistock, who was by then the Duke of Bedford. Head of its research department was Harold Lockwood, a former member of Arnold Leese's Imperial Fascist League. This new BPP, with offices at 33 Maiden Lane, WC2, produced a journal, the *People's Post*, and campaigned for clemency for William Joyce while condemning the Nuremberg War Crimes Trials.

The BPP ceased to exist after the death of the Duke of Bedford. A respected naturalist and authority on birds, he was out on the grounds of his Endsleigh estate in Devon when he died of gunshot wounds in 1953, aged sixty-four. Despite a coroner's verdict that the death was accidentally self-inflicted, his elder son, John, who inherited the dukedom, suggested it may have been suicide. In his book *A Silver-Plated Spoon*, he described his father as 'The loneliest man I ever knew, incapable of giving or receiving love, utterly self-centred and opinionated. He loved birds, animals, peace, monetary reform, the park and religion.'[52]

The British Council for a Christian Settlement in Europe (founded 1939)

On 19 September 1939, just over a fortnight after the declaration of war against Germany, British People's Party members John Beckett and Ben Greene lunched with Admiral Domvile. The three then went to the London home of another of the party's mainstays, Captain Robert Gordon-Canning, formerly of the British Union of Fascists (BUF). Here they met with five members of The Link and together formed the British Council for a Christian Settlement in Europe (BCCSE), with the intention of working for a negotiated settlement with Hitler. Becket became its secretary, Lord Tavistock its chairman, and its headquarters were in Greene's Hampshire home in Berkhamsted. Although the organisation worked with members of the Peace Pledge Union and even some left-wing pacifists, the operative word here is 'Christian'. The prime movers in the BCCSE were strongly anti-Jewish, and their actual aim was to unite Christian Europe against non-Christians, meaning Jews. Attempts to bring in key members of Mosley's BUF and Maule Ramsay's Right Club foundered on account of long-standing factional differences. However, support from Lord Beaverbrook and from several notable members of the Independent Labour Party made it look briefly as if there was mileage in their campaign to curtail the war, but the Tyler Kent spying scandal (implicating the Right Club and other Jew-haters) put paid to the BCCSE. Many of its key members were arrested and interned in late May 1940.[51]

The last BCCSE meeting was probably the one held at the Kingsway Hall in London on 3 April 1940, with John Beckett in the chair. Lord Tavistock spoke too quietly for many of the audience to hear, outlining his efforts to negotiate a peace, particularly his unsuccessful discussions in the German Embassy in Dublin. Hugh Ross Williamson of the British Union of Fascists then spoke against Churchill and in favour of the chivalry of the German Navy, to mixed audience reactions. The final speaker, John McGovern of the Independent Labour Party, made himself equally unpopular by praising Hitler for all he had done for the working classes in Germany. All three speakers were heckled. Outside the hall, communists, pacifists, anti-communists, Jew-haters and others sold their journals and handed out their anti-war literature. With the rest of Europe resigned to the reality of war, the BCCSE constituted a very disparate and rather desperate gathering of eccentrics, misfits and malcontents.[54]

Main sources

Background and general information on all these organisations and individuals can be found in Wikipedia, Metapedia and a host of more specific websites. These have been used extensively throughout – occasionally as a primary source, very frequently to cross-check details gleaned from elsewhere. For anyone wanting to extend more information than that given here, a series of internet searches using key words is an obvious starting point. To find specific books, especially those now out of print – many can now be read online at little or no cost – Forgotten Books (www.forgottenbooks.com) is particularly recommended. To buy hard copies, try the American Book Exchange (www.abe.com and www.abe.co.uk). Documents marked with an asterisk are original copies in the private collection of the author.

1. Independent Labour Party Information Committee (1921), *Who Pays for the Attacks on Labour?*
2. Peter Barberis, John McHugh and Mike Tyldesley (2000), *Encyclopedia of British and Irish Political Organisations: Parties, Groups and Movements of the 20th Century*
3. Steven Dorril (2006), *Blackshirt: Sir Oswald Mosley and British Fascism*
4. *Information*, Vol. XIII, No. 41, 16 December 1938★
5. John Simkin, 'National Political League', http://spartacus-educational.com
6. These five National Political League leaflets (from a package sent to The Britons, addressed to Major Rich) were sold recently on eBay
7. Race Matthews (2014), *Prejudice: Anti-Semitism in the Distributist Weeklies*, www.kobobooks.com
8. Geoffrey Alderman, 'Can this Jew-Hater G. K. Chesterton be a Saint?', *Jewish Chronicle*, 18 September 2013; Metapedia, *National League for Clean Government*
9. Metapedia, *National League for Clean Government*
10. Geoffrey Alderman, 'Can this Jew-Hater G. K. Chesterton be a Saint?', *Jewish Chronicle*, 18 September 2013
11. Bryan Cheyette (1995), *Constructions of 'the Jew' in English Literature and Society: Racial Representations, 1875–1945*
12. Gill Bennett (2009), *Churchill's Man of Mystery*
13. British Empire Union, *The Empire Annual 1930*★
14. *British Empire Union Monthly Record*, 4(44), July 1920★
15. Wikipedia, *Economic League (United Kingdom)*
16. Wikipedia, *British Empire Union*
17. Wikipedia, *British Workers League*
18. G. C. Webber (1986), *The Ideology of the British Right, 1918–1939*
19. Thomas P. Linehan (2001), *British Fascism, 1918–1939: Parties, Ideology and Culture*
20. Wikipedia, *Middle Class Union*
21. *The Britisher*, no.1, 15 September 1937★, and no. 5, June 1938★; *Christian Free Press*, no. 28, March 1939★
22. Richard Thurlow (1998), *Fascism in Britain*

230 Appendix 2: Peer groups of The Britons

23 Loyalty League (c.1923), *The Jewish Menace to Christian Civilisation*
24 *The Patriot*, January 1923★
25 *Hidden Hand*, 2(12), January 1922★
26 *Hidden Hand*, 3(1), February 1922★
27 *Canadian Jewish Review*, 24 February 1922
28 *Hidden Hand*, 4(8, August 1923★
29 *Loyalty*, July 1923★
30 *British Guardian*, September 1924★
31 Robert Benewick (1969), *Political Violence and Public Order*
32 *British Guardian*, 5(6), June 1923★
33 Roger Eatwell (2003), *Fascism: A History*
34 British Fascists (c.1926), *Objects* [policy leaflet]★
35 Janet Elizabeth Dack (2010), *In from the Cold? British Fascism and the Mainstream Press 1925–1939*
36 Martin Pugh (2006), *Hurrah for the Blackshirts! Fascists and Fascism in Britain between the Wars*
37 British Fascists, *Mass Meeting at Kensington Town Hall*, leaflet, 24 February 1927★
38 British Fascists, *Mass Meeting at Town Hall, Canning Town*, leaflet, 2 March 1927★
39 Wikipedia, *British Union of Fascists*
40 Association of Art Historians, *Bulletin*, October 2005
41 Richard Griffiths (1983), *Fellow Travellers of the Right: British Enthusiasts for Nazi Germany 1933–39*
42 Security Services documents on Rudolph Gottfried Rosel, National Archives, Kew
43 Anglo-German Information Service, *The Women's Movement in Germany*★
44 Anglo-German Information Service, *Speech by the Führer and Chancellor of the German Reich before the Reichstag on January 30, 1939*★
45 Anglo-German Information Service, *Herr Hitler's Avowals of Peace (A Collection of Extracts from his Speeches)*★
46 Anglo-German Information Service, *Art in Modern Germany*★
47 Anglo-German Information Service, *German Labour Service: Lecture given by General Tholens, Deputy Chief of the German Labour Camps to the Anglo-German Fellowship in London on October 19th 1938*★
48 Anglo-German Information Service, *Hitler's Speech to the Diplomatic Corps at the New Year Reception on January 11th, 1937*★
49 Anglo-German Information Service, *Address to the German Führer and Reich Chancellor by the Apostolic Nuncio, Monsignor Cesare Orsenigo, Doyen of the Diplomatic Corps, at the New Year Reception in Berlin on January 12, 1939*★
50 Mary Kenny (2008), *Germany Calling – A Personal Biography of William Joyce*
51 Francis Beckett (1999), *The Rebel who Lost his Cause: The Tragedy of John Beckett, MP*
52 John, Duke of Bedford (1959), *A Silver-Plated Spoon*
53 Robin Saikia (ed.) (2010), *The Red Book: The Membership List of the Right Club, 1939*
54 *Free Press*, no. 40, October 1939★ and no. 46, April 1940★

Other sources providing general back-up details include Eugene C. Black (1988), *The Social Politics of Anglo-Jewry, 1880–1920*; Gisela C. Lebzelter (1978), *Political Anti-Semitism in England, 1918–1939*; Kenneth Lunn and Richard C. Thurlow (eds) (1980), *British Fascism*; A. W. B. Simpson (1995), *In the Highest Degree Odious: Detention without Trial in Wartime Britain*; Tom Villis (2006), *Reaction and the Avant-Garde: The Revolt against Liberal Democracy in Early Twentieth-Century Britain*; Robert Skidelsky (1975), *Oswald Mosley*; Gavin Bowd (2013), *Fascist Scotland*; *The New Age Supplement*, no. 3, 22 November 1934, and numerous internet sites.

APPENDIX 3
SOME INDEPENDENT RIGHT-WING BRITISH JOURNALS

For ease of access, these journals are listed simply in alphabetical order. In truth, their date of founding is much less relevant than the details of the role and relevance of each.

Eye-Witness

In 1911 the writer Hilaire Belloc founded the weekly newspaper *Eye-Witness* with the intention of using its pages to expose political corruption. It featured literary and political contributions from Belloc's friends and associates, among them G. K. Chesterton, H. G. Wells and George Bernard Shaw. Belloc soon realised, however, that he was too busy working on other projects to run the paper properly and so he allowed Cecil Chesterton (brother of G. K. and cousin of A. K.) to take over most of the editing and general office work. At the end of its first year Belloc quit completely and passed the ownership of the paper to Cecil, who renamed it *New Witness* (see below).[1]

While there remains controversy over the extent to which G. K. Chesterton's occasional anti-Jewish literary snipes amount to proof that he was actively anti-Jewish, no such doubts exist where Hilaire Belloc is concerned. His *The Jews* (1922), which he dubbed 'my admirable Yid book', was written with the declared intention of debunking anti-Jewish ideas. However, its initial thesis reads:

> The Jews are an alien body within the society they inhabit – hence irritation and friction – a problem is presented by the strains thus set up – the solution to that problem is urgently necessary. An alien body in any organism is disposed of in one of two ways: elimination or segregation.[2]

And here is a rhyme Belloc wrote about the large London home of the wealthy (Jewish) Rothschild family:

> At the end of Piccadilly is a place
> Of habitation for the Jewish race.
> Awaiting their regained Jerusalem,
> These little huts, they say, suffice for them.
> Here Rothschild lives, chief of the tribe abhorr'd
> Who tried to put to death Our Blessed Lord.
> But, on the third day, as the Gospel shows,
> Cheating their machinations, He arose:
> In Whose commemoration, now and then,
> We persecute these curly-headed men.

Even Belloc, however, had no time for *The Protocols* or its proponents. Of Nesta Webster he wrote:

> She is one of those people who have got one cause on the brain. It is the good old 'Jewish revolutionary' bogey. But there is a type of unstable mind which cannot rest without morbid imaginings, and the conception of a single cause simplifies thought. With this good woman it is the Jews, with some people it is the Jesuits, with others Freemasons and so on. The world is more complex than that.

He would have said the same of Beamish and The Britons.[3]

Cecil Chesterton's aversion to Jews was more open and extreme than that of Belloc, and yet he too shied away from outright hatred while accepting it in others. In one of the only references to Jews in his posthumously published *A History of the United States* (1919), he stated: 'The problem of the Jew exists in America as elsewhere – perhaps more formidably than elsewhere. This, of course, is not because Jews, as such, are worse than other people: only idiots are anti-Semites in that sense.'[4] However, without Belloc there to rein him in, Cecil Chesterton placed contributions in *Eye-Witness* which dismayed even Belloc and contributed to the journal's early demise. And his own writing slipped far too readily into precisely the type of Jew-hatred he labelled (above) as the realm of idiots.[5,6]

G.K.'s Weekly

The pilot edition of this popular literary and campaigning journal, which was edited and published by G. K. Chesterton, appeared in 1924. The first proper edition followed in 1925. *G.K.'s Weekly* rose out of the ashes of his late brother's journal, *New Witness* (see below), and continued until G. K.'s death in 1936. Thereafter it became the *Weekly Review*, which lasted until 1948. In 1926, those closely associated with *G.K.'s Weekly* founded the Distributist League. Although the magazine became increasingly right-wing, it wasn't as overtly anti-Jewish as its two predecessors, Belloc's *Eye-Witness* and Cecil Chesterton's *New Witness*.[5,6,7]

The *Morning Post*

This daily newspaper was founded by Lord Glenesk. When he died, on 24 November 1908, ownership passed to his only surviving heir, his daughter Lilias, Countess Bathurst, and to her husband, Lord Bathurst.[8] The couple were both vice-presidents of the xenophobic and pro-fascist British Empire Union. Lady Bathurst was overtly Jew-hating. During the First Balkan War (1912–13, noted for its brutal treatment of Jews) she wrote to the editor of the *National Review*, Leo Maxse, who shared her dislike of all things Jewish: '*One* Samuel is going to catch it. We *are* being governed by Jews and Celts. I think it's time the former were sent back to Asia like the Turks.' And five years later, on 28 September 1917, also to Leo Maxse, she wrote:

> I heard from London that the panic and selfishness of the Jews, Russian and otherwise, is disgraceful and that they crowd all the public houses. Can't these vermin be sent back to their happy Fatherland to cut each others throats. What a glorious opportunity to get rid of them.[9]

From 1911 until 1937, the ultra-Conservative and often anti-Jewish *Morning Post* was edited by H. A. Gwynne (Howell Arthur Keir Gwynne, 1865–1950; a close friend of Rudyard Kipling, he was a pall-bearer at the latter's funeral in 1936). Gwynne, Ian Colvin and Nesta Webster (along with other members of staff at the paper) co-wrote eighteen articles under the collective title of *The Cause of World Unrest*. Serialised in the paper during July 1920, these detailed supposed Jewish plots behind key world events and repeatedly referenced *The Protocols*. All the quotations came from a translation of *The Protocols* specially commissioned by Gwynne and produced by Victor Marsden, the paper's Russian correspondent. (This is the version, later published by The Britons, which has since become the standard text worldwide). In the autumn of 1920, a collected edition of the eighteen articles was published in book form with an introduction by Gwynne. Although this volume, also entitled *The Cause of World Unrest*, did much to imbue the myth of a global Jewish conspiracy with authority and legitimacy,[10] it was no isolated slice of bigotry. Indeed, it must be viewed in context.

Fear of a threat from international Jewry was widespread, due in no small part to the popular belief that the recent Russian Revolution had been fermented by Jews. Thus, for example, in August 1919, a special investigation team commissioned by the US War Department had compiled and published a secret report entitled *The Power & Aims of International Jewry*. In Britain, an article appeared in the 8 February 1920 edition of the *Illustrated Sunday Herald* under the title 'Zionism versus Bolshevism: A Struggle for the Soul of the Jewish People'. And here is Winston Churchill writing on 'the schemes of International Jews':

> The adherents of this sinister confederacy are mostly men reared up among the unhappy populations of countries where Jews are persecuted on account

of their race. Most, if not all of them, have forsaken the faith of their forefathers, and divorced from their minds all spiritual hopes of the next world. This movement among the Jews is not new. From the days of Spartacus-Weishaupt to those of Karl Marx, and down to Trotsky (Russia), Bela Kun (Hungary), Rosa Luxemburg (Germany), and Emma Goldman (United States), this world-wide conspiracy for the overthrow of civilisation and for the reconstitution of society on the basis of arrested development, of envious malevolence, and impossible equality, has been steadily growing. It played, as a modern writer, Mrs. Webster, has so ably shown, a definitely recognisable part in the tragedy of the French Revolution. It has been the mainspring of every subversive movement during the Nineteenth Century; and now at last this band of extraordinary personalities from the underworld of the great cities of Europe and America have gripped the Russian people by the hair of their heads and have become practically the undisputed masters of that enormous empire.

Later, in the same article, Churchill stated:

There is no need to exaggerate the part played in the creation of Bolshevism and in the actual bringing about of the Russian Revolution, by these international and for the most part atheistical Jews. It is certainly a very great one; it probably outweighs all others. With the notable exception of Lenin, the majority of the leading figures are Jews. Moreover, the principal inspiration and driving power comes from the Jewish leaders.

In 1924, the *Morning Post* was sold by Lord and Lady Bathurst to a consortium headed by the Duke of Northumberland,[8] founder of both the Boswell Publishing Company and *The Patriot*. In 1937 it was sold again, this time to the *Daily Telegraph*, whereupon it was absorbed into that paper and so ceased to exist as a separate title.[11]

The *National Review*

In 1883 two English writers, Alfred Austin and William Courthope, founded the *National Review* as a platform for the Conservative Party. Leopold Maxse served as its editor from 1893 until his death on 22 January 1932. In the run-up to the Great War, his monthly magazine took on a fiercely anti-German tone. Maxse himself was particularly vehement in his concern about German Jews in Britain and about 'international Jewry' supporting Germany. At the end of the war, Maxse argued that the terms of the peace were far too lenient for Germany. He pushed too for Western intervention in Russia to defeat Bolshevism, frequently extending this anti-communism to include patently anti-Jewish sentiment.[12]

New Age

Founded in 1894 as the journal of the Christian Socialist movement, this weekly was bought by A. R. Orage and Holbrook Jackson in May 1907 with financial backing from George Bernard Shaw. Jackson stayed for one year, after which Orage ran and edited the magazine until he sold it in 1922. It ceased publication in 1938. Under Orage, the magazine became a platform for British literary, social and political ideas. What is interesting in the context of this book is the way it gradually drifted from the left to the anti-Jewish right.

Here is a brief and simplified picture of the political left during this period. Fabianism, as embraced by Shaw and Orage and most of the early *New Age* circle, tackled socialist ideas and produced its own political body, the Labour Party. There was a strong thread of nostalgic romanticism within the Fabian movement which led its adherents to favour guild socialism over trade unionism. If Fabian socialism strove to represent all classes, trade unionism strove on behalf of the working class and produced as its political wing the Independent Labour Party (ILP), to the left of which, pitted against wealth and capitalism, was the Communist Party. Between each of these was bitter and often destructive factionalism.

Writing in the mid-1920s, Orage described his own early politics as follows:

> Like every intellectual in those days – I refer to the earliest years of the twentieth century – I began as some sort of Socialist. Socialism was not then the popular or unpopular vogue it has since become; but it was much more of a cult, with affiliations in directions now quite disowned – with theosophy, arts and crafts, vegetarianism, the 'simple life', and almost, as one might say, the musical glasses. (William) Morris had shed a medieval glamour over it with his stained-glass 'News from Nowhere'. Edward Carpenter had put it in sandals. Cunningham Graham had mounted it on an Arab steed to which he was always saying a romantic farewell. Kier Hardie had clothed it in a cloth cap and a red tie. And Bernard Shaw, on behalf of the Fabian Society, had hung it with innumerable jingling epigrammatic bells – and cap. My brand of Socialism was, therefore, a blend or, let us say, an anthology of all these, to which from my personal predilections and experience I added a good practical knowledge of the working classes, a professional interest in economics which led me to master Marx's 'Das Kapital, and an idealism fed at the source – namely, Plato.[13]

If Orage had a political strength, it lay in his experience of northern working-class life. Before his purchase of *New Age*, he had been a schoolteacher in Leeds. His political weakness lay in his naive nostalgic romanticism. Thus, again pre-1907, influenced by Arthur Penty (with whom he and Holbrook had founded the influential Leeds Arts Club), he had been the co-founder and secretary of a Guild Restoration League.

Penty, Hilaire Belloc, Cecil Chesterton and G. K. Chesterton together pioneered distributism, an economic theory which suggested that the means of production should belong to all (as in communism), but that this should go hand in hand with the right to have personal property (as in capitalism), so long as it was non-productive.

Belloc and the Chestertons were anti-Jewish, rabidly so in the case of Cecil Chesterton and his immediate circle, and Orage, always in awe of Penty, gradually took on board their anti-Jewish views. In 1918 he met C. H. Douglas, who was developing economic theories based on his observation that, in successful businesses, the total costs of production always exceeded the total expenditure on wages and dividends, meaning that workers could never afford what they produced. Though they are now widely discredited, Douglas's theories, which Orage dubbed social credit, initially gained popular credence.

Douglas, especially in his later writings, openly embraced the idea of a threat from international Jewry and believed that Jews controlled finance. He had, however, long been privately anti-Jewish. A handwritten letter by him dated 25 November (no year given, but around 1925) includes the sentence: 'There is no doubt in my mind that we are going to be handed to the Jews, lock stock & barrel.' He then goes on to discuss two prominent international bankers and how the one has been 'put into office and kept there' by the other.[14] And, though Douglas was never openly extreme in his views, his social credit movement quickly became closely associated with the anti-Jewish far right and has remained so ever since.

When Douglas died in 1952, a brief obituary of sorts appeared in Arnold Leese's Jew-obsessed journal *Gothic Ripples*. Because Leese was an acolyte of Arthur Kitson, who admired Douglas, it was nothing like as savage as it might otherwise have been:

> Clifford Hugh Douglas, the Jew who invented Social Credit, died on 29th September. He was a bit of a mystery. His features were 100 per cent. Jewish (see portrait in his own paper *Social Credit*, 17th May 1935). The late Arthur Kitson, monetary reformer, knew him well; in 1925, Douglas had a Jewish accent, and when asked where he came from, said 'Kirkcudbright', pronouncing the name as spelled, which no native of that Scottish county would do. Late in life Douglas became what the Jews would call 'anti-semitic', but, although seemingly genuine in this, like the Jew H. H. Klein in New York, his own Jewishness would not allow him to accept Hitler, and he and his followers spread many ridiculous stories about the German leader. We think Douglas must have had some blood relationship with the Mond family; they had the same caste of feature, and the names Clifford, Hordern and Douglas crop up in both families.[15]

All these shades of anti-Jewry were reflected in the *New Age*. In 1913, just six years after Shaw helped Orage to buy the paper, the Fabians were so disappointed with it that they founded a replacement, the *New Statesman*. After the Great War, the *New Age* became a mouthpiece of social credit and a platform for the writing of the anti-Jewish right, with regular contributions from Belloc and the Chestertons, Arthur Kitson (of The Britons), Anthony Ludovici (a Hitler enthusiast and author of *The Jews, and the Jews in England*) and Ezra Pound.

After 1922, though Orage no longer edited the *New Age*, he stayed on as its *éminence grise*, and anti-Jewish themes persisted. Thus, for example, the 6 December 1923 issue carried a piece written by C. H. Douglas, entitled simply 'Social Credit', in which he draws on *The Protocols* as a 'substantially accurate' document containing prophesies which are 'moving rapidly towards fulfilment'.

The *New Age* serves as a clear illustration of how nostalgic romanticism can turn committed young left-wingers into older right-wing bigots. The nostalgia divorces them from their old loyalties while romanticism lets them embrace what would once have been utterly alien to them. It's why an ILP stalwart such as John Beckett could become a fascist, and it's precisely why Hitler and Mussolini could take socialism and turn it into that very different thing, National Socialism.[17]

New Pioneer

This fascist and anti-Jewish monthly journal was launched in December 1938 by John Beckett and Viscount Lymington (who became its editor). Contributors included A. K. Chesterton, Major General Fuller, Anthony Ludovici, Rolf Gardiner, Ben Greene, H. T. Mills, Philip Mairet and the pro-Nazi historian Sir Arthur Bryant.[16] *New Pioneer* reflected the interests of the British Council Against European Commitments which Beckett and Lymington also founded, and so it promoted non-involvement in European conflicts.[18]

New Witness

Founded in 1912 by Cecil Chesterton, *New Witness* was Hilaire Belloc's *Eye-Witness* under a new name. This journal quickly took on an even more overtly anti-Jewish tone than its predecessor. Some letters from an anti-Jewish writer and former MP called Frank O'Donnell had appeared in *Eye-Witness*, but Belloc had been wary of the man. Not so Cecil Chesterton, who, impressed with O'Donnell's writing, made him a columnist for *New Witness*. O'Donnell, who would, in later life, come wholly to believe in an international Jewish banking conspiracy, contributed pieces which outraged Jewish opinion. The upshot was that Cecil Chesterton and his journal were sued for libel by a Jewish businessman. The case reflected badly on the reputation of Belloc even though he was no longer involved in the journal, having sold all his shares. While publicly supporting Cecil, he wrote critically about him in private to another friend:

> the detestation of Jewish cosmopolitan influences, especially through finance, is one thing, and one may be right or wrong in feeling that detestation or in the degree to which one admits it; but mere anti-Semitism and the mere attack on a Jew because he is a Jew is quite another matter, and I told him repeatedly that I thought things he allowed O'Donnell to publish were unwise and deplorable ... The national term 'Jew' had been used simply as a term of abuse, much as a Lower Middle-class American will use the term 'Irish'.

Cecil Chesterton edited the *New Witness* from 1912 to 1916, when he joined the Highland Light Infantry as a private soldier. Thereafter, the journal was run by his wife, Ada, who served as its secretary and business manager, while his brother G. K. Chesterton served as its editor. Three times wounded, Cecil refused to leave his post until the armistice was declared on 11 November 1918. Less than four weeks later (6 December) he died of nephritis in a French military hospital.

Ada and G. K. jointly kept *New Witness* going until 1923. One year later, G. K. Chesterton published the pilot edition of his new journal, *G.K.'s Weekly*, as the successor to *New Witness*.[5,6]

Plain English

This deeply anti-Jewish journal was founded in 1920 by Lord Alfred Douglas, who, as an ex-lover of Oscar Wilde, had gained notoriety when that relationship became central to the high-profile trials in 1895 that led to Wilde's imprisonment for homosexuality. Assisting on the magazine was Harold Sherwood Spencer, whom Beamish had brought into Noel Billing's Vigilante Society, in which Douglas had also been an active member.

In a curious turn of events, Douglas appeared as a witness for the defence when Billing was taken to court by Maude Allen for accusing her of lesbianism. At the time Allen was appearing in *Salome*, the Oscar Wilde play which Douglas had helped Wilde to translate.

Edited by Douglas, *Plain English* was prominently advertised in early issues of The Britons journal *Jewry Über Alles*. Articles published in *Plain English* talked of Jewish ritual murders and endorsed *The Protocols*. Douglas and T. W. H. Crosland (author of *The Fine Old Hebrew Gentleman*) were mentioned in an article in the *Jewish Guardian* of 21 April 1922: 'It must no longer be a paying proposition to men like Mr. Crosland and Lord Alfred Douglas to invent vile insults against the Jews.' The sentence was later repeated in a letter from the editor of the *Jewish Guardian* that appeared in the *Morning Post*. Douglas then took libel action against both the *Morning Post* and the *Jewish Guardian*, a case which he won.[19]

Throughout his life, Douglas was involved in numerous court cases, not all of which turned out in his favour. In 1923 he went to jail for six months after having been found guilty of libelling Winston Churchill. The case was discussed in the December 1923 issue of the *Hidden Hand*. While Douglas was in jail, *Plain English* was edited by Spencer – who, it should be remembered, was also a founder member of The Britons. The magazine folded soon after Douglas came out of prison.

Plain Speaker

This was founded in London towards the end of 1957 by the right-wing Russian émigré George Knupffer. Peter Marriott, former chairman of The Britons, was Knupffer's co-editor. There was also a three-man honorary advisory committee consisting of Sir Charles Petrie and two retired American military men, both active right-wingers – Lieutenant General P.A. del Valle and Colonel Eugene C. Pomeroy. For further details, see the entry for Anthony Chavasse in Appendix 4.

Saturday Review

This popular magazine, founded in 1855, was owned and edited from 1933 until her death in December 1936 by the millionaire Lady Lucy Houston. From 1930 until 1936 she also controlled the overtly anti-Jewish Boswell Press, and from 1924 until 1936 she was responsible for the publishing of the Boswell Press magazine the *Patriot*.[20]

The 26 December 1936 issue of the *Saturday Review* is a typical one from that period in that it is relentlessly anti-communist, focusing on the relationship between Russia and war-torn Spain. Throughout, it sides with Franco. The first page begins with a parliamentary exchange between Foreign Secretary Anthony Eden and the MP Captain Maule Ramsay. The journal sides with the latter. Inside is a picture showing Hitler and Mussolini shaking hands in front of a large swastika flag. Beneath are the words 'Hitler and Mussolini, real friends of England and enemies of Bolshevism'. Selling at 2d a copy, this large-format weekly was essentially a high-circulation platform for those who would have had England join forces with fascism to fight Judeo-Bolshevism.[21]

The inside front page of the issue of 2 January 1937 is given over to a full-page article reprinted from the *Daily Mail* headed 'Make Terms with Germany'. Here is an extract:

> Strong pressure is being put by the Reds upon the British Government to abandon its policy of non-intervention … All the world knows that the Spanish civil war was engineered by Moscow … Is there any wonder that Germany and Italy have declared their determination not to tolerate the establishment of a Red regime in the Peninsula? … And agreement with Italy … is on the point of completion. The time has now arrived when Britain should come to terms with Germany also. That great nation is one of the strongest armed Powers in the world. She has met, and defeated, the subversive influences of Communism within her own borders and, by a series of resolute actions, has demonstrated her strength and her formidable influence.

The piece concludes with fulsome and uncritical praise for Germany and Nazism.

In each issue of the *Saturday Review* during the late 1930s we find further evidence of an absolute commitment to the Nazi cause in the small ads, under 'Miscellaneous'. One regular and seemingly innocuous advertisement reads: 'Germany's desire for peace and general recovery. Read the facts. Free literature in English from Dept. S, Deutscher Fichte-Bund, Hamburg 36, Jungfernsteig, 30.'[22] This deserves further attention. The Deutscher Fichte-Bund (German Fichte League or Fichte Association, also known as the Union for World Veracity) supplied free 'information sheets' worldwide in a variety of languages. It had been founded on 29 January 1914 by Heinrich Kessemeier to propagate German thought and aims abroad and was named after the German nationalist Johann Gottlieb Fichte. By the 1930s, under the directorship of Dr Theodore Kessemeier (son of the founder), it had become fervently Hitlerite, pro-Nazi, anti-Bolshevik and anti-Jewish, distributing articles critical of Russia and the left in Europe along with translations of major speeches by Hitler, Goebbels, Rosenberg, Darré and other leading Nazis.[23] From the mid-1930s onwards it rivalled World Service as an essential international propaganda vehicle of German Nazism, eclipsing overseas Nazi propaganda operations such as the London-based Anglo-German Information Service. Much of its effort in the late 1930s, and even into the early 1940s, was directed at America in an effort to prevent its becoming involved in the war.

As war approached during the late 1930s, the Deutscher Fichte-Bund supplied propaganda to British Nazi sympathisers and helped them to network with like-minded organisations in other countries. Thus, G. Woods, writing on behalf of Arnold Leese's Imperial Fascist League to the All Russian Fascist Party in Berne (led by Boris Toedtli, who was also the head of the Swiss branch of World Service) stated:

> We have heard of your movement, and should very much like to establish relations with your party. We understand from the *Deutscher Fichtebund* of Hamburg, that your movement is against the Jews. On this point we shall have common ground. So that you have a chance to study our movement I enclose some leaflets, and by the same mail am sending you a copy of our monthly paper, *The Fascist*.

They were also in touch with Mosley's British Union of Fascists, whose January–April issue of *British Union Quarterly* carried the following in its editorial:

> Readers who are desirous of learning something of the new Germany without being able to visit her for themselves will receive assistance from the Deutscher Fichte-Bund. This organisation is concerned not with the dissemination of political propaganda, but with the task of giving to people outside Germany information which they may require about the cultural, political and economic developments in Germany under National-Socialism.

Another UK Fichte-Bund contact was the British Protestant League, a small Scottish anti-Jewish and anti-communist organisation run from Bearsden, near Glasgow, by Alexander Ratcliffe. The September 1943 issue of their journal, *Vanguard*, bore the front-cover wording 'Communism with the mask off'. This was the title of a speech by Goebbels as translated and distributed by the Deutscher Fichte-Bund. The text which followed quoted directly from that leaflet. Throughout the war and after, Ratcliffe regularly used the Fichte-Bund and other German propaganda as direct source material for his publications.

The Deutscher Fichte-Bund even distributed the work of British Jew-haters. One such work was *Great Britain's Policy after Munich: A Well-Known Scotsman's Unheeded Warning*, which had been written by Dr A. P. Laurie, a founder member of The Link.[24] We know that much of its literature distributed in Britain came via The Britons, however, as everything that passed through the latter's office carried their stamp.

Truth

Founded by Henry Labouchère, a diplomat and Liberal politician, this periodical first appeared on 4 January 1877, specialising in investigative journalism and the exposure of fraud. After the First World War it became closely associated with the Conservative Party and grew increasingly right wing, so much so that in October 1941 it became the centre of a short-lived scandal, when the Labour MP Josiah Wedgewood accused it, in Parliament, of being a fascist and pro-Nazi journal and called for an end to its publication. But the controversy subsided, and the journal continued to appear under the editorship (1940–53) of Collin Brooks, whose deputy editor was A. K. Chesterton, previously of the British Union of Fascists and subsequently founder of the National Front. Both under his own name and under the pseudonym Philip Faulconbridge, Chesterton was also a frequent contributor. His and other pieces were often overtly anti-Jewish.[25] When in 1953 Ronald Staples bought the journal, he sacked Brooks, Chesterton and other right-wing staff. Chesterton responded with an angry essay entitled *Truth Has Been Murdered* (published by The Britons) and then by launching his own far-right replacement, *Candour*. *Truth* ceased publication in 1957 following the death of Staples.

Main sources

Throughout, Wikipedia and other internet sources to cross-check details. Documents marked with an asterisk are original copies in the private collection of the author.

1. A. N. Wilson (2004), *Hilaire Belloc*
2. Hilaire Belloc (1922), *The Jews*
3. Robert Speaight (1957), *The Life of Hilaire Belloc*
4. Cecil Chesterton (1919), *A History of the United States*
5. Race Matthews (2014) *Prejudice: Anti-Semitism in the Distributist Weeklies*, www.kobobooks.com
6. Geoffrey Alderman, 'Can this Jew-Hater G. K. Chesterton be a Saint?', *Jewish Chronicle*, 18 September 2013
7. Wikipedia, *G.K.'s Weekly*; various copies of *G.K.'s Weekly*
8. The Bathurst Estate and Cirencester Park, www.cirencesterpark.co.uk
9. Keith Wilson (1992), 'Hail and Farewell? The Reception in the British Press of the First Publication in English of the Protocols of Zion, 1920–22', *Immigrants & Minorities: Historical Studies in Ethnicity, Migration and Diaspora*, 11(2): 171–86

Appendix 3: Some right-wing British journals **243**

10 Howell Arthur Gwynne (1920), *The Cause of World Unrest*
11 Wikipedia, *The Morning Post*
12 Wikipedia, *National Review (London)*; Wikipedia, *Leopold Maxse*
13 *The New Age Supplement*, no. 3, 22 November 1934
14 Letter from C. H. Douglas to 'H. E.' dated 25 November (written *c.*1925)★
15 *Gothic Ripples*, no. 94, 16 November 1952★
16 *New Pioneer*, 1(3), February 1939★
17 Wikipedia, *The New Age*
18 Steven Dorril (2006), *Blackshirt: Sir Oswald Mosley and British Fascism*
19 *Hidden Hand*, 4(8), August 1923★
20 G. C. Webber (1986), *The Ideology of the British Right, 1918–1939*
21 *Saturday Review*, 162, 26 December 1936★
22 *Saturday Review*, 163, 2 January 1937★
23 Fichte-Bund leaflets (in English)★: no. 812, *The German Winter Help* [speech by Erich Hilgenfeldt]; no. 852, *The General Staff's Report of a European Great Power: About France's Iron-clad Eastern Frontier*; no. 862, *Adolf Hitler's Contribution to the Promotion of European Peace*; no. 872, *To the Poilu of Verdun: An Open Letter from a German Front Line Fighter*; no. 922, *Who are the Rulers of Russia?* [speech by Rosenberg, listing Jews in power]; no. 952, *What is Germany Going to Do?* [speech by Hitler]; no. 962, *Bolshevism and the Farm Class*★
24 Louis W. Bondy (1946), *Racketeers of Hatred*★
25 Wikipedia, *Truth (British periodical)*; various copies of *Truth*

APPENDIX 4
KEY FIGURES IN THE BRITONS

Years before I even envisaged writing this book, I began making notes for my own use on the backgrounds of individuals associated with The Britons. Almost as soon as I began the book, I realised that this information would greatly help readers, hence this appendix. What I failed to do in compiling this list was to keep a record of my sources. All I can say is that I checked and rechecked every single detail, deleting anything about which I was remotely unsure. Many of the characters listed here are worthy of further biographical research.

Leading members, 1920s and 1930s

Joseph Banister said that he 'first came up against the Jewish menace as a journalist in America before the Boer War'. A founder member of The Britons, he was the author of their pamphlet *Jews and the White Slave Traffic* (1924). They also distributed his self-published book *England under the Jews*. In the late 1930s Banister was a columnist for and prominent contributor to the Militant Christian Patriots' journal *The Britisher*.

Henry Hamilton Beamish – see Chapter 1.

Mr C. Beaumont spoke at a London meeting of The Britons held at Kensington Town Hall on 14 December 1921.

Miss Meredith Beaumont lived in Putney and was the main organiser, for the women's committee of The Britons, of the meeting held at the Star and Garter Assembly Rooms, Putney Bridge, in January 1922. The theme of the meeting was 'The Alien Menace to our Homes'. An active member of The Britons, she later joined the Imperial Fascist League.

Brigadier General R(obert) B(yron) D(rury) Blakeney (1872–1952), as a lieutenant in the Royal Engineers, was involved in the Battle of Omdurman in Sudan (in which British forces under Kitchener defeated the forces of the Mahdi). At the time he had been serving as a subaltern on the Sudan Military Railway. During the Second Boer War (1899–1902) he commanded the 3rd Balloon Section of the Royal Engineers, after which he worked in railway administration. In 1906 he was appointed deputy general manager of the Egyptian State Railway and in 1919 was promoted to manager, a post he held until 1923. His activities on the British political right began in the early 1920s when, after returning to Britain, he joined The Britons, became an early member of the British Fascisti (BF) and also joined the Nordic League. In 1924 he replaced Lord Garvagh as the BF president and took on the editorship of its journal, the *Fascist Week*. Helping to organise the BF on strict military lines, he forged alliances with the Anti-Socialist Union and other right-wing groups. Under his guidance, the BF was a mainstream conservative and patriotic group implacably opposed to communism and the unions. In the run-up to the 1926 General Strike, Blakeney and Rear Admiral A. E. Armstrong argued that the BF should suspend its fascist identity and devote its energies to supporting the strike-breaking Organisation for the Maintenance of Supplies (OMS). Defeated in this move by a contingent led by Rotha Lintorn-Orman and the BF Grand Council, Blakeney and his supporters (including Armstrong, the Earl of Glasgow and Lord Earnest Hamilton) left the BF and formed The Loyalists, a group which was absorbed into the OMS once the General Strike began. After the General Strike, Blakeney became associated with the Imperial Fascist League (IFL) and spoke at several of their events. At one of these gatherings, he and the IFL leader Arnold Leese were beaten up by supporters of Oswald Mosley's British Union of Fascists (of which the IFL had been deeply critical, having labelled Mosley a kosher fascist and called his organisation the British Jewion of Fascists). Despite this beating, Blakeney later played a minor role in the BUF, as well as contributing occasional articles to their journals, *Action* and *The Blackshirt*. During the Second World War, while many of his fellow right-wingers were interned, Blakeney, seen to be a less of a threat, remained free and served with the Home Guard.

Lord Cardross, otherwise known as Shipley Gordon Stuart Erskine, 14th Earl of Buchan (1850–1936), was a member and supporter of The Britons. In 1922 he gave £30 towards the cost of new printing machinery. An entry in the December 1922 issue of the *Hidden Hand* states: 'We have the permission of Lord Cardross to say that he is the donor of the generous gift recorded recently, and we hope that his example will be imitated by many others, so as to enable us to extend the good work.' A letter from him about the (Jewish) Labour MP Emanuel Shinwell was printed in the December 1923 issue of the *Hidden Hand*.

Dr J(ohn) H(enry) Clarke (1853–24 November 1931) chaired the meeting that founded The Britons and went on to serve as its vice-president and chairman from its inception until his death in 1931. His anti-Jewish writings included *White Labour Versus Red*, *The Call of the Sword* and *England under the Heel of the Jew*. Clarke was a doctor who, having taken up homeopathy, became the chief consulting physician to the Homeopathic Hospital in London. He also ran a successful clinic at 8 Bolton Street, Piccadilly, and had numerous private patients from throughout the world. A workaholic, he was the editor, for twenty-nine years from May 1885, of the journal the *Homeopathic World* and the author of numerous influential books on homeopathy. Among these was the seminal and widely read volume *The Prescriber: A Dictionary of the New Therapeutics*, which, to this day, remains essential reading for any lay practitioner. Before the formation of The Britons, Clarke and Beamish had been leading members of the Vigilante Society.

Captain R(ichard) T. Cooper (1884–1957) was a founding member and mainstay of The Britons who was also active in the Imperial Fascist League. Educated at Julien's Atelier, a leading Paris art school, he became a professional artist and designed posters for the Underground Group (1924–35). As the cartoonist 'Goy', he contributed a series of notoriously anti-Jewish cartoons to the *Hidden Hand*, the *British Guardian* and other Jew-hating journals. Cooper became the official president of The Britons in 1948 after the death of Beamish, a post he retained until his own death.

Mr Cowper-Todd was at the 11 May 1923 Britons meeting which Beamish attended.

Walter Crick, who served as vice-president of The Britons (1925–36), was a wealthy Northampton boot manufacturer who ran the company founded in St Giles Street, Northampton, by his father, Walter Drawbridge Crick. He was also the uncle of Francis Crick, the Nobel Prize-winning co-discoverer of the double helix structure of DNA. Walter Crick caused controversy in 1925 when, at a gathering of Northampton businessmen, he gave a speech in which he urged them all, as loyal Britons, to rise up against the power of Jewish financiers – which, he claimed, was a bigger danger than Germany had been in 1914. On 19 March 1925 he was quoted in the *Northampton Daily Echo*: 'Jews can destroy by means of finance. Jews are International. Control of credit in this country is not in the hands of Englishmen, but of Jews. It has become the biggest danger the British Empire has ever had to face.' The response of the *Jewish World* was to call on Jewish people in Britain to boycott footwear by Crick & Co. The Britons then carried an advertisement for the shoe company on the front page of the *British Guardian* (3 April 1925), and appointed Crick their vice-president. But by the mid-1930s, Crick & Co. had become a failing enterprise. In 1939, Walter Crick and the Nobel laureate Frederick Soddy co-authored a small book entitled *Abolish Private Money – or Drown in Debt*. At the start of the Second World War, Walter, blamed by his family for the failure of the shoe firm, emigrated to the USA, where he spent the rest of his working life as a sales agent for a rival shoe company before retiring to a California orange farm.

J(ames) D. Dell was a solicitor who became the full-time office manager of The Britons in the spring of 1923 and its honorary secretary in 1924. Following the death of J. H. Clarke in 1931, he remained as secretary but took over much of the administration of the society. After twenty-five years in the post, Dell retired in 1949 (a year after the death of Beamish) and went to live in South Africa. His position was taken (briefly) by A. F. X. Baron and then by Anthony Gittens.

Harry MacLeod Fraser co-founded and then led the Silver Badge Party. Before that he had served in India and risen to the rank of lieutenant commander. He was an early member of The Britons. A fervent campaigner on anti-Jewish issues, he worked closely with Beamish, and the two men co-compiled *The Jews' Who's Who* and became co-defendants in the Mond libel trial. Shortly after the trial Fraser spent a couple of years living in India, from where he produced a series of anti-Jewish pamphlets. After returning to Britain he continued this work, which included an unpublished manuscript that he described as 'a kind of concordance to The Protocols'. He was killed in a motoring accident on 15 July 1924 and was buried in Rosemarkie parish churchyard, Scotland.

L(eslie) Fry was born Louise A. Chandor in Paris, France, on 16 February 1882. Both her parents were American. In St Petersburg in 1906 she married Feodor Ivanovich Shishmarev, a Russian aristocrat who was an officer in the Russian Imperial Army. He was murdered by Bolsheviks during the Russian Revolution, having previously sent his wife out of the country with their two sons and his family's fortune. For the rest of her life his widow was committed to anti-communist and anti-Jewish activity, networking tirelessly, often using her wealth to fund organisations and publications. Using her married name, Paquita Louise Shishmareff, she lived first in Britain, then in Canada, then moved to New York and finally settled in California. She claimed to have met Henry Ford in or around 1920 and to have presented him with a copy of *The Protocols of the Learned Elders of Zion*. In 1931, under her pen-name L. Fry, she published her highly influential book *Waters Flowing Eastward*, in which she attempted to prove that *The Protocols* were part of a vast and genuine Jewish plot to destroy Christian civilisation. In Britain she became involved with The Britons, and in 1935 she revived the Militant Christian Patriots (MCP) and launched their first magazine, *Free Press*. After returning to America in 1936, Fry set up the American MCP in Glendale, California. The following year, the inveterate far-right organiser George Deatherage (klansman, founder and leader of the Knights of the White Camellia) attempted to unite Hitlerian Americans by creating a single umbrella party, the American National Confederation. Among those who joined him were Fry (for the MCP), William Pelley (founder and leader of the Silver Shirts) and Donald Shea (director of the National Gentile League). On 21 July 1942, twenty-eight leading figures of the American extreme right were indicted as German agents in what was to be called the Mass Sedition Trial. Six months later, in early 1943, Fry was one of five further far-right activists to be added to this group of indictees. The charges against her, however, were dropped before the case went to court.

248 Appendix 4: Key figures in The Britons

Reverend A. W. Gough was a prebendary of St Paul's Cathedral. An active member of The Britons, he was also the London and Home Counties chairman of the British Workers' League. Despite having its roots in the left wing of the Labour Party, this 'patriotic labour' group was, from its founding in 1916, both anti-socialist and pro-empire. Gough was also an active member of the National Citizens' Union. In 1924 the Boswell Printing and Publishing Company issued his 94-page book *The Fight for Man*.

Mr H. E. Granger was at the 11 May 1923 Britons meeting which Beamish attended.

Miss Greig was the honorary secretary of The Britons in the early 1920s. A letter that Beamish wrote to her from P.O. Sinoia, Rhodesia, on 30 March 1922 reads:

> Dear Miss Greig, As I gather that you have not been able to collect anything from Cox, & as I shall get thrown out of my Clubs if my Subs are not paid, I am enclosing P.O.S for £4/4/0, out of which I will be grateful if you will pay the Royal Societies Club & Sports Clubs £2/20/ each. I have written as per copy enclosed to Justice Salter & I hope he will like it. From the M.P. account S must have conducted his case none too well, but of course it is difficult to criticise when one was not present. I was glad to see Ian Colvin's letter. It certainly was a vindictive sentence. I am writing to tell Henry Ford what I think of him too, for though I live in the wilds I always keep a running fire. I have just written to that arch Bolshevik Smuts, suggesting that now he has mowed down a few hundred 'Reds', perhaps he will turn his attention to the Jews who organised our recent S.A. revolution. Mail just off. Hope to hear from you soon. Best love, & let me know about Cox. Your sincere friend, H. H. Beamish

Notes: During 1920, Henry Ford had serialised The Protocols *in his* Dearborn Independent *newspaper; Sir Arthur Clavell Salter was made a high court judge in 1917; Ian Duncan Colvin was the leader writer for the* Morning Post *('M.P.' above); Cox may well be Ernest Sevier Cox, the American white supremacist who, in 1922, co-founded the Anglo-Saxon Clubs of America and, in 1923, published his seminal racist book* White America; *Smuts is Jan Christiaan Smuts, the racial segregationalist and pro-Zionist (hence Bolshevik) who, in September 1919, was elected prime minister of South Africa ('S.A.'); 'S' might be Harold Sherwood Spencer, Jew-hater and homophobe, whose book* Democracy and Shylocracy *was published by The Britons in 1922. If so, the case referred to may well have been the one brought against him by Mond's brother.*

Captain A. E. N. Howard was another member of The Britons who went on to join Arnold Leese's Imperial Fascist League. While he was an active member of The Britons he spent time out in China, where he promoted the society and its publications.

William Morgan Jellett (19 May 1857–27 October 1936) was the Unionist MP for Dublin University (1919–22). In October 1921 he sent a letter to The Britons in which he enclosed his membership fee but expressed his regret at being unable to attend their 3 October meeting at Caxton Hall.

Arthur Kitson (1861–1937) was an inventor and entrepreneur, writer and journalist, and an increasingly anti-Jewish currency reformer. He was managing director of the Kitson Lighting Company of Stamford, Lincolnshire. In 1901 he had invented the vaporised oil burner, in which fuel, vaporised at high pressure, heated a gas mantle, giving six times the luminosity of traditional lights. Despite this and many other patents, Kitson was declared bankrupt in 1925. He was the member of The Britons through whom Arnold Leese was introduced to *The Protocols*. When Leese, having then embraced Jew-hatred, co-founded (and later led) the Imperial Fascist League, Kitson (along with Beamish) became an early member. His books included *A Scientific Solution of the Money Problem* (1895), *The Money Problem* (1903), *Industrial Depression* (1905), *The Circumnavigator: Captain Cook* (1907), *An Open Letter to the Right Hon. David Lloyd George* (1911), *Trade Fallacies* (1917), *A Fraudulent Standard* (1917), *Money Problems* (1920), *Unemployment: The Cause and the Remedy* (1921), *A Letter to HRH the Prince of Wales* (1931) and *The Bankers' Conspiracy* (1933).

Mrs Laing, of 53 Camden House Court, hosted the 5 July 1921 meeting of The Britons at which Captain T. R. Cooper spoke on 'France, England and the Jews'.

Lieutenant Colonel A(rthur) H(enry) Lane had served in Egypt under Kitchener and then in South Africa under Milner. His book *The Hidden Hand: A Plain Statement for the Man in the Street* was published in 1902. As well as being active in The Britons, Lane was a member of the Imperial Fascist League and an early member of the Unity Band. In 1927 he became the chairman of the National Citizens' Union. His influential anti-immigration book *The Alien Menace: A Statement of the Case* was published by the Boswell Printing and Publishing Company in 1928. During 1928–9 he founded the Militant Christian Patriots. He also wrote *A Life of Service* (1929) and *War Debts* (1934).

T. Lane was a speaker at Britons meetings during the early 1920s and is singled out in the July 1923 issue of the *Hidden Hand* with reference to a series of open-air meetings following the Hammersmith Town Hall event (at which he had been a platform speaker alongside Beamish): 'Large audiences collected every Wednesday evening to hear our speakers and of these Mr. Lane is a prime favourite.'

Victor Emile Marsden (1866–28 October 1920) was a journalist and translator born in Salford. Little is known about the first fifty years of his life. According to the journalist, broadcaster and conspiracist Stanley Monteith (in his book *Brotherhood of Darkness*), Marsden was 'a man with heavy ties to the English occult or illuminist Movement'. In 1914, Marsden's translation of the play *The King of the*

Jews, a Sacred Drama, from the Russian of 'K.P.' was published in New York by Funk & Wagnalls ('K.P.' was the Grand Duke Constantine). Marsden also published a translation of Vsevolod Vladimirov's *The Revolution in Finland under Prince John Obolensky*. During the First World War he was the Russian correspondent of the *Morning Post*. He was married to a Russian woman and was still in the country when the Russian Revolution began. Critical reports that he sent back to England led to his arrest on 31 August 1918. Thrown into the notorious Peter-Paul Prison, Marsden expected to be executed. He was eventually released, but the brutality of the conditions and his treatment during his incarceration severely damaged his health. When he returned to Britain, with an understandable hatred of Bolshevism (for which he less understandably blamed the Jews), though still ill, he painstakingly translated *The Protocols of Zion* into English. Nursed back to apparent health by his wife and friends, he was deemed well enough to return to work, and the *Morning Post* rehired him as their correspondent to accompany the Prince of Wales on his tour of the empire. On his return Marsden fell ill, and he died a few days later. A 48-page account of his trip, with the odd title of *Crossing the Line with His Royal Highness the Prince of Wales: in H.M.S. Renown, Friday–Saturday, 16–17d (Victor E. Marsden)*, was published posthumously in 1920 by Angus & Robertson. His pamphlet *The Jews in Russia, with the Names of the 477 Jews of the 'Russian' Soviet* was published by the Britons in 1921, and his translation of *The Protocols* was first published by them in 1923.

E. J. Montgomery was appointed the South African representative of The Britons and translated their publications into Afrikaans.

Lady Moore (1874–1941) was the Irish-born wife of Major General Sir John Moore and the great granddaughter of the pioneer John Batman, who founded the city of Melbourne in Australia. She and her husband spent many years in India, where he served with the Army Veterinary Service. He received his knighthood in 1919. The couple returned to England in 1921 and took up residence in Hampstead; Sir John retired in 1923. Shortly after their return from India, Lady Moore spoke on the subject of alien influence in Ireland at the meeting of The Britons held at Caxton Hall on 3 October 1921. She later presided over and spoke at a series of the society's meetings. In a talk entitled 'Need of Activity', she urged members to 'attend the Bolshevic Sunday Schools, which are all conducted by Jews, and observe how the poison is being spread'.

George P(ercival) Mudge (1870–17 September 1939) was an important early member of the Eugenics Education Society, a co-founder of the Order of the Red Rose, a founder member of The Britons and a co-founder of the Loyalty League. He was professor of zoology at the University of London, and his *A Textbook of Zoology* (1901) remains a classic text. He also contributed to the *Encyclopaedia Britannica*. As a geneticist, he was a follower of Gregor Mendel, and in 1909 he co-founded the *Mendel Journal*.

W. A. Peters was an early member of The Britons. In December 1923, he, Clarke and Cooper together set up the Britons Publishing Company.

H. M. Pimm proposed a vote of thanks at the meeting of The Britons held at Caxton Hall on 3 October 1921.

John Pollock (26 December 1878–22 July 1963) was a historian, journalist and translator whose full title was Sir Frederick John Pollock, 4th Baronet. He served in Poland and Russia from 1915 until 1919 as chief commissioner of the Great Britain to Poland and Galatia Fund. On Monday 1 November 1920, addressing a monthly meeting of The Britons, he told his audience that, based on his experiences in Russia, the only key that fitted to explain events there was *The Protocols*.

Capel (George Pett) Pownall (1869–8 February 1933) was born in Pimlico. In 1908 he was a British archery competitor in the summer Olympics in London. His pamphlet opposing the use of paper money, *Give Back Our Gold* (1920), was published by the *Malvern News* and sold through The Britons. He was another member of The Britons who later joined the Imperial Fascist League.

Brigadier General Cyril Prescott-Decie (4 August 1865–1953) was a career soldier who was a cadet at the Royal Military Academy, Sandhurst (1883–5) before joining the Royal Artillery in which he served as a lieutenant (1885–93), a captain (1893–1900) and then a major. He fought in the Anglo-Boer War (1890–1900) and was an artillery commandant during the Great War, initially in Peshawar (1915) and then in France, where he was severely wounded in 1917; he was awarded the DSO. Throughout the Irish Civil War (1919–22) Prescott-Decie served as divisional commissioner in the Royal Irish Constabulary in Munster, during which time he gained a reputation as an advocate of a policy of pre-emptive shooting to kill and of reprisal killings, although he stopped short of supporting the use of secret murder squads. A member of National Fascisti, he was co-founder and president of the short-lived Loyalty League and an active member of The Britons, both of which gave him the chance to voice his Jew-hatred. In the general election of November 1922, Prescott Decie stood in Putney, on behalf of the Loyalty League, as an Independent Conservative candidate. In response to an appeal made on his behalf by the then vice-president of The Britons, J. H. Clarke, many members of the society gave money towards his election expenses. Though unsuccessful, he achieved a creditable 27 per cent of the vote.

Bessie Pullen-Burry (1858–September 1937), an early and active member of The Britons, was an author and much-travelled explorer who was also a member of several geographical societies. Her books included *Jamaica as it is: 1903*, *Blotted Out*, *Nobly Won: A Novel*, *Eleanor Lewknor*, *Ethiopia in Exile: Jamaica Revisited*, *In a German Colony; or, Four Weeks in New Britain* and *From Halifax to Vancouver*.

Major Rich worked in the office of The Britons during the 1920s. He seems to have been responsible for contacts with other organisations and for arrangements concerning many of the society's early publications. Some of the packages of sample publications sent by other organisations to the Oxford Street or Great Ormond Street offices of The Britons during the 1920s were addressed to him. In 1934, Arnold Leese contacted J. D. Dell concerning the anonymous pamphlet *Jew's Ritual Slaughter*, which The Britons had first published in 1923. Unable to help Leese, Dell wrote to Rich on 19 May 1934. The letter read:

> Leese, of the Imperial Fascist League, writes me asking for details re Burton's unpublished MS. referred to on p. 9 of enclosed pamphlet, and how the Jews got his papers. I don't know who drew up the pamphlet, nor can I tell Leese what he wants to know. Can you throw light on the matter? Leese advises withdrawal of the pamphlet because of the error in stating that Burton was in Damascus in 1840, when he was only 19. He would seem to be right here. Personally, I avoid this question of ritual murder altogether, for various reasons, and have not got the pamphlet down on our list. I should be obliged if you could help Leese. He says he is getting an article out on the Damascus case in the June 'Fascist'.

P(hilip) J(ames) Ridout (1877–1960) was born in Castle Cary, Somerset, and lived in Warwickshire, where he was employed as a cabinet maker. He was an active member of Arnold Leese's Imperial Fascist League and later of Archibald Maule Ramsay's Nordic League and is credited with inventing the Jew-haters' rallying cry of 'Perish Judah!' (based on his initials), which was usually accompanied by a Nazi-style salute. Returning to the fray after the war, Ridout founded his own British Empire Party (BEP) in the summer of 1951. BEP progress was reported regularly in the pages of The Britons journal *Free Britain* and was boosted when, following the collapse of the British Workers' Movement, Arnold Leese urged his followers to join the party. In the 1951 general election the BEP put up just one candidate, Trefor David, in the Welsh constituency of Ogmore. A colourful local character, David initially gained considerable support. However, after a local paper revealed Ridout's fascist past, most of that support evaporated.

A. Toulmin Smith was the honorary secretary of The Britons from its founding in 1919 until his sudden death around 1924, when his post was taken by J. D. Dell.

Harold Sherwood Spencer was born in Wisconsin in 1890 of British parents. In 1913 he published a collection of poems, *The Flood of Youth*. He arrived in Liverpool on 18 January 1915 aboard the *Franconia*, recorded in the ship's passenger list as an engineer of 5 St James Place, in West London. Having volunteered for the British Army, he was commissioned in 1915 into the Royal Irish Fuseliers, where he rose to the rank of captain and served on three fronts. He claimed to have worked for the

British Secret Service. Obsessed with the idea that Germans were sexually corrupting British civilians, Spencer was invalided out in September 1917, having been judged mentally unstable. Soon after this, he befriended Beamish and joined the Vigilante Society, contributing anti-German, Jew-hating and homophobic articles to its magazine. In 1918 he self-published an anti-Jewish book, *Democracy or Shylocracy?* A year later he was a founding member of The Britons, who, in 1922, republished his book with the added subtitle *Shall the Jew Win?* During the early 1920s, Spencer was first assistant editor and then editor of the anti-Jewish journal *Plain English*. Twice married, frequently caught up in legal action, once jailed, he eventually returned alone to America in 1927.

Mr Stuart 'of Putney' was reported in the August 1923 issue of the *Hidden Hand* as having spoken on Jewish control of the musical world at a meeting of The Britons held on 2 July 1923.

Colonel Thomas Robert Swinburne hosted (with his wife) a meeting of The Britons at their London home, 23 Eaton Place, on 6 June 1921, at which George P. Mudge spoke on 'Pride of Race'. Swinburne was lord of the manor of Pontop, and the couple's main home was Pontop Hall in Durham. Following a long military career, Swinburne reached the rank of major in the Royal Marine Artillery and retired just before the start of the First World War, when he was made an honorary lieutenant colonel. Also a semi-professional artist, he had been both author and illustrator of *A Holiday in the Happy Valley, Kashmir*, published in 1905 by Smith, Elder & Co. In 1919 he co-founded and became treasurer of the Plumage Bill Group, which campaigned to ban the import of feathers for millinery purposes. In 1914 his wife became treasurer of the French Wounded S.O.S. Society. The couple's only son, Thomas, was killed in action in France on 1 April 1918.

Lord Sydenham of Combe (4 July 1848–7 February 1933) was an army officer and colonial administrator. As George Sydenham Clarke he joined the Royal Engineers in 1868 and served both in the 1882 Egyptian Expedition and as assistant political officer during the subsequent campaign in Sudan. From 1885 to 1892 he was secretary to the Colonial Defence Committee, for which he was knighted in 1893. In 1888 he was also secretary to the Royal Commission on Navy and Army Administration. During the late 1890s he was superintendent of the Royal Carriage Department at Woolwich. Clarke retired from the army in 1901, having been appointed governor of Victoria in Australia. After leaving this post in 1903, he went on to serve in India as governor of Bombay (1907–13), for which service he was made Baron Sydenham of Combe in Devon. A former Liberal, in his later years he became increasingly reactionary. Following the Great War, Sydenham became not only a prominent diehard in the Conservative Party but also a leading member of The Britons and a prominent promoter of *The Protocols*. In *The Enigmatic Edwardian*, his biography of Reginald, 2nd Viscount Esher, James Lees-Milne paints a singularly unpleasant picture of Sydenham, describing him as 'an insensitive, clumsy, uncouth and infinitely boring man'. Phyllis Angelina Reynolds, Lady Sydenham of Combe, his second wife, was an early member of the British Fascisti.

Lord Templeton attended the meeting of The Britons held on Saturday 5 March 1921 in the drawing room of 4 Elm Park Gardens, 'by the kind invitation of Miss Wyatt and Miss Hunt'. The report in the April issue of the *Hidden Hand* describes him as 'our former patron'.

Mr Varnals seconded a vote of thanks at the meeting of The Britons held at Caxton Hall on 3 October 1921.

Arnold White (1 February 1848–5 February 1925) was an author, journalist and unsuccessful election candidate. See Chapter 2.

H. F. Wyatt was a keynote speaker at the meeting of The Britons held at Caxton Hall on 3 October 1921, and he spoke again at a meeting in Kensington Town Hall on 14 December 1921.

Leading post-war members

A(nthony) F(rancis) X(avier) Baron (4 October 1913–1974) was described as 'a stocky man with the features of a professional boxer'. He could be intimidating. A supporter of Arnold Leese, he lived in Framlingham in Suffolk. In 1948, he and a group of other Leese supporters attempted to found the National Workers' Party, but the whole thing fell apart, mainly because of internal struggles between Baron and another leading member, Anthony Gittens. In 1949, J. D. Dell, the honorary secretary of The Britons and the Britons Publishing Society, retired, and his place was taken by Baron, who appears to have upset almost everyone else in the organisation. More than two years of internal strife followed for The Britons. Part-way through, Baron gave up his secretarial post, only to take the nominal presidency. He bowed out of The Britons in January 1951, but it took legal action against him before Gittens et al. were finally able to resume normal business at 40 Great Ormond Street in late April. A new edition of *Free Britain* appeared on 22 April 1951, the first in three months. It didn't paint an impressive picture of Baron (see Chapter 3). Baron then joined forces with Peter Huxley-Blythe, who had been part of Oswald Mosley's post-war regrouping. Huxley-Blythe had subsequently worked for the enigmatic Francis Parker Yockey, had briefly mentored Colin Jordan, and had then helped Roger Pearson to found the Northern League. Together, Baron and Huxley-Blythe established NATINFORM (the Nationalist Information Bureau), which ran from around 1954 until 1958. However, the two men quarrelled, Huxley-Blythe accusing Baron of being a Nazi. Baron and his close ally Karl Smets, who headed the German branch of NATINFORM, were both expelled – only to set up their own NATINFORM, which rapidly eclipsed its predecessor.

Baron also worked closely during the mid-1950s with Oswald Pirow, the South African far-right leader and wartime Nazi who had recently (1953) fallen out with Oswald Mosley.

Anthony James Wykeham Chavasse (25 July 1925–June 2004) was an anti-Jewish and pro-white racist whose activities demonstrate the minutely factionalised nature of the far right in the UK. During the late 1950s he was an enthusiastic supporter of the British Israelite Church and an active member of A. K. Chesterton's League of Empire Loyalists (LEL). Towards the end of that decade he joined the Patriotic Party (PP), a breakaway group from the LEL, which was chaired by Major General Richard Hilton, with Major A. R. Braybrooke as its vice-chairman. The PP's treasurer was Oliver Gilbert, a veteran fascist and Jew-hater whose pre-Second World War activities had included stints as a prominent member of Arnold Leese's Imperial Fascist League and Archibald Maule Ramsay's Nordic League. The PP broke with LEL because its members wanted to contest elections rather than agitate. However, Hilton and Braybrooke soon had an acrimonious falling out, and Hilton formed his own separate group, True Tories (TT). In 1967, after A. K. Chesterton founded the National Front, Chavasse joined it along with almost all the other members of the LEL, the PP and the TT. Meanwhile, in 1965, he had begun working with another long-standing anti-Jewish campaigner, a Russian émigré called George Knupffer. Since 1957, Knupffer had been editing and publishing his own right-wing monthly journal, *The Plain-Speaker*, originally subtitled 'A Review of Facts, Events and the Required Action'. By the mid-1960s, *The Plain-Speaker* had become the monthly 'Organ of the Institute for Political and Economic Studies and the World Integralist Association'. The latter (sometimes known as the Integralist World Association or just the Integralist Association) was founded by Knupffer, with Braybrooke as its president and Chavasse as its 'British Representative'. By January 1968 Chavasse had become Knupffer's assistant editor on the journal, a post he held well into the early 1970s. By the summer of 1982 Chavasse was a leading member of the Voter's Association for a Free Society (commonly called simply Free Society), on behalf of which he regularly placed advertisements in far-right journals such as *Candour* (founded by A. K. Chesterton). During the mid-1990s, he and Free Society's co-founder, Mary Staunton (also a veteran racist and a British Israelite), were two of the three people behind the financing of the London-based New Age journal *Rainbow Ark*. Free Society had by then become Free Society to Save the Planet. During the early 1990s Chavasse immersed himself in catastrophism and the revision of ancient history, becoming a prominent member of the Ancient History Studies Group of the Society for Interdisciplinary Studies. He spent his last ten years working on an unpublished book on his theory of evolution. Throughout this period he was also a director and administrator of the Good Earth Publishing Company.

Mrs J. Collis-Bird was secretarial assistant to Anthony Gittens and worked in the office of The Britons during the early 1950s. By the early 1960s, she and Gittens were co-proprietors of the Clair Press, The Britons' printing enterprise, which, as well as being the imprint of several Britons titles, offered a commercial letterpress, colour and photolitho service.

Hilary James Coughtrie Cotter (b. 20 March 1918) was a former naval man who became a prominent contributor to the far-right press during the 1950s and began contributing to The Britons journal *Free Britain* in 1953. He had previously been involved with NATINFORM, until falling out with its co-founder, Anthony Baron, after they had published (in 1951) his book, *World Dictatorship by 1955? Why Forrestal Threw Himself out of the Window*, which The Britons were distributing.

Trefor David was a Welsh engineer and blacksmith who was elected a Plaid Cymru councillor in Bridgend in 1931 and then a Glamorgan county councillor. His belligerence saw him nicknamed 'the stormy petrel', and his confrontational style resulted in frequent court appearances. Found guilty of slander in one case, the heavy damages left him bankrupt. A subsequent separate case at Swansea Assizes saw him acquitted on a charge of publishing scandalous and defamatory libel. David took up numerous issues and was seldom out of the local limelight for long. He was the candidate for The Britons 1951 spin-off British Empire Party in the 1951 general election and might even have won with a popular vote if the local press hadn't exposed the fascist history of his party leader, P. J. Ridout.

Admiral Sir Barry Domvile (1878–1971), a career naval officer whose father was also an admiral, joined the Royal Navy in 1892. He was appointed assistant secretary to the Committee of Imperial Defence in 1912 and was commander of four different battleships (destroyers and cruisers) during the First World War. After the war he became director of plans (1920), chief of staff to the commander-in-chief, Mediterranean (1922), commanding officer of the battleship HMS *Royal Sovereign* (1925), director of the Department of Naval Intelligence (1927–30), commander of the Third Cruiser Squadron (1931–2) and president of the Royal Naval College, Greenwich (1932–4). Throughout the 1930s he contributed anti-Jewish pieces to *The Patriot*, some of which were reprinted in leaflets and pamphlets issued by the Boswell Publishing Company. Impressed by Nazism during a visit to Germany in 1935, Domvile attended the September 1936 Nuremberg Rally as a guest of the German ambassador Joachim von Ribbentrop and became a council member of the Anglo-German Fellowship. He helped found The Link and became one of the most prominent members of this pro-Nazi organisation. In the 1939 Hythe by-election, he supported St John Philby, the anti-Jewish candidate for the British People's Party. Domvile was arrested and interned (7 July 1940–29 July 1943), after which he resumed his anti-Jewish activity, supporting A. K. Chesterton's League of Empire Loyalists and becoming a regular contributor to *Free Britain* during the early 1950s. In the late 1960s he sat on the national council of the newly formed National Front. A prolific writer and diarist, Domvile published two autobiographical books, *By and Large* (1936) and *From Admiral to Cabin Boy* (1947; published by the

Boswell Publishing Co.), and a history British naval and merchant seamen, *Look to Your Moat* (1932). He also produced several specifically anti-Jewish works, including *The Great Taboo: Freemasonry, Straight from the Jew's Mouth* and *Truth about Anti-Semitism*. In the mid-1950s The Britons published his slim pamphlet *Appeal from Sir Barry Domvile*.

Anthony William Gittens (1904–17 November 1973), a Catholic, was educated at the Cardinal Vaughan School in Kensington. In the early 1920s, having read *The Cause of World Unrest* series that appeared in the *Morning Post*, he undertook research work for Nesta Webster. Gittens joined The Britons in 1924 and served as its secretary from 1950 until his death almost a quarter of a century later. He was also involved with many other far-right groups. During the 1930s, as a prominent member of the Imperial Fascist League, he founded their Kentish Town branch. Along with Arnold Leese and five others, Gittens was jailed for a year in 1947 for aiding two escaped Dutch soldiers who had been imprisoned after being captured while serving in the German Army. After The Britons' long-term secretary, J. D. Dell, retired in 1949 and his post was taken by Anthony F. X. Baron, Gittens joined the latter's recently formed National Workers' Party (NWP). Things quickly went very badly wrong between the two Anthonys, which killed the NWP stone dead and very nearly did the same for The Britons (see Chapter 3 for Gittens's emotional version of what happened within The Britons). On the death of Arnold Leese, Gittens took over the publication of *Gothic Ripples*. The late 1960s and early 1970s saw the aging Gittens join the National Front (NF) and work closely with its founder, A. K. Chesterton, who was out of Britain most of the time and therefore needed someone to watch what went on with his organisation and report back to him. He needed a spy. Gittens was that man.

Edwin B. Horton (31 January 1911–March 1982) was a speaker (alongside Anthony Gittens and P. J. Ridout) at the 24 September 1950 nationalist rally in Trafalgar Square. In 1951 he was an active member of Ridout's British Empire Party (BEP) and contributed to its journal, *Bridgehead*. Alongside The Britons' Great Ormond Street address, Horton's home at 103 Lower Oldfield Park, Bath, was a BEP contact address.

Colin Jordan (19 June 1923–9 April 2009) began contributing to *Free Britain* in 1951. That December, he formally merged his journal *Defence* (full title: *Defence Against Alien Control*) with *Free Britain*. See Chapter 7 for far fuller details on Jordan.

Arnold Leese (1878–18 January 1956), though he was never actually a member of The Britons, worked very closely with them, especially in the post-war years. He regularly subsidised their work, gave them office space in premises he owned, and became a regular contributor to *Free Britain* during the early 1950s. See Chapter 6 for much more on Leese.

Peter Marriot was chairman of The Britons for eight months from mid-1952 until he resigned in March 1953, intending to pursue reforms within the Conservative Party.

H(erbert Victor) T. Mills (26 April 1896–1982), who was known to his associates as Bertie, was the post-war honorary treasurer of The Britons and became a regular contributor to *Free Britain* during the early 1950s. His extensive involvement in far-right activities is outlined in Chapter 4.

Archibald Maule Ramsay (4 May 1894–11 March 1955), known to his friends as Jock, was a Scottish aristocrat who was schooled at Eton and Sandhurst. He joined the Coldstream Guards in 1913 and served in France for the first two years of the Great War before being invalided out with a severe head injury. During the late 1920s he became active in the Conservative Party and in 1931 was elected MP for Peebles and Southern Midlothian. The nearest he came to high office was to serve as a government member of the Potato Marketing Board. It was probably his political extremism that prevented him going any further. A fervent pro-Franco nationalist during the Spanish Civil War, Ramsay formed the United Christian Front to protect Christianity from Russian communism. From 1938 onwards he became obsessively anti-Jewish: he founded the Right Club and was involved in a number of other far-right and anti-Jewish groups. Ramsay supported The Britons financially as well as contributing to *Free Britain*, and the society published his book *The Nameless War* in 1952.

Timothy J. W. Tindal-Robertson (b. 1940) assisted Anthony Gittens in running The Britons during the 1960s and the early 1970s. A convert to Catholicism, he graduated from Trinity College in Dublin and entered the Catholic Church in 1964. Following the death of Gittens in 1973, he took over the running of The Britons. In 1976 he and his wife, Andrea, founded a Catholic imprint, the Augustine Publishing Company, which they ran jointly until 1995, publishing and supplying books on orthodox Catholicism. Tindal-Robertson writes and lectures on Fatima and is the author of several books on this theme. He is also active in the New Jersey-based World Apostolate of Fatima (also known as the Blue Army).

Major B. Wilmot-Allistone, as chairman of The Britons in the mid-1950s, presided over the society's annual dinner at the New Horticultural Hall, London, on 23 April 1955. He wrote popular war stories, claimed to have photographed the ghost of a kitten, and was active in the British Road Federation. He also led the Mosley-linked right-wing Ex-Service Party, which put up candidates in constituencies in East Lewisham and Central Wandsworth during the 1945 general election but gained very few votes.

APPENDIX 5
DRAFT CONSTITUTION OF THE BRITONS

I own an original draft copy of the constitution of The Britons, which I assume was the work of Henry Hamilton Beamish himself. The manuscript, dating from 1919, consists of a series of sheets stuck together with glue and tape to make one long sheet, with parts of the text on both sides. The whole thing is an untidy mix of typed text, printed text and handwritten alterations, amendments, substitutions and additions in black ink.

The first sheet is typed and headed 'Constitution of The Britons', above which are two handwritten lines. The first reads 'The Companies Act 1908–1917', the second 'Company-not-for-profit-and-limited-by-guarantee'. Below the heading is handwritten 'founded by H. H. Beamish. 1919'. Written in blue pencil to the left of this is '3 Copies'. The typed text follows (italics below indicate handwritten text).

***

NAME. The name of the Society shall be 'THE BRITONS'.

MOTTO. The motto of 'THE BRITONS' shall be 'LOVE YOUR COUNTRY'.

The registered office will be in England.

OBJECTS. *The objects for which* The Britons *is established are*

> To insist that in future Britain shall be governed by our own native-born people *only.*

> That only citizens who are born of British-born parents shall be permitted to vote or sit in Parliament.

> That all Aliens be removed from the Privy Council.

> That the present inadequate Naturalisation Laws be drastically amended.

That the Alien Immigration Laws be made more stringent, thus preventing our Country being swamped with undesirable aliens and cheap foreign labour.

That our workers and industries require to be safeguarded against dumping and foreign goods produced by underpaid foreign labour.

That all positions, civil, naval, and military, be filled by Britons i.e. citizens of British born parents.

That Britons be assisted to acquire agricultural freehold land that land settlement and land banks be encouraged to prevent urban congestion and unhealthy living conditions.

That all Aliens who have changed their names during the 1914–18 War, be compelled to revert to their original names.

That all Merchants and Shopkeepers be compelled to display the proprietor's name in a prominent position, and that all companies and firms publish the names of their directors and partners on all communications.

That all Britons be assisted to fight the Alien menace.

That the ACT OF SETTLEMENT of 1700 be re-enacted.

(End of first sheet. Sheet 2 is a page of printed text that was originally part of the memorandum of association of the Remembrance League. As we know from Chapter 1, Beamish was directly involved with similar First World War ex-servicemen's organisations, including the Silver Badge Party, the National Association of Discharged Sailors and Soldiers, and the National Federation of Discharged and Demobilised Soldiers and Sailors, so it is no surprise to find him using a constitutional document from such a body as a partial template for the one he was founding in 1919. This section, in which (throughout, with a couple of accidental omissions) the word 'League' is deleted and replaced with the word 'Britons', begins with the following printed text.)

(H) Subject to the provisions of section 19 of the Companies (Consolidation) Act 1908, to purchase, take on lease or in exchange, hire or otherwise acquire any real or personal property and any rights or privileges which The Britons may think necessary or convenient for the purposes of its business, and in particular any lands, buildings, or works, and to construct, maintain and alter any buildings or works necessary or convenient for The Britons business.

(I) To sell, let, mortgage, dispose of or turn to account, all or any of the property, rights or privileges of The Britons.

(J) To undertake and execute any trusts which may lawfully be undertaken by The Britons and may be conducive to its objects.

(K) To borrow or raise money for the purposes of The Britons on such terms and such security as may be thought fit.

(L) To invest the moneys of The Britons not immediately required for its purposes in or upon such investments, securities, or property as may be thought fit.

(M) To establish and support or aid in the establishment and support of any charitable or benevolent associations or institutions, and to subscribe or guarantee money for charitable or benevolent purposes in any way connected with the purposes of The Britons or calculated to further its objects.
(N) To draw, make, accept, indorse, discount, execute and issue promissory notes, bills of exchange and other negotiable or transferable instruments.
(O) To do all such other things as are incidental or The Britons may think conducive to the attainment of the above objects or any of them.

(New sheet)

Provided always that The Britons shall not support with its funds or endeavour to impose on or procure to be observed by its members or others any regulation, restriction or condition which, if an object of the League [sic], would make it a trade union.

Provided also that in case The Britons shall take or hold any property subject to the jurisdictions of the Board of Education or Charity Commissioners for England and Wales, The Britons shall not sell, mortgage, charge, or lease the same without such authority, approval or consent as may be required by law, and as regards any such property the

(New sheet)

Council or Trustees of The Britons shall be chargeable for such property as may come into their hands and shall be answerable and accountable for their own acts, receipts, neglects and defaults, and for the due administration of such property in the same manner and to the same extent as they would as such Council or Trustees have been if no incorporation had been effected, and the incorporation of The Britons shall not diminish or impair any control or authority exercisable by the Chancery Division or the Board of Education or Charity Commissioners over such Council or Trustees, but they shall as regards any such property be subject jointly and separately to such control and authority as if The Britons were not incorporated. In case The Britons shall take or hold any property which may be subject to any trusts, The Britons shall only deal with the same in such manner as allowed by law having regard to such trusts.

4. The income and property of The Britons, whencesoever derived, shall be applied solely towards the promotion of the objects of the League [sic] as set forth in this Memorandum of Association, and no part thereof shall be paid or transferred, directly or indirectly, by way of dividend, bonus, or otherwise howsoever by way of profit to the members of The Britons.

Provided that nothing herein contained shall prevent the payment in good faith of reasonable and proper remuneration to any officer or servant of The Britons, or any member thereof not being a member of the Council of Management, in return for any services actually rendered to The Britons, nor prevent the payment of interest at a rate and not exceeding £6 per cent. per annum on money lent or reasonable and proper rent for premises demised or let by any member of The Britons; but so that no member of the Council of Management of The Britons shall be appointed to any office of The Britons paid by salary or fees, and that no remuneration shall be given to any member of such Council except repayment of out of pocket expenses and interest at the rate aforesaid on money lent or reasonable and proper rent for premises demised or let to The Britons provided that the provision last aforesaid shall not apply to any railway, tramway, gas, electric lighting, water, cable, or telephone company of which a member of the Council of Management may be a member, or any other company in which such member shall not hold more than one hundredth part of the capital, and such member shall not be bound to account for any share of profits he may receive in respect of any such payment.

5. The liability of the members is limited.

6. Every member of The Britons undertakes to contribute to the assets of The Britons, in the event of the same being wound up during the time that he is a member, or within one year afterwards, for payment of the debts and liabilities of The Britons contracted before

(End of sheet. 'P.T.O.' is written below right in blue pencil. Overleaf the printed text begins as follows, all of it crossed out in blue pencil.)

The Companies Acts 1908 to 1917.
COMPANY NOT FOR PROFIT AND LIMITED BY GUARANTEE.
Memorandum of Association
OF
THE REMEMBRANCE LEAGUE
LIMITED.

1. The name of the League is 'The Remembrance League Limited'.
2. The registered office of the League will be situated in England.
3. The objects for which the League is established are –
   (a) To assist discharged sailors and soldiers, and to take all necessary steps to obtain adequate pensions for them, and for their widows, children and other dependents.
   (b) To assist them to obtain agricultural land in the United Kingdom for the purpose of settlement thereon, with a view to cultivating the same, and to supply them with the necessary housing and buildings thereon, and to provide the necessary machinery and stock.
   (c) To assist those who so desire to emigrate to the Colonies, and as far as possible to aid them in obtaining land.
   (d) To promote and assist in the further development of the

(Here the crossed-out script stops abruptly, resuming as follows at the top of the fourth page of the Remembrance League document.)

Appendix 5: The Britons **263**

4 the time at which he ceases to be a mem~~osts, charges and expenses of winding up the same and for ~~the rights of the contributories amongst themselves, such~~ be required not exceeding one shilling.

(This must have been the end of clause 6. The~~, as it applies to The Britons, seems to continue here. It is still t~~document, but, once again, each time the word 'League' oc~~ossed out and 'Britons' handwritten abov~~

7 If upon the winding up of The Britons t~~h the satisfaction of all its debts and liabilities, any property w~~e shall not be paid to or distributed among the members of T~~ and so far as effect can be given to the next provision, shall b~~rred to some other institution or institutions having objects s~~ects of The Britons, and which shall prohibit the distributio~~ncome or property, among its or their members to an extent~~ is imposed on The Britons by virtue of Clause 4 hereof, s~~r institutions to be determined by the members of The Brito~~e time of dissolution, or in default thereof by such Judge of the~~ustice as may have or acquire jurisdiction in the matter, and if i~~t cannot be given to such provision, then to some charitable c~~

Accounts – and – Audit –

8 True accounts shall be kept of the sum~~ved and expended by The Britons and the matters in respect ~~ceipt and expenditure take place, and of property, credits and l~~Britons and, subject to any reasonable restrictions as to the time~~specting the same that may be imposed in accordance with the~~e Britons for the time being, shall be open to the inspection o~~ Once at least in every year the accounts of The Britons shall b~~ the correctness of the balance sheet ascertained by one or mor~~ed Auditor or Auditors.

(End of sheet. The next attached sheet i~~e entire manuscript is typed with handwritten c~~k ink.)

1 A financial obligation of members is ~~ayment of an Entrance Fee of One Shilling and an Annual ~~One Shilling. Voluntary donations are accepted.

2 Membership is confined solely to Brit~~men over eighteen who can prove that their parents and gra~~of British blood. Before being accepted as Members all appli~~the approved enrolment form proving that their parents and g~~e of British blood.

Constitution of The Britons

3. Th[e Society shall be strict]ly non-party and non-sectarian.
4. Me[mbership shall be] effected either by direct application to the Head Office or t[hrough the med]ium of any Branch.
5. Eve[ry candidate for] enrolment shall state the Branch to which he or she wish[es to belong.] Failing this, such Member shall be considered a Member of t[he Head Office B]ranch.
6. A m[ember shall be at li]berty to withdraw his or her membership at any time upon givin[g three cal]endar months' previous notice in writing to that effect.
7. The [Council of Manage]ment may at any time on the request of a Member, transfer s[uch Member from] one *Branch* to another.
8. In th[e event of any M]ember being guilty of conduct calculated to bring discredit [upon THE BRITO]NS, the Executive Committee of his or her Branch may make [representations] to that effect to *the Council of Management* of the Head Offic[e, which] shall afford the Member whose conduct is in question an op[portunity of expl]anation, and if the same shall be unsatisfactory, the name of such [Member shall] be expunged from the Roll of 'THE BRITONS'. A Memb[er who h]as been expunged shall not be entitled to be re-enrolled as a m[ember without th]e express sanction of *the Council of Management* of the Head O[ffice.]

(End[notes: This sh]eet begins with many handwritten corrections. Through[out, 'Executive Co]mmittee' is deleted and 'Council of Management' handwritt[en. Likew]ise, throughout, 'President, Treasurer, Secretary' is altered [to... 'Secreta]ry' deleted and 'Vice-President' handwritten. [Amende]d, the typed text reads as follows.)

[COU]NCIL OF MANAGEMENT

The C[ouncil of Mana]gement of 'THE BRITONS' shall consist of [a Presiden]t, Vice-President, and Treasurer.

[Th]e first Members shall be:-

PRESIDENT:

VICE-PRESIDENT:

SECRETARY:

Each of whom [shall continu]e until his or her death or resignation, or until the happening of [something which] would by the English Law disqualify him or her from acting as [such. And] as vacancies occur in the aforesaid offices the same shall be filled f[rom per]sons appointed by the Council of Management of the Head Offic[e without] qualification as aforesaid.

9. The Coun[cil of Managem]ent of the Head Office shall be at liberty to appoint an[y othe]r officials as they may from time to time think fit, to hold [at the p]leasure of the Council of Management of the Head Offic[e.]

COUNCIL OF MANAGEMENT AND BRANCHES

(The following text is crossed out in ink.)

10 Shall consist the President, Vice-President, and Treasurer for the time being of 'THE BRITONS', each of whom shall act in the same capacity for Executive Committee of Head Office, and such other persons as may be from time to time be [sic] co-opted by the Executive Committee of the Head Office.

(Deleted text ends. Typed text continues.)

The President, Vice-President, and Treasurer, for the time being of 'THE BRITONS' shall be ex-officio Members of the Committee of every Branch established under this Constitution.

11 The Council of Management of the Head Office shall be responsible for the establishment, maintenance, and extension of the organisation of 'THE BRITONS', and shall be a supreme Court of Appeal for the settlement of all questions in dispute arising upon the Constitution, or between Branches, or as to the rights, powers and duties of Committees and their Officials.

12 A Meeting of the Council of Management of the Head Office may be summoned at any time by the President or by any two of its Members.

MEETINGS OF COUNCIL OF MANAGEMENT

Meetings of the Council of Management shall be held as often as is considered necessary by the members, but not less than once a month.

VOTES OF COUNCIL OF MANAGEMENT

Each member shall have one vote, and in the event of an equality of votes, the President shall have the casting vote.

BRANCHES

Local Branches may be established anywhere within the British Isles by Warrant of Constitution, under the authority of the Council of Management of the Head Office, addressed to any ten Members, and every such Branch shall be given a name and registration number. Every Warrant of Constitution must be under the hands and seals of the President, Treasurer, and Secretary for the time being of 'THE BRITONS'.

13 Any Warrant of Constitution may at any time be withdrawn by the Council of Management of the Head Office if *in their opinion it is thought advisable to do so*. In the event of the withdrawal of the Warrant of Constitution from a Branch, the Members thereof shall have the right to select, or may be assigned, another Branch Council of Management of Head Office. Any

surplus funds of a Branch whose Warrant of Constitution shall be so withdrawn shall be taken over by ('Executive Committee of' deleted) Head Office, to be applied (*The following text is deleted.*) either within the late sphere of action of the dissolved Branch, or in the establishment of a new Branch, in substitution for the dissolved Branch. Any surplus funds of a Local Branch whose Warrant of Constitution is so withdrawn shall be taken over by Executive Committee of Head Office, and shall be applied (*End of deletion. Typed text continues.*) in the establishment of a new Local Branch in the same district.

14 Every Warrant of Constitution of a Branch shall appoint its first President, Treasurer, and Secretary, each of whom and their successors, shall hold office in accordance with the Warrant of Constitution.

15 The management and direction of affairs of a Branch shall be vested in a Council to consist of its President, Treasurer, and Secretary, who shall be ex officio Members, and of such other persons as may be indicated in the Warrant of Constitution.

16 The Committee of the Branch shall have the power, subject to confirmation by Council of Management of Head Office, to make Bye-laws for the regulation of its proceedings.

AFFILIATION FEES

For the purposes of probaganga [sic] work and for the support of Head Office, Branches shall forward an affiliation fee of £1 for every complete 100 members (the minimum affiliation fee to be £1) If the number of branch members exceed 500, the fee shall be £10. All affiliation fees are to be paid annually to Head Office.

Responsibility of Head Office

The Head office shall not be responsible for any liabilities incurred by a Branch, unless written sanction has been given by Head Office prior to incurring the expenditure.

FINANCE of Branches

17 Publication of the full name and address of every person donating or bequeathing to 'THE BRITONS' *Five Pounds* sterling is compulsory.

18 A Foundation Fund shall be established for propaganda and administrative purposes. All Entrance Fees, Donations and Bequests to 'THE BRITONS' shall be devoted to this Fund.

19 The Foundation Fund shall be under the sole control and administration of Council of Management of Head Office, but subscriptions may be made to Branches to meet working expenses, subject to the aforesaid conditions as to publication.

20 The Accounts of all Branches shall be submitted to audit annually, *and copies of the audited accounts sent to Head Office.*

21 The Warrant of Constitution of a Local Branch shall provide for the payment of an annual subscription to its funds by its Members, and the funds thus

raised, together with any donations or bequests in favour of the Branch, shall be under the sole control and administration of the Committee of that Branch, subject to such conditions and obligations as may be laid down in the Warrant of Constitution.

22 Nothing in this Constitution shall be deemed to impose any obligation on a Member of 'THE BRITONS' to join a local Branch.

CANDIDATES FOR PUBLIC BODIES

All Candidates seeking election with the support of 'THE BRITONS' to any public body within the sphere of influence of a Branch, shall be selected by the Committee of such Branch, in accordance with the Warrant of Constitution.

APPENDIX 6

PUBLICATIONS BY THE BRITONS

This listing consists only of first editions.

Judaic Publishing Company, 1920–1922

1919–20: A short-lived series of anonymous introductory leaflets under the collective title 'English Order'. These included sheets entitled *The English Birthright*, *The Alien Peril*, *Pride of Race*, *What the Jews Say about Themselves*, *Is a Christian Civilisation Possible in a Nation Influenced by Jews?* and *Can a Jew be an Englishman?*

1920: Anonymous, *The Code of The Jew* (4 pp.)

1920: Anonymous, *Is the Jew to Enslave the World?* (c.4 pp.)

1920: Anonymous, *The Conquering Jew* (c.4 pp.)

1920: H. H. Beamish (with H. M. Fraser) *The Jews' Who's Who: Israelite finance – its Sinister Influence* (255 pp.) [published anonymously] ★

1920: Anonymous [George Shanks, with Major Burdon], *The Jewish Peril: Protocols of the Learned Elders of Zion* (96 pp.)★

1920: Dr J. H. Clarke, *White Labour Versus Red, with a Synopsis of The Protocols* (c.16 pp.)

1921: Anonymous, *A Short History of the Jewish Race* (c.4 pp.)

1921: Victor Marsden, *The Jews in Russia, with the Names of the 477 Jews of the 'Russian' Soviet* (24 pp.)

1921: Dr J. H. Clarke, *The Call of the Sword*

1921: Lord Sydenham, *The Jewish World Problem*

1921: Anonymous, *4 Protocols of Zion* (24 pp.)★ [*not The Protocols* of Nilus]

1922: Bessie Pullen-Burry, *Letters from Palestine, February–April, 1922* (137 pp.)

The Britons Publishing Co.

1922:	Dr J. H. Clarke (ed.), *England under the Heel of the Jew: A Tale of Two Books* [a new edition of a volume originally published by C. F. Roworth, anonymously, in 1918]
1922:	Harold Sherwood Spencer, *Democracy or Shylocracy?* (88 pp.)
1923:	Joseph Banister, *Jews and the White Slave Traffic, or Lords of the Hells of Gomorrah* (12 pp.)
1923:	Victor E. Marsden (trans.), *Protocols of the Learned Elders of Zion* (76 pp.)★
1923:	Anonymous, *Kol Nidre: The Jews' Immoral Prayer* (c.4 pp.)
1923:	Anonymous, *Jew's Ritual Slaughter* (c.12 pp.)
1923:	Otto Von Kursell and Alfred Rosenberg, *The Grave Diggers of Russia: Is the Jew to Enslave the World?* (31 pp.) [published by the German People's Publishing House, issued by The Britons]
c.1923:	Anonymous, *The Jewish Bolshevism* (32 pp.)
1924:	'Apionus' [Harold Sherwood Spencer], *The Bolshevists of Ancient History* (30 pp.)
1927:	F. Roderich-Stoltheim, *The Riddle of the Jew's Success* (288 pp.)
1931:	Joseph Banister, *Our Judeo-Irish Labour Party: How the Interests of the British Working Men are Misrepresented and Betrayed by Politicians who are Neither British nor Working Men*
1933:	A. Homer, *Judaism & Bolshevism: A Challenge & a Reply* (8 pp.)
1936:	Anonymous, *A Plot for the World's Conquest* (16 pp.)★
1937:	Anonymous, *Why Are the Jews Hated?* (16 pp.)★
1937	H. H. Beamish, *South Africa's Kosher Press* (7 pp.) [A response by Beamish to a piece by Arthur G. Barlow in the Johannesburg *Sunday Express* of 29 August 1937]
1938:	Captain Arthur Howard, *The Beast Marks Russia* (28 pp.)
1950	Anonymous, *Russia and the Jews* (4 pp.)★
1951:	Jubelum, *Freemasonry and the Church of England Reconciled*
1951:	Anonymous, *Atomic News! The U.S.S.R. is and Has Been under Jewish Domination* (6 pp.)★
1951:	Rev. Walton Hannah, *Why Shouldn't I Be a Freemason?* (14 pp.) [Augustine Publishing Co.]
1951:	Trefor David, *The Bloody Red Streak* (32 pp.)
1952:	Monsignor George E. Dillon, *Grand Orient Freemasonry Unmasked: As the Secret Power behind Communism* (174 pp.)
1952:	Captain A. H. M. Ramsay, *The Nameless War* (116 pp.)★
1952:	Rev. Denis Fahey, *Humanum Genus: Encyclical Letter of His Holiness Pope Leo VIII on Freemasonry* (24 pp.)
1952:	Rev. Walton Hannah, *Darkness Visible: A Revelation and Interpretation of Freemasonry* (228 pp.) [Augustine Publishing Co.]
1952:	Anonymous, *The Britons*

c.1952: P. J. Keith, *English Masonic Isolation: A Myth Exploded*
1953: L. Fry, *Waters Flowing Eastward: The War against the Kingship of Christ* (267 pp.)★
1953: A. K. Chesterton, *'Truth' Has Been Murdered: Open Letter to Mr Ronald Staples* (4 pp.)
1953: Anthony Gittens, *To Who it May Concern* [one-sided sheet]
1954: Frau Ilse Hess (trans. Meyrick Booth, ed. G. Pile), *Rudolph Hess, Prisoner of Peace* (152 pp.)
1954: Lieutenant Colonel J. Creagh Scott, *Hidden Government* (76 pp.)★
1954: Rev H. Thornton Trapp, *Christian or Freemason* (4 pp.)
1955: Nesta Helen Webster, *Secret Societies and Subversive Movements*
1955: Colin Jordan, *Fraudulent Conversion: The Myth of Moscow's Change of Heart* (143 pp.)★
1955: Thorburn Muirhead, *Searchlight on Britain* (338 pp.)
1955: H. T. Mills, *Money, Politics and the Future*
c.1955: G. Pile, *The White Races*
1956: Wing Commander Leonard Young, *Deadlier than the H-Bomb* (88 pp.)
1957: H. Franklin Knudsen, *I Was Quisling's Secretary* (192 pp.)★
1958: F. J. P. Veale, *Crimes Discreetly Veiled*
n.d.: Anonymous, *The Great Jewish Masque, or The Ass in the Lion's Skin* (36 pp.)

Britons Publishing Company

1960: Mark Ewell [Marie Endean], *Manacles for Mankind* (96 pp.)★
1961: Professor W. George, *Race, Heredity and Civilisation: Human Progress and the Race Problem* (48 pp.)★
1961: Commander J. S. Drummond, *The Twentieth Century Hoax* (187 pp.)
c.1962: Dr Michael F. Connors, *Dealing in Hate: The Development of Anti-German Propaganda* (86 pp.)★
1962: Harold McCrone, *Should We Join the Common Market?* (2 pp.) [the Clair Press/The Britons]
1962: P. Clavell Blount, *Ideas in Action* (192 pp.) [the Clair Press/The Britons]
c.1962: Lieutenant Commander T. W. Bridges, *Is Freemasonry a Religion?* (4 pp.)
1963: Walton Hannah, *Darkness Visible: A Revelation and Interpretation of Freemasonry* (231 pp.)★
1964: Vindex, *Light Invisible: The Freemason's Answer to Darkness Visible* (125 pp.)
1964: Dr R. McNair Wilson, *Promise to Pay* (110 pp.)
1964: Walton Hannah, *Christianity by Degrees: Masonic Religion in the Light of Faith* (216 pp.)
1964: Charles Kingsley, *The Roman and the Teuton* (173 pp.)
1964: P. Clavell Blount, *Compulsory Mass Medication* (151 pp.) [the Clair Press/The Britons]
c.1965: Arnold Leese, *The Legalised Cruelty of Shechita: The Jewish Method of Cattle Slaughter* (12 pp.)

Appendix 6: Publications by The Britons

1965: Arnold Leese, *The Rothschilds' Rise to Rule* (140 pp.) [previously published as *Gentile Folly: The Rothschilds*, 1940, and dedicated to Henry Hamilton Beamish]*

1965: Léon de Poncins, *Le Problème juif face au concile* (40 pp.) [published jointly with Ediciones Acervo, Spain]

1966: Arthur de Gobineau, *The Inequality of Human Races* (218 pp.) [trans. Adrian Collins, from 1854 original]

1966: Richard Wagner (trans. Vivian Bird), *Judaism in Music* (46 pp.)

1967: Bernard Lazare, *Antisemitism: Its History and Causes* (208 pp.) [anonymous translation]*

1967: Anonymous, *Free Speech Defence Committee* [leaflet]

1967: Franklin Knudsen, *I Was Quisling's Secretary*

1967: Vicomte Léon de Poncins (trans. Timothy Tindal-Robertson), *Judaism and the Vatican: An Attempt at Spiritual Subversion* [paperback]*

1968: Major General Richard Hilton, *Imperial Obituary: The Mysterious Death of the British Empire* (160 pp.)*

1968: A. K. Chesterton (ed.), *Not Guilty: An Account of the Historic Race Relations Trial at Lewes Assizes in March 1968* (29 pp.)*

1968 A. J. A. Peck, *Rhodesia Condemns: The Perfidy of Albion* (192 pp.)

1968: Vicomte Léon de Poncins (trans. Timothy Tindal-Robertson), *Freemasonry and the Vatican: An Attempt at Spiritual Subversion* [hardback]

1969: Patrick J. Gearon, *The Wheat and the Cockle: The Liberal Assault within the Post-Conciliar Church* (168 pp.)*

1969: Hugh Ross Williamson, *The Modern Mass: A Reversion to the Reforms of Cranmer* (32 pp.)

1970: Anonymous, *The Diary of an Unborn Child* (4 pp.)

1971: Tito Casini (trans. Scott McCallum), *The Last Mass of Paul VI: An Autumn Night's Dream* (184 pp.)

1971: Nesta Webster [aka Julian Sterne], *World Revolution: The Plot against Civilisation* (374 pp.) [edited and brought up to date by Anthony Gittens]

1973: Henrietta May Carribea Strickland Bower, *Challenge to Godliness with Vigil, Prayer and Penance: The Story of the All Night Vigil Movement*

1975: Count Léon de Poncins (trans. Timothy Tindal-Robertson), *State Secret: A Documentation of the Secret Revolutionary Mainspring Governing Anglo-American Politics* (192 pp.)*

1977: Michael Davies, *The Tridentine Mass* (32 pp.) [Augustine Publishing Co.]

1979: Anthony Michael Fides, *Man's Origins* (34 pp.) [Augustine Publishing Co.]

1983: Abbot O. S. B. Gueranger, *Liturgical Year: Time after Pentecos, Book 5* [The Britons Catholic Library]

1983: Abbot O. S. B. Gueranger, *Liturgical Year: Time after Pentecost, Book 6* [The Britons Catholic Library]

1986: Michel de la Sainte Trinité, *The Third Secret of Fatima* (38 pp.) [Augustine Publishing Co.]

Others

Five anonymous pamphlets, *c.* mid-1950s: *Some Strange Cults, Despotism in Disguise, Disraeli, the Destroyer of Toryism, Some Heresies and their Founders* and *Work and Objects*

Mid-1950s: Sir Barry Domvile, *Appeal from Sir Barry Domvile*

APPENDIX 7
ADDRESSES OF THE BRITONS

Many of the leaflets, pamphlets and other documents issued by The Britons are undated but carry a contact address. These provide some help in working out roughly when they were produced.

From summer 1920: 62 Oxford Street, London W1
From March 1923: 40 Great Ormond Street, London WC1 (demolished in 1965)
From January 1951: 46–48 Princedale Road, London W11
From June 1954: 74 Princedale Road, London W11
From 1959/1960: 111A Westbourne Grove, London W2
From 1964: South View, Chawleigh, Chulmleigh, Devon
From around 1975: Chulmleigh, Devon, EX18 7HL

Also, during the mid-1920s The Britons Printing Co., Ltd, was at 28 Milkwood Road, Herne Hill, London SE. Other imprints used by The Britons were the Judaic Publishing Company, B.P.S., the Clair Press, the Britons Catholic Library and the Augustine Press.

SOME SELECTED FURTHER READING

For those interested in reading more on the history of immigration into Britain during the late nineteenth and early twentieth century, I can recommend Eugene C. Black's *The Social Politics of Anglo-Jewry, 1880–1920*, published by Blackwell in 1988. Despite a few glaring errors, it's a comprehensive and detailed work. For a broader sweep, focusing on the period from 1850 to 1980, there's the revised edition of the well-researched *Racial Violence in Britain in the Nineteenth and Twentieth Centuries*, edited by Panikos Panayi (Leicester University Press, 1996).

The only person who has previously published some excellent research on Beamish and the Britons is Gisela C. Lebzelter. Her book *Political Anti-Semitism in England, 1918–1939* (Holmes & Meier, 1978) offers another take on many of the areas that I've covered in this volume. She also contributed a chapter on Beamish and the Britons to another book I highly recommend, *British Fascism*, edited by Kenneth Lunn and Richard C. Thurlow (St Martin's Press, 1980).

Two earlier books that are true classics are Louis W. Bondy's brilliant and seminal volume *Racketeers of Hatred* (Newman Wolsey, 1946), which, immediately post-war, still manages to be clear-cut, painstakingly detailed and professionally objective. It's an object lesson in how to write about the history of bigotry, being at once richly detailed and highly readable. As such, it's far and away my favourite book on the subject. The second, also essential reading, is George Thayer's *The British Political Fringe* (Anthony Blond, 1965). Thayer covers the racist right, the radical left, and Scottish, Welsh and Irish nationalism. What makes both of these books particularly informative is that their authors made a point of getting close to the individuals and organisations about which they were writing. Bondy got direct access to hundreds of journals, leaflets, speeches, etc., while Thayer simply visited the premises of his subject organisations and interviewed some of their key activists.

There has been so much written about *The Protocols* that it's not easy to choose specific titles. However, Lucien Wolf's slim exposé *The Myth of the Jewish Menace in*

World Affairs; or, The Truth about the Forged Protocols of the Elders of Zion (Macmillan, 1921) was one of the very first and remains an excellent indictment. And for a clear and excellently researched view of how *The Protocols* fared in America, Neil Baldwin's masterpiece *Henry Ford and the Jews: The Mass Production of Hate* (Public Affairs, 2003) is essential reading.

For more on the Vigilante Society and its milieu, I thoroughly recommend two well-researched but very different books. In 2004, Barbara Stoney published her authoritative and thorough biography *Twentieth Century Maverick: The Life of Noel Pemberton Billing* (Bank House Books). Equally detailed and accurate, but a more scandalously rollicking read, is Philip Hoare's *Oscar Wilde's Last Stand: Decadence, Conspiracy, and the Most Outrageous Trial of the Century* (Arcade, 1997).

Among the best general books on British fascism are Colin Cross's *The Fascists in Britain* (St Martin's Press, 1961), Richard Thurlow's *Fascism in Britain* (I. B. Tauris, 1998), Martin Pugh's *Hurrah for the Blackshirts! Fascists and Fascism in Britain between the Wars* (Jonathan Cape, 2006) and, because it offers detailed listings of far-right publications, Philip Rees's *Fascism in Britain: An Annotated Bibliography* (Harvester Press, 1979).

I've included very little about Oswald Mosley and his pre-war and post-war fascist groups. Two further books which cover this subject in detail are Robert Skidelsky's classic work *Oswald Mosley* (Holt, Rinehart & Winston, 1975) and Stephen Dorril's revealing (though poorly proofread) *Blackshirt: Sir Oswald Mosley and British Fascism* (Viking, 2006).

Finally, here are five excellent books which shed light on very specific subjects while including a great deal of broader information: *Collar the Lot! How Britain Interned and Expelled its Wartime Refugees* by Peter and Leni Gillman (Quartet, 1980); *Beyond the Pale: The Christian Political Fringe* by Derrick Knight (Caraf, 1982); *Fellow Travellers of the Right: British Enthusiasts for Nazi Germany 1933–39* by Richard Griffiths (Constable, 1980); *The Red Book: The Membership List of the Right Club, 1939*, edited and introduced by Robin Saikia (Foxley Books, 2010); and, lastly, *The Rebel who Lost his Cause: The Tragedy of John Beckett, MP*, written with surprisingly skilled detachment by his son Francis Beckett (London House, 1999).

As many of these books are now out of print, you may well be looking for second-hand copies. I would start by searching on Google, Amazon, eBay, AbeBooks and their ilk – or, if you don't need to own a copy, inter-library loans, of course. Good hunting!

CONCLUSION

We're all guilty of prejudice of some kind, though we usually deny it, and seldom understand the distorted logic behind it.

We can learn from those who exhibit extreme prejudice. They immerse themselves in a culture – and above all a literature – that re-enforces their dogma, that tells them they're right, even when it's obvious that they're wrong. Faced finally with failure, they persist by clinging to a naïve quasi-religious faith in the heroic righteousness of what they're doing.

John Tyndall was a founder-member of the National Front (NF), becoming its chairman in 1972. He was ousted after the 1979 General Election in which all 303 NF candidates lost their deposits. That year, David Brennan, the NF candidate for the parish council in Kings Walden, Hertfordshire, actually managed to secure zero votes! Absolutely undaunted, Tyndall founded the British National Party (BNP) in 1982, leading that organisation until Nick Griffin ousted him in 1999.

In 1988 Tyndall published a book, *The Eleventh Hour: A Call for British Rebirth*, much of it written while in prison for his beliefs. In it he expresses his faith as follows:

> Not for us the cosy tranquillity of the political soft option; for us only the long march through the cold night – which must precede the glorious dawn.

There was, of course, no glorious dawn for Tyndall in the real world. He was found dead in his home in Hove, Sussex on 19 July 2005, less than a week after his seventy-first birthday and just two days before he was due to stand trial at Leeds Magistrates' Court on charges of incitement to racial hatred.

In truth, the fate of the extremist – ever the outsider – is self-sacrifice, devoid of glory… having publicly marched that whole distance to a different rhythm. That was the course taken by Tyndall. It was also the one taken by Beamish. The Mond case didn't banish him. Despite the unpaid fine, he was back in Britain less than four years later with no consequences. His exile was self-imposed martyrdom. Instead of facing the reality of The Britons as a tiny impoverished version of what he'd envisaged, he opted for a nomadic illusion of popularity and importance. Likewise, after just seven-and-a-half months of internment he was offered very reasonable terms of release. On the pretext of solidarity with other internees half a world away, he remained in further custody for just under two-and-a-half years, while in the real world his last hope, Hitler, exterminated as many Jews as he could before finding defeat and suicide. The Japanese called it kamikaze. And, in our world, we see it persisting most graphically in the suicide bomber.

If we hope to counter extreme prejudice, we have first to study and understand it. That's precisely why I'm writing this and other books on the subject. Without understanding, there are not only more victims, but more perpetrators… some of them former victims…

The eventual creation of a Jewish homeland, as once advocated by both Beamish and Hitler, can be traced back to the Balfour Declaration. This was the letter written on 2 November 1917 by the UK Foreign Secretary, James Balfour, to Baron Walter Rothschild, a leading British Jew. In it Balfour wrote:

> His Majesty's Government view with favour the establishment in Palestine of a national home for the Jewish people, and will use their best endeavours to facilitate the achievement of this object, *it being clearly understood that nothing shall be done which may prejudice the civil and religious rights of existing non-Jewish communities in Palestine…*

The italics are mine.

Nick Toczek
April 2015

AFTERWORD

Since the completion of this book, several pertinent pieces of information have come my way.

Days after submitting the finished manuscript, I was contacted out-of-the-blue by Raymond Roberts, a former professor of history at the University of Zimbabwe. He'd been doing extensive research into the life of Henry Hamilton Beamish in Southern Africa.

From him I learned that Beamish's wife, Francis, had remained in Bloemfontein where she was still living when her husband died in 1948, so it seems that they must have separated, presumably before or just after the 1934 Greyshirts trial. Thereafter, Beamish doesn't appear to have spent time in South Africa.

Ray also told me of a book he was trying to locate: *Canada Raw: The Adventures of Henry Hamilton Beamish in The Canadian North-west, 1891–1895*. Intrigued, I scoured the internet and obtained a copy.

It's a poorly proof-read account – detailed though somewhat dull – of what happened to Beamish during his five years in the wilds of Canada. Having been sent out there by his father to learn farming, the whole experience proved to be an extremely tough one. Indeed, he came close to death several times as he eked out a hand-to-mouth struggle against the twin extremes of poverty and the elements. What he endured in those years vividly illustrates his blend of stubborn pig-headedness and rugged perseverance.

The book also confirms my suspicion that he was no writer. The whole account – actually written in Ceylon in 1899 – was the work of a friend, Lionel Haweis, who persuaded Beamish to narrate the tale while he took copious notes during a series of fairly drunken nights that they spent together.

Having tried but failed to get the work published, Haweis eventually lodged the manuscript (and his correspondence with publishers) in Canada with the British Columbia Archives and Records Service. Here it was accidentally discovered in 1993 by P. Stephen Haack (after he'd made a numbering error when filling in a request form for documents). It was Haack's edited version which was published in 1996 as *Canada Raw*.

In a phone conversation, Ray also informed me that, during his wartime internment, Beamish fell in with a number of younger pro-Nazi internees – most of whom will presumably have been from German families settled in Rhodesia – and that they'd idolised him.

Lastly, I also obtained a copy of Karina Urbach's excellent 2015 book *Go Betweens for Hitler* in which she discusses the post-war interrogation of Ribbentrop's assistant, SS-Oberfuhrer Wilhelm Rodde, by his Russian captors in 1947. Rodde was a rabid Jew-hater who'd become a Nazi Party member in 1932 and had joined Ribbentrop's Bureau in 1934. Towards the end of 1937 he was appointed Germany's Canadian Consul, becoming very active in pro-Nazi circles – especially as a Bund member – and rapidly establishing himself as Hitler's most prominent representative in Canada. He will therefore have met and worked with Arcand and many of Beamish's other Canadian Nazi associates, if not with Beamish himself.

Questioned about Hitler's supporters in Britain, Rodde talked about the key role played by members of the Anglo-German Fellowship. He then went on to name five British subjects who 'carried out intelligence work for us' – Arnold Wilson, Thomas P. Conwell-Evans, Captain Kennedy, Henry Hamilton Beamish and Ernest Tennant. Of Beamish, Rodde said that he'd arrived in the spring of 1936 'in Germany without money and shabbily dressed. He was fully looked after by Count Dürckheim'.

This then is a yet another visit to Germany by Beamish and certainly backs up my assertion that he was a German agent. His association with Dürckheim is also interesting. Karlfried Graf Dürckheim had spent six months in South Africa during 1934 with a mandate to foster support for Nazism. In 1935 he became Ribbentrop's chief assistant. A Buddhist and a Jew-hater, he was then found to have had a Jewish grandmother and to have been related to both the Oppenheim and Rothschild banking families. As a result, he was quietly removed from office and, in June 1938, sent to Japan. It seems highly likely that Beamish and Dürckheim would have become acquainted in 1934 during the Greyshirts trial.

Rodde died in his Russian prison on 6 April 1949. Dürckheim, changed by post-war imprisonment in Japan, returned to Germany to become a leading authority on Zen Buddhist spirituality. He died on 28 December 1988.

INDEX

Note: **bold** page numbers indicate photographs.

4 Protocols of Zion 88

'A Casualty of 18B' 156
A History of the United States (Chesterton) 233
Ackerman, Carl William 182
Act of Settlement 91
addresses 273
Akers-Douglas, E. 203, 204
Alexander III 75–6
Alexander, Kenneth 41
Aliens Act, 1905 77
aliens, proposed treatment of 22–3
All Russian Fascist Party 241
Allen, Maude 239
Almost in Confidence (Barlow) 7
America: anti-Jewish sentiment 183–4, 185; links with 111
American Bulletin 42
American Nationalist Confederation 57
American Nationalist Party 41
American Nazi Party 131
Ampthill, Lord 198–9
Anglo-German Fellowship (AGF) 97, 218–19, 221
Anglo-German Information Service (AGIS) 221–2
Anglo-German Review 225
Anglo-Saxon Federation 101
Angriff Press 130
anti-Bolshevism 197

Anti-Bolshevist Publishing Company 35–6
anti-Catholicism 19, 126
anti-fascism 163
anti-German demonstrations 197
anti-German sentiment 7–8, 12–13, 212–13
Anti-Jewish Information Bureau 107, 120
anti-Jewish riots, 1190 74–5
anti-Jewish sentiment: British Empire Union (BEU) 197; history of 74–81, 192; nineteenth century 3; South Africa 4–6; Western Europe 74
anti-Jewish violence 79–80
anti-Muslim sentiment 74
anti-Semitism, Beamish on 49, 54
Anti-Socialist and Anti-Communist Union (ASACU) 194–5
Anti-Socialist Union 194
Arcand, Adrien 51, 55, 57, 68–9
Arnold Leese House 121, 161
Askwith, Lord 200
Aufbau 56, 68
Augustine Publishing Company 132
Austin, Alfred 235
Australian League of Rights 131
Authors' Syndicate 174–5

Baillie, Major J. 147
Balfour Declaration 25, 277
Banister, Joseph 79, 83–4, 94, 244
Barker, Col. Victor 210
Barker, Robert Hewitt 19

Barlow, Arthur G. 7, 16, 28–9, 46–7
Barnes, Major James Strachey 147
Baron, Anthony Francis Xavier 105–9, 254–5
Bathurst, Lord and Lady 196–7, 234
Battersby, James Laratt 156
Bax-Ironside, Sir Henry 172
Beacon Light 39
Beamish, Blanche Georgina (née Hughes, mother) 2
Beamish, Frances Winifred Lingard (née Green, wife) 35
Beamish, Henry Hamilton **139**, **140**; activity in custody 67–8, 69; address to German Fascists 31; alleged extortion 32; alleged role in rioting 16; in America 30–1, 39, 42, 56; anti-British 56; anti-German sentiment 7–8; anti-Jewish sentiment 17–18; on anti-Semitism 49, 54; Barlow's portrayal 7, 46–7; birth 2; and British Union of Fascists 36–7; business enterprises 4, 7; campaign for rights of former combatants 18; in Canada 43, 55–6, 278; Clapham by-election 21–3; on concentration camps 50–1; correspondence with Huggins 59–60; correspondence with Tredgold 58–9, 60, 61–6; death 70, 100; death of father 3–4; developing reputation 35–6; disputes 93; documenting 'Jewish influence' 18; early career 3; education 2–3; election policies 22–3; evidence in Billing's court case 20; evidence to Select Committee on Incendiarism 8–16; exchanges with Salomon 29–30; extreme views 19; failing health 69; family background 2; finances 31; financial difficulties 28; in Germany 31, 43–5; as go-between 42–3; held in custody 57–67; and Imperial Fascist League (IFL) 36, 45; influences on 5; informing on 'spies' 13; International Congress of Anti-Semites 50–1; Judge Graham on 30, and Leese 146; legacy 190–1; letter to Kositzin 56–7; Levy slander case 37–9; listing of German companies 16; loss of interest in The Britons 39; marriage to Frances 35; meets Mussolini 31–2; memorandum to Tredgold 65–6; Mond libel case 24–5, 26–8, 47; move to London 17; on Mrs Fry 213; nationalism 13–14, 15; as Nazi agent 39, 40; and Nazi Party 35; in New York 51–5, **140**; note to Ramsay, 1947 99; in Nuremberg 44–5, **139**; Palestine proposal 44, 48; parents 2; in Paris 32–3; personal account of years 1891-1918 17; personality 3, 50; political activities 7–8; predisposition to bigotry 6; reactions to 46; relations with Hitler 93; release from custody 66–7; resigns from Vigilante Society 23–4; resigns presidency of The Britons 69–70; response to Barlow 48–9; return to London 31, 92, 93; returns to England 42, 43; returns to South Africa 28–9, 35, 37; in Rhodesia 6–7; Rhodesian Parliament 56, 57; siblings 2; sources 70–3; in South Africa 4–5, 6–8, 278, 279; South African Infantry 16; in Southern Rhodesia 29; speech at Berlin University 43; speech at Hammersmith 33–4; speech at Munich University 44; as stateless 190–1; support for Arcand 68–9; support for Hitler 38–9; terms of release 60–1; in Tokyo 43; will 70
Beamish, Henry Hamilton (father) 2, 3–4
Beamish, Tufton Percy Hamilton 2
Beamish Collection 17
Beamish House 115, 121, 163
Bean, John 121, 161
Beaumont, C. 244
Beaumont, Meredith 244
Beckett, John 18, 34, 99, 160, 223–4, 226, 227, 228, 238
Beckwith Company 87, 183
Beckwith, Peter *see* Houghton, Harris Ayres
Beek, Gottfried zur 177
Belloc, Hilaire 80, 210, 232–3, 236–7, 238
Belsher, A.S. 24
Ben Israel, Menasseh 75
Bennett, Harry 186
Bernstein, Herman 178
Bertin, Capt. H. 67
Biarritz (Goedsche) 168
Biff Boys 215
bigotry: logic of 81; predisposing factors 6; promotion through literature 20
Billing, Lilian Maud Pemberton 23
Billing, Noel Pemberton 22–4; prosecution 19–21
Birmingham Nationalist Club (BNC) 101, 118–19, 160
Birth of a Nation (Griffiths) 183
Bitter Harvest: A Modern History of Palestine (Hadawi) 116
Black Book 20–1
'Black Jews' 90

282   Index

Blackshirt (Dorril) 98
Blakeney, Brig. Gen. Robert 194, 208, 244–5
blood libel 74, 150
Bloomfield Books 132
Blue Book on Incendiarism 49
Blumenfeld, R.D. 194
Board of Deputies of British Jews 213, 223
Boche and Bolshevik (Webster and Kerlen) 86–7
Boer War, anti-Jewish sentiment 5–6
Bogory, Natalie de 182
Bolshevism: as Jewish 192; threat of 25–6
Bolshevism from Moses to Lenin: A Dialogue between Adolf Hitler and Me (Eckart) 80–1
book, background to 1
Borsch, Col. Friedrich 162
Boswell Publishing Company 104, 194, 203, 240
Bottomley, Horatio 196
Boulton, Col. Oscar 213–14
B.P.S. Printing Co. 115, 118–19
Brasol, Boris 182–3
Braybrooke, Major A.R. 255
'Breaking the Silence' 116
Brennan, David 276
Bridgehead 109, 111, 113
British Brothers League (BBL): background to 75–6; end of 77; founding of 76; growth 79; meetings and activities 79–80; public meeting, 1902 76; sources 81–2; support for 79
British Citizen Movement (BCM) 7–8, 11, 15
British Commonwealth Union (BCU) 198, 199
British Council Against European Commitments (BCAEC) 223, 226
British Council for a Christian Settlement in Europe (BCCSE), 228
British Empire Fascist Party 218
British Empire Movement (BEM) 111
British Empire Party (BEP) 109–10, 154, 252
British Empire Producers' Organisation 17
British Empire Union (BEU) 196–8, 234
British Empire Union Monthly Record 197
British Fascism 207
British Fascisti (BF) *see* British Fascists (BF)
British Fascists (BF) 36, 94–5, 194, 204–9, 214; Leese in 146–7
British Guardian 33, 79, 94–6, **136**; *see also* Hidden Hand
British League of Ex-Servicemen and Women (BLESW) 159–60

British League of Rights 131
British Lion 207, 208, 214
British Movement 128, 164
British National Party (BNP) 103, 161–2
British Patriotic Traders' and Consumers' Alliance of South Africa 8, 9, 11, 14–15
British People's Party (BPP) 160, 224, 227
British Protestant League 241
British Southern Africa Company 6
British Union 216
British Union of Fascists (BUF) 36–7, 80, 97, 148–9, 209, 215–16, 217, 241
British Workers League (BWL) 198
Britons Publishing Company (BPC) 131, 251
Brittain, Sir Harry 193, 200
Broadhurst, Mary Adelaide 195
Brooks, Collin 242
Brunner, Mond company 35
Bund Völkischer Europäer 39
Burdon, Major 173–4
Burgess, Victor 159
Burke, Emory Carney 42
Burroughs, John 183
Butler, Eric 131

Cambridge University Nationalist Club 160
Cameron, William John 31–2, 184, 185–6
Canadian Nationalist Party (CNP) 43
Candour 116, 124, 127, 242
Cardross, Lord 245
Carroll, C.E. 99, 224, 225, 226
Catholic Herald 125
Catholicism 125–6
Centre International d'Études sur la Fascisme (CINEF) 147, 211
Chavasse, Anthony James Wykeham 255
Cherep-Spiridovich, Count 36
Chesterton, Ada 239
Chesterton, A.K. 115, 116, 122, 124, 126–8, 131, 160, 190, 223, 224, 242
Chesterton, Cecil 195, 232, 233, 236–7, 237, 238–9
Chesterton, G.K. 210, 233, 236–7, 239
Chestertons 80, 195
Christian Nationalist Crusade of America 101
Christian Reformers 156
Churchill, Winston 97, 234–5
Clair Press 124, 255–6
Clan-Briton 111–12
Clapham by-election 21–2
Clarke, John H. 19, 23, 24–5, 83, 85, 88, 96, 170, 175–6, 245–6; publications 86; vice-president of The Britons 28, 29

Clarke, Rev. Fielding 111–12
Clifford's Keep siege 74–5
coin clipping 75
Cole, Comm. E.H. 222–3
Cole, H.A. 6
Collier, Vincent 223
Collings, James Horace 23
Collis-Bird, Mrs J. 255–6
Colonial College, Hollesley 2
'Colour Comes to Britain' 115
colour prejudice *see* race relations
Colvin, Ian 176
Combat 162
Common Sense 128–30
communism, as Jewish 110, 192
Communist Party 236
Conan Doyle, Sir Arthur 80
concentration camps, Beamish on 50–1
conspiracy theory 6, 77–8
constitution 259–67
Consumers' Alliance (CA) 8, 9, 11, 14–15
Cook, John 110
Coolidge, Calvin 183–4
Cooper, Richard T. 109, 246
Cooper, Sir Richard 88, 198–9
Cotswold Agreement 162–3
Cotter, Hilary 109, 256
Courthope, William 235
Cowper-Todd, Mr 246
Cowrie, Mr 68
Cox, Sir Richard 2
Crewe, Lord 6
Crick, Walter 246
Croft, Henry Page 198–9, 201
Cromwell, Oliver 75
Crosland, T.W.H. 239
Cust, Robert 173–4

D. P. Lapham Bank 184
Dalton, Hugh 35
Danziger, Max 63, 65
Darling, Justice 47
David, Trefor 110–11, 252, 256
Davies, I.I.J. 119
de Heekelingen, Herman de Vries 211
Dearborn Independent 31–2, 87, 90, 184–6
Deatherage, George 56
Defence Against Alien Control 113, 160
Dell, J.D. 32, 96–7, 105, 175–6, 247, 252, 254
Denbigh, Fred W. 8
Der Angriff 43
Der Fränkische Tageszeitung 45
Der Sturmer 44
Deutsche Textil Zeitung 221

Deutsche Zeitung in Grossbritannien 221–2
Deutscher Fichte-Bund 240–2
Die Un?schuld der Jenseitigen (*The Innocence (?) of Those on the Other Side*) 88
Diebel, Hans 42
Dies Committee 39–40, 55
Dies, Martin 40
Dior, Françoise 163; letter from **141**
Disraeli, Benjamin 75
distributism 210–11, 236–7
Distributist League 233
documents **136**
Domvile, Admiral Sir Barry 104, **138**, 219, 221, 224, 226, 228, 256–7
Dorril, S. 98
Douglas, C.H. 237, 238
Douglas, Lord Alfred 34, 239
draft constitution of The Britons 259–67
Dürckheim, Karlfried Graf 279

early years of The Britons: Beamish's role and effect 93, 94; Caxton Hall meeting 1921 88–9; constitution 83; finances 92, 95, 96; founder members 83; Herne Hill meeting 95–6; hostility 93; inaugural meeting 83; inter-war years 97–8; internal conflict 94; international perspective 84–5; links with German organisations 85; meeting, May 1920 84; meetings and activities 83, 93; networking 85; political aspirations 88; post-war associates 101; publications 93–4; relocation 90; size of organisation 93; sources 102; stasis 96; women's committee 88
East Finchley by-election 23–4
Eckart, Dietrich 31, 80, 87
Economic League (EL) 198, 201
Eden, Anthony 240
Edict of Expulsion 75
Edmondson, Robert Edward 51–2, 57
Edward I 75
Efficiency and Empire (White) 5, 77–8
'Efficiency and Vice' (White) 21
Elmhurst, Ernest 42
Empire Tea Rooms 48
Empire Windrush 100
Endell Street Military Hospital 204–5
Enemies of the Human Race (Butmi) 169
enemy-born subjects, proposed treatment of 22–3
England under the Jews (Banister) 79
English Array (EA) 215, 223
English Mistery (EM) 215, 217, 223
Erfurt Conferences 56

espionage 41–2, 221
Eugenics Education Society 193–4, 250
European Liberation Front 108
Evans-Gordon, Major Sir William 76–7
eviction 121
'Experiences of Mr. H. H. Beamish in connection with Land Settlement Work and Employment of Labour' 17
Eye Witness 232–3, 238
Eyre & Spottiswoode 170–1, 175; letter from **141**

Fabianism 236
factionalism 162
Farquharson, Margaret Milne 195
Farran, Capt. Roy 103
Fascism for Old England (Leese) 146
Fascist Gazette 210
Fascist League *see* Imperial Fascist League (IFL)
finances 92, 115, 120, 175–6; early years 95
First Balkan War 234
Fischer, Theodor 178
Fleischhauer, Col. Ulrich 50, 179
Flynn, T.O. 58, 62
Ford, Henry 38, 87; acquisitions 184; anti-Jewish sentiment 183ff; apology to Sapiro 186–8; *Dearborn Independent* 184–6; Grand Cross of the German Eagle 188; libel case 185–8; politics 184; pragmatism 187–8; sources 188–9
Fountaine, Andrew 103, 161
Fowler, F.D. 170–2, 175
Frank, Leo 183
Fraser, Harry MacLeod 18, 21–2, 29, 247
Fraudulent Conversion: The Myth of Moscow's Change of Heart (Jordan) 119, 160–1
Free Britain 100–1, **136**; January 1950 103–4; October 1950 104; November 1950 105; January 1951 105; April 1951 105–6; May 1951 109; September 1951 110; December 1951 113; February 1953 114; December 1953 115; January 1954 115; February 1954 116; November 1954 116; March 1955 118; May 1955 119; July 1955 120; and *Defence Against Alien Control* 113; end of 120; finances 120; improved production quality 115; irregular publication 113–14, 120, 121
Free Press 43, 212
Freemasonry 98
Fritsch, Theodor 35, 177, 185
Fry, Mrs Leslie 212, 213, 247
fund raising 88, 89, 95

Galton, Sir Francis 193
Garner, Elmer J. 67–8
Gaster, John Marston 159
General Strike 207–8
Gentile Christian Front 101
Gentile Folly: The Rothschilds 150
George, Wesley Gritz 124–5
German-American Bund 39, 40–2, 43, 45–6, 51
German espionage 41–2
German Nazi propaganda **138**
German People's Publishing House 87
Germans, as sexual predators and perverts 21
Germany, anti-Semitism 50
Gilbert, Oliver 226, 255
Gittens, Anthony 98–9, 104, 105, 119, 120–1, 124, 125, 128–9, 130, 131, 157, 163, 254, 257
Gittens, Joyce 124, 125
G.K.'s Weekly 210, 233, 239
Glenesk, Lord 234
Glinka, Yuliana 169
Goebbels, Joseph 178
Goedsche, Hermann 168
Goetze, Sigismund, libel case 34
Gohier, Urbain 33
Golovinski, Matvel 169
Gore, Charles 150
Gothic Ripples 101, 107, 109, 114, 116, 120–1, 153, 154–5, 156–7, 165, 237, 257
Gough, Rev. A.W. 248
Graham, Judge, on Beamish 38
Granger, H.E. 248
Graves, Philip 178, 179
Gray, Arthur 199
Great Sedition Trial 40, 42
Great War, anti-German sentiment 7–8
Greater Britain Movement 163
Green, George 188
Greene, Ben 227, 228
Greer, Harry 22–3
Greig, Miss 248
Grenfell, Capt. Russell 116
Griffin, Nick 276
Griffiths, D.W. 183
Griffiths, Peter 164
Gwynne, H.A. 176, 234

Hall, Sir William Reginald 198
Hamm, Jeffrey 159, 160
Hammersmith Town Hall, Britons' meeting 33–4
Hancock, Anthony 165–6
Hannett, D.G. 209

Hannon, Patrick 199
Harding, Warren G. 183–4
Harrison, Louisa Mary Ann 2
Harvard Club 51–2
Hauen, Capt. Müller von 177
Haweis, Lionel 278
Henry III 75
Hidden Government (Scott) 124
hidden hand 192
Hidden Hand September 1920 86; October 1920 86; December 1920 87; May 1921 88; September 1921 88; January 1923 89; March 1923 90; April 1923 92; May 1923 93; June 1923 93; November 1923 94; boycott 92; circulation 93; final issue 94; *see also British Guardian; Jewry Über Alles*
Hilton, Major Gen. Richard 255
Hirschfeld, Magnus 99
Hitler, Adolf 80–1; Beamish on 49–50, 51; correspondence with 96–7; Leese's attitude to 153; relations with Beamish 93
Hobson, J.A. 5
Hogge, James Myles 18
Holland, Catesby 8
Holmes, C. 104
Holmes, T.V. 116
homosexuality 19, 21
Hooded Men *see* White Knights of Britain
Horton, Edwin B. 109, 257
Houghton, Harris Ayres 87, 182–3
House Committee on Un-American Activities 40–1
Houston, Lady Lucy 203, 240
'How Israel Treats Her Arabs' 116
Howard, Capt. A.E.N. 248
Huggins, Sir Godfrey 57, 59, 62, 68
humanity 122
Huxley-Blythe, Peter 108, 254

Illustrated Sunday Herald 234
immigration and settlement 76, 77
Imperial Fascist League (IFL) 36, 37, 42, 45, 147–8, 200, 209, 232; Great Portland Street meeting 148–9; political programme 148; rivalry with BUF 148–9
Inch, Harry Victor 37
Independent Labour Party (ILP) 236
Independent Nationalist 101
India, accusations against Jews 29
Industrial Intelligence Bureau (IIB) 196
Industrial Problems and Disputes (Askwith) 200
internal conflict 94, 105–8

International Congress of Anti-Semites 50–1
international perspective 84–5
internment 22–3, 57, 97, 151–3, 224, 226
Isaacs, Rufus Daniel 29
It is Close at Hand: At the Gates 169
Italy, as friendly towards Jews 99

Jackson, Holbrook 236
January Club 220
Jeffery, Robert Key 115, 127
Jellett, William Morgan 249
Jewish Guardian 239
Jewish Naturalisation Act 1753 75
Jewry Über Alles 83–6, **136**; *see also Hidden Hand*
Jews: association with wealth 192; and Bolshevism 25–6, 192; in Britain 74–7; spreading venereal disease 21
Jews and the White Slave Trade or Lords of the Hells of Gomorrah (Banister) 79
John Bull 196
Joly, Maurice 168
Jordan, Colin 101, 105, 113, 115, 117–20, 124, **141**, 155, 157, 257; arrests 165–6; biography 159; in Birmingham 160; in Coventry 161; death 166; education and early career 159; imprisonment 162, 163, 164; and Leese 160–1; Leyton by-election 164; marriage 163; police raids 165; politics and activism 159–66; at Princedale Road 161; remarriage 166; shoplifting 164–5; sources 166–7; World Union of National Socialists 162–3; writings 160, 166; in Yorkshire 165
Jordan, Mrs Colin, letter from **141**
journals 232–43
Joyce, William 97, 206, 223, 224
Judaic Publishing Co. 29, 83, 88; *see also* The Britons Publishing Company
Justice in Rhodesia 57–8

Karadja, Princess 57
Kaufman, Gerald 165
Kentish Rooms, meeting 36
Kerlen, Kurt 86–7
Kerr-Richies, Ian 163
Kessemeier, Heinrich 241
Kessemeier, Theodore 241
key figures 244–58
Kingdom Herald 156
Kitson, Arthur 145–6, 237, 249
Klapproth, Johannes 57
Knight, Maxwell 196
Knights of the Ku Klux Klan 131

Knupffer, George 239–40, 255
Kosher War 56
Kositzin, Mr 56–7
Ku Klux Klan 89–90, 101, 183–4
'Ku Klux Klan' (article) 89
Kullgren, William 39, 68

La Vieille France 32–3, 85
Labouchère, Henri 242
L'Action Française 32, 93
Lagarde, Paul de 44
Laing, Mrs 249
Lane, Col. A.H. 200, 212, 249
Lane, L. 249
Lawson, Gerald 164
Le Fasciste Canadien 56
League of Empire Loyalists (LEL) 116–17, 120, 121–2, 127, 161, 255
League of Gentiles 39
League of Nations 84
Leese, May Winifred 120, 121, 144, 161, 162
Leese, Arnold 36, 37, 43, 98, 105, 107, 109, 110, 116, **134**, 200, 207, 209, 237, 252, 257; arrest 151; attitude to Hitler 153; and Beamish 146; biography 143; British Fascists (BF) 146–7; and The Britons 155; Centre International d'Études sur la Fascisme (CINEF) 147; death 119–20, 156; engagement 144; in France 144; health 151, 153; hunger strike 151–2; Imperial Fascist League (IFL) 147–8; imprisonment 150, 151, 154; in India 144; internment 151–3; in Kenya 144; Kitson's influence 145–6; legacy 190; libel charge 154; literature **135**; marriage 144; military career 144–5; personality 145; politics 145–6; racism 154–5; refused passport 153; retirement 145; in Somaliland 144; sources 158; Stamford Council elections 146–7; veterinary career 143–5; workload 150–1; writings 154, 159, 190
Leese Memorial Fund 156–7
lesbianism 19
Levy, Rabbi A. 37
Levy slander case 37–8
Leyton by-election 164
Liberty Restoration League 220
Liebold, Earnest Gustav 184, 188
Lintorn-Orman, Rotha 204–6, 208
Lipman, V.D. 77
literature: promotion of bigotry 20; role of 80

literature exchange 85
Liverpool Abercrombie by-election, 1917 18
Lloyd George, David 22
London offices **137**
Londonderry, Lord 219
Loyalty League (LL) 95, 203–4, 250
Loyalty News Debate 204
Ludovici, Anthony 237
Lusitania riots 8–9, 48–9
Lymington, Viscount 223, 226, 238
lynching 183

Macchiavelli, Niccolò 168
Maclean, Neil 35
MacNab, John Angus 223
Madagascar Plan 44–5, 51, 53, 55
Makgill, George 196, 198
Marriott, Peter 115, 239–40, 258
Marsden, Victor 94, 176, 177, 179, 249–50
Martin, Don 131–2
Maxse, Leopold 93, 234, 235
May Laws, Russia 75
McGinley, Conde 129
McGovern, John 228
McLaughlin, Michael 165
meat supplies 17
Meister, Wilhelm 177
Melchett, Lord *see* Mond, Sir Alfred
mercenaries 40–1
Meyer, Judge Walter 179
Meyjer, Herman 153–4
MI5 147, 213, 220
Middle Class Union (MCU) 200
Militant Christian Patriots (MCP) 200, 212–13, 220
Military Service (Review of Exemptions) Bill 18
Miller, James M. 185–6
Mills, Herbert T. 109, 258
Milner, Alfred 25–6
Mond, Sir Alfred 22, 51; alleged profiteering 34–5; Beamish on 49; libel case 24–5, 26–9, 47; wheeler-dealing 34
Montagu, Edwin Samuel 29
Monteith, Stanley 249
Montesquieu 168
Montgomery, E.J. 250
Moore, Lady 88, 250
Morning Post 86–7, 176, 234–5
Morrison, William 130–1
Mosley, Oswald 36–7, 80, 148, 160, 190, 209, 214–15, 223
Mosley Manifesto 215

Mount Temple, Lord 219
Mudge, George P. 88, 95, 193–4, 199, 203, 204, 250, 253
Mussolini, Benito 31, 99
'Mussolini's Critics' 95
My Irrelevant Defence: Meditations Inside Gaol and Outs on Jewish Ritual Murder (Leese and Gore) 150

National Association of Discharged Sailors and Soldiers (NADSS) 18
National Citizens' Union (NCU) 200, 203, 207–8, 220
National Fascisti (National Fascists) 207, 209–10
National Federation of Discharged and Demobilised Soldiers and Sailors (NFDSS) 18–19
National Forum 101
National Front 103, 117, 127, 128, 255, 257
National Front Constitutional Movement 103
National Front After Victory 109, 160
National Labour Party 161
National League for Clean Government (NLCG) 195–6
National Liberal Club 18
National Party 198–9
National Political League (NPL) 195
National Political Reform League (NPRL) 195
National Review 235
'National Socialism (Racial Fascism) in Practice in Germany' 45
National Socialist **142**
National Socialist League (NSL) 223–4
National Socialist Movement (NSM) 162, 164
National Union of Ex-Servicemen (NUX) 18–19
National Vanguard 129
National Workers' Movement (NWM) 101, 105, 154, 216–18
National Workers' Party (NWP) 217, 257
National Workers' Union (NWU) 217
Nationalist Information Bureau (NATINFORM) 108, 109, 254–5
Nationalist Workers Movement 110
Nationalzeitung 221, 222
naturalisation, call to rescind 22–3
Nazi Anglo-German Fellowship 194
Nazi Party 31; Beamish' relations with 35; in Britain 222; rise of 90
Nazi propaganda **138**

Ness, Neil Howard 39, 40–1
networking 85, 90, 111, 153
New Age 236–8
New Christian Crusade Church 131
New Party 36, 209, 214–15
New Pioneer 223, 238
New Statesman 237
New Witness 195, 232, 238–9
New Witness League 196
Newman, John Pretyman 200
Nilus, Sergei Aleksandrovich 169, 174
Nordic League (NL) 42, 212, 213, 220, 252
Nordische Gesellschaft 220
Northern European 124
Not Guilty: Historic Race Relations Trial, Lewes Assizes in March 1968 128
Notting Hill riots 161
NUPA 36–7

objectives 90–1
O'Donnell, Frank Hugh 195, 238
O'Flaherty, A.E. 8
Ogmore election 110–11
Okhrana 169, 174
Oliver, Revilo Pendleton 128–9, 130, 132
Olivier, David 37
Omni Publications 130
Orage, A.R. 236–8
Orange River Colony settlers 6
Order of the Red Rose 199, 250
Organisation for the Maintenance of Supplies (OMS) 207, 210
Otway, Loftus William 2
Otway, Robert Waller 2
Our Judeo-Irish Labour Party: How the Interests of the British Working Men are Misrepresented and Betrayed by Politicians who are Neither British nor Working Men (Banister) 79
Out of Step: Events in the Two Lives of an Anti-Jewish Camel-Doctor (Leese) 156

paki bashing 128
Paladin League 217
Palma, Joseph 186
paramilitarism, BNP 162
Parliamentary Report 68
passports, refusal of 153
Patriot 240
Patriotic Fund 88, 89
Patriotic Party (PP) 255
Patriotic Publishing Company 188
pauper migration, opposition to 77
Peace and Progress Information Service 227

Peace Pledge Union 227
Pearson, Sir Cyril Arthur 193
Pelley, William Dudley 41
Penty, Arthur 236–7
People's Defence League 201
Peoples' League 196, 200
People's Post 160, 227
Percy, Alan, 8th Duke Northumberland 203
perversion, Vigilante Society obsession 21
Peters, W.A. 251
Petitioner's Committee (PC) 8, 9, 11–13, 15
Petrie, Sir Charles 239–40
Phoenix Press and Bookshop 162
Phoney War 97
Pile, Bertram 'Duke' 110
Pimm, H.M. 251
Pipp, Edwin G. 184
Pirie, Denis 163
Pirow, Oswald 255
Plain English 34, 239
Plain Speaker 115, 239–40, 255
Plane Tree Restaurant, Britons' meeting 32
pledge 92
pogroms 75–6
police raids 163, 165
Political Corruption and How to End It 172
political offshoots 110
Pollitt, Harry 207
Pollock, John 251
Poncins, Comte Léon de 130, 131
Portman Papers 116
post-war associates 101
Pound, Ezra 237
Powell, Enoch 117
Pownall, Capel 251
prejudice 80–1
Prescott-Decie, Brig. Gen. Cyril 203–4, 251
pro-Nazi activists 97
Procès-verbaux de réunions secrètes des Sages d'Israël 33
Property and the Nation: A New Conservative Philosophy (Marriott) 115
Protocols of Zion: Trilingual Spanish, English, Arabic (Yahya) 179
Public Ledger 182
public opinion 163
publications 83–4; 1960s 128; exchanges of 85; list of 268–72; literacy 112–13; pirating 130; for sale, 1920 86; for sale, 1923 90; for sale 1949 100; for sale 1955 119; sales 111, 114, 119
Publicity 67–8
publishing, 1960s to 1970s 131–3

Pulitzer, Paul 128–9
Pullen-Burry, Bessie 251

Race, Heredity and Civilisation (George) 124–5
race relations 104; *see also* colour prejudice
Rachkovsky, Pyotr 169, 174
racial prejudice 100, 114, 115
Racial Preservation Society 127–8
racism 117–19, 122, 128, 164
Ramsay, Archibald Maule 42, 68–9, 105, **134**, 220, 223, 226, 240, 252, 258
Rand Daily Mail 8
Ratcliffe, Alexander 241
Reading, Lord *see* Isaacs, Rufus Daniel
Reconstruction Society 194, 200
relocation 115, 121, 124, 125
'Restore the Act of Settlement of A.D. 1700' 91
Rex versus Leese (Leese) 154
Rhodesia 6
Rhodesian Herald 66–7
Rich, Major 252
Ridley, Samuel Forde 77
Ridout, P.J. 104, 109, 252
Right Club (RC) 97, 220, 226
riots: Notting Hill 161; South Africa 8–9, 48–9; Trafalgar Square 162
rivalry, between organisations 148–9
RMS *Lusitania* 8, 10–11
Rodde, Wilhelm 279
Romanoff House Boys' School 2
Rosel, Rudolf Gottfried 221–2
Rosenberg, Alfred 35, 87, 177, 217, 220
Rowe, T. Victor 226
Royal Commission on Alien Immigration 77
Ruddiman, Mrs Stanley 186
Rushbrook, J.F. 212
Russia 45, 169
Russian Empire, anti-Jewish sentiment 75–6
Russian Revolution 234

Sackville Russell, Hastings William, Duke of Bedford 160, 227–8
Salomon, Mr, exchanges with Beamish 29–30
Salt Lake City Tribune 42
Samuel, Sir Harry Simon 77
Sanderson, William 199, 215
Sapiro, Aaron, libel case 185–8
Saturday Review 240–2
scapegoating 6, 192

Schirach, Baldur von 185
Schnell, Silvio 178
Schwimmer, Rosika 183
Schwinn, Herman Max 40, 41–2
Scott, Lieut. Col. John Creagh 124
Scottish Women's Hospital Corps (WHC) 204–5
Searchlight 163
Second Boer War 25
Segel, Binjamin 178
Select Committee on Incendiarism 8–16
Sempill, Lord 219
Serpico, Philip C. 130
Seton Hutchison, Lieut. Col. Graham 216–18
Shanks, George 170–1, 173, 174–6, 179
Shaw, George Bernard 236
Shaw, William Stanley 76
Sherrard, L.H. 147
Shlesinger, Theodore 49
Silesia Revisited (Seton Hutchison) 217
Silver Badge Party (SBP) 18
Silver Shirts 39, 41
Silverman, Sidney 111–12
Simmons, William J. 183
Simpson, Harry 36, 146, 207
Skeels, Serocold 218
Skinhead Moonstomp 128
Smets, Karl 254–5
Smith, Percival Frere 7, 27, 58
social credit 237
Socialism Explained (Fowler) 172
Socialist National Defence Committee (SNDC) 198
Society for Upholding Political Honour (SUPH) 171–2
Sons of Liberty Press 131
Sosnowsky, Gen. G.J. 182
South Africa: Beamish on 49–50; effects of annexation 25; land settlement 6
South African Farmer's Advocate and Home Magazine 4
South Africa's Kosher Press 48
Spearhead 103, 162–3
'Special Notice To Our Readers' 92
Spencer, Harold Sherwood 19, 20–1, 23, 24, 239, 252–3; Goetze libel case 34
Spiridovich, Alexander Ivanovich 174
Spivak, John J. 41
Stamford Council elections 146–7
Staples, Ronald 242
State Secret: A Documentation of the Secret Revolutionary Mainspring Governing Anglo-American Politics (Poncins) 131

'Statutum de Judeismo' 75
Stoddard, Lothrop 100
Streicher, Julius 44
Stuart, Mr 253
Sunday Times Book Exhibition 119, **135**
Swinburne, Col. Thomas Robert 253
Sydenham, Lord and Lady 253–4

Tait, Euphemia 24
Tariff Reform League 193
Tavistock, Lord 228
Taylor, James 159
Templeton, Lord 254
Tennant, David 118
Tennant, Ernest W.D. 218–19
The Account Book of Judah (Meister) 177
The Alien Immigrant (Evans-Gordon) 77
The Alien Menace (Lane) 200, 212
The American Mercury 116
The Bloody Red Streak (David) 110–11
The Britisher 212
The Britons 163; background to 24; Beamish resigns presidency 69–70; demise 131; draft constitution 259–67; eviction 121; Hammersmith Town Hall 33–4; increased activity 33–4; key figures 244–58; launch of 28; legacy 190–1; literacy 112–13; objectives 90–1, 112–13; peer groups 202–3ff; Plane Tree Restaurant meeting 32; planned re-organisation 32; pledge 92; precursors 192–3ff; proposed expansion 114; *The Protocols of the Learned Elders of Zion* see separate heading; early years
The Britons 114
The Britons Publishing Company 89, 94; *see also* Judaic Publishing Co.
'"The Britons" Ready for Expansion' 114
The Cause of World Unrest (Gwynne et al.) 176–7, 234
The Code of the Jew 84
'The Colour Question Has Suddenly Burst On Britain' 100
The Coloured Invasion (Jordan) 164
The Cross & the Flag 101
The Destitute Alien in Great Britain: A Series of Papers dealing with the Subject of Foreign Pauper Immigration (White) 77
The Distributist League 210
'The English Crown Witness of Adolph Hitler' 32
The English Democracy: Its Promises and Perils (White) 77
The Fascist 147, 148, 150

The Fascist Bulletin 207, 208
'The First 47,000' 20
The Golden Book of the Los Angeles Bund 42
The Grave Diggers of Russia 87, 93–4
The Great within the Small and Antichrist: An Imminent Political Possibility: Notes of an Orthodox Believer (Nilus) 169
The Helmsman 223
The Hidden Hand (White) 78
The History of a Lie: The Protocols of the Wise Men of Zion (Bernstein) 178
The Imperialist 19, 20
The International Jew 32, 90, 185, 187, 188
The Investigator 96, 98
The Jewish Bogey and the Forged Protocols of the Learned Elders of Zion (Wolf) 178
The Jewish Cemetery at Prague 169
The Jewish Peril 169–71, 173–4, 176, 177
The Jewish Question: How to Solve it (White) 78
The Jewish War of Survival (Leese) 153
The Jews (Belloc) 232
The Jews' Who's Who (Beamish and Fraser) 18, 29, 44, 85, 172, 177
The Lid Lifts (Walker) 163–4
The Link 97, 221, 224–6, 228
The Modern Jew (White) 77
The Myth of the Jewish Menace in World Affairs; or, The Truth about the Forged Protocols of the Elders of Zion (Wolf) 178
The Nationalist 161
The Norther European 161
The Outline of Sanity (Chesterton) 210
The Patriot 203, 214
The Power & Aims of International Jewry 234
The Problems of a Great City (White) 77
The Protocols of the Elders of Zion, Critically Illuminated (Segel) 178
The Protocols of the Elders of Zion and Jewish World Policy (Rosenberg) 177
The Protocols of the Learned Elders of Zion 1, 29, 68, 86, **137**, 192–3; in America 182–3; authenticity 178–9, 187; background to 168–9; in British Museum 174; and The Britons 170–1; Clarke's talk 85; contents 169; continued circulation 179–80; continued publication 98; creation of text 169; early versions 169; editions and sales 124, 177, 183, 188; first appearance 169; French translation 33; as *The Jewish Peril* 169; negotiations for 170–1; publication in Britain 169–70; published by The Britons 177; reactions to 178; royalties 174–5; serialisation 169; sources 180–1; translations 94, 174, 176, 177, 179, 182, 250; trial 178–9

The Queen's Necklace (Dumas) 168
'The Red Bible' 182
The Referee 78
The Secret of the Jews 169
The Secret World Government or The Hidden Hand (Cherep-Spiridovich) 36
The Secrets of the Elders of Zion (Beek) 177
The Servile State (Belloc) 210
The Spectator 171
The Storm 42
The Superman 217
The Tablet 98
The Vigilante 19, 21
The War in South Africa: Its Causes and Effects (Hobson) 5
The Zionist Protocols – The Program of the International Secret Government 177
'This Nigger Stuff' 154–5
Thomas, G.E. 96
Tiecken, Henry 154–5
Tindal-Robertson, Timothy 124, 128, 131, 258; letter to Catholic Herald 125–7; writings 132
Toedtli, Boris 241
Tomlinson, Leonard 111–12
Toulmin Smith, A. 83, 175, 176, 252
Tozer, Derek 116
Tredgold, R.C. 57, 58–9, 61–6, 68
True, James 57
Truth (Fraser) 29
Truth (journal) 127, 242
Truth: The Evidence in the Case (Seton Hutchison) 217
Tulloch, T. Erskine 147
Tyndall, John 121, 161–3, 276

UK Independence Party 81
Union Movement 160
United Christian Front Committee 220
United Empire Fascist League 218
United States, anti-Jewish sentiment 183–4, 185
United We Stand, Divided We Fall: The Protocols of the Meetings of the Learned Elders of Zion 188
Unity Band 200, 213–14
Universal Anti-Bolshevist League 35–6

Van Hyning, Lyrl Clark 101
Vanguard 241
Varnals, Mr 254
venereal disease 21
Vigilante Society 19, 239, 253; activities 79–80; end of 24; ideas of 'perversion' 21; resignations from 23, 24
Völkischer Beobachter 35, 44, 45

Von Kursell, Otto 87
Von Moltke, Johannes 37
von Ribbentrop, Joachim 45, 218–19, 221–2

Walker, Patrick Gordon 163–4
Warner, James 130–1
Waters Flowing Eastward (Fry) 212
Webster, Martin 121, 162
Webster, Nesta 86–7, 128–9, 130, 172, 176, 208, 233
Wedgewood, Josiah 242
Wellington, Lord 219
White, Arnold Henry 5, 20, 21, 36, 77–80, 254
White, John Baker 196, 198
White Defence League 122, 161
White Knights of Britain 213, 220, 222–3
Whitehead, Walter 150
Whitley, Rhea 40
Whittaker, William 43
'Who Wants War?' 50
Wiener Morgenzeitung 32
Wilhelm of Wied, Prince 20–1
Williamson, Hugh Ross 228
Wilmot-Allistone, Major B. 119, 258
Wilson, Harold 164

Wilson, Woodrow 183
Wodehouse-Temple, C.G. 218
Wolf, Lucien 178
women's committee 88
Women's Voice 101
Woods, G. 241
World Integralist Association 255
World Revolution (Webster) 130
World Service 40, 41, 42, 43
World Service 42, 50, 56, 241
World Union of National Socialists 162–3
World War I, anti-German sentiment 7–8
World War II 97
Wyatt, H.F. 88–9, 254

Yahya, Hasan 179–80
Yockey, Francis Parker 108, 254
York, Clifford's Keep siege 74–5
Young, Fred 101
young people, appealing to 122

Zachary, Roy 41
'Zionism versus Bolshevism: A Struggle for the Soul of the Jewish People' 234
Zionist Record 67
Znamya 169

Taylor & Francis eBooks

Helping you to choose the right eBooks for your Library

Add Routledge titles to your library's digital collection today. Taylor and Francis ebooks contains over 50,000 titles in the Humanities, Social Sciences, Behavioural Sciences, Built Environment and Law.

Choose from a range of subject packages or create your own!

Benefits for you
- Free MARC records
- COUNTER-compliant usage statistics
- Flexible purchase and pricing options
- All titles DRM-free.

Benefits for your user
- Off-site, anytime access via Athens or referring URL
- Print or copy pages or chapters
- Full content search
- Bookmark, highlight and annotate text
- Access to thousands of pages of quality research at the click of a button.

REQUEST YOUR FREE INSTITUTIONAL TRIAL TODAY

Free Trials Available
We offer free trials to qualifying academic, corporate and government customers.

eCollections – Choose from over 30 subject eCollections, including:

Archaeology	Language Learning
Architecture	Law
Asian Studies	Literature
Business & Management	Media & Communication
Classical Studies	Middle East Studies
Construction	Music
Creative & Media Arts	Philosophy
Criminology & Criminal Justice	Planning
Economics	Politics
Education	Psychology & Mental Health
Energy	Religion
Engineering	Security
English Language & Linguistics	Social Work
Environment & Sustainability	Sociology
Geography	Sport
Health Studies	Theatre & Performance
History	Tourism, Hospitality & Events

For more information, pricing enquiries or to order a free trial, please contact your local sales team:
www.tandfebooks.com/page/sales

Routledge
Taylor & Francis Group

The home of Routledge books

www.tandfebooks.com